BEST SEAT IN THE HOUSE

SPIKE LEE

with Ralph Wiley

A BASKETBALL MEMOIR

BEST
SEAT
IN THE
HOUSE

CROWN PUBLISHERS, INC., NEW YORK

*This book is dedicated to
my loving wife, partner, and
fellow New York Knicks
season ticket holder—
Tonya Lewis Lee*

Special photography from George Kalinsky
Back page of the *New York Post* reprinted with permission from the *New York Post*.
Copyright 1994, NYP Holdings, Inc.

Published by Crown Publishers, Inc., 201 East 50th Street, New York, New York
10022. Member of the Crown Publishing Group.

Random House, Inc. New York, Toronto, London, Sydney, Auckland
http://www.randomhouse.com/

CROWN and colophon are trademarks of Crown Publishers, Inc.

Printed in the United States of America

Design by Lauren Dong

Library of Congress Cataloging-in-Publication Data
Lee, Spike.
    Best seat in the house : a basketball memoir / by Spike Lee
with Ralph Wiley. — 1st ed.
    1. Basketball—United States.   2. New York Knicks (Basketball
team)   3. Lee, Spike.   4. Sports spectators—United States—
Biography.   I. Wiley, Ralph.   II. Title.
GV885.7.L44   1997
796.323'0973—dc21   97-5887

ISBN 0-609-60029-X

10   9   8   7   6   5   4   3   2   1

First Edition

ACKNOWLEDGMENTS

Thank you to Steve Ross at Crown Publishers who approached me at a Knicks-Bulls playoff game to do this book. At the time I didn't even know I had a basketball book in me.

Special thanks to Ralph Wiley. This is the second time we collaborated on a book, and I think the working relationship is getting better all the time. Nonetheless, Ralph, you're a great writer, period.

Much props go to the ballplayers and coaches who lent me their valuable time. In some instances it was our first time meeting, others are old friends. You guys are the reason I wanted to play ball growing up in Brooklyn. I owe y'all one. Bob McAdoo, Dave Stallworth, Bob Cousy, Cornbread Maxwell, John Havlicek, Phil Jackson, Bill Bradley, Walt Frazier, Bill Walton, Rick Pitino, John Starks, Michael Jordan, Derek Harper, Larry Brown, Donnie Walsh, Jeff Van Gundy, Buck Williams, George Gervin.

And to the nonplayers, love also—Super Knicks fans Fred Klein and Stan Asofsky, Woody Allen, and my grandmother Zimmie Shelton.

I would like to thank the New York Knicks and their people who assisted Ralph and me in every way possible. They are Dave Checketts, Ernie Grunfeld, John Cirillo, Dennis D'Agostino, and Chris Weiller. George Kalinsky and Betsy Becker came through like champs, providing me total access to the photographic archives of the New York Knickerbockers.

CONTENTS

PRE-GAME INTRODUCTIONS

*Knickerbocker—
a descendant of the
Dutch settlers of
New York. A New Yorker.*

I'm busy here. I'm making promises to my wife. Promises I don't know if I can keep.

"I'm just gonna sit here."

"Um . . ."

"No, I am."

". . . We'll see."

Tonya knows I'm not exactly under oath. We are sitting courtside, Thirty-first Street side, Eighth Avenue end of Madison Square Garden, and it's beginning to heat up in here. The Knicks' bench is directly across the floor. "Watch me," I say. "I'm staying cool this evening. And I'm not saying anything. I'm just gonna sit here. I swear. I don't care what the score is or what's happening out on the court. I don't care how bad the calls are. I'm just gonna sit here. I'm too tired tonight."

I look down at a copy of *Hoop,* the official National Basketball Association magazine. Then I hear a change in the pitch of the crowd's drone. I take my time looking back up. The visiting team is entering from the dark square passageway to the locker rooms, on the Thirty-third Street side. Tonight the visitors wear—could be the blood-red road warm-ups of the Chicago Bulls; the purple with gold trim of the Los Angeles Lakers; the Kelly green of Boston; the Seattle emerald; the tricolor of Houston or the Washington Bullets-soon-to-be-Wizards; the cardinal red of the Philadelphia 76ers; Orlando's natty pinstripes; Indiana blue. But in my mind's eye, it all comes back around to the World Champion Bulls. That's what I see. Blood red. Hope the Knicks have the Answer tonight.

I half-lid my eyes, look up without raising my head as the opposition jogs onto the court, greeted by a smattering of boos and the booming hip-hop that the Knicks warm up by.

> > >

Last October, before the 1996–97 season began, I shot a commercial with Michael Jordan. This one wasn't for Nike. Bill Gray, the former U.S. senator from Pennsylvania and now the head of the United Negro College Fund, called me and asked me to direct Michael in a spot for UNCF. I gladly went out to Chicago. It was the umpteenth commercial we had done together over what is now a nine-year collaboration. This was the same day the New York Yankees had a ticker-tape parade in lower Manhattan, celebrating their first World Series championship in eighteen years. While driving back from the Bulls' suburban Chicago practice facility, the Berto Center in Deerfield, Illinois, in his Range Rover, Jordan and I talked. There I was, riding shotgun with the greatest ballplayer in modern sports history, probing his mind. Surprisingly, Michael answered every question I asked. He told me in coldly analytical terms why he believed the Bulls would repeat as World Champions in 1997. He said it wouldn't be easy, no guarantee, because many teams had improved. He included the Knicks. Mike is a cold-blooded appraiser of talent—like a nuclear physicist he can break down a player's game to an atom.

"So it's gonna be the Knicks and Chicago in the Eastern Conference finals, right?" I ask.

"I think that. If the Knicks don't—if they don't fall asleep on Washington."

What about Orlando? The Magic lost Shaquille O'Neal to free agency—and to market forces and circumstances that had little to do with winning ball games and NBA titles, like making movies, commercials, and rap videos and revealing one's ego and pride. Used to be only team owners were able to exhibit such acumen. Wilt Chamberlain, Moses Malone, Kareem Abdul-Jabbar—all traded by their original teams. This time a dominant center had traded himself, signing a contract with the Lakers. But after Shaq broke up the Magic, Jordan said, *"The Magic is still a good team."*

I knew Jordan was talking about Penny.

Penny Hardaway is like Michael and his teammate Scottie Pippen in this way: if you ask them, "What do you play?" meaning position, they say, "What do you need?" meaning they can do everything. The other

Magic players are unmagical, catch-as-catch-can. Not enough this year. Not with Penny nursing a surgical knee.

Seattle is a different beast. The Sonics have Rain Man, 6-foot-10 forward Shawn Kemp, whose total game has grown by leaps and bounds in reliability since he came to the league, a year out of high school, in 1989, at the age of nineteen. Shawn has one of the more fitting nicknames that are always handed out in sports—Shawn plays in Seattle, and he falls from the sky. The Sonics have Gary Payton, second-best defensive guard in the league (Money is primo), and Hersey Hawkins, pure shooter, and ageless, Brooklyn-born, 6-foot-9 Sam Perkins, and the 6-10 German, Detlef Schrempf, best German ballplayer ever. The league is international now. The Sonics are tough to match up with. I've seen them do some things. See them if they get there.

The Houston Rockets brought in thirty-three-year-old Charles Barkley to help thirty-four-year-old Clyde Drexler and Hakeem Olajuwon, who'll be thirty-four by the time of the 1996–97 playoffs. Charles is still explosive, still in charge on the boards, probably be able to rebound from his rocking chair. Hakeem and Glide already have their rings. The Rockets have experience, but no young legs or proven point guard to carry them through the active mine field of eighty-two regular-season games, then eighteen, nineteen, twenty more, conducted with far, far more intensity, in the playoffs. One injury, and . . .

Philadelphia has young legs, 6-foot-5 Jerry Stackhouse, second year from North Carolina, and rookie Allen Iverson from Georgetown. At six feet even, Iverson is a revelation in the way David Thompson and Isiah Thomas were once. But the Sixers aren't going anywhere. Dues to pay. They don't know what it's about yet. It's one thing to play thirty games a year, two or three a week, twenty-minute halves, against less talented twenty-year-olds who are sitting in passive zone defenses. It is quite another thing to play one hundred games a season against the best ballplayers in the world every night; hard men defending the basket, their means in life; playing four forty-eight-minute games in five nights on the road, or six in eight days. You are going to hit the wall.

The Bullets have young legs, too, 6-foot-9 Juwan Howard and Chris

Webber, and now they have Strick—Rod Strickland, the ex-Knick from the Bronx—out high. The Bullets have as much talent as anybody. On paper. It takes more than that to become World Champions. Webber still shows aftereffects of coaching himself in college at Michigan. C. Web and Juwan have good futures, if they keep learning. What they *cannot* do is step out on the perimeter and guard the 6-foot-6 Jordan, 6-foot-8 Scottie Pippen, 6-6 Ron Harper, and 6-10 Croatian Toni Kukoc on the perimeter, *and* keep 7-2 Australian Luc Longley and 6-8 Dennis Rodman off the glass.

"Don't sleep on Washington, now," Jordan warned me. *"Don't sleep on them."*

The Lakers loom on the horizon. They have Shaq, Shaq Fu, *Kazaam, Steel*—a team's worth of personalities, talent, payroll, and ego, all in one dark, impressive body. They have Nick Van Exel and rookie Dexter Fisher at point, 6-10 Elden Campbell, 6-6 Eddie Jones, and an eighteen-year-old rookie out of an Ardmore, Pennsylvania, high school, 6-6 Kobe Bryant, at two-guard. Bryant can play anywhere. Jerry West, the Lakers' general manager, hopes Kobe can be like Mike one day. Even Michael Jordan tells me, *"The young kid, Kobe. Don't sleep on him, either. He's got some skills. It'll be a couple of years, but he's got some skills. He's got a lot to learn, though."*

L.A. has much talent, but there's more to it. Hard to out-talent Jordan. The question is, do the brothers *recognize*? Do they *represent*? Can they get out of their own self-absorption long enough to understand each other's strengths and weaknesses, enhance the strengths, compensate for the weaknesses? Can they be what an NBA World Championship winner should be—a *team*—so quick? Many players rarely use that word. They say "squad," maybe "crew," maybe would rather be hanging with the homeys than hanging with the craft that made them famous in the first place.

Crew, squad, *team*. Not the same things.

"So, Mike, do you think Shaq will win a ring?"

". . . I think he will."

"This year? Can the Lakers beat Seattle this year?"

". . . No. But I think eventually Shaq will."

"Think he wants to win? Think he cares enough, with all the other stuff he's got going?"

"He does. But I don't think it's going to be just because of him. I think it's going to be because of his other players around him. Because he can't play in the fourth quarter."

I don't mention missed free throws. Mike assumes I know what he means.

"So Seattle is going to come out of the West this year?"

"Easy. Easy."

For the Knicks, it comes down to Chicago, maybe Indiana, or Washington, Atlanta, or Detroit may surprise. Atlanta is coached by Lenny Wilkens, who, with arms folded and a sour look, has won more games than any coach in NBA history. Ran point for the Hawks once. Has Mookie Blaylock out high, 7-2 Dikembe Mutombo inside, Steve Smith, Christian Laettner. Atlanta is no day at the beach. Gotta get stops there before thinking of the Lakers, Houston, Seattle, Portland. Gotta get out of the East first. That means stops on Chicago. Maybe Miami. Maybe Indiana.

"No," says Jordan. *"Indiana has too many injuries."*

But the Pacers re-signed 6-foot-7 Reggie Miller, my old nemesis. Reggie thrives in the spotlight. I could've seen him playing in the orange-and-blue. But Knicks' general manager Ernie Grunfeld and Garden president Dave Checketts both said to me, "Allan is six years younger," so the Knicks went another way and signed Allan Houston, another free agent two-guard.

"The Knicks would have had a better chance of winning now with Reggie than with Allan Houston. It depends on how you play it. If you're trying to win now with Patrick, while he's still around, then Reggie. Reggie's been in clutch situations—he's another clutch player and has respect on the offensive and defensive end no matter who he plays. I mean, he plays me tough. He's totally underrated. I respect Reggie as a defender. He moves his feet well and on the other end he can get your two-guard in foul trouble. Reggie Miller can get me into foul trouble more times than I can get him into foul trouble. He does a lot of flopping. He leans into you on offense. You've got to respect that three-point

shot. He's got so many weapons to work with. I was shocked the Knicks got Allan, not Reggie. I'm telling you, Spike, with Reggie you would have won it. Y'all would have won it. You would have. You'd have a veteran who can adapt."

But Reggie is still in Indiana. Is Mike saying between the lines that the Pacers will be tough? Is he hiding in the weeds like a snake in the grass, talking about their injuries? Or is he already starting the psychological war with Allan Houston? He respects Larry Brown, the Pacers' coach. Beginning the season, Indiana had a lot of 6-foot-7 flexible players. Flexible enough to guard talented size averaging 6-8 on the perimeter—Jordan, Pippen, and Kukoc? That's the problem. Does Indiana have the Answer? It has two on the boards—the Davis Boys, Antonio, Dale. But 7-foot-4 Rik Smits waited until the season began to have surgery on his feet. He'd be back in plenty of time for the playoffs. Indiana's rookie, Erick Dampier, a big Willis Reed–like 6-11, had surgery, too. He was back before all the leaves fell off the trees last fall, 1996. Rare is the rookie who can help you in the playoffs. Maybe, if you are only asking them to give a starter a blow, not get in the way. Rookies have no concept of how hot it gets when the Bulls crank up the RPMs on full-court pressure D, rebounding, the running game, run you through thickets of screens with elbows for thorns in the half-court set.

Indiana does have the good coach in Larry Brown. *"Negative, because they're going through a problem with Larry Brown,"* said Jordan. *"I don't think they like Larry—"*

"He wears out his welcome after a while, right?" I ask.

"I think he gets tired. He gets complacent with what he has to work with. He wants to change. He's a man of change. When he stays in one place too long, maybe he wears out his welcome a little bit. But I like him. I would play for Larry Brown in a heartbeat."

"Did you ever think that [Bulls' coach] Phil Jackson might be leaving the Bulls?"

"Sure."

"You thought so? Was it ever a chance for you and him to be in New York?

"There was a chance."

"You mean . . . that could have happened?"

Michael's eyes become burning copper. *"Before I signed with Chicago last year, after we won, it came down to thirty minutes. New York was right downstairs. The Bulls—all they had to do was mess up."* He signed for $30.14 million for one year in Chicago, but my pulse skips anyway. "So if you'd worn the orange-and-blue, would the Knicks have won the title?"

"I don't know."

"You don't know?! Wait a minute. You're telling me—"

"My coach is everything. Don't know what kind of coach [Jeff] Van Gundy is. I know Phil." Before the season began, Coach Larry Brown had said to Roscoe Nance of *USA Today,* "Where we have a problem with Chicago is, yes, they are great, well-coached, but [Chicago] has tremendous perimeter players. So our game is changing in that direction. I think we've improved ourselves, but only time will tell if we can close the gap on Chicago."

Later on, Larry Brown told me, "Spike, what I think, and I've looked around this league, is this: when you put Scottie, Michael, Kukoc, and Harper out there, you've always got three big guys on the perimeter who can guard a lot of people and create plays for themselves and their teammates. That is *so* hard to match up with. That's my problem."

No, Coach, I think to myself. That's *our* problem.

Tonight, Bull is on the menu in the Garden. At the end of their line of talent . . . there he is. Michael Jordan. Black Jesus. Money. Black Cat. Air. High Pharaoh. Jordan flows onto the court with a rhythmic pigeon-toed gait that he, Jackie Robinson, Bullet Bob Hayes, John Elway, Dominique Wilkins, and I share, along with a few million other people, including our two-year-old daughter, Satchel. I think being pigeon-toed gives you character. Tonya is inclined to say "Corrective shoes." Well, no one walks as confidently as Jordan, except maybe Naomi Campbell.

Jordan looks over and winks, about to apply his multidimensional game, steel-edged will. Plans to put on a show. He calls this the Mecca of basketball. He's done it before, to the Knicks and to me—come in and defiled Mecca. I saw Jordan drop a double nickel—55 points—on March 28, 1995, in the fifth game he played after he came out of retirement. He signed the Air Jordans he wore that game for Satchel. For now his Bulls are defending World Champions, and they've won the NBA title four of the last six seasons. And I'm thinking, "This time we've got the Answer."

But I'm just going to sit here.

"Um—*hm.*" Tonya isn't going for it.

Now the Knickerbockers come out. My hometown team. Hard for me to sit here. Charles Oakley, co-captain of the Knicks, at the head of the line, tosses me the rock. I dribble it twice, run my hands over the pebble grain, then toss it back. I look around and see John McEnroe, Johnny Mac, is here. Ed Bradley, Woody Allen, the Baldwin brothers (how many of them are there?), Kevin Bacon, Tom Brokaw, Richard Lewis, Matthew Modine, John F. Kennedy Jr. The regulars. Plus the stars who come out because Jordan is in orbit, who come out to the game with sunglasses on. If NBA commissioner David Stern sees me, he'll say: "Spike, are you behaving yourself?" Like I'm two years old. Like it's not my league, too. Stern's been saying that to me ever since Reggie Miller dropped . . . Well, let's not spoil it. Be patient. Let the Game come to you.

During the pre-game introductions last season at Air's Crib, the United Center in Chicago, Steve Ross, the editor of this book, came by and said he thought I had a story about basketball in me. He asked me to think about it. I thought about it. I thought that in many ways I came of age with this NBA game; it was a game and league whose development had in many ways paralleled my own. I had learned what the Game is all about: relationships. . . . Now the Bulls are introduced to the awe of courtside stars and seeming disinterest of the regs. The lights bounce off Jordan's head. Then they dim.

The Knicks are introduced. The rookies aren't the Answer. Almost never are. The Bulls have none. We have three: John Wallace, 6 feet 10, Syracuse; Walter McCarty, 6-10, Kentucky; Dontae Jones, 6-7, Mississippi State. Wallace can score, but sat back in zones at Syracuse. Jones can see, but a screw in his foot is the question. He's on injured reserve. McCarty is . . . interesting. Might be able to use him one day. He's light in the ass, legs as skinny as mine, but he's flexible, he works hard on D, rotates well. He could deny—maybe make Kukoc put the ball on the floor.

The rest of the bench could be part of the Answer. Herb Williams, number 32, is a steadying influence in the locker room, backing up Patrick Ewing at center. Herb has good karma. Intelligent brother. Smart, well-read, will be thirty-nine by the time the playoffs start. The griot, I call him. The Obi-Wan Kenobi of the team. He needs glasses. He's always squinting. He refuses to wear goggles, or even contacts, on the court. Buck Williams. Number 52. Quiet as it's kept, Buck could be key for the Knicks. This brother was a great ballplayer in his day, a Hall of Famer to me, still has quality minutes in him. Can rebound. He's thirty-seven. His game bothers Dennis Rodman. Always has.

Charlie Ward, backup point guard, number 21. Third year. I love Charlie. Like his game. I think he should be an NFL quarterback, and this is not to negate his basketball talent, but it was a crucial mistake when somebody gave Charlie Ward, the Heisman Trophy–winning quarterback on the national championship Florida State football team, the advice to tell the NFL that if you don't draft me in the first round, don't draft me. How come a guy who won the national championship of college football running a pro offense like Florida State's, who has the arm, the tools, and who has the *gift*, the vision, to see passing lanes no one else can see, who can intuitively feel blind-side pressure, who is a quiet leader, a solid citizen, devoted Christian, humble and confident, whose game was loved by Bill Walsh, the guru of modern pro football offense—how come a special quarterback like that isn't drafted by the NFL? Well, if he says, if you don't draft me in the first round, don't draft me, the NFL says, okay. We won't. (Why give them an out when they don't want black quarterbacks in the first place?) This may be a blessing in disguise. Nobody understands passing better than Charlie. He gives New York a set second rotation backcourt with John Starks. Together they give us an edge. And Charlie is *still* the best quarterback in all of metropolitan New York City. Easy. Easy.

Number 3. John Starks. My man. I have almost every Knick player's jersey. Starks's is the one I wear. Not the most talented two-guard ever to come down the ramp, but he has a huge heart, no fear. He doesn't even call it playing. He calls it "putting in work." John has quickness, good jumping ability, deep shooting range, but again I go back to his ticker. He is going from being a starter, dealing with Jordan, to backup, the second rotation, where he can dominate. Here's someone who was born the third of seven children in impoverished conditions in Tulsa, Oklahoma, the third boy, whose older brothers beat the caterwauling shit out of him, then told him never to accept it; raised by a grand-mother who made him see the glory in work; he went on to four junior colleges trying to play; he was bagging groceries at Safeway at nineteen, out of school. But Starks never gave up. Even after he made it to top level, the NBA, he got cut by several teams, got caught up in the politics of the game, but he kept on pushing. He's going into his seventh year as a New York Knick. I've never been prouder of anybody who has worn the orange-and-blue.

His determination, optimism, zeal, and heart, that's partly the reason why he acts crazy sometimes. It comes with the package when you have to play over your head. In the second rotation, he can calm down; he will be better than any second-rotation two-guard in the league. He isn't bet-ter than Michael Jordan. No sin in that. Starks is not great, but a very good player who at times, for stretches, can seek and find greatness, who is going to work hard, play defense, and score, and give his all. Once, after he became a starter and made the NBA All-Star team, he said, "two-guards like me and Michael Jordan." I had to laugh. But I'm look-ing for a big year from John now that he doesn't have to stay with Jordan for forty minutes a game. I think he can be at his best as a role player. And he knows it. "As a player you have to sit back and think about your career and realize what's important to you," he told me. "The one thing I don't have is the championship. With Allan here, my minutes might go down, but my production will go up."

Now the starters, the first rotation. Chris Childs. *Numero uno.* Run-ning point this season. Free agent from Jersey. Broke his leg, was out for the first six games of the season. I worry about his base, his ankles, his legs—they look a little shaky. Can they take the stress? Never saw much of Childs with the Nets. I don't watch the Nets except when they play the Knicks. I was surprised when the Knicks went after him. He's quick, has a nice stroke. He has to run the club, hold down the opposing point guard, make open shots, set the table. The Knicks front office could've gone after a package of Miller, Barkley, and Strickland, or the Childs–Houston–Larry Johnson hookup, and decided to go with youth. Ideally, you need a mixture, a blend of youth and experience. We're old enough.

"Chris is a good point guard," said Starks. "Thinks pass first. He's a leader. Strong-minded. Even if he hasn't taken a shot all game, when a big shot comes, he's going to knock it down."

Number 34. Charles Oakley. Oak. Power forward. Been here a few years. Only thing that bothers me about Oak is he's been getting hurt, where before he was indestructible. He's thirty-three. I hope he won't break down before the end of the year. Oak is the heart and soul of the team.

L.J. Number 2. The Knicks got Larry Johnson from Charlotte, along with a $12-million-a-year salary, for Anthony Mason in the off-season. L.J. brings offense. Glad he got rid of the gold tooth, hope he's not doing that Grandmama character in those Converse ads anymore. Hope he can guard one of the Bulls on the perimeter. He's only 6 feet 5.

This is what Jordan told me: "*Spike, those are good moves the Knicks made. It's not like the Bulls are automatically going to win. No. We're the oldest team in the league. That could be a factor. The biggest thing for the Knicks is if they can jell—people in certain roles. Larry is not the go-to guy every single time. He may be in certain situations. Allan Houston may be in certain situations. Or Patrick. Or even Starks. They've got to be able to share that role. If they can do that, then defensively they're going to be all right. Although you do have some loopholes over there. People may say the Knicks won't be as strong defensively, like they were in the past, but I think they will, because the core of their defense is still there: Patrick, Oakley, and Starks. I'm pretty sure Scottie is glad [Anthony] Mason's gone, but he's got a difficult matchup with Larry Johnson. Larry posts him up and can get him in foul trouble. But Larry can't play the other end.*"

Starks thinks otherwise: "A 248-pounder, chasing threes around?

Hey, anybody would get tired. Larry's finding out his place within the team. He's going to work. They say he can't play D. He's capable. Allan too. They both can defend the three-spot. Remember that. Larry, once he gets rolling in his natural position, the four-spot, the way he is capable of playing, we're going to be hell to beat."

Patrick Ewing. Number 33. The captain. Can score—24 points per game over his eleven-year career. The Knicks' best player in the twelve years he's been on the scene. Not a quick jumper. And his hands are small, not much bigger than mine, and nothing like Michael's fishing nets. Those hands, and what's going on inside his head, are Jordan's secrets. Patrick doesn't have the ball control Michael does. Lobs to him are tricky, and his turnover ratio is always high. Getting along now. Every time the Knicks lose in the playoffs to Chicago—four times in the last six years—Patrick says, "I still think we're the better team." Wonder if he's getting tired of saying that. I'm tired of hearing it. Once I asked him if he really believed it. Patrick told me, "Not really, Spike, but I've got to say something." Jordan appreciates Ewing's career: *"If I could pick one player I'd like to see win the NBA title, if I couldn't—I couldn't pick one, but I could pick three: Patrick, Charles Barkley, and Oakley."*

Allan Houston. Number 20. The Knicks' 6-foot-6 starting two-guard. X factor. Unknown quantity. Free agent out of Detroit. From Louisville, Kentucky. Home of Muhammad Ali. He has to hit the three, go to the hole when they stay up and deny the deep j. He's got to play D. Allan is looking for a breakthrough year. He's got the stroke. Great form. Very sweet. Jordan's matchup?

"Allan is a good offensive player," Jordan said. *"But . . . he has yet to prove that he can play solid defense against some of the good two-guards in the game. . . . I love Allan. He is . . . a little bit timid. When his shot is going great, he's fine; when his shot is not, then you may lose him on the other end as well."*

Starks disagrees, naturally. "Allan is an All-Star caliber player. With him in here, I don't have to pace myself. When I go out, I know Allan is in there. Allan was a go-to guy in Detroit. He's a one-on-one player, can go get his shot. He's just not accustomed to playing with big men in Detroit. He has to get used to it. Pick his spots."

I wouldn't mind if it wound up in a seventh game, the ball on Allan's shooting hand, on a kick-out from Patrick, and quick ball rotation from Starks—one good look by Allan from 22 feet, for all the marbles, with Jordan flying at him. I think I could live with that this year.

"Michael Jordan has a heart like a lion. With him you have to compete every single night, or he's going to put you to shame," said Starks. "I think about this all the time. Chicago is about psych. They try to get into your head. They know at the end of the day they have one of the greatest players ever to play. They use him to get inside the other team's heads. Can't get caught up in what Michael's doing. He's going to get his. I've got him. Let me have him. Stop the others. . . . The key to beating them—let me guard Jordan, and everybody else get theirs. . . . It's going to be the Knicks and the Bulls in the Eastern Conference finals, Spike. And it *ain't* gonna go seven."

The buzzer sounds. My senses heighten. The run is on.

> > >

"All ball! Aw, no! That's all ball, Ref! Terrible call! All ball!"

The ref smiles at me and wags his finger back and forth. *Ah-ah-ah.* His teeth look filed down. Maybe he wants my blood. The Knicks are down one. In Tonya's eyes I see reflected what she calls madness. I've promised. Five minutes later I'm jumping up and down. I'm a Knicks fan. I'm looking for the Answer—to recapture the championship seasons of 1969–70 and 1972–73, the only two NBA world titles the Knicks have won. Happened back when I was a kid, so it's not right that New York has won only the two. Judging from the roar, I'm not alone. We're hungry. We're impatient. We're loud. We boo. We shout. We are dyed-in-the-wool, unregenerate, no flip-flopping Knicks fans. Like it or lump it as long as you don't jump it—our view of the court, I mean.

That would be hard to do, now that I've got the best seats in the house.

We're here game after game, watching the rotations; watching wheels begin to wobble and fall off the rookies as they find out what it is like, how insignificant they are in the history of the Game; watching the rotation of the teams as they pass through the Garden, the rotation of the substitution pattern of the Knicks, the players off the bench within a game; watching the rotation of the ball during a deep j or a free throw, backspinning just right if the shot is reliable; watching the defensive rotations, critical when you double-team, play team D, because everybody who plays the Bulls—or any team with a special player—must do this well, if it is going to have a chance to win. Winning the NBA title is about will, luck, and understanding the *other* guy's game. The Game itself is about skills, problems, answers, unselfishness, rotations . . . it all comes back around.

FIRST QUARTER

"Welcome to the magic world of Madison Square Garden, the world's most famous arena. And now for tonight's starting lineups . . ."

T here was something promising in the voice of John F. X. Condon, public address announcer of Madison Square Garden, the New York Knickerbockers, and my youth. Something irresistibly trust-worthy was in the uptick of his familiar nasal tones. I can hear them now, filling the Garden air, announcing the starting lineups, on January 26, 1968. Defending national champion UCLA, coached by the Wizard of Westwood, John Wooden, had invaded the magical world. My younger brother Chris and I watched this panorama in awe from our vantage point near the rafters atop the new Garden, itself atop Thirty-fourth Street's Penn Station. UCLA faced what the newspapers had called upstart Holy Cross. "Upstart" meant Holy Cross had no prayer against UCLA and its 7-foot-2 center, Lew Alcindor. I didn't need a newspaper to tell me that. But I'd been reading the papers for a while by then, following the fortunes of New York ball clubs. I knew the hacks' lingo and codes.

The seats at the Garden were sectioned off in cascading colors—blue on top, green, orange, yellow, red, beige down at courtside. Sitting up in the nosebleed cheap seats, general admission, the blue seats in the Garden, lair of the rowdy, boisterous working-class fan, we saw Alcindor, in the powder-blue UCLA hookup, rise and flick the ball into the basket with a disdainful motion, his wrist pronated, broken as if painted on the dark ceiling of the Garden by the hand of God.

Dunking had been outlawed in college ball by the NCAA, mostly because of the threat of Alcindor's dominance. Fear of a single player's dominance had spurred rules changes before. The lane had been widened from 6 to 12 feet to prevent 6-foot-11 George Mikan of the Minneapolis Lakers from dominating. Mikan still dominated. A three-second lane violation had been enforced to keep 7-foot-1 Wilt Chamber-lain from dominating. Big Dipper dominated anyway. In 1961–62, he had averaged 50.4 a game for the NBA Philadelphia Warriors. *Averaged* fiddy. Dropped 100 points on the Knicks one night that year in Hershey, Pennsylvania. His hard-handed point guard, Al "the Destroyer" Attles, from Newark, was eight for eight from the field that game. Layups. He never shot 100 percent again. His man was trying to help on Wilt. We got this skinny from our elders, almost by osmosis. Whenever my father, Uncle Cliff, and Uncle Len took Chris and me to the old Garden in Manhattan, at the corner of Forty-ninth Street and Eighth Avenue, for East Coast Athletic Conference triple-headers on bright Saturday afternoons, we heard these stories. And they were often well-told and good stories, too; good, like Nedick's, and Chris and I even got to stop at the Nedick's stand for a hot dog after the games, at least in flush times we did.

When he was young, Chamberlain could sprint, high jump, run all day, coming out of Overbrook High in Philly, then Kansas, then the Globetrotters for a while. Hall of Fame baseball pitcher Bob Gibson had also been a Globetrotter. Wilt was leading the league in assists in 1967–68, simply because he wanted to. He'd been better than the league. Yet Russell and the Boston Celtics had limited him to one NBA title, with the Philadelphia 76ers in 1966–67. For the 1968–69 season, Dipper was in L.A., traded from Philly to the Lakers. Wilt was in L.A. the way Shaq is in L.A. now, as the Laker center, minus the movies, the rap videos, the "TWISM" tattoo: The World Is Mine. For his sake, I hope Shaq hasn't boned 20,000 women, though, the way Wilt said he did.

With the retirement of Bill Russell after Boston's 1968–69 NBA title win over the Lakers, L.A. expected a dynasty. The thirty-two-year-old Wilt was still the most dominant figure in the Game.

But one day Alcindor was going to be better. As our elders insisted on the accuracy of this information, I looked at Chris, half-lidded my eyes, and gave a quick vibrating nod, like one of those bobble-headed dolls. On this the old men were right, my nod said. We knew our elders were wise about certain matters, but we were becoming wiser quicker, of that we were sure. I was nearing eleven, and Chris was nine. Alcindor was closer to our age than theirs. Didn't take long for me to adopt him. Alcindor was a New York ballplayer before he became the King. Not inch-for-inch the best player. But the King. Oscar Robertson, the Big O, the 6-foot-5 guard, would name Lew that when they played for the

Milwaukee Bucks one year hence. Whether at UCLA or as a rookie in the NBA in 1969, Alcindor and his Afro were imperious and inevitable. What happens when a New York ballplayer grows to 7 feet 2, is coached by Wooden, gets fed in the post as an NBA rookie by the O, then years later by Magic Johnson? Skyhook happens, the ultimate weapon, the most unstoppable force—outside of Michael Jordan, who was getting his first grade school picture taken in Wilmington, North Carolina, at the time—in the history of the Game. The skyhook came into being because of a rule designed to stop a brooding, tall "yute" from Harlem, Ferdinand Lewis Alcindor, from getting his game on. It was an improvisation of historic proportions. My father and his comments on hoop and his trade, jazz musician, had made Chris and me aware.

Jazz musicians also lived by improvising within structure. Bill Lee had played the Game and his music; he seemed to understand their nature. I know my father simply transferred his own love of sports to his eldest son—me. To his next eldest son, Chris, the legacy was less clear. My mother always said Chris had crawled backward, even rode his tricycle backward, whenever an explanation for Chris's behavior was in order, which was beginning to be often. I took his occasional lack of animation in cheering the Knicks as a temporary condition—like chicken pox, without the disfigurement. It was not long after those trips my brother and I took beneath the marquee to the old Garden, and then the one to the new Garden to see Lew Alcindor dispose of Holy Cross, that I began my own journeys, going solo to see the Knicks if need be. And the need became greater as Chris became more distant from the Game. But it's always much better to have company when you see something amazing.

UCLA ran rings around Holy Cross, 90–67, to the awe of at least two of the 18,106 at the Garden. A week before that game, our father let us stay up late and watch a basketball game on TV. Our mother, Jacquelyn Shelton Lee, hated that, sometimes, but he would overrule and let us stay up to watch the games. At times, she would tell us to turn off that TV, she wasn't trying to give Con Ed any more money than it was getting already. And then, for whatever reason—maybe he saw my growing passion for it—my father would then say, "Aw, Gem, leave them boys alone. Leave them watch the game in peace."

My mother would relent, but not without comment: "*Those* children need to go to *bed*, get some *rest*. They have school in the morning."

The game we watched that night was the biggest regular-season college game ever at that time—UCLA and Lew Alcindor vs. the University of Houston and Elvin "Big E" Hayes, January 20, 1968. At Houston. Big E was 6 feet 9, had good extension on his jumper. Got *way* up there. Alcindor had a scratched cornea, wore a patch over his eye. During ensuing seasons, as an NBA star in Milwaukee and Los Angeles, he wore safety goggles. That night Big E made over 50,000 in the Astrodome happy, 71–69. *I* wasn't happy. I thought Alcindor was a better ballplayer, UCLA a better team. But that's the beauty of it. The people with the best individual players don't always win. The people who play best as a *team—they* win. Hoop is unlike football or baseball that way.

When they met in the NCAA semifinals at the L.A. Sports Arena on March 22, 1968, UCLA won, 101–69, and went on to win one of the three consecutive NCAA titles with Alcindor. That was proper. Basketball and Houston didn't seem to go together. This, of course, was before we knew of Hakeem Olajuwon of Texas by way of Nigeria—before hoop blew up worldwide.

Tiny Archibald was a New York ballplayer. Tiny went to De Witt Clinton High, up in the Bronx, then went on to Texas–El Paso—Texas Western back then—collegiate home of five black starters who had beaten Kentucky's all-white starting five for the NCAA title in 1965. Kentucky was coached by Adolph Rupp. They had two or three future pro players on that team. But for Texas Western Coach Don Haskins, the brothers played better that day. So Tiny went down there too. He'd be a rookie in the NBA with the Cincinnati Royals, in 1970–71 (the Royals would leave Cincinnati to be the Kansas City Kings in 1972, eventually becoming the Sacramento Kings).

It was Tiny's game then. New York City's game, no matter where it was played. To me, it represented the city and youth, the tired and poor struggling upward in a vertical cylinder between concrete and sky— creating workable space and constructing dreams out of nothing much more than thin air. Dr. Naismith hung up the peach basket in Springfield, Massachusetts, 105 years ago. Men like Rupp, Hank Iba, Clair

Bee, and Phog Allen were credited with teaching it best at state universities. Men like Joe Lapchick, former original Celtic and Knick coach
who signed Nat "Sweetwater" Clifton, the first black player in the NBA,
who came in the same year, 1950, as the Celtics' Chuck Cooper and
Detroit's Earl Lloyd, fostered the pro game; men like Lapchick and
Bob Douglas, coach of the New York Renaissance Five, the matchless
Rens, who fought their way out of gyms in hellholes of racism like
Cicero, Illinois, but who kept playing because, as I was told, Douglas
said "no one was going to deny [them] the right to earn a living."

At first, the foothold of the pro game was in the sticks, the chitlin circuit for modern pro basketball, only it wasn't in the South and they
weren't serving chitlins; Oshkosh, Flint, Toledo, Rochester, Fort Wayne,
Minneapolis, Syracuse. But I believe it was brothers from the city, like
Alcindor and Tiny, who imprinted the Game with a distinct style and a
life of its own, who made it Broadway as an entertainment spectacle,
whose athletic artistry and creativity lifted pro hoop from the distant
outposts of its origins and ethnic urban subculture base into the worldwide consciousness today. The Game has always danced in the blood of
New Yorkers. And in the city, we know that when the Game is played
both creatively and well, it can become an art form.

I followed the Knicks. They had gotten good by the time I was twelve, in
the fall of 1969, and seemed ready to challenge the dominance of the
Celtics, led by Bill Russell, who had won ten of eleven previous NBA
titles. But by the beginning of the 1969–70 season, Russell had retired.
And the Knicks had not won a title in the twenty-year history of the
NBA. Yeah, 1969–70 was going to be a good season, all right. The Game
was dancing in my blood by now. Time to bring the world championship
of the city's Game home. I felt this with all the fervor of youth. Why were
my passions so directed? Well, as I say, my father was serious about sports,
his basketball, almost as serious as he was about music. Almost. He was
reverential toward both, and I was encouraged to participate in both mind
and body. It was the fate of men such as the Lees, my father said, without
a hint of pride about it, rather with something tending toward resignation.

So duty called. The Knicks would get there if I had to carry them on my back.

Celtic fans thought otherwise, Russell or no. Russell was complex, intelligent, eccentric. He'd played mind games with Chamberlain, inviting him to dinner before championship games, letting him play with his Lionel train set, then playing him close, playing him distantly, finessing Goliath. Russell, from Oakland, California, became the greatest winner the NBA has known, with eleven NBA world titles to his credit, all won in Boston in a thirteen-year run. Wilt, all of 7 feet 3, and I don't care what the program says, invited Russell to Thanksgiving dinner six straight years with his family in Philly, and then, in Russell's words at the NBA's celebration of its fiftieth year, "proceeded to kick [Russell's] brains in. I tried to return the favor when he came to Boston."

Maybe, in the end, Wilt only had killer instinct for the two years his teams won the NBA title, when the opposing players had somehow aroused Goliath. If Wilt had displayed what is called killer instinct all the time, he might have actually killed somebody out there. He wasn't the assassin that Michael Jordan is—Agent Double-O-Soul. "I had to change the way I played [Wilt] every single game," Russell said. "If I hadn't done that, it would have been over."

Some people are born old, or have an old soul. Russell's like that. Had an old man's laughter, a cackle, an old man's look and approach, was difficult to follow in the way his mind worked. Made the blocked shot a weapon. If Chamberlain and Russell played today, you wouldn't see as many dunks. You'd see as many *attempts*, but not as many dunks. The most electrifying play in pro hoop is not the dunk. It is the *blocked* dunk. Charles Barkley is adept at it—freakish for a man only 6-4. Russell cleaned up his teammates' mistakes, led the Celtics' defense, and in 1968–69 took over coaching for a year and became the first black coach to win a world title in a pro sport in American history—saying more about American history than black men. The Celtics were grooming a successor, a 6-9 player with steel springs for legs and what Muhammad Ali called "the complexion for the connection." Dave Cowens. He was what was becoming an American rarity—a big white dude who had lift and could play. The Celtics wouldn't get him until 1970–71.

The European immigrant tired and po' had been assimilated, but some of their ex-yutes were still involved. Early pro teams in the '20s and '30s made no bones about the ethnicity of their players. Pro clubs from defunct leagues had names like the New York Celtics, the Original Celtics, the Cleveland Rosenblums, the SPHAs (the South Philadelphia Hebrew Association), the Buffalo Germans, the Brooklyn Arcadians, the New York Hakoahs. The NBA Boston Celtics' longtime coach and then still its general manager was a shrewd, tough, bullet-shaped Jew from Brooklyn, New York, named Arnold "Red" Auerbach, a trader of professional talent. From the upper reaches of the Garden, I watched him light up fat victory stogies, adding to the haze of smoke in my habitat. Auerbach had retired from the bench, but I still saw him during the 1969–70 season.

That was *our* year. The Knicks' coach was a quiet little man, also Jewish, named William "Red" Holzman, who had played at City College of New York under Nat Holman, one of the original Celtics, long before the point-shaving scandals of 1950. Holzman was from Brooklyn. *Our* Red.

The Knicks' chief scout in 1969 was Dick McGuire. He coached the team and Holzman was chief scout until they switched jobs two days after Christmas, 1967. McGuire had a slice of the Ireland map on his face, as did Danny Whelan, the trainer who redefined "ruddy" and was trainer of the 1960 Pittsburgh Pirates world champion baseball club. Whelan jumped out of baseball and landed, a bit unsteadily, on his feet with the Knicks. Whelan used to say he could communicate better with the basketball players—maybe because the Pirates' Hall of Famer Roberto Clemente, from Puerto Rico, spoke Spanish as his first language. Whelan knew athletes well—how to keep them loose, when to make them laugh, when to get serious, and he knew their bumps, bruises, and sprains.

One of the best ball handlers of the era just past was another little guy who had played for Boston, early in the Russell dynasty. Hirsute. Looked Italian. Bob Cousy. Da Cooz, they called him in Brooklyn. Little ethnic guys were known to have handle in their day. Quick, some of them, like Holzman, Holman, Chet Forte at Fordham, or Da Cooz, and guys who went to college in the Carolinas, where the state universities went north for coaches and players. By the time I saw him, Da Cooz, from Queens, New York, was done as a player and was coaching Tiny Archibald as a rookie in the NBA, in 1970, in Cincinnati, then in Kansas City. The Cooz could relate to Tiny's game, gave him a free hand. Tiny took it from there, leading the NBA in scoring (34.0) and assists (11.4) in 1973.

Anyway, like I said, the Game danced in everybody's blood in New York.

Radio had a lot to do with it. It was the same way later for fans in Los Angeles listening to Chick Hearn describing Magic Johnson's Showtime L.A. Lakers of the '80s, or for people today in the Midwest, listening to Johnny "Red" Kerr describing the latest derring-do of the Bulls and Air Jordan. When I was younger, it was watching the Knicks' road games on television, on WOR, Channel 9, with Bob Wolff and Cal Ramsey commentating, or listening in to the Knicks' home games via their play-by-play man on radio station WNBC, that other easily identifiable voice, this one belonging to a former Knick ball boy from Lincoln High in Brooklyn, named Marv Albert: "Now the Knicks, down by one, going right to left at the Seventh Avenue end of the Garden. Frazier . . . to Barnett . . . Barnett stops . . . *Yess!*"

Back then, when I thought of a New York ballplayer, I didn't think first of Tiny or Lew Alcindor, as Kareem Abdul-Jabbar was christened, even though he was from Power Memorial High, upper Harlem, and even though his skyhook would score 38,387 points in regular season NBA action, more than anybody in the history of the Game, more even than Michael Jordan, who, don't forget, was born at Cumberland Hospital on Myrtle Avenue, in Fort Greene, Brooklyn.

Back then, when you said "New York ballplayer," you thought of a guard—a strap of brown leather who played taller than he was, played calm, knees bent, ready to flex, burst, and pick your dribble or grab your j. All arms and legs. High waist. You didn't think of him with the ball. Never had it long. Right to the rack, first chance. By you. Educated around the basket, variety of close-in shot-making; good jumper, could rise above the rim, above the square, maybe. Pass it or shoot it, his look said, but do something. And don't be bringing no trash up in here. He never smiled. He never showed much in the way of a deep jump shot.

Always looking for the layup, or the dunk, looking to blow by with a monster first step or to methodically break you down with a bounce or three, changing direction like a fish. Or he could play with his back to the basket, down low, put the pin-down on you underneath, lock you on the low block. If you were content to play behind him, he shot right over the top of you. Then you were candy. If you reached in for his dribble from behind, better not lead with your face, or an elbow would remind you it's not polite to reach.

The New York ballplayer had every evasive dribble. You rarely saw them because, like his deep j, he rarely had to use them. Handle? He had the ball-handling ability of any guard today—and this was over twenty-five years ago. He never used his dribbling skill to waste time out away from the hoop unless it was the end of a regulation game and that was the thing to do. Dribbling exhibitions were for Marques Haynes, Curly Neal, and them, the Globetrotters, the Magicians, other comic-relief barnstormers. Kept the big white folks laughing. No. Do it in the *real* flow, against serious D, to make a hoop, set one up, make a guy miss, highest level—that's when handle meant something. Reverse, crossover, hesitation, yo-yo, spin, between-the-legs, wraparound, wraparound both ways—a New York ballplayer had them twenty-five years ago. When I was twelve, this New York ballplayer was a dream. *The* Dream. Dean "the Dream" Meminger.

Dream was born in the Carolinas—Walterboro, South Carolina—but he grew up in New York, and the city was writ large on his game. He'd graduated from Rice High School in 1967, the first guard and, at the time, the only player other than Lew Alcindor to make the New York prep All-City team three years running. Dean didn't go on to St. John's or any other New York institution of higher learning, but to Marquette, in Milwaukee, in the distant upper Midwest. Why? Well, for one thing, Dick McGuire's brother, Al, was head coach at Marquette.

Dream was legit. I heard of playground legends like "Pee Wee" Kirkland, Earl "the Goat" Manigault, or Herman "the Helicopter" Knowings, who, when you jumped with him, would say, "Floor, please," and still be rising as gravity brought you back down. I'd heard of them, but I never went to Harlem for Holcomb Rucker's tournaments. Never saw them. Helicopter had hops, Pee Wee had handle, Goat got game, but they were lore to me. They never made it to the NBA. Connie Hawkins, from Boys and Girls High in Brooklyn, was the one of them who did. Hawk finally made it to the Phoenix Suns of the NBA in '69, but by then he was twenty-seven, and an old twenty-seven. Even though he averaged 24.6 a game that year, he might as well have been finished, because he was way out in Phoenix, and back in New York we rarely got to see what he had left. The Dream was *real*. We knew he had game. City Game. No deep j, they always said, but plenty game. There was no way for me to know if he'd play for the Knicks one day, and on that day Dream would not be like 'Copter, Pee Wee, or Goat, but the hard, rock-ribbed truth. And you could look him up.

> *If your sneakers slip and slide,*
> *Get the ones with the star on the side*
> *Ask your moms to empty her purse*
> *To get the ones that say Converse.*

It would be difficult to overstate the impact of sports on our lives in Brooklyn. Basketball was another piece of fabric in a crazy quilt of games. Back then even the way we followed sports was different. Kids growing up today like whichever team is winning because they can see every team play on television. SportsCenter, 24–7. But back in the day, you only saw your local teams on the news, so there was much more loyalty to the team you grew up with. You were more inclined to follow the teams in your hometown, felt connected to and represented by them in a personal way, which was why Brooklyn took it hard when the Dodgers left for Los Angeles after the 1957 season, the year of my birth. And that was the moment when ball really began to change.

Ask the Colts fans in Baltimore after their football team left for Indianapolis. Or the fans in Cleveland after the Browns went to Baltimore—it was like getting a divorce you really didn't want.

But the games themselves were still and always right on our block. We lived at 186 Warren Street in Brooklyn, smack dab in the middle of a quiet block of four-story brownstones, on a rise between Henry and Clinton Avenues, the middle of the neighborhood called Cobble Hill. It was a working-class neighborhood, mostly Italians, some Puerto Ricans, some Jews, but mostly Italians, and along Court and Smith Streets, the storefronts had names like Staubitz Market, Campobello Pizzeria, Cusimano & Russo Funeral Home. Then there was us, the Lee clan. There was my father, Bill; my mother, Jacquelyn; then me, the oldest child; and then my brother Chris; my brother David; my sister, Joie; and my brother Cinque. We had the Five Stairsteps covered, as long as they didn't break out Cubie on us. The Lee kids had our own squad, our own club, our own team.

Before we moved to Cobble Hill in 1962, we lived on Union Street in the Crown Heights section of Brooklyn. When we moved to Cobble Hill, we were the first black family in the neighborhood. The day we moved, we got called nigger a couple of times, but halfheartedly, and we were only kids, and kids call each other everything under the sun and then forget about it. I don't recall any adults doing it at the time, although you know they did behind closed doors or the kids wouldn't have learned it. We weren't really much of a threat because we were the only ones up in there and we were quickly accepted. My friends were representative of the peoples surrounding us. Italian, Puerto Rican, Jewish. If there had been ten black families behind us, then we would've caught hell. We moved into our duplex. The Lilienfelds, who were Jewish, lived below us. Quickly I became good friends with Hugo Lilienfeld. Down the block was another one of my good friends, an Italian-American, Louie Tucci, along with his brother Joe and their family. My siblings and friends did everything together. Hoop was part of it.

There were Catholic schools around. St. Peter's, St. Paul's parish school down the street from us. We didn't go to Catholic schools; we went to the public school around the corner, P.S. 29, which we called 29s. We played ball in the school yard at 29s—punchball, boxball, softball, stickball, two-hand touch football, and always hoop. My brothers and I played stoopball in front of our house; then we went around to 29s, people chose up sides, and we went half-court for hours, both spring and fall. I never played any organized sports, just choose up sides in the school yard. I was on the small side, so I tried to use my speed to get around people and for defense. We didn't travel around Brooklyn to play. We weren't that good.

In winter, snow meant two things: one, school might be closed and, two, it gave you a nice ground cover so you could play tackle football on the cement, though I preferred two-hand touch. The season would decide what sport we played, argued over, loved. We were all sports fanatics, and every block had a team, and that's what we would do. I remember reading that my idol, Walt Frazier of the Knicks, had grown four inches between his junior and senior year in high school. I secretly believed it might happen to me. It never did. Instead, people just seemed to keep getting taller around me.

When we were young, we played for the pure love of playing. Once you got into high school, the stakes changed. Girls came into the equation, and girls liked guys who could sing and guys who could play sports—particularly basketball. It became a manhood thing, who had game. After that I never tried to play the game anymore, at least not at an organized level, just shooting around. But before I became a teenager, we all played—Hugo, Louie, Pino, Paulie Moe, Botz, Joe, Chuckie, Dennis Blake, *everybody*. My sister, Joie, likely thought we were all lunatics, but I remember her getting her licks in at stoopball. We played constantly, stopping only to eat, sleep, and argue about who was better, Yankees or Mets, Jets or Giants, Willie Mays or Mickey Mantle, Joe Namath or Fran Tarkenton, Frazier, Big O, or Jerry West.

The night owl edition of the *Daily News* came around eight in the evening, after dinner. At the corner of Warren and Henry there was a store called Willie's. Some called it Jack and Bill's. That's who owned it before Willie. Everybody would congregate there at about eight, waiting for the paper. The older men were waiting to see what number had hit, and the yutes waited for the box scores to come in. We'd all be hanging out there, waiting, a mix of ages and colors, on a corner of Brooklyn that was peaceful and quiet before we all showed up there at once and gave it life. Then the truck would careen up, grind its gears, the driver would call out, "Yo!" and then throw bundles of papers off the back. The papers quickly disappeared, accompanied by "Jeez" because the wrong number came up or "Told yas!" if Mays, Mantle, or Frazier did well. An egg cream would set you back fifteen cents. And they are still the most delicious potable I've ever had. That was our SportsCenter: read the box scores out of the night owl edition of the *Daily News* while gulping down an egg cream.

A pair of high-top Converse Chuck Taylor All-Stars cost eight bucks. I normally wore P. F. Flyers or Keds, but I begged my parents for my first pair of Cons. Only little kids wore those sissy P. F. Flyers or Keds. I was an athlete and I needed to wear what the other athletes wore. There is something about a new pair of sneakers that makes a boy feel he can run faster and jump higher, and they also made a fashion statement not so different from how it is today, although there's much more to covet in this day and time. But back then the most coveted legitimizing agent for the discerning youth was white high-top canvas Chuck Taylor All-Stars. The Knicks wore them. So did the Lakers. Everybody did. They were the only right thing to wear. If you wanted to get fancy, you'd adorn them with colorful shoelaces. I vividly recall getting my first pair of Chucks and wearing them proudly as all my friends' eyes sought out their glory.

I'd also wanted this baseball glove, a sweet leather MacGregor, a Claude Osteen model. I would go and stare at that glove, right there in the window of Modell's, the sporting goods store on Fulton Street in downtown Brooklyn. This was back in 1965. The Los Angeles Dodgers were still Brooklyn's team as far as most of Brooklyn saw it. Koufax, Drysdale, and Osteen were the money pitchers. My father said it was important to have left-handed starters if you were going to win. The Dodgers did win the World Series that year over the Minnesota Twins, behind Koufax, Drysdale, and the crafty lefty, Osteen. I wanted that glove. Only problem was, it cost fifty dollars, a ton of money back then. But to my surprise my father bought it for me. My mother said he was crazy. He replied, "If the boy wants that glove, I'm gonna get it for him." And he did, too. My eye was good, even then. There was an older guy, a teenager, a Puerto Rican named Carlos. He liked my glove. Everybody did. It was sweet. Carlos had a big softball game coming up, he said, and he wanted to borrow it. No way was I giving it up. I wasn't doing it. Carlos tells me if I let him use my Claude Osteen MacGregor, he'll take me to the first game of the World Series.

Imagine this. Carlos must have thought I was crazy. But the first game of the World Series was a grand temptation. Carlos did have friends named Oliva, and the fine hitter from Minnesota was named Oliva. Mind you, we would have had to get on a plane and fly to the Twin Cities to go to this World Series game. I was young and dumb—I had to be, because I believed him and gave him my glove. Of course he didn't go to any such thing resembling a World Series game, let alone take me. Finally I got my glove back. But my bag was packed, *ready* to go to the World Series, just in case.

I wore that glove out over the next decade. Played catch with my father wearing it. A father playing catch with his son. I don't want to sound like Eisenhower, but there is something powerful in that. One day I'll play catch with our daughter, Satchel.

Tonya wanted that name. She knew nothing about baseball, didn't know of Satchel Paige, the great pitcher of the Kansas City Monarchs and the Cleveland Indians. She liked the name. Satchel will be athletic. Maybe soccer. She has a good left foot. At the age of two, Satchel can kick a ball proficiently. You have to start 'em young.

There's been this big misconception that I came from a well-to-do family, and that is not the case. We were highly educated—our history mandated it. My great-grandfather William Edwards Williams studied under Booker T. Washington at Tuskegee and started the Snow Hill Institute in Snow Hill, Alabama. A distant cousin of mine, Frank McDuffy, was part of the origination of the Laurinburg Institute in North Carolina, where Dizzy Gillespie and quite a few basketball players got their scholastic finishings. My father had gone to Morehouse College in Atlanta. My paternal grandfather also went to Morehouse. My mother went to Spelman College, just across from Morehouse. Her mother, my grandmother, also went to Spelman. But as far as money went—we didn't have much. We were rich in ideas. In talents. Our parents made sure we sought them out.

My father is a jazz musician. And jazz musicians do not make a lot of money. The only ones who ever did were Miles Davis and, more recently, Branford and Wynton Marsalis. To make matters worse, my father was a traditionalist, a believer in acoustic music. He refused to play electric bass. He would compose on piano, but his instrument of choice and craftsmanship was the acoustic upright bass. Because he would not play electric bass, his work got cut in half. Yet he was such a staunch traditionalist as far as music was concerned that we went hungry a few times—not a lot, but enough to remember. One of my earliest images is of my father, who is my size, lugging that big bass around. My mother, who stopped working at one time to raise my brothers and sister and me, supported his principles in the matter. But she had to start working again. So she became a teacher at St. Ann's in Brooklyn Heights. She taught Afro-American literature, English, and art. All along, she was a strong supporter of my father. Though I believe artists should have integrity, I also know my father had five kids and a wife, and you think about that, as I'm sure he did. But no matter what, he was not going to play no electric bass for nobody. Our lights were cut off by Con Ed several times. I remember eating dinner by candlelight. It wasn't romantic. I remember the gas being turned off, and thinking, "Brooklyn Union don't play." I remember that.

Mostly, I was carefree. The only problem kids had in those days was finding money to buy candy or baseball cards. If there was a fight, somebody might end up with a fat lip or a black eye, but the combatants would be friends again the next day. Or brothers again the next day.

Chris proved this to me. We were playing two-hand touch football one day, and the Lees had been broken up, and Chris was playing for the opposition. I was the quarterback, and David was my receiver. David always was the best athlete among us. He was more muscular, had a better base, more strength, and he ran and changed direction well, would become a good tennis player one day. Chris may have had such aspirations, but now they were crushed with finality as I threw the deep ball to David, our younger brother, who reached up over Chris, took the ball away, and scored a touchdown. I ran down to celebrate with David, and a good thing, too, for now I was in position to break up the fight between them. Chris had not hesitated. As David scored, Chris raced to him and waded in with both hands, his face a mask of anger and grief. At first

David covered up, but then he began to apply himself in return and they were going at it hammer-and-tongs when I got to them and broke it up. "Quit it! Quit it!" I stood between my younger brothers, pushing out with both hands, trying to keep the pillars of a temple from crumbling. I made no mention of this fracas at dinner. Chris was already in Dutch with my mother. He gave her a lot of trouble. Chris resented authority. He was looking for a place to express himself, as I look back on it. That place was not the classroom; it wasn't the football field, as he had just found out. But by the next day, the incident was forgotten. There was another ball game to play. Or watch.

I was at Shea Stadium for Willie Mays's first game as a New York Met. He hit a home run, too, and I think it was his first time up. My friend Eric Wilkins and I had gone to Shea Stadium, and Eric was a Willie Mays fanatic, as many New Yorkers and sons of New Yorkers were and still are. But when the Giants (and Dodgers) moved away in the late 1950s, that took Mays away. Back then, as today, the teams came east twice a year for four-game sets, and Eric, he would go to every game when the San Francisco Giants came to town. He loved Mays so much. He liked Willie McCovey, Juan Marichal—could imitate Marichal's high leg kick perfectly—and the Perrys, Gaylord and Jim, Jim Davenport, Tito Fuentes, José Pagan, and Jim Ray Hart, but he liked them because they played with Willie. Eric insisted Jim Ray was going to be a great hitter, and he would have been if he hadn't offended Bob Gibson by digging into the batter's box too deep for too long at Candlestick Park one day. Gibson, the St. Louis Cardinals' fireballing right-hander and former Globetrotter, was a notoriously fast and ill-tempered worker on the mound. He waited with arms akimbo while Hart had called time and dug in, dug in, dug in with his spikes, and after he'd gotten himself comfortably situated and settled in, Gibby looked in and said, "You finished?" Hart looked up, confused, had no reply. "I said, are you through?" Gibson snarled. He wound up and brushed Jim Ray back with a heavy, blazing fastball. Actually, Jim Ray was dug in too deep and couldn't evade, so Gibson's pitch hit Hart in the shoulder blade, broke it, and Jim Ray never was the same after that. Mays and his teammates had probably warned him about digging in so deep against Gibby, but Hart didn't listen to veterans telling him how the game is often played on the highest level.

Joe Morgan, the former All-Star and two-time MVP second baseman, now a great baseball television commentator, recalls that he got a line drive base hit off Gibson once, a shot right past Gibson's ear into right center on a fastball tailing away from Morgan. When Morgan later scored a run after the hit and arrived back in the dugout looking for hand slaps and pats on the back, he was surprised when his teammates shunned him. Absolutely shunned him. Would not even look him in the face. Because nobody wanted to be seen by Gibson celebrating with some guy who had just nearly taken off Gibson's ear. The shunning gave Joe pause. No wonder Gibson had quit the Globetrotters. No need for killer instinct there. I took these stories as lessons. Of what, I was not sure, but I knew they were lessons. Never dig in too deep against a mean guy throwing high heat. Take the outside pitch the other way. And sometimes brothers will fight over a lousy touchdown pass.

Most of us liked the Mets instead of the Yankees in those days—most of us in Brooklyn and Queens, at least. Oh, we *knew* the Yankees. Great teams up there in the Bronx. But historically it seemed that the Yankees didn't want any black or Latin players, so they represented an elitist, country-club mentality and were not of the working classes, although they would make exception for a DiMaggio, a Rizzuto, or a Berra. The Yankees had the same chances to sign the Mayses, the Dobys, the Hank Aarons, the Ernie Bankses, and the Roberto Clementes as the National League teams had, but it never happened. Del Webb and Dan Topping, the Yankees' brain trust back then, seemed to have blinders on. Then in 1954 they grudgingly got the catcher Elston Howard, and then they brought him in to back up the guy who outside of Mickey Mantle was their best player. Yogi Berra. But the Yankees never did receive the benefit of the doubt in Brooklyn, even after Howard hit a home run in his first World Series at-bat in 1955. That was the year Brooklyn finally beat the Yanks in the World Series. Ellie's fault, is what the Yankee fans probably said. Never should have signed him. In Brooklyn we'd had Roy

Campanella. Three-time MVP. The Italians in the 'hoods rooted hard for Campy. When he got a hit, he was a *paisan*. But when he whiffed— *moolan yan*.

The Yankees seemed to think "Negro" ballplayers would offend the sensibilities of their season ticket holders from Westchester and Connecticut. Appearing on a show called *Youth Wants to Know,* Jackie Robinson was asked if he thought the Yankees were a racist organization at the time. When Robinson answered, simply and honestly, "Yes," it caused a brouhaha.

This all changed when the Dodgers moved to L.A., even more when the Yankee ownership moved to George M. Steinbrenner. People called him a tyrant. Sometimes you end up being a tyrant in business. George brought in Jim "Catfish" Hunter, Lou Piniella, Chris Chambliss, Mickey Rivers, Oscar Gamble, Willie Randolph, Reggie Jackson. When Reggie hit three home runs on the first three pitches he saw in the last game of the 1977 World Series at Yankee Stadium to win it over the Dodgers— the Los Angeleez Dodgers—the Yanks were down and I was a fan. In the 1996 season, when the Yankees got ex-Mets Darryl Strawberry and Dwight Gooden to go with brilliant center fielder Bernie Williams, slugger Cecil Fielder, rookie phenom shortstop Derek Jeter, David Cone, and crafty lefties Andy Pettitte and Jimmy Key, it was a magical season. I went to a few regular-season games and all of the home playoff and World Series games.

While growing up, I never cared for the New York football Giants, as they were called back then. For so long there were two New York Giants franchises, the baseball and the football team, until the baseball Giants went to San Francisco for the 1958 season. In baseball, I was a Mets fan, the Dodgers a distant second. But I was a Jackie Robinson fan, born the year Jackie retired, on being traded from the Dodgers to the Giants. I knew this as lore. I never saw Jackie play, but it seemed I did because I was told stories about his grit, tenacity, and skill, his significance as the first black ballplayer in the big leagues. In Brooklyn I already knew sports had a social significance. That was one reason I didn't care for the New York football Giants or the reputation they held.

In the early '60s, the New York football Giants had a reputation as a redneck team, more Birmingham Giants than anything representing New York. They had some cool guys, like Frank Gifford and Andy Robustelli, Erich Barnes, Emlen Tunnell, then Spider Lockhart, but they had a proclivity for ignoring the obvious. In 1965 they had a chance to draft a back everybody knew would be great, a brother from Kansas named Gale Sayers. If Sayers had played in New York, he'd still have billboards up. The Giants picked out a guy named Tucker Fredrickson from Auburn. Slow guy. White. Gimme a break. No problem with him being a white boy. It was the slow part that made him and the Bobby Duhons unacceptable. Ain't we trying to win here?

By 1967 I had already become a New York Jets fan. And so 1969 was a great year for me all around. The Jets were in the AFL, the American Football League. Played at Shea. They had Joe Willie Namath, one of my heroes. Joe *guaranteed* the Jets would beat the Baltimore Colts in the third Super Bowl game. I believed him, although the sportswriters and oddsmakers favored the Colts by as much as 17 points. But with backs like Emerson Boozer and his whirling dervish spin move, the battering ram power of Matt Snell, and the pass-catching ability of George Sauer Jr. and Don Maynard, Namath came through like a champ, the Jets won Super Bowl III, 16–7, in Miami, in January, to kick off 1969. Sportswriters have searched for a guy to give 'em a guarantee ever since then, like Namath and Ali, give 'em something they can use to fill pages in the papers. Guarantees make for good copy the day after. Win or lose, it makes a good story. Back page.

The Jets' Super Bowl victory got '69 off on the right foot, and Namath became my man for life. Then the pitching-rich Mets, the Miracle Mets, won the World Series that fall.

I went to a bunch of Mets games in 1969. What a year. During that season, if you cut the panels out of half-gallon cartons of Borden's milk— Elsie the Cow—and got a certain number of them, you got to see a Mets game for free—designated games where you could get in and go sit up in the grandstand. I drank me a whole lotta milk that year. My best friend Kwame Olatunji and I were at the game when the Mets clinched the Eastern Division, against the St. Louis Cardinals. Next up, in the playoffs, were the Atlanta Braves. The first two playoff games were in

Atlanta—Bad Henry Aaron hurt us, as I recall, and we had to be very careful with him—and then they came back to Shea for game three. The Mets beat the Braves three straight. Seaver, Koosman, Gentry. Nolan Ryan. Our parents let us miss school; all the post-season baseball games were held in the daytime back then. When Davey Johnson flied out to Cleon Jones for the last out of the last game and the Mets were World Champions, I ran out on the field like all the rest. And for a long time I kept my patch of outfield sod until my mother finally made me throw it away. About sod in the house, my mother was not so romantic.

To a young man to whom each sport was a passion, who was, like most, thinking maybe it could be me out there one day, it all seemed like fate. Destiny. And the Knicks were next.

We moved away from Cobble Hill into Fort Greene in September, a month or so before the beginning of the 1969–70 NBA season. My mother was a trailblazer in real estate matters. The best thing was to buy a brownstone while the buying was good. I entered Rothschild Junior High 294. After I enrolled in seventh grade my father took me a few blocks away from home to Long Island U., on the corner of Flatbush and DeKalb Avenues. LIU was playing Niagara University.

My father wanted me to go for two reasons. The first was so I could see the 5-foot-9 guard for Niagara who was leading the nation in scoring. Daddy said his name was Calvin Murphy. The second reason for taking me came to light at halftime. LIU's gym was once the stage of the old Brooklyn Paramount Theater, where Frankie Sinatra sang and all the girls would faint, fall out, and carry on, across the street from Junior's, home of the world-famous cheesecake. On this day, my father said, "C'mon, Spike, we're going to see Calvin Murphy." Who? During warm-ups, Calvin looked harmless. The other players were much bigger. Once the game started, though, no one could stay with him. He hit for nearly 50 on LIU, so much quicker than the other players it looked as if he was moving under a strobe. At halftime we went down to the floor. I was soaking up the angles when suddenly I found myself standing by a black man with white hair and rheumy eyes.

My father said, "Spike, I want you to meet a great man. This is Jackie Robinson."

At the time, Jackie was doing color commentary on LIU games. Of course, he had been a baseball, basketball, track, and football star at UCLA. My father pushed me up to him. I shook the great man's hand. Now in my mind, Jackie Robinson was a coal-black man with coal-black hair, a barrel chest, quick, strong, with piercing eyes. This couldn't be the same man, white-haired, with such weakened eyes. I shook his hand and thought about my black Louisville Slugger bat, the Jackie Robinson model. I'll never forget it—my father, Calvin, Jackie, all at once, in Brooklyn.

With the Jets in the Super Bowl that January and the Mets Miracle in the World Series in October, I already felt good about 1969. As the leaves on the poplar trees turned, it was time for basketball season, the NBA, and the Knicks. The Nets were stationed farther out on Long Island. In a few years they'd get the Doctor, Julius Erving. If people had tried to outlaw dunking with Julius around there would've been a riot, and I'm not just talking black people here. Billy Cunningham, the Kangaroo Kid from Erasmus High in Brooklyn, sixth man on Philadelphia's 1966–67 NBA champions, loved to watch Doc operate. In spite of Julius and the Iceman, George Gervin, I never embraced the American Basketball Association in quite the same way I had the AFL. The ABA had very interesting innovations, like the three-point shot, but I think what threw me was that hideous red-white-and-blue ball. You could see the bad rotation on a clank shot. Ugly.

Besides, I had never needed another basketball team or league to follow. When Chris and I would sit transfixed in front of the television set for a Knicks game during the 1969–70 season, we'd take turns saying, "Dad-day! Who do you want to win? Who do you want to win the game?" trying hard to contain our excitement. I suppose everybody likes company when they are cheering their team on, when everybody in the house is on the same page. My father would frustrate Chris and me constantly because he'd say, "Boys, I just want to see a good game." We must have asked my father that question a million times, didn't matter what sport, which team, or who was playing. My father would never say which team he wanted to win. Even though we believed he was pulling for one team over the other—even though in my heart of hearts I knew deep inside he was pulling for the Knicks—he would always answer the same way: "Just want to see a good game, boys."

Looking back, it would be *impossible* to overstate the impact of sports on my life—on many lives in Brooklyn. It may seem we had encyclopedic knowledge of sports, but we were steeped in them too, and very willingly so. And in that way Brooklyn was no different from a lot of places. Brooklyn had its own ambience and its patois, its dialects, but maybe we were not so different. Maybe we were emblematic. It's said some standardized tests like the Scholastic Aptitude Test (SAT), the LSAT, and the GMAT are culturally biased against black people here in America. Well, you can go across this nation, and ask any black man my age, younger, or older, and be that man from Brooklyn, Barstow, Boston, Birmingham, or Benton Harbor, Michigan, be he rich or poor, executive or panhandler, dyslexic or Denzel, if you ask that man, "Who was the forerunner of Michael Jordan in style of play?" that man will not hesitate saying, "Dr. J." It is automatic. If you ask, "Who was the forerunner of Dr. J?" that man will say "Elgin Baylor" or "Connie Hawkins." It should be that way in many fields of endeavor. Maybe it will be, one day. But this is what we were allowed, so this is what is of the fabric. All I know is, nothing meant more to me, nowhere in my life of twelve years was I more willing than when late fall arrived and I was going to junior high school and it came time to follow pro hoops, the 1969–70 Knicks, and we got Student Government Association cards allowing us to buy discount tickets to the Garden.

Walt Frazier was my favorite ballplayer, not only on the Knicks but in the entire NBA. He was my hero and idol. The only ones on his level were Joe Namath—Clyde in football version—Jackie, Mays, and Ali. The method of Frazier's game drew me in. I wanted to emulate his cool professionalism and style. I admired everything about him. He made me see that producing while making it look easy was the epitome of skill. We were both born in Atlanta, him on March 29, 1945, me on March 20, 1957 (Pat Riley was born on March 20 but in 1945). Despite this age difference, I felt we had a lot in common. Clyde scored the first Knick basket in the history of the new Garden, on Valentine's Day 1968.

Part of what made him a great ballplayer was his unselfishness. It was well within the scope of his game to try to score 40 points every night and to accomplish it often. But it would not have been in the best interests of the team, as it was then constructed. The 1969–70 Knicks starting lineup had some very good shooters in it, and that was part of the beauty of how they played. The Knicks were not the fastest or the jumpingest team in the NBA. They had to play team ball to win. They had to move it to the open man, force the defensive rotation, pass until they found the open Knick for the quick look at an 18-footer or maybe the cut to the hole. They had to play as a unit because they were not the most talented team in the concentrated dose of talent that was the NBA, which had "grown"—shrunk—from seventeen teams to fourteen in the twenty years since the merger of the National Basketball League and the Basketball Association of America in 1949.

At the beginning of the 1969–70 season, the Celtics were defending champions but had a void in the middle with Russell retired and Cowens a senior at Florida State. It would take Cowens a couple years to get acclimated once he came in. But they had a good backcourt. They had John Havlicek. I hated him because I hated the Celtics and he was now their greatest player. I use the word "greatest" advisedly. People have forgotten how great Havlicek once was.

In Milwaukee, the Bucks had Lew Alcindor at center and thirty-one-year-old Oscar Robertson at point, and they had drafted Lucius Allen, a guard on Alcindor's UCLA dynasty, and Bob Dandridge, a willowy 6-7 rookie with a fluid j from Norfolk State. My father and my uncles said Norfolk State was in the "See-Aye-Double-Ay," the CIAA, the Central Intercollegiate Athletic Association, a group of eastern black colleges. My father said that the CIAA tournament had all the pomp and circumstance of the Atlantic Coast Conference tournament, only more colorfully so, and the cheering occurring there was not of the mechanical, all-right o-kay go-team variety, but heartfelt, full of love and soulful rhythmic stomping. The CIAA tournament was something to see, all right, he said. And the players weren't bad, either. He told me it was up to me to know things like this, because I wouldn't get it from the press. It would be up to me to know about my history and to investigate it for myself. My father may have been more of a college hoop fan, which may also explain why I adopted the professional Knicks. The same but different. A child always needs a difference. My father would often say, "He ain't got nothing," whenever I got excited about some flash-in-the-pan pro prospect.

Dandridge was a rookie and would take a while baking. Along with this sweet-shooting rook, the Bucks had shooters like Jon McGlocklin, rebounders like Curtis Perry and Greg Smith. But the Big Bad Wolf that year was the Lakers, with Chamberlain, Jerry West, and Elgin Baylor.

The Knicks would have to play as a team, rotate, one through eight, to have any chance against the collections of superior individual talents on the Lakers, Bullets, Celtics, and Bucks.

Not that the Knicks were without talent. Far from it. John F. X. Condon would tick off the starters, one by one: "At guard, six-foot-four, from Southern Illinois, Walt Frazier."

To me, it nearly all began and ended with Condon's introduction of Frazier, but since he was my sporting hero, I may be biased in my perceptions—although, come to think of it, he averaged 20.1 points and shot .501 from the field during 1969–70 and played every game. Yet it seemed that Frazier was often at his best without the ball, on the defensive end. To put it in perspective, nothing made me calmer or more reassured than watching Clyde smoothly bring the ball upcourt against would-be pressure. Never showed any panic, he might have had the ball stolen from him here or there, but not very often, because I can't recall a single case. But he could steal it from you in a second. Nothing turns a game quicker than a steal and layup at the other end, and cool Clyde would look so calm pulling off the caper. The louder the Garden got, the calmer—and quicker—Frazier became. He would spend a quarter setting up the opposing point guard, just watching his moves, checking his dribble for the flaw. Then, when the Knicks went on a run, or needed a steal and a basket either to get back into a game or to put one away, Clyde knew how to go about getting it and when to go for it. "God gave me quick hands," Frazier would tell me later. He chuckled as he told me. "Like I always say, I was the oldest of nine kids, so it helped to have quick hands."

The high screen-and-roll is a tenet of basketball. It was hard to run on Frazier, particularly if his man set the pick. Clyde would wait until the man with the ball dribbled around the screen, then flash out as the ball left the ball handler's hand heading to the floor. When the ball was in possession of no one, Walt stuck out his hand, picked it, and he was gone the other way. He was a good jumper, and his drives were automatic. If Clyde took it to the hole, if he saw it, it was there. He got decisive rebounds by anticipating and often took the opposition's best guard on D—but never Jerry West. Dick Barnett always guarded West, although there was always room for switching on a good team. If you got close enough, you could even hear them: "Got yours." "Get mine."

Back then the dunk was just beginning to become the form of self-expression Julius Erving was to make it. Frazier would rise above the rim and lay the ball in with either hand, according to the defender's position. I felt like he was saving his energy for the next steal. I don't remember him ever dunking. He was like Jim Brown had been as a running back with the Cleveland Browns in the NFL—efficient in his use of energy. I became aware of Frazier and his game during the National Invitational Tournament his senior year, 1967, when he led the Salukis of Southern Illinois to the title at the old Garden. As fate had it, the Knicks then drafted him. Clyde had the size to play Big O. After Frazier was seasoned by a couple of years in the league, I knew we had an Answer.

Clyde even got me up out of Chuck Taylors. Later on in his career, when he began to wear low-cut white Pumas with the distinctive black stripe, I couldn't wait to get me a pair. Of course, because of Clyde, there was a run on the white low-cut Pumas, so my first pair was red suede with the white stripe. Eventually I had to get up out of those when I noticed that when it rained, or when you played in those and your feet sweated, your socks would be stained pink by the running of the dye. And I wanted to look like I might have a little bit of game.

Willis Reed was the captain. He came from Grambling University in northern Louisiana. Willis looked as if he could've played football for Eddie Robinson, too. He was 6 feet 9, with a high chest like a pigeon's, long, thick arms, could suit as a defensive end very well. Wonder how he got away from Coach Robinson down there? He was quiet and, being from Hico, Louisiana, and all, ashamed of his dialect, I'd imagine, needing work on his game, but a specimen of gigantic proportions at 245 pounds when the Knicks drafted him in 1964. At first the Knicks tried to use him at forward, since he was agile for his size, with Walt Bellamy at center. Bells was okay, but I never got the feeling we could win with him. Willis looked lost at forward. The footwork, and being taken out away from the basket on defense, bothered him. The Twin Tower theory didn't work. The Knicks would try it again, years later, with Bill Cartwright and Patrick Ewing. It didn't work then, either. But Willis caught on, made it apparent he had more potential than Bells as a center. Bells was already thirty, nearly shot, limited. Reed, besides size and rebounding ability, had a lefty j, accurate and surprisingly soft, launched from so imposing a figure such a distance from the hoop. He was automatic from 18 feet away.

Reed and Johnny Bench, then a young catcher with the Cincinnati Reds, had a TV show called *MVP.* They were taped in New York, over in Manhattan. I can remember sitting in the audience for some of those old shows, which occurred after this season. A lot of people recall Willis as the MVP of the Knicks that year, 1969–70, maybe rightly so, since you can't win the NBA title without big people against Chamberlains, Unselds, Alcindors. Willis was our center, and it was his job to battle with them, night in and night out, on even terms. We didn't ask him to outplay them every night. We'd outplay them at the other positions and in the way we played together. These Knicks were, to me, the first and truest definition of the word "team."

Going into the season I wasn't as big a fan of Dick Barnett, the 6-4 guard from Gary, Indiana, who started opposite Frazier. I remembered him from being a Laker. Played with Jerry West, and he would say, "Fall back, baby," whenever he launched one of those left-handed j's, the ones where he would pull his feet up into a tuck beneath him. When he felt it, he'd yell, "Fall back, baby." He would be running back down to the defensive end before the ball landed with a pop into the net. The Knicks traded to get him the day before the 1965–66 season began. He looked old. Had this sleepy-eyed countenance, a sort of down-in-the-mouth look. His teammates called him Skull. He often looked it; while playing, his face resembled the one in the painting by Munch, *The Scream*. But he had an unerring corkscrew jumper, lefty, and had become something of a legend in two years with the Syracuse Nationals, then three with the Lakers. He'd gone to Tennessee State, playing there for a legendary coach, John McLendon, and was two-time NAIA Player of the Year. Coming from under the wing of McLendon, it was not surprising that Barnett, in addition to being a player of professional abilities, was an articulate brother who went back to school and got his doctorate and who while playing had a grasp of the Game, his future, and a dry wit. He had a way of leveling the other Knicks with the latter. He told Bill Bradley he would never be mugged because he dressed as if he'd *already* been mugged. He told Frazier it was just as well that Frazier outdressed him, being as how he could never outshoot him anyway. Skull kept everybody loose, and thinking.

"We were a very bright team," said Bradley. "Dick was *very* bright. He'd been around. Experienced. And then Frazier, Reed, DeBusschere, Phil Jackson, Cazzie—all of them were very smart men. And we had a unique group of personalities." Some of the old Knicks say Barnett is still the most original personality they've ever encountered. "Barnett was my idol," said Frazier. "He and Red Holzman were the catalysts for my success. They gave me a lot of confidence at a time when I was doubting that I should even be in the league. Dick said defense was my forte. Red gave me confidence about it, too. I was just happy these men even thought I *had* a forte."

I couldn't see all this then. I was hanging from the rafters. My appreciation for Barnett didn't develop until he was retired. Being a callow youth, I equated experience with being old. I just knew Barnett was old—thirty-three at the start of the 1969–70 season. Frazier was twenty-four; Reed was twenty-seven. They were the age that hoopers should be as I saw it. Now I know Dick was at the height of his powers, in control of his game, known as an ace defender, not an easy thing in the NBA. With Frazier, he gave the Knicks the best defensive backcourt in the league at the time, and men who could score 30 points each on a given night.

This multidimensional backcourt is mirrored today, but at the average height of 6-8 instead of 6-4, and in vertical airspace as well as on the floor, by the world champion Bulls. Today is their era. When the Bulls go to their end-game win rotation, it is Jordan who goes to point guard, controlling the action and flow, where Frazier once was, even though Jordan is the prototypical size of a two-guard, just as Frazier was once. It is now Scottie Pippen, the 6-8 forward, who can play two-guard if necessary, where Barnett once was. And in this configuration there are nights when the Chicago Bulls can shut down the other team's backcourt, and they will not let the game get below the free-throw line in the heated final minutes of the fourth quarter.

So, in 1969, the Knicks were set at three positions—both guards, Frazier and Barnett, and Reed in the middle, at center. But to borrow from one of my father's idols, Mr. Duke Ellington, it don't mean a thing if it ain't got that swing. And when you say "swing" in basketball, both then and now, you are talking about somebody who can play forward. Guard too.

No position was more provocative than small forward, given over to a former Princeton All-American and Rhodes scholar, Bill Bradley, over Cazzie Russell, from Chicago and the University of Michigan. The Knicks won a coin flip with the Detroit Pistons in 1966 for Cazzie's draft rights as the number one pick. The Pistons didn't do as badly as other losers in subsequent coin flips. When the Phoenix Suns lost in the flip to Milwaukee three years later, losing Alcindor, the next pick was a 6-foot-11 stiff from Florida named Neal Walk. But in 1966, Detroit's consolation was better; a 6-3 guard out of Syracuse and D.C. named Dave Bing, who ended his playing days with a scoring average of 20.3 over twelve seasons and 901 games—ended his playing days so blind in one eye that he would make 20-footers by looking down and gauging the distance and release of his shot by his position on the floor. He later owned a successful steel company, Bing Steel.

The dynamic between Russell and Bradley was interesting and profitable. This was a place where styles and cultures clashed and made noise and people paid attention, especially if they sensed the drama was playing out along racial and class lines. It sold tickets, and it always has. Russell came to the Knicks in 1966 after his illustrious collegiate career at Michigan. Cazzie could be streaky, but whenever he got hot—lights out. He was a siege gun shooter, like Reggie Miller is today. Cazzie went about 6-5, was very bowlegged—straighten out his legs and he might have been 6 feet 7. He was a "tweener" in the papers. Not big enough to do damage inside as a forward, not enough handle or quicks to play outside. But he could fill up the cup.

Bradley's career at Princeton tracked right alongside Russell's. In fact they had faced each other in the 1964 Holiday Tournament up at the old Garden. Princeton had led by 12 points with three minutes to play. Then Bradley fouled out, and Cazzie hit a jumper at the buzzer to win it for Michigan. After graduation, Bradley went off to Oxford on a Rhodes scholarship, then he came back and joined the Knicks roster in 1967. The Knicks ran his record at Princeton in the press guide, not Cazzie's from Michigan; when Russell, the starter, was injured on January 21, 1969, breaking an ankle as Joe Kennedy of Seattle fell on him in a scramble at the Garden, Bradley, who had been playing mostly at guard, was inserted as a starter at small forward.

It stayed that way in the fall.

In some ways this foreshadowed the Larry Bird–Magic Johnson struggles ten years later, only this rivalry occurred on one team, at one position. The impact, rather than being national, was more provincial. But the Game always was played in middle America, too, Indiana being a hotbed. There, and in other places like Missouri, Bradley's home state, the game was played in a different style. There was more of a reliance on outside shooting, patterned play, less reliance on what people called flash, creativity, and man-to-man matchups on defense. In those days many black Knicks fans thought Cazzie should have gotten his starting job back and Bradley should have been coming off the bench. "Oh, I don't know about that," Bradley told me. "There were a lot of black people in my corner, too." Bradley was a mirror image of Cazzie at 6 feet 5— as Bird and Magic were both 6-9. No matter the reason, many black people wanted to see Cazzie play, and whites—especially the newer white Manhattan crowd—Bradley was one of theirs, they wanted to see him do well. This was why the Knicks put his Princeton record in the guide in the first place. Bradley enabled them to tap into a new market for the Game played by the vagrant classes.

Of course, it wasn't that cut and dried for either man.

"There was mutual respect," Bradley would tell me years later. "Every practice was a war, in terms of competition. As an athlete and a human being, I felt Cazzie was absolutely dedicated to the game and that we were in this circumstance of competition. Ultimately the coach would decide. Of course, my so-called break came when Cazzie broke his ankle. I stepped in at the end of the 1968–69 season. We ended up losing to Bill Russell in the playoffs in his last year."

They genuinely seemed to respect each other, Caz and Dollar Bill. Later I found out Bradley had suffered social ostracism himself while at Princeton for playing basketball, the lower-class sport where blacks could have an equal foothold with whites. Some of his fellows derisively called him Old Satin Shorts at Princeton. So I figure envy must know no color.

"My first year I noticed some of the people called me White Hope. I knew I wasn't any white hope," said Bradley. "There's only one hope. There were great expectations for me. And I failed badly my first year. I was put at guard, and I was too slow to play guard, couldn't keep up. And so things were difficult. At the same time, I was receiving these rather sizable offers. The Dairy Association wanted me to be a spokesperson for milk. Olivetti wanted me to be its national spokesperson. I felt these things were coming to me not because I was the best player on the team, which I wasn't, but because I was white. And that was the perception of how to market. So I just decided, I'm not going to do it, and I never did, throughout my time in the league."

Bradley worked on his game, his defense, his shot. The summer after his rookie year he played in the Baker League in Philadelphia. In the last game of the Baker League season, Bradley, playing for Gaddis Real Estate, scored 46. Earl "the Pearl" Monroe, the star guard of the Baltimore Bullets, scored 62, and his team, Jimmy Bates, won. Bradley's game got better. His stroke was as sweet as any of the others to begin with. Bill—Dollar Bill, we called him—had to work to get his off because his money shot was not a jumper that got him away from a defender, as Cazzie's could, but often a set shot. Bradley would stick out his rump and line the shot up off his shoulder. He was as deadly as any when they ran him off a few bumps, a few picks, and if he got a good look at it and he could get that shot off, he wouldn't miss. Looking back on it, I can see he had to work hard to get the starting slot, and by the beginning of the 1969–70 season he was entrenched at starting small forward, with Caz performing as the sixth man—instant offense—and with a lot of people believing Caz had gotten a raw deal—a lot of people, except the public Cazzie, who seemed to have a perpetual smile crawling across his spreading Asiatic features. He embraced his role and named the Knicks' subs "the Minutemen." It was the right thing, what Holzman did with Cazzie, Bradley, and the rotation. I think Bradley turned out to be a better starter, but we wanted some style and Cazzie had it. We got that, too, in the end. Cazzie lit up the Garden many a night that season, averaging 11.8 points per game. Over the last 28 games of the year, Cazzie averaged 18.4. There is an axiom in sports that you can never lose your starting job to an injury. You can only lose it by being outperformed. Bradley and Cazzie turned that around. Neither outperformed the other, but both generally outperformed the opposition.

So that was four out of five starters. But the big forward position had been hurting us before, which was why we had tried the Twin Towers experiment with Reed and Bellamy. You could not have such a glaring weakness in your starting lineup and hope to beat the Bullets, the Celtics, the Bucks, or the Lakers. You needed a horse inside, a strong rebounder, a physical presence to take some of the load and the pressure off your center—in the Knicks' case, the stoic Reed. The Knicks would not have been a factor in the playoffs at the end of the 1969–70 season if they hadn't pulled off the trade. On December 19, 1968, the Knicks sent Bellamy and Howie "Butch" Komives, who was just a jump-shooter, to the Detroit Pistons for their best player and one of the best all-around athletes in the league, a former major league pitcher with the Chicago White Sox, a 6-6, twenty-eight-year-old named Dave DeBusschere. And for the Knicks, DeBusschere turned out to be the answer. The final one. I loved his game from the get-go. I loved his superior athletic ability—very strong, very willing to bang and board, combining a great base, good legs, with touch outside. He and Frazier may have been the best athletes on the team. DeBusschere was the missing link. He could stroke it from the corner, the wing, up top, great range. And since he played forward, he forced the other team's best rebounder away from the basket when he went outside. He was also a fierce defender, could back up Reed at center if need be, and we needed it because our next best big forward after Dave the Rave Stallworth, a 6-foot-8 guy from North Dakota named Phil Jackson, was hurt. The league, then and now, is physical, punishing down low. A body *can* get hurt.

The Knicks won a lot of games that year with the second rotation off the bench, Cazzie Russell's Minutemen. No one of any age can play a whole forty-eight-minute NBA game and retain his optimum performance capacity the entire time. No matter what your condition is, sooner or later you're going to get tired if you are playing flat out. Your second rotation is going to win or lose you a lot of games. The second rotation in 1969–70 worked itself out beautifully.

First, there was Cazzie, who had a starter's firepower. When he subbed for Bradley, there was no dropoff. At the other forward in the second rotation, behind DeBusschere, we had Dave Stallworth, from Wichita State, and originally from Dallas, Texas, like Dennis Rodman. Stall had been out of ball for two years after having had a heart seizure on March 7, 1967, in Fresno, California. Before that he'd averaged 13 points and six boards a game and had played opposite Cazzie before Bradley and then DeBusschere arrived. For the 1969–70 season, Dave the Rave had returned, and we needed his flexibility bad. He gave us a live body inside—6-7, could run, could get on the boards, could hop, not a shooter but a scorer, and he knew that, and the Knicks needed somebody who could drive, play the lanes, crash the boards, create havoc. Dave the Rave rarely took the 18-footer on which the Knick offense was based. Hard worker. He'd average 7.8 points.

In the backcourt, Mike Riordan crashed around into people, was our intentional fouler—this being back in the day of the two-for-one foul strategy—and they'd put him in to foul somebody and take him right back out if we were behind late, and he gave a blow to Frazier or Barnett as needed. Riordan was hard-nosed on the defensive end and could score with a hellbent drive and even a j.

Donny May was All-American at Dayton, but no more than a scrub on this most professional team. Nate Bowman, Reed's caddy, was a crowd favorite and a scrub, too, at this level. Bill Hosket and John Warren probably could have played for Vancouver today. Back then they could usually be represented in the box score this way—DNP-CD: Did Not Play, Coach's Decision.

The current Chicago Bulls coach and Zen master, Phil Jackson, was on the Knicks' roster in 1969–70. Nice player. Tall, gangly, long arms, clean-cut, though in a year or two he grew an Age of Aquarius white boy Afro; hook shot, good timing, not real robust, but you can't have it all. Had a basketball player body, long arms, coat-rack shoulders, sinewy legs. I remember the shoulders. Never seen any like them, before or since. He'd hurt his back, but he was around. He would've been a backup at center and forward. He took up photography, and that's what he did that year.

So in the end we had a classic eight-man rotation that Red could extend to ten at times. And everybody who played had a reliable j or, in the case of Stallworth, didn't shoot jumpers. All the fans had a stake in the game, a personal stake, and many ethnicities were represented, and classes too. Bradley was followed by the elites, some of whose ilk had given him a hard time at Princeton. He'd brought in a whole new crowd—and an opinionated one, at that. Immigrant classes spawned DeBusschere, Riordan, Holzman. Then you had the brothers, ranging from deep southern rural to midwestern to Chicago slick to Gary, Indiana, hard. It didn't seem curious at all to me that there was not a single native New Yorker on the roster. Couldn't carry people just to be carrying them.

Bottom line, there was no formal affirmative action then or, if there was, it was not the kind that favored black people. You earned your way into the Knicks rotation. No matter who they were or where they were from, it was like the politics of the city and the nation were revealed in their backgrounds, their games, and by those who followed them. This is a reason they are remembered so fondly. For we saw how they made it work. They represented something. There was something there for everybody, too. So this was the team that took hoop upscale to Broadway. Whatever differences they had as individuals, you never saw them revealed in their play. They put differences aside for a higher purpose. They were a team. They were the best. The best *team,* I'm saying. They were the best not because they had the most talent but because they had great chemistry.

> > >

The Knicks began the season 23–1, still the best start to a regular season in the history of the NBA, including the then record streak of nineteen wins in a row. Eighteen wins in a row! Red Holzman had his preferred substitution pattern right from the beginning. The starting five were rarely outplayed. Then Riordan would come on to give Frazier or Barnett a blow, depending on who needed it most—probably Barnett, who was older—or who wasn't going well. Dave the Rave would give a reddening DeBusschere a rest, Cazzie would check in for Bradley, and the tempo of the game would often pick up. Many times the second rotation would put games away in the second quarter, for all intents and purposes. Depending on who we were playing, DeBusschere would then go back in, and maybe Reed would come out. Or maybe Bowman would go in for Reed, if we had a lead and could afford to play him. The ball movement was on time, Swiss movement. The Knicks worked you until they got the open shot. Even from 20 feet away, they were exceedingly reliable. The lead dogs, Frazier and Reed, averaged 20.9 and 21.7 points that season, and shot a combined .514 from the field, in an era when Milwaukee's .488 team field goal percentage led the league. The Knicks' scoring was balanced: Bradley, 14.5 a game, DeBusschere at 14.6, and Barnett, 14.9. These were *seasonal* averages. Can't have a better spread.

It began paying off with the streak of twenty-three wins out of the first twenty-four games. I was ecstatic. DeBusschere had gotten acclimated in the second half of the previous season, and where it took other teams time to jell, the Knicks were already solid in approach, all with league experience, and every essential man but Barnett still in his twenties. They defended as a team, too, starting out high with Barnett and Frazier. Bradley and DeBusschere overplayed the passing lanes, and the Knicks turned it over very rarely and never seemed to miss an open shot.

I watched the road games on WOR with a fascination bordering on autistic fixation. When my sister, Joie, and younger brother Cinque came to me years later with the script for *Crooklyn,* it took me back to that time. Our house being a democracy, we voted on which shows to watch on the one television set we owned. On most Friday nights the Knicks played on the road. And those were the only games that were televised, then only on WOR, no cable TV back then. But also on Friday nights, *The Partridge Family* and *The Brady Bunch,* both of my sister's favorite shows, came on back-to-back, starting at eight o'clock, and they were definitely what my sister would choose if left to her own devices. I couldn't just lob on my sister. She would grab my lob, say she had rights. There was only the one TV. But if the Knicks were on, the game would be on at the same time as what she wanted to see. Chris was usually with me. Cinque was usually with Joie.

The swing vote was David.

Naturally, I had to resort to that staple of politics—bribery. As soon as Cinque saw David was bribable, he let it be known that he was open for business too. I gave up a few nickels and dimes, some twos and fews. Chris was usually loyal without benefit of the vigorish. Some nights Joie would prevail, though, and I had to endure an hour of schmaltz-ridden ABC family shows before seeing the Knicks. Even today, to my horror, I know the themes to those shows by heart. I was not far from killing my sister. While the Knicks are on Channel 9, I'm watching David Cassidy, and my siblings are singing along with "I Think I Love You" and "I Woke Up in Love This Morning."

The Knicks' winning nineteen regular-season games in a row set an NBA record that lasted all of two whole years before Chamberlain and the Lakers won thirty-three in a row in their championship season, 1971–72. That record is still on the board. Nineteen in a row seemed impossible then. But the Knicks did it. The last win came in Cleveland against the Cincinnati Royals, who had a 12-point lead with two minutes to play. Led by Frazier's defense, the Knicks came back and won 106–105, as I fell over myself in front of the only television in the brownstone in Fort Greene. Da Cooz was the Cincy coach. He must have had a flashback, because he put himself into the game to try and ice it late, but he could not, and committed a decisive turnover. He was too old to play now, and never did again. He got Tiny Archibald the next season. And the Knicks had their win. Said Bradley, "Da Cooz. By then it was 'Yeah, right.'"

It was nothing for me to go to the Garden alone. No point in even asking Chris by then. He just wasn't interested in it as much anymore. Once, on one of my trips over to the Garden, I saw Emile Francis, who was then the New York Rangers' coach and general manager. He smiled, and at first I thought he was going to ask me if I could skate, if I was a Rangers fan. Instead he rubbed my head for luck. It was an insulting tradition among some people, rubbing a pickaninny's head for luck. Didn't take, though. The Rangers hadn't won the Stanley Cup since 1941, and after Francis rubbed my head in 1969, they were cursed with twenty-five more years of futility until they finally broke through and won the cup in 1994. Old Emile rubbed the wrong nappy head. Never been a Rangers fan since that incident.

We—the Knicks—finished the regular season 60–22. Whatever jealousies and conflicts there were on the team—I'm sure they had them—did not surface publicly and never showed up on the court. Now the playoffs began. It would be a struggle, though the Knicks were number one in the NBA in average margin of victory, averaging 9.1 points more than the opposition. In the playoffs, the Knicks would face the Bullets, with a 50–32 season record, then the Milwaukee Bucks, a 56–26 team, with rookie Lew Alcindor as its focal point, and aging Big O at point. If form held and the Knicks won, they would face the Lakers for the title. The Lakers had finished second in the Western Division to the Atlanta Hawks and Lou Hudson, he of the formful jumper and a 25.4 scoring average that year, hitting 53 percent from the field, amazing for a man who almost exclusively used a deep j. Hudson would have chewed on a three-point line. Sweet Lou.

Everybody figured the Lakers were biding their time. West averaged 31.2 points a game, and the Lakers also had Chamberlain *and* Elgin Baylor, no older then than Charles Barkley is in the 1996–97 season. As I look back, of the twenty players in the starting lineups for Milwaukee, Baltimore, New York, and the Lakers that year, ten of them made the NBA's Fifty All-Time Greats list in 1996. Some of the starters on those four teams who didn't make it, like Baltimore's forward, the knock-kneed

Gus "Honeycomb" Johnson, could have made it. I can still hear Condon: "That is goaltending," after Gus grabbed a shot. Barnett didn't make it. The rook from Milwaukee named Bob Dandridge didn't make it, though he averaged 18.5 points a game over thirteen seasons, played on two teams that won NBA titles. Fred "Mad Dog" Carter didn't make it. He averaged 15.2 for eight years—three straight years averaging 21 per game. Neither Bradley nor Russell made it, but taken together, as they played the same position on the same team, they could have made it, too.

All ball. That's what I'm talkin' 'bout.

The Knicks began their quest with a best-of-seven series against Baltimore. The Bullets had never won an NBA title, but they matched up with us better than anybody. "It was uncanny," said Frazier. "Every matchup was dramatic." For Reed, they had 6-8 Wes Unseld, as wide as he was tall. He matched Willis in rebounding. The Bullets also had Gus Johnson at power forward. He was an equal match for DeBusschere. "I can still see DeBusschere slumped in a corner of the locker room, drinking a beer, barely able to get the can to his mouth, he was so tired after playing Gus Johnson," Frazier says. At small forward, the Bullets threw Jack Marin at us. Fluid, mobile at 6-5, built to run, gave Bradley fits. Had a big brown birthmark on his shoulder. "Bradley and Marin ran so much they made you dizzy," Frazier said. "Don't even talk about Havlicek."

For Frazier, the Bullets had Earl "the Pearl" Monroe, one of the greatest one-on-one players of all time. They called *him* Black Jesus first. He was the original. Game was so original and poetic that it won him converts. Black Jesus from North Philly, Baker League, Winston-Salem State, Coach Bighouse Gaines, CIAA tournament. Legendary. Creative. Went to college during the Greensboro lunch-counter demonstration era down in North Carolina. People said there were no social conflagrations in Winston-Salem during this time. They credited Monroe's artistry with cooling out the masses. It might get tense on Main Street, but, black and white, people turned out to the Winston-Salem Coliseum to see if Earl might drop 50 on somebody's dome that evening. Original spins, sleight of hand, flat, tiptoe j, and any kind of layup you can think of and some you can't. Monroe averaged 23.4 points that season, 1969–70. You usually whispered his name.

At the other guard, the Bullets had Mad Dog Carter, who now waxes eloquent on ESPN, and Kevin Loughery. This was not a watered-down league of minor talents. There was a pitched battle every fuggin' night, and the differences in talent between teams were not great.

The first game went double-overtime at the Garden. Mad Dog went for 21. Pearl dropped 39 on Clyde, who had 16 points, 11 boards, and 8 assists, yet was outplayed. Unseld snatched off 31 boards, shocking us, and had 5 assists. If not for Reed, DeBusschere, and Bradley, we would have gone down in flames under this firepower. DeBusschere had 24 boards and 22 points, Bradley rang up 21, Willis had 30 and 21 boards, and the Knicks prevailed, 120–117. Then the Knicks won game two, 106–99. Clyde stuck to his knitting on Pearl, held him to 19, but now Gus Johnson went off—28 points, 12 rebounds. Still, the Knicks balance— six players in double figures—got it done. The Knicks were up 2–0. The Bullets had us right where they wanted us.

Game three was a classic, if you were a Bullets fan. Unseld, in his second year in the league, made his playoff bones that night. He went off like a Roman candle, scoring 23 points, grabbing 34 rebounds, and even dishing dimes—4 assists. The Knicks seemed stunned by the ferocity of his play. He'd snatch a rebound, and before his feet lit he'd done a half-turn in the air and fired an outlet pass to Monroe, who was nearly to half-court. Showtime. Unseld was lithe, amazingly so for a man who made Charles Barkley look anorexic. The Bullets had six in double figures, four with 20 or more. Mad Dog had 23, Marin 20, Pearl 25. The Knicks lost, 127–113. What we expected to be the beginning of the end was just the beginning. Unseld kept pace the next game at Baltimore with 24 rebounds. The brother was *housing* the boards. The Bullets outrebounded the Knicks by 11, Pearl went for 34, Gus for 18 and 13 boards.

Two up. Back to the Garden.

Willis stepped up big-time in game five—36 points and 36 rebounds, Knick playoff records. Unseld had only 15 rebounds that night, three more than DeBusschere. Frazier had 16 points and 16 rebounds, and the Knicks outrebounded the Bullets by 37 to win at home, 101–80.

Game six was a tight defensive struggle. They were playing as if for their lives. Gus took the Bullets over in that game, exploding to the rafters at the Baltimore Civic Center for 31 points and 14 boards. Pearl had his 29, and the Bullets sent it to a seventh game with a 96–87 win. There was no telling now. The Bullets concentrated their defensive attention on Reed, Frazier, and Bradley. Without high-scoring games from those three, they reasoned, they could outscore the Knicks. But Knick ball saved New York. The Knicks smoothly moved the ball to the players left completely one-on-one. Skull Barnett went for 29, and DeBusschere had 28 points and 13 rebounds, to get a little bit of an edge on the minute-weary thirty-four-year-old Gus Johnson, who had 24 and 13 (Gus died in 1987 at the age of fifty-one). Pearl had his 32. Marin, who later became a lawyer, got the better of Bradley, who later became a senator, but Caz came off the bench to score 18, Riordan had 10, and by getting a little something from everybody and getting 6 more assists than the Bullets as a team and holding Unseld to 16 boards, New York won the game and the series, 127–114.

Yowsuh! Unseld had played his game. So did Gus, Jack, Mad Dog. Pearl was unbelievable, averaging 28 points per game over the seven-game series, all against Frazier. But when it was over, the Knicks were still standing. At the time, a tired Frazier said of Monroe, "Glad I don't have to see his face anymore."

"He was my nemesis," Frazier says now. "I had a reputation as a ladies' man. Somewhat deserved. But Earl Monroe was the only *man* I would dream about. He gave me nightmares."

Milwaukee was up next. The Bucks would win the NBA title themselves the next season, but Alcindor was a rookie this year, and Willis took full advantage, averaging 27.6 points per game, pulling Alcindor away from the hoop and popping in that lefty jumper and knocking Lew off the low block for the boards. Lew Alcindor, soon to become Kareem Abdul-Jabbar, had to find out what it was really like first, and the Knicks were too balanced. In the first game, won by the Knicks 110–102, Bradley, Cazzie, and DeBusschere had 18 each, complementing Reed's 24, offsetting Alcindor's 35 points and 15 rebounds. Cazzie and Bradley combined for 26 a game over the five-game set, too quick for Smith and

Perry, too savvy for rookie Dandridge. Milwaukee was disposed of, though Alcindor averaged over 32 points a game. Nothing you could do to stop the King. Just slow him down, get on top, and stay up on the other Bucks. It worked like a charm.

So now it came down to the series with the Lakers for the World Championship.

I followed these proceedings with mood swings following each victory or loss that caused my mother to wonder if I was ill, or maybe insane. Chris was no longer as die-hard as I was, at least not on this subject. On others, he could be intractable. Once, well after the football incident, we were on one of our bike runs into Manhattan—eight of us from the block, including Chris and me. It was great fun to race across the Brooklyn Bridge and go up Sixth Avenue all the way to Fifty-ninth Street and Central Park, jumping potholes, popping wheelies. We did it often. It's how I learned the streets of Manhattan well. On this trip, Chris—a good cyclist—ran over a broken bottle and ended up with a flat. As his tire expired, we stood astride our bikes. I got off mine. I'd walk home with him. Chris looked up at us. Veterans in our party wore looks of superiority, as if they had too much savvy to ever have a flat tire. Chris looked at them, and then at me. Then he picked up his bicycle and heaved it into the East River.

As he stormed off in a crosstown direction I looked at my brother with mingled contempt and awe. When Chris finally got home, my grandmother Zimmie asked him where was his bike? "I threw it in the river." She said, "*What?* What river?" Chris replied, "I threw it in the East River. I had a flat tire. I wasn't going to push that thing home all the way." Only the Knicks could inspire me to such heights of foolishness, heights that, once my mother found out, would test the limits of her patience. And I would never, ever test my mother's patience in matters involving expense. Bicycles were not disposable. But Chris and I were polar opposites. He talked nonstop. I was quiet, hardly spoke. I loved sports. He left them lying there.

But now as the NBA finals neared, I made a bold statement of my own at the dinner table: "We're gonna beat the Lakers." Chris nearly dropped his fork. I was being vocal and certain of something at the same time? "First you are going to clear that plate," said my mother. "And what the hell is a Laker anyway?"

For Chris's transgression of bike-tossing, he caught more flak. But not from my father. When my mother expressed concern about Chris's stability, my father would scoff: "There's nothing wrong with Chris. Leave him alone. He's fine." Nine times out of ten, my father would not let anybody touch Chris. He felt everybody in the world was crazy but Chris and him. Later on, when Chris became a bicycle messenger for over five years, it may have been to prove something. To himself.

The NBA championship series best-of-seven finals began at Madison Square Garden. Jerry West and Elgin Baylor combined for 54 points in the first game. Baylor and Wilt combined for 44 rebounds. Whatever Lakers were, I hoped they were not all like *that,* not *all* the time. But Willis Reed had himself a terrific game with 37 points and 16 rebounds and 5 assists, and Riordan came out of nowhere with 19, most over the head of Johnny Egan and Keith Erickson, a former volleyball player. He was looking to help, away from Riordan. Knicks with ease, 124–112. I thought, "We got it. We got it. We're better than them." Even when the Knicks lost game two, 105–103 at the Garden as West went for his normal 34, I thought it was okay. The Knicks shot only 43 percent, with Frazier the only starter even close to 50 percent from the field. The Knicks had still outrebounded them, 59–46. We would get one in L.A. Maybe two.

We got the first one, 111–108, although not without heart palpitations. Willis had 38 points and 17 rebounds. His ability to step away from the basket for his shot was bothering Wilt, whose game, both defensively and offensively, was exclusively down low, especially with his advancing age. He wouldn't effectively step out and hound Willis's j. As long as we had Willis, we had the equalizer for the Big Dipper. Let West have his 34. So the Knicks did. West had 32, the Knicks were up by two, two seconds left, Laker ball under the Laker basket, out of time-outs. We had 'em licked. West took the inbounds pass near his own free-throw line. He heaved up a runner. Looked like desperation, a 62-foot shot. Went in like he practiced it. *Swish.* The Knicks looked stunned. All except Clyde, who sauntered back to the bench like "Yeah." Almost like he expected it. Almost like he appreciated the improv on West's part. Like he was saying, "Sweet. Now let me show you what I got." Clyde took us through the overtime—19 points, 11 rebounds, 7 assists, estimated 5 steals for the game. And somehow we won, 111–108, at the Forum. Under today's rules, the Knicks would have lost that game. West's shot would've counted for 3.

The next game, West got 37. Baylor got 30, with 13 boards. The Lakers outrebounded the Knicks, 66–51. Willis had 23, DeBusschere 20 and 11, Barnett 29, but Wilt's 18 points, 25 boards, 4 blocks, and 7 assists were the key to victory. The Knicks were never out-assisted. That was *our* game. But the Lakers had 10 more and came away to the good, 121–115.

Two games each. "Right on schedule," I thought.

But the best-laid plans went awry. Reed went across the lane with Chamberlain early in the fifth game at the Garden. Massive forces met. Willis was thrown off-balance, missed landing on his feet, and crashed into the Garden floor directly on his hip. A deep, painful, nerve-inflaming, muscle-locking bone bruise and muscle pull. He couldn't even walk. Red decided to go small, move DeBusschere to center, with help from Stallworth, bring Cazzie off the bench, play him and Bradley at forward. The Knicks escalated pace, played a 1-3-1 offense suggested by Bradley at halftime. "That was a mark of Red as a coach," said Bradley. "A lot of times we'd come to the bench during a time-out and Frazier would say, 'Let's run BF,' or 2-1F or 2-3F or backdoor. Red would never dictate plays. He was open, responsive. I suggested it. Red said, 'I don't know what else we're gonna do.' We tried it, and it worked." Cazzie was hot. Stallworth was in back, running the baseline, a mosquito Wilt couldn't swat. Rave had 12 points, 6 boards, 3 assists, a nasty reverse lay, and we escaped, 107–100. Willis only played eight minutes. Baylor, West, and Wilt combined for 63, but Caz had 20 and Clyde had 21 and 21 boards. DeBusschere kept Wilt in the building, held him to 22 points and 19 rebounds. Clyde played in a quiet frenzy and helped Barnett limit West to only 20 while becoming, behind Wilt, the dominant player on the floor.

Knicks, 107–100, up three games to two, going back to L.A. But without Willis we were in trouble. It was great to see us win game five. But at the same time, I was subdued. Willis didn't look like he'd be able to come back. With time to prepare, the Lakers were a lock in game six. DeBusch did his best—25 points, 9 rebounds. But he had no chance against Wilt, who had 45 points on 20 of 27 from the field, 27 rebounds, and 4 blocks. The Lakers outscored the Knicks 36–16 in the first quarter and won, 135–113. "Shows why Red was a wise coach, by not coming back with that same 1-3-1 offense when Willis was out," said Bradley. "We wouldn't have been able to pull the same thing. I'm sure [Laker Coach Joe] Mullaney had them working on it on the day off. They clearly had us outmanned. So Red was right to buy some time with that game."

We had the same problem when they came back to New York for game seven, May 8, 1970.

I know I went to an earlier playoff game before the seventh and final game, but I don't have the ticket stubs to remind me which one. The reason is that I scalped my playoff ticket. Scalped it and slipped in. I had gotten to know the Garden quite well by then. I knew there was a door where, if it was left ajar, you could sneak in. Maybe the guard might not be able to resist taking a peek at the festivities. The crowd noise might lure him from his station. Sold my ticket for a premium, pocketed the loot, and waited by the door. I only missed half of the first quarter. I wasn't going to miss that game just because I didn't have a ticket. Didn't have a seat and didn't care. Stood up in the blue haze of cigarette and cigar smoke wreathing the blue seats, listened with amusement to changing and acidic descriptions of the ballplayers. One might be "ya stinkin' bum!" one game and "da best dere is!" the next. Raspberries splattered like rain around me, and smiles, too. For many fans in the blue seats, the game from the blue was a welcome haven from a harsher everyday life.

This is how I got a ticket to game seven of the NBA Finals that year: My father's lawyer, Peter Eichenberry, lived down the block. He'd gone to Ohio State, was a big Buckeye basketball fan. They'd had some good teams there, with Jerry Lucas, the center, and Havlicek, now a part of the hated Celtics; Bobby Knight was a sub on that squad. By then Knight had started coaching at Army and was going on to coach at Indiana; not many knew who he was. I believe Peter Eichenberry was in the same class with Havlicek and Lucas. He had season tickets. His son David and I were friends. When Peter couldn't make it, he'd give us his tickets and we'd go. Somehow I got him to promise if there was a game seven in the NBA finals that year, he would give me—I mean, let me buy—a ticket. Lo and behold, there was a game seven, and there I had a ticket—not just a ticket but one down in the yellows, the lower promenade, where I didn't need an oxygen mask, not in the blue heaven nosebleed seats anymore bay-bee! For game seven! But I had another dilemma.

On that same exact night, May 8, 1970, weeks after my thirteenth birthday, my father was giving a jazz concert at Cami Hall. And I was torn over what to do. After all, I love my father, and I always respected his work. But I was just as serious and even more insulated in my devotion to the Knickerbockers. We'd never won a World Championship before. In my mind, my father would have another concert one day soon, and I could go to that one. But the Knicks would never again have a chance to win a first—our first—NBA title. So even though I had to wrestle with it in my mind, all along I knew. My mother said, "Look, Spike, I think you are old enough to make this decision on your own. Hopefully, you will make the right decision."

I think she thought I was going to the concert.

My father probably thought so too.

I opted to go to the game. I felt I had no choice. My blood ran that way too.

> > >

I took the A train from Lafayette Avenue. The A would take you straight in to Manhattan, to Thirty-fourth Street and Madison Square Garden. There was nothing like being a kid and going to a ballpark or stadium in New York City. The smell of warm chestnuts, pretzels, the excitement, the humanity, the unpredictability, crowds of people yammering and buzzing along with the sirens, jackhammers, and pile drivers. Game seven, Knicks' first real shot at the NBA championship, and this was against the Lakers, as mighty as the Celtics had been, mightier even, with Russell retired; the Lakers, with Chamberlain, West, Baylor, Happy Hairston jumping out of the gym. They had run us into the ground in game six to tie the series. But even if Willis couldn't play, everyone there that night believed the Knicks would win. It seemed important that every fan felt as I did: if we cheered loud enough, long enough, encouraged the Knicks, somehow we would make the difference. I can still hear people: "Gonna win it all ta-night! Right?" Even without Willis, we'd will them through.

Both teams came out for the pre-game warm-ups and introductions. We were all looking for Reed, hoping, but he was nowhere to be found at first. There was this incredible hum in the air, like riding a tuning fork. It was almost tribal. There was this palpable, continuous hum, people talking excitedly, strangers greeting each other like neighbors with "Whaddaya tink? Tink so?" Then there was a flash of a tall man in the white warm-up with orange piping. Willis Reed was on the runway. He was limping, but coming out on the court. "We didn't know, either," said Bradley. "Wilt, West, and Baylor had taken their shots and were standing at the top of the key. Suddenly there's a little rumble, and it gets louder. And louder. Then Willis emerges from the tunnel. And the place goes berserk. So for all of us, it was Oh, my God, here, look at this! Incredible!"

It was like an explosion went off in my eardrums. It was the loudest I've ever heard it in the Garden, before or since. The crowd was at full throat. At that moment the knowledge was secure in my mind, inside that storm of noise. The real Knicks fans knew we were going to win. We had waited. Now we were positive. A completely positive feeling. A completely positive sound. The Lakers stopped taking their warm-up shots and turned around and watched the grim captain limp out onto the court. Then Clyde sort of smiled a little and tossed the captain a ball. Willis took it without a hint of an expression on his face. You'd never know that mere moments before, he was in the Knicks' locker room, lying on a training table, being injected with Xylocaine or lidocaine or something called Carbocaine, plus a cortisone shot; injected with a needle the size of an ice pick. Phil Jackson had taken a picture of it. "They waited till the last second before the game was going to start. And the doc put a needle in his leg," Jackson told me. "It was a long fellow, and he gave him one injection and then he stuck another syringe in and gave him a second." Willis could not even feel his leg now. He lifted the ball into shooting position and took the first of two warm-up shots. His signature left-handed j's, from 18 feet away, extended and at an angle. Both found the bottom of the net. The explosion of sound became a rolling wave. It was over. I'm telling you, it was over then and there, though West led the league in scoring that year and averaged 34.3 against the Knicks, though they had Baylor, though Chamberlain was dominant. Why did the Lakers turn and look at Willis? They got psyched, right there. They had to know—no way, nohow, not tonight, baby. Not in the Garden.

"For me, when I saw that, I said to myself, 'We've got these guys,'" said Frazier. "They were mesmerized, standing there, watching Reed, and they just stopped warming up. Wilt did it. Elgin did it. West did it. I gained a lot of confidence when they did that. They should have ignored him, like 'Yeah, Reed is on the court now. And so what?' But they seemed very concerned."

"The Lakers turned around and looked because they didn't think it was going to happen," said Bradley. "They were like everybody else—curious to see if this man was really going to be able to play. When they saw him come out, then heard the reaction, they realized they were in slightly different circumstances than they had spent the last twenty minutes anticipating."

The game began. Willis rebounded a Chamberlain miss, and the crowd roar heightened, making your senses sharper, like a light going on in a room. Willis got it to Clyde, then dragged his bad leg downcourt. Clyde brought it up like a show pony into the teeth of the sustained roar—Clyde might have been at his height as an athlete at that moment, at his height physically because he had just turned twenty-five, with the reflexes of a twenty-five-year-old, at his height mentally for this one night, with the sure knowledge of a player ten years older. He could've taken West or Garrett right there—taken them right to the hole. Chamberlain might have grabbed what to him would have been trash, and the floor would have been out of balance and West would have been halfway to the other end. No. Not now. Not yet. Clyde knew to get Willis off first. I can still see Clyde bouncing the ball confidently, waiting as Willis dragged his useless leg to the frontcourt. Willis stayed out beyond the free-throw line. Wilt was slow to follow. He should have followed quicker, stayed up on Willis. No way was Willis going by him. But if Wilt had stepped out, Clyde could've gone to the hole. In retrospect, Wilt should've done everything he could to deny Willis's shot. But he didn't. "A leopard can't change its spots," Frazier says. "Chamberlain was unaccustomed to going out on the perimeter. He wasn't comfortable out there. So he did what he normally did. He stood under the basket. But those days were over."

Willis Reed couldn't really jump off his leg and couldn't move laterally at all. If Chamberlain had come out and touched him, Willis would not have been able to get his shot off without Wilt grabbing it. The middle would have been open, a Barnett or a Bradley backdoor cut for a layup would have been worth the same two. A pass to Bradley, executing the X cut, a return pass to Frazier—it all might have worked. But none of it would have had the same emotional impact.

Willis rose up on his toes and shot the lefty j. While the ball was in the air, there was a change in the sound of the crowd, into a long *e* of anticipation, then a burst of sound—*Wooop!*—as the ball split the net and made it dance. The roof seemed to lift right off the Garden. Knickerbockers by two. The Lakers missed again. DeBusschere swept the glass. Barnett had the ball now, coming across. Willis popped out, a good 20 feet away, on the right wing, Barnett fed him the pass, then there was the change, the *e*, the tribal sound, as the shot was launched, rotating in a brief arc.

Eeeeeeeeee woop!

Another 18-footer by Willis. Knicks by four.

We were never headed after that.

"When he hit the first two shots, oh, my, it was like 'Well, maybe this is their year.' The Lakers weren't beaten when Willis hit those first two shots," said Bradley. Except maybe in their minds. They were beaten by halftime, though. Momentum shifted dramatically when Willis hit those two shots. Red took him out after that because he couldn't run. "But that was all we needed," Bradley said. "Frazier took over at that point, and the rest of us played solid games. And the rest is history."

The Knicks blew the Lakers away. Reed played only twenty-seven out of a possible forty-eight minutes. DeBusschere did the trench work, putting a body on Wilt, pushing him off his favorite spots. Suddenly Wilt looked old. And even looking old, he had 21 points and 24 rebounds. Baylor and West combined for 47. But Barnett and Bradley, then Riordan, Caz, and Rave were flashing into the passing lanes all night. Barnett and Bradley combined for 38 points. DeBusschere had 18 points and 17 rebounds. And Clyde—Clyde was great. I can honestly say I've never seen a player have a better game than the one Clyde had that night. At the end of the first quarter the Knicks led, 38–24. By halftime it was 69–42, and the second half was the celebration of what had become merely a happy formality. Red had Clyde on Dick Garrett, the guard opposite West. Garrett ended up 3 of 10 from the field. Garrett was Clyde's old homeboy—like a little brother. He had Garrett in his back pocket, no problem whatsoever, like he owned him. Three times Walt stripped him or West clean off the dribble. Clyde went to another level—36 points, 19 assists, an unheard-of number for a 36-point scorer, 7 rebounds, 4 steals, and shot the lights out—12 of 17.

"That game was one of destiny," said Frazier. "I always said it was meant to be. Nothing about it was planned. It just evolved that way, that Willis hit the first two shots, that him doing that lit a fire that swept through me, the whole arena. I always said if we'd played the Lakers ten more times, we would not have beaten them. But for this one game, it all happened for us. The crowd galvanized us, and it . . . words won't do. It was just meant to be."

I never saw Oscar Robertson in his prime. In 1961–62, Oscar had averaged a triple-double—30.8 points, 12.5 boards, and 11.4 assists— over the eighty-two-game season. I know he was a great player. But he couldn't have been any better than Clyde was on May 8, 1970. And, led by Frazier, they played classic Knickerbocker basketball, played it as if they had created it, and in a sense they had. They created it on this night, an original composition of basketball. It *was* like music! New York had 30 assists, Los Angeles 17. And that, along with defense and rebounding, was the Answer.

The lead swelled. The Knicks took curtain calls in the fourth quarter, letting the Lakers have that one, 30–19. Even Nate Bowman made three field goals. The crowd roar sustained me deep into the night, and far into the future. The New York Knicks were World Champions, 113–99, over the Los Angeles Lakers. The Knicks were the best basketball club on the planet. They ran leaping off the court to a champagne bath and interviews with Howard Cosell. The smile on Frazier's face reflected mine. I went down into the subway catacombs with other happy fans. The A train carried one contented soul back to Brooklyn. For an hour, all was right with the world.

> > >

When I got home, my family was back from the concert. Very few people had attended. Folks were trying to be buoyant, trying to lift my father's spirits, talking about how great the music had been. I know it was, because he was and still is a great musician. Sometimes when we went to my father's concerts, the families of the musicians would be the only ones in the audience. He founded two groups, the New York Bass Violin Ensemble, a group made up solely of bassists like Ron Carter, Richard Davis, Milt Hilton, Lyle Atkinson, great musicians like that. My father had another group called the Descendants of Mike and Phoebe, they being the earliest descendants we can trace our lineage back to in slavery. Uncle Cliff was on trumpet, Aunt Consuela was on piano, with Aunt Grace on vocals. So at an early age I gained respect for musicians, and I found that a lot of people didn't respect their music like I believed they really should. On some nights, when I didn't have school the next day, my mother would let me go with my father to clubs where he played—the Village Gate, the Bitter End, and the like. People would be yelling, talking, drinking, laughing, and clinking their glasses all the way through his sets, and it was all I could do to keep from shouting, "Shut up and listen!" so you could hear the music, and give due respect to my father's craft. It would kill me to go to these clubs, listen to these performances, and it was like nobody cared. But even then my father would put it into perspective for me: "Spike, I'm not playing for nobody else. I'm playing for myself."

Sometimes my father played at a spot with sawdust on the floor called West Boondock. That was where Clyde used to hang out sometimes. His was the first Knick autograph I ever got as a kid. Frazier signed a check from the restaurant. Signed it for me and smiled. I was eleven. It was then I decided I would appreciate the craft the brothers brought to the game, not be like people at the clubs, talking when they should've been paying attention. Nobody chastised me for missing the concert. Nobody celebrated over the prodigal son's return, either. In retrospect I know it hurt my father that I didn't go to the concert. He never let on, though. In fact, he made me give him a blow-by-blow account of the game. The Knicks' performance had been so magnificent! I had to tell somebody, play by play. I also told Chris. And he listened to me, with about a half-smile playing across his face. As I think back on it, he didn't care so much as he knew how much I did.

> > >

The euphoria of the Knicks' winning the championship must have lasted, oh, at least until I went to John Dewey High out on Coney Island in 1972, an hour's transit each way. That same year the United States lost the Olympic gold medal in basketball to Russia for the very first time. It seemed that structured, patterned ball with no room for creativity had given the Russians a chance, and they shocked old Hank Iba and his team in the Olympic gold medal final in the Munich Games. I went to high school with my man, Earl Smith, who loved the game as much as I did. Our school had only intramural sports. Dewey was a small, experimental school concentrating on academics. This was when Chris began a furtive occupation as a graffiti artist. His tag was "the Shadow." It got him into hot water with my mother all the time. My father was more forgiving. I had hoop.

In 1970–71, the season after the Knicks won it, they went 52–30. Milwaukee, behind a determined thirty-three-year-old Big O and Kareem, won the NBA title. They deserved the ring. Kareem was now King. The Knicks didn't make it past the Bullets. Monroe, Unseld, Marin, Mad

Dog Carter, and Gus beat the Knicks, 4 and 3. Same kind of war, only this time the Bullets were left standing. Bradley missed his shot at the end of the seventh game, and the Knicks lost.

"It had taken us seven games to beat the Bullets the year we won," says Bradley. "So in the seventh game of '71, we're down by one, eight seconds left. The play was to Frazier. Get the ball, do his thing. Not a set play. They immediately double-team Frazier. Three seconds left. He throws it to me. I'm headed toward the corner. I've only got one place to go with three seconds left, that's one dribble and a jumper from deep in the corner. Meanwhile, Unseld realizes this too. He comes out and he leaps, sweeps at the shot, and actually ticks the ball. He blocked the shot, but the ball gets to the backboard. We lose by one. No, I didn't think it was going in after Wes ticked it. Before? You always think it's going in. If you get the ball in the last minute and you don't think it's going in, you're not a shooter. The mood was down afterward. I was down. We thought we'd repeat. That was 1971. Now it's 1996, a quarter-century later. I can come to New York, get in a cab, and have some guy say to me, 'What the hell did you miss that shot against the Bullets for?'"

I don't know how much, if anything, winning the title the year before had taken out of the Knicks, but I'm sure there were egos that ballooned and ran amok, and partying like crazy. These were young men, after all. Pictures of Clyde's boudoir with the round bed and mirrors adorning the ceiling above it were published in various newspapers and magazines. Willis was deified for coming out for the seventh game. Never does a man's head much good to be deified. Some measure of resentment seemed to be brewing between him and Frazier. It was Frazier's team, to me and many others. Just that little bit of dissonance was enough to make the difference.

After the 1970–71 season, the Knicks made another big deal, sending Stallworth, Riordan, and $100,000 to the Bullets for Earl Monroe. There was hoopla over it. Frazier and Monroe, in the same backcourt. Quietly we made another addition that year. A rookie out of Marquette. Dean Meminger.

I loved Monroe's game—but I always thought of him as a Bullet. Feared his game. Baltimore had always been one of our toughest matchups, individually. They seemed to mirror us to the letter, and nowhere could we claim a clear edge going in. The series against them always seemed to go seven games, and out of maybe three hundred total ball possessions, the Knicks, playing at their optimum, might be three possessions better. It can get that fine.

I liked the *idea* of Monroe playing for the Knicks, though. Barnett had given his all in the drive to the first title. He was still around, helping to coach, but of little use as a player anymore. There was speculation, most of it negative, about whether Monroe—who sometimes in Baltimore would take over a game—would blend with the other Knicks, who played with each other so unselfishly. Was Pearl going to play Knick ball? Would he sacrifice his game to fit into the Knicks' team concept? Earl did sacrifice a lot, because, all that wild magical stuff he was doing in Baltimore, well, I won't say he was pulled onto the carpet, but he wasn't as flashy with the Knicks as with the Bullets. The Knicks were all about team efficiency then. So there would be glimpses of his style, but he really wasn't encouraged to be as creative as he could have been. I still think, in retrospect, you can be just as creative and not have it be detrimental to the team. I think when it's your turn in the logical progression of play, in the playing of the improvisational composition of the game, then you can create. But there are times when creativity should be stifled for the sake of efficiency, especially if the object of the game is to win. The Knicks had Pearl handcuffed sometimes, and he talked about this. Pearl was the Miles Davis of hoop. But in the end he gave up a part of his individual style for classic Knick ball. "Because of his ability to control his body, one of the most original players I've ever seen," said Bradley. "Always the shot was an inch higher than the defender. And the way he played that year—Monroe refuted every pundit in the books. Earl demonstrated he could play any kind of ball you want to play. Tough D, team concept, one-on-one. Earl elevated his game, I think. He contained his individuality in the flow of the team play."

"What people overlooked, when they said Earl and I couldn't play together, was our mutual respect for each other, born out of our battles," said Frazier. "It was no problem. If he was having a good game, I got him the ball. And vice versa. It was a credit to him that he toned down his game. And after his first year he had games when he erupted. He could ignite the crowd, get people involved. Trying to deny him took a supreme effort. Believe me. I know. We didn't have designations like one or two. We were backcourt men. Whoever had the ball brought it up."

Whoever had the ball. So Earl's sacrifice was small compared to what Dream did. He had to give the ball up completely. If he were playing today, imagine the ego Dean Meminger could display compared to some of these young boys who come into the league now thinking they're supposed to get shoes named after them and TV commercials and movies because they got their game off on other teenagers. They have no idea, some of them. Rare is the talent of a Ken Griffey Jr. in baseball or a Tiger Woods in golf, a Jordan in basketball. They come along once or twice in a life span. But now, every year during the NBA draft, you've got twenty-eight guys sitting behind a curtain, insulted if they get drafted too low. They have no concept of humility, of sublimating their game to the needs of the team. I doubt whether any rookie in recent memory came into the NBA with Meminger's credentials back in 1971–72. Dean had started three varsity seasons at Marquette—freshmen were blessedly ineligible back then—and averaged 16.4, 18.8, then 21.2 points per game his senior year, on blistering .508 shooting. Marquette won the National Invitational Tournament (NIT) at the Garden in the spring of 1970, in his junior season, and Dream was named MVP, capping off a season in which Marquette went undefeated, 26–0, the last big-time college team to do so, outside of Indiana U. in 1976.

Meminger was the number one pick of the Knicks. He came in knowing he wasn't going to play, or would play very little. The Knicks had Frazier, Barnett, and Monroe, three 6-foot-4, world-class, championship-caliber guards. Dean was barely six feet—although when asked about his lack of height after the Knicks drafted him, he did say, "It's not how tall you are, it's how tall you play."

Meminger took one for the team—took a backseat because he was a rookie, because it was expected, and mostly because it was fair. In the end, he was no Frazier, Monroe, or even Barnett. But it wasn't like he didn't have game. "A *great* defensive player," said Bradley. In the fifth game of the 1971–72 season, Frazier took sick. Dream started in Baltimore. Monroe's first trip back to the town where he'd been legend. Dream was supposed to be Monroe's caddy, a second rotation guard. All Dream did was make twelve of fourteen shots, drop 25 points on the Bullets, and dominate the floor game with 9 assists and 7 boards. He played forty-five out of a possible forty-eight minutes, and after the game Earl Monroe, celebrating his twenty-seventh birthday, said, "That was like watching *me*!"

Clyde got better in a hurry. "Dean the Dream. He knew so much about the game that Barnett and then the rest of us took to calling him Coach," says Frazier.

Imagine a rookie guard with a similar résumé coming in today with that kind of knowledge and then doing that kind of number off the bench in his fifth regular-season NBA game. Why, his agent would expect a quick contract renegotiation, a starting job, an All-Star slot, a guest shot on *Martin* or *Moesha,* and a recurring role on *Homeboys in Outer Space* on UPN-U People's Network.

Dream went back to the bench, to guarding Frazier and Monroe in practice.

In 1971–72, we had Frazier, Barnett (mostly as assistant coach), Phil Jackson, Willis, DeBusschere, and Bradley. Now we had Monroe and Meminger, a big, rough player named Charlie Paulk from Memphis, another named Luther Rackley, and a cagey veteran big-man scorer, Jerry Lucas, who the Knicks had given up Cazzie for, to my chagrin. It was not the blend. Not only were Baltimore, Milwaukee, and Boston still good but the Lakers were great that year. The Knicks beat Baltimore four games to three in the playoffs, steamrollered Milwaukee, defending champions, four games to one, then faced off with the Lakers again in the 1971–72 NBA finals. Jerry West had never won an NBA title, and Chamberlain only had the one with the 1966–67 Philadelphia 76ers—with the Kangaroo Kid, Billy Cunningham, Chet "the Jet" Walker, big Luke Jackson, and the guards Wali Jones, Hal Greer, and Matty Goukas. But now the Lakers had a small forward from Columbia named Jim McMillian, and they brought in Gail Goodrich to pair with Jerry West. The once great Baylor, at thirty-seven, played in only nine games, but he got his ring, too. The 1971–72 Lakers had a sixth man in

Erickson, a backup guard named Pat Riley. These Lakers won an NBA record sixty-nine games, lost only thirteen. That held as the NBA record, up until the Bulls went 72–10 in 1995–96. So it was the Lakers' turn, and they routed the New Look Knicks in five games in the NBA finals of 1971–72, winning game four in overtime on May 5 at the Garden, 116–111, and winning the World Championship two days later at the Forum, 114–100. That Laker team is often trumpeted as one of the all-time best teams for their outstanding record of 69–13 and for winning those thirty-three games in a row during the regular season. Chamberlain, West, McMillian, Hairston, Goodrich, and the rest were brought back to defend their title for the 1972–73 season.

Looking back on it, I wasn't jaded about the 1972–73 Knicks team, I just always felt that the first championship team was better. It was special, and I was and probably always will be an idealist about it. The first time can't be duplicated, no matter what you're talking about, but I just . . . well, I *liked* that first team better. "It was the drama, Spike," says Bradley. "That's the difference. That's why the fans remember that one most memorably. Willis's injury, appearance, and shots in the seventh game is Bobby Thomson hitting the home run for the Giants in the '51 playoffs against the Dodgers. It's one of the moments that live in the minds of fans forever, because it had all the elements: human drama, courage, competence, excellence, team play, overcoming great odds. But frankly, for me, the 1972–73 team was the most enjoyable, satisfying team. I was kind of at the top of my game."

But Frazier says, "There's no comparison to be made. In 1972–73, we had Earl, and Dream, but I don't think we had the cohesion that we had on the first team. The second championship is vague, where the first one I can remember like yesterday, because of the dramatic way that it played out. I had perhaps my best game as a player, and it was the first championship for the Knicks. Anything that's first, like your first love, you remember more than the second."

Some of the more negative aspects of winning, like inflated pride and inflated egos, had their insidious effect, as did time, on both the team and me. Reed was hurt for much of the 1972–73 season, barely averaging 11 points a game. Lucas was on the team, and 6-foot-11 John Gianelli.

Gianelli could rebound, and Lucas was money from up top with his shot. We had gotten bigger and deeper. But the league was faster. The league was always seeming to get better then. We had speed in a rookie guard named Henry Bibby from UCLA, but he was a rookie, so . . .

It looked like 1972–73 would be the year of the Celtics. Boston ripped off sixty-eight regular-season wins—one short of the record set the year before—behind a superior backcourt set of Jo Jo White and Don Chaney, with Paul Silas rebounding, Don Nelson shooting, and that jumping jack Dave Cowens, and he was 'bout ripe. And they had Johnny Havlicek. Cowens was hopping through the roof, Havlicek was coming off two seasons when he'd averaged 28.9 points, second in the league to Kareem, and 27.5 points, third to Kareem Abdul-Jabbar and Tiny. If white men can't jump, it must be something they came down with lately. Cowens could definitely sky. Havlicek was one quick, tireless Dobre Shunka. Paul Silas was crawling all over the boards, Don Chaney (currently Knicks assistant coach) and Jo Jo White had size and spring in the backcourt. Chaney could score, and Jo Jo could shoot.

The sixteen-team league distilled itself down to five truly superior teams in 1972–73. Boston mounted that 68–14 mark. Baltimore went 52–30, Milwaukee with Abdul-Jabbar went 60–22. The aging Lakers, coasting through the regular season, also went 60–22. The Knicks went an almost pedestrian 57–25, seemed to be bridesmaids in some heavy-weight competition. Then into the breach stepped Dream. He was our quickness that year. Dean had averaged 4.3 points off the bench his rookie year, playing little behind Barnett, Frazier, and Monroe. But Meminger got 185 rebounds and dished 103 assists in his limited playing time. He did not play in a pout. Then in 1972–73, with barely four more minutes per contest than in his rookie year, he averaged not quite 6 points a game, with 229 rebounds and 133 assists. Clyde was twenty-eight and had played a lot of minutes in the last four seasons. Monroe was a year older and had had both bursa sacs beneath his knee joints removed, so he was playing on knees that moved like tectonic plates— bone on bone.

We faced the Bullets in the first round of the playoffs. Abe Pollin and his people had a plan in sending Monroe to the Knicks and Carter to the

76ers. The Bullets had acquired the services of a streak-shooter named Archie Clark. Everybody called him Shake 'n Bake. Bowlegged. Lot of Cazzie in his game. They had also gotten Phil Chenier, a 6-4 guard from Cal, in the physical mold of Frazier. He'd left school early and made it, he was that good. Chenier was a fine player. But during one regular-season game, he must have gotten frustrated against Clyde. He might have been *like* Clyde, but he was *not* Clyde. Clyde was better. No sin in that. Most nights Clyde was better than any guard in the NBA. But Chenier lost his cool, and he hit Clyde in the face, kind of a half-slap, half-punch, as Clyde was playing D on him. At first Clyde looked shocked. What was this fool doing? But I would see it happen again. Years later the most gentlemanly Dr. J ended up grabbing Larry Bird in a straight-arm choke-hold. It was unlike Dr. J to act like that on the court, but Julius was past his prime then, and Bird told him, "I'm gonna drop 50 on you tonight, Doc." He probably was about to do it, too. Doc grabbed him in frustration. Clyde didn't grab Chenier—actually, he grabbed him in a different way. Instead of rumbling with Chenier, he put him in his place. Clyde was not past his prime. On eight consecutive possessions, Clyde came down the court and scored on Chenier every single time. Long jumpers. Mid-range. Layups. Clyde took him every time. The other Knicks just moved out of his way. They knew full well what he was doing. No doubt some of them were thinking like I was: "Yeah. Take him, Clyde. Take him again. Take his ass again. One time, baby. One more time. And these last two . . . are for ya mama!"

Clyde always responded the way a true champion responds. Which is, don't divert my energies into this stupid personality conflict, *mano a mano*, but let me beat your brains in and then walk off the floor laughing, and you'll have lost, trying to figure out what happened. Yeah, you were the toughest guy on the block. But I beat you, so what does that make me?

I liked that.

"We knew Clyde had to get the ball," said Bradley. "You knew it was happening."

"Well, I thought at first he was swinging at Bradley and inadvertently hit me as I ran past," said Frazier. "Plus, the ref called the foul on *me,* said he would throw me out of the game if I did anything, so I said nothing. I just made eight straight baskets. I wouldn't say it was because he hit me. I don't know. Might have happened anyway. But a lot of fathers have mentioned that to me in years since. They say, 'Man, I try to tell my son, that's the way you handle a situation like that. You don't retaliate, you remain cool, take over, take it out on them in the game.'"

Chenier turned out to be a model citizen, and now does TV commentary for the Bullets.

The Bullets were no longer the Bullets. Monroe, Carter, Marin, and Gus were gone. But they had Big E, Elvin Hayes. No matter. Frazier and Monroe combined for 48 in the first game and 61 in the second. Bradley and DeBusschere combined for 42 in game three, just as the Bullets tried to concentrate on the backcourt. Clark, Chenier, and Hayes combined for 73 in the Bullets' only win. The Knicks closed them out, 109–99 at the Garden, winning four and one, behind a combined 67 from Monroe, Frazier, and DeBusschere. Willis, struggling, injured, scored 12 in twenty-seven minutes. Meminger was quietly perfect from the field and the line: 6 points, 3 rebounds, 3 assists, several unrecorded steals. The NBA did not keep records of steals and blocked shots at the time.

The Knicks met the Celtics in the Eastern finals, the mighty 68–13 Celtics, winners to meet the Lakers for the title. It was an epic confrontation. In the first game, at Boston, the Celtics won in a romp, 134–108. You didn't beat the Knicks like that back then. It was the most points and largest margin of victory over the Knicks that season. Phil Jackson, showing his potential, got a tech in the second quarter while scoring 11 points but getting only one rebound. Silas and Cowens made him disappear. The Celtics cleaned the Knicks on the boards, 52–35, shot 57 percent from the field. Havlicek had 26 points, 11 assists, and 9 rebounds. Jo Jo White went for 31, and Nelson, with what we then called that "fag" foul-shooting style of his, had 21. When Don Nelson got 21, you were in trouble. Cowens had 18 points and 15 boards. The Celtics were coming at us in waves. Red Holzman knew our only way in that series: he had to get Dream in there more. Either Dream would do it or he wouldn't, but we had to get him in there. Frazier had 24 in the first game, but Barnett, now thirty-six, was only 2 of 9 for 4 points, and Monroe had but 12.

In the second game, at the Garden, the Knicks romped, 129–96. Touché. What was the difference? Well, Frazier had his steady 24, and 10 assists. But Barnett was shut out, and Monroe still had only 12. So three things did it. First, the Knicks hit the boards as a team. Ten players had 2 or more rebounds. Second, the ball movement picked up. They had 12 more assists than Boston. And third, Dream played twenty-two minutes, scored 11 points, with 3 rebounds and 2 assists, and with Dream around, Jo Jo had only 15, on 6 of 14 shots.

With Dean solidly in the rotation now, the Knicks turned up the floor game and the D and improbably won the next two, 98–91 at Boston and 117–110 at the Garden, and were up 3–1. In the latter game, it helped that Havlicek didn't play due to an injured shoulder. Cowens and White combined for 67 points, and Silas had 23 rebounds, but Frazier had one of his games, with 37 points, 9 boards. Dream played thirty-eight minutes. Monroe didn't play, and Barnett played four minutes. Dream came up large with 10 points, 7 assists, 5 rebounds. When he fouled out, the Garden crowd gave him a standing O.

Now the Celtics brought out the mamas-in-law. That's what you call those games in the playoffs when you're down 3–1, or 2–0. That's a mother-in-law game. You never play harder than you play then. Talk about backs to the wall. Havlicek came back, a grim look on his face. Cowens had 32 points and 16 rebounds, Havlicek had 18 through gritted teeth, and the Celtics prevailed by one at Boston, 98–97. Then the Celtics evened matters by winning 110–100 at Madison Square Garden. Cowens with 26 points and 14 rebounds, White with 25 points. Frazier had 29, Monroe 22. Surely the Celtics, playing much better than New York across the front line, had the Knicks measured now. But privately, Red Auerbach fretted about Meminger. "The little s.o.b., he's *killing* us!" he confided to some Celtic players. Meanwhile, Knicks President Ned Irish was telling the veteran Knick players that they were finished, that they were cooked. They could never beat Boston in Boston.

In the seventh game, Meminger, in for Monroe, played thirty-six minutes alongside Frazier; scored 13 points, got 6 rebounds, 3 assists, and 4 steals; and was assigned to hound Jo Jo White into an off-shooting performance, 10 of 22. Cowens had his 24, but Havlicek had only 4 in twenty-three minutes, his arm dangling useless at his side, obviously hampering his play.

In 1969–70, the Knicks had managed to overcome the loss of their star player. The Celtics did not this time. The Knicks won going away, 94–78. After the Celtics' return to the World Championship was held in abeyance—for a year, as it turned out—Auerbach snarled, "The little s.o.b. did us in."

And he didn't mean *his* leprechaun.

And so, to me, drubbing the Lakers in Chamberlain's final year for the NBA title in 1972–73 was anticlimactic, even though the Lakers were defending World Champs. Baylor was gone. The Lakers felt it. The Knicks switched from being guard-oriented against the Celtics to being forward-dominated against L.A. Meminger went back to being a caddy. The Knicks lost the first game as Bradley and DeBusschere combined for 49, then never let the Lakers score more than 100 points in any other game as they won four straight, but never won by more than 5 points until game five, the last one, May 10, a 102–93 win over the Lakers in Los Angeles. DeBusschere was injured, shot horribly—1 for 9—before he left. But Bradley scored 20 points, had 7 rebounds, 5 assists. Monroe had 23, Willis 18, Frazier 18, Lucas 10. Dream balanced the floor, was 2 of 2 from the field, 5 points. Just enough. The Knicks were World Champions.

I haven't been able to say that since.

Maybe I'd gotten a little spoiled. That was a fine team. Lucas was throwing that stuff in from above the top of the key. We were playing Knick D, Knick ball. Even though Willis was injured and could not contribute much, we were faster, with Dream and Frazier and Monroe and Bradley and even Phil Jackson, who averaged 8.7 points in the playoffs and had 6 points, 7 boards, and 2 assists in the final game against the Lakers. But it was almost too businesslike, or maybe I was older and didn't believe in Santa Claus anymore.

They had a story in the press that Lucas had the Manhattan phone book memorized. He played memory games, could have made a living on it later, but I doubted whether he had memorized the entire Manhattan phone book. Although they say he did it to Bobby Fischer, the chess champion, in front of the players in the locker room one night. Asked Fischer to pick any page from the New York phone book, go down the left column any number of names, give him the name. Fischer scoffed, then said, page 362, line 14, Albert Smith; and Lucas gave him the correct number. Had to be some trick. I do know he could bomb from deep with that half-set. That was no trick. That helped. Frazier was Frazier, Bradley was Bradley, Monroe reined in his game, averaged 16.1 in the playoffs on .524 shooting from the field. Dream got us over, playing D, handling, rebounding, killing the opposing second rotation, whoever they put on him, shooting .554 from the field. Layups. Dean Meminger never averaged better than 6 points a game for New York. But no Knick implemented the team concept any better.

> > >

High school was *Superfly* in 1972, Watergate, the Vietnam War ends, all happening fairly far away from John Dewey High. I was very quiet in high school and on top of that, I looked very young, about twelve. In fact, when I later went on to Morehouse College, I looked like I was in junior high school. This youthful appearance had a devastating effect on girls: it devastated their interest. In four years of high school I didn't have a girlfriend. There were plenty of girls I liked, even one or two I got up enough courage to rap to, but to no avail. They weren't having it. I wasn't getting any rhythm, nothing, zip, nada.

I became close with a friend named Larry Tucker. One reason we became close was that he was a ladies' man. He had girls left and right, up and down. I looked up to him and admired him for this, and he also gave me encouragement. There was a girl I liked named Rebecca Kelly, and although I was not vocal about my interest in her, Larry sensed it. I was too terrified even to say hello to her, shy as can be. Well, one day he told me that she had said she liked me, so why didn't I speak to her. Hearing this, I finally got up enough courage to rap to her. My rap was weak. It did me no good with her, but it boosted my confidence. Larry had made up the part about her saying she liked me, just to soup me up. He knew there was nothing to be afraid of. I wanted to kill him for that at first. He set me up. But he explained that it was the only way I would have ever spoken to her. He was right. So it was worth it. He was a good friend.

One night during this time I was awakened in the wee hours. "Psst. Psst. Hey." Chris's finger was poking my back. "C'mon." He was fully dressed. I was fuzzy with my dreams.

"Where you think you're going?"

"C'mon," he said. "Just . . . c'mon."

I dressed quickly, and we slipped out of the house. We ran around a few corners and ended up in front of a construction wall. The wall was laced with graffiti. I saw Chris's tag in one corner—the Shadow. I heard the pebble shake in the spray can. I turned and was about to lace him with some verbal graffiti of my own. What if Mommy found out? But instead, I said not a word. Because then I saw my brother was looking at the wall, looking at his own handiwork, and what stopped me from speaking was the look on his face. It was a look of fierce pride and . . . peace. I'd never seen Chris look at anything like that before in my life. Not with such care, with such joy. I looked back at the wall. And I saw it differently. It had changed. I no longer saw trouble. I looked and saw the depth that had been applied to it, the making of this flat wall into a three-dimensional space. I saw things that were on my brother's mind, things only he knew. I looked at that wall for a long time. When I looked back at my brother, he was looking at me. And he was looking at me for . . . *something*. And I think that was when I realized that my brother had not cared about the game so much as he saw I did. So I nodded quickly, like one of those bobble-headed dolls—the look of conspiratorial acceptance and approval. And Chris broke into the broadest of grins.

One thing happened during my high school years that I do think is relevant to basketball. It happened one Saturday in the spring of my junior year. UCLA and Wooden were still in the dynasty business. They had a center named Bill Walton. They played North Carolina State in the NCAA tournament semifinals in 1974. North Carolina State won, ending a string of eight straight NCAA tournament championships by the Bruins. You will not see that again. N.C. State was represented by a 5-6 point guard named Monte Towe, a 7-4 center named Rick Burleson, a 6-5 forward who seemed to be in the DeBusschere athletic mode named Tim Stoddard, later to become a major league pitcher. But mostly what they had—what you could not take your eyes off of—was the lift of a 6-foot-4 player who wasn't really a guard, wasn't really a forward, but he was definitely a player.

David. That's all they said. That's all they had to say. David O'Neil Thompson. He was the first player who jumped so high they actually tried to quantify it with a measurement called the standing vertical jump—how high a person can jump up from a standstill, without a lead step, without a running start, without adrenaline. In a strict—and probably irrelevant—scientific sense, they said David Thompson had a vertical jump, I believe, of 44 inches.

There were always great jumpers. You had to be able to jump to get game. But some were especially well known for it—Jumping Joe Caldwell of the Hawks, for instance. Doc was flying then, too, in the ABA with the Virginia Squires and then with the Nets; Kangaroo Kid; Al McGuire kept one up at Marquette, like Robert "Elevator Man" Lackey and, later, Earl Tatum; Helicopter; and Goat. David seemed to go higher, though, and then float on the perimeter. Once, his feet got tangled up around somebody's head during a game—somebody who was standing erect at the time, somebody tall, and this occurred far away from the basket—and David started falling, falling from what seemed like the top of the arena, then landed on his own head, not quite flush, luckily for David and N.C. State.

I didn't know it then, but I had seen the future. They called him Skywalker.

I graduated from John Dewey High in June of 1975, the year the Golden State Warriors from Oakland won the NBA title. That summer I worked at a Baskin-Robbins in Brooklyn Heights. It was mad crazy hot that summer. Scooped a lot of ice cream. In August I went off to Morehouse College in Atlanta, home of my maternal grandmother, a couple of months after the Warriors won their only NBA title, some two years before George Lucas released *Star Wars,* long before I ever thought about becoming a filmmaker. I was just getting out of Dodge. My father drove me to La Guardia airport, shook my hand, and left me to fend for myself. Dean Meminger had been similarly released by the Knicks the year before, taken in the expansion draft. League was watering down. Meminger would wind up in Atlanta too, coming to play for the Hawks.

What I remember about the summers before I went away to college is that they seemed to last forever. I didn't spend all summer in New York City. Like most black parents who had relatives in the South, my mother and father would get rid of us; they were tired and needed a break. So they took us south, and we would spend half the summer with my mother's mother, Zimmie Shelton, in Atlanta, and then we would spend the other half of the summer with my father's mother, Alberta G. Lee, down in Snow Hill, Alabama. Once, during one of these summer voyages south in my father's Citroën to stay with our grandparents, Chris was running his motormouth so much that my father finally said in exasperation that he'd give Chris five dollars if he'd just shut up for five minutes. Five dollars was a lot of money. Chris couldn't do it. Even for five minutes, he couldn't be silent. It was like he was trying to hold his breath underwater for that long or something. My brother's big mouth never ceased to amaze me. Finally he just let out a yell. He couldn't do it. Not even for five bucks. Five bucks could buy a whole lot of candy back then too.

Snow Hill is the *real* country, everything fresh, clean, pure, and that's probably one reason why my grandmother Alberta is still alive today. Both of my grandmothers are, in fact.

My maternal grandfather, Richard Jackson Shelton, after whom I'm named—Shelton Jackson Lee—died when I was in high school. He had been a big, big baseball fan, so when we both were younger, he would take Chris and me to the Atlanta Braves games at Fulton County Stadium just so we could see Hank Aaron hit, and we sat together and saw some good visiting teams, and watched and listened to the Hammer hit baseballs so hard that it almost made your teeth hurt. It was good I would now be in Atlanta, able to keep tabs on my grandmother. With her good graces, of course.

I recently asked my grandmother if she remembered how I got the nickname Spike. "I don't know how you got Spike," she said, "because I asked your father, 'Well, why in the world you calling him Spike?' He said, 'I don't know.' I said, 'Well, I need to know, because we had just thought we were going to call you Pascal.' When I got to the hospital that morning, already they were calling you Spike."

Again, there is a perception of "how can Spike Lee make films about the working class when he comes from a well-to-do family?" Well. My parents didn't have the money to accompany me to Morehouse to help me settle in. They didn't have the money to put me through Morehouse. My grandmother Zimmie put me through Morehouse. She was not a rich lady; she had been a teacher, and she had saved her money for her grandchildren. She lived alone, only a few blocks from the Morehouse campus, and when the plane landed, I headed directly to her house. It must have been over 100 degrees that day in Atlanta. I spent the night sleeping on her porch because it was too hot to sleep inside. She warned me to keep my chest covered. I was asthmatic growing up, and that had been a handicap on the school yards of Brooklyn. But it was so hot I slept uncovered and woke up wheezing like a bagpipe. It was the first day of registration at the college. Registration day is chaotic at Morehouse—incoming students on line, parents demanding their children get served, people scrambling for rooms. There I was, wheezing, dragging my bags around, trying to get registered, in 100-degree weather, humid, muggy. Oh, I was *so* miserable. Thought I was dying. How I got through it, I don't know, but I did. Got a room in Hubert Hall, where I was to reside the entire four years. Luckily, my grandmother was there for Sunday dinner. You had to fend for yourself on Sundays at Morehouse as far as eating dinner was concerned: last meal was at 3:00 P.M. My roommate for three years was from Chicago, James Mack—big brother, 6-6, cared nothing much for basketball. Never played sports. His thing was chemistry. Brainiac.

While I was away for four years in college at Morehouse, I saw the Knicks only when they came to Atlanta or when I went home for the Christmas holidays. But the team was crumbling before my disbelieving eyes. I was getting older. So were the Knicks, and the replacements were not as shrewdly obtained. In short, it was other people's turn. We just didn't have the championship firepower or the championship psyche anymore.

> *Tom Riker . . . Jesse Dark . . . Kendall Mayfield . . .*
> *Eugene Short . . . Jim Barnett . . . Mel "Killer" Davis . . .*
> *Neal Walk . . . Larry Fogle . . .*

Sometimes the Hawks would practice in the gymnasium at Morehouse. I stopped in out of curiosity a time or two. One day I heard Hubie Brown, the Hawks' coach, cursing out John Drew, a 6-5 forward and high scorer of those Atlanta teams. Hubie called Drew everything but a child of God. I never knew it happened—when you watched from the blue seats, you never knew coaches spoke that way to the players. From where I sat in the blue, I felt like talking that way at times, when a guy was messing up, but I was shocked when I found out it happened. Later, after watching Rick Pitino and John Thompson operate, I remembered. They could curse left and right too, but you could tell they were teaching. It wasn't vicious. Hubie was vicious. I collared him at a Knicks game, in the early '90s. He'd been the Knicks' coach for five years and is currently an analyst for TNT. I told Hubie I'd actually been surprised when he cursed out John Drew so profoundly. Hubie just laughed, then said, "The only time Drew was an All-Star was when he was with me."

After my freshman year, the Olympics were held in Montreal. The U.S. Olympic basketball team was coached by North Carolina Coach Dean Smith. I noticed a big man with a big Afro helping him. Who was that tall brother? His name was John Thompson? Hmn. The U.S. team won the gold, though they got much trouble from the Puerto Rican team, featuring another New York ballplayer, thick little guy named Alfred "Butch" Lee, who dropped 35 on whoever got in his way. I remembered him the next spring, toward the end of my sophomore year, when he and Dick McGuire's brother Al led Marquette to the NCAA Final Four at the Omni in Atlanta. Marquette won the national championship behind Butch.

That same spring, Meminger played his last game in the NBA. After two years in Atlanta he had come back to the Knicks. Played thirty-two games. Gone after only six years in the league. "He didn't have a deep jumper," says Bradley. "But he could play."

"Didn't have a perimeter shot, but was an excellent penetrator, an integral part of the second championship team," says Frazier. "Dean was headstrong. He had his concepts, always tried to get coaches to utilize plays, always suggesting. Not all coaches were like Red. Some may have resented it."

I rarely went to games in college. Caught the Knicks a few times and the Lakers once. I could no longer afford to follow sports like some kind of lunatic. I had to concentrate on my studies; my grades were not good. By the end of my sophomore year, I'd run out of elective classes to take, and now I would have to decide what I was going to do with myself. I declared a major in mass communications. That meant taking classes at Clark College, now Clark–Atlanta University, directly across the street. Morehouse didn't have the major. Mass-comm encompassed film (Super 8), TV production, print journalism, and radio.

At the same time, the spring of 1977, the NBA finals pitted the Portland Trail Blazers against the star-laden Philadelphia 76ers, led by Dr. J, big George McGinnis from Indiana, and the 7-foot-1 Caldwell Jones, one of a family of five brothers from McGehee, Arkansas, all of whom played in the NBA (Caldwell said his sister was better than any of them). The Sixers had a project from a Florida high school, a 6-foot-11 kid named Darryl Dawkins, who liked to be called Chocolate Thunder, but he would provide evidence of such only sporadically and was better at making copy for the papers with his flights of verbal fancy. He liked to say he was from another planet: Lovetron, he called it. And he had a full quiver of names for his dunks—he was the first man I saw shatter a backboard and have it be regarded as a skill, somehow. That was his "Chocolate Thundering–Building Rumbling–Glass-Breaking–Rim-Shaking–High-Flying–[Bill] Robinzine-Crying–Jam-I-Am Dunk." Or something like that. He had a million of 'em. But you know, he never did get a ring. The Sixers had another New York ballplayer, Lloyd Free, called World and the Prince of Mid-Air. Later in his career he legally changed his name to World B. Free. From Canarsie High in Brooklyn.

Sportswriters had a ball with him, too. Possibly was the single most selfish gunner in history, but that was his job, to come in and score. He wasn't multidimensional. Just a jump-shooter, with ungodly lift, though.

Portland was coached by Dr. Jack Ramsay, led by the 6-foot-11 center and Grateful Dead devotee, Bill Walton, and 6-9 forward Maurice Lucas from Pittsburgh. Mo was a serious brother. Lucas went to Marquette, lost in the NCAA finals to David "Skywalker" Thompson and N.C. State in '74, when Al McGuire got a tech. Mo was the kind of brother who'd go up to McGuire after a game and say, "You lost this game, Coach." Which he did do then. Luke had already lost to the Skywalker. So Chocolate Thunder and the Prince of Mid-Air were not going to be a problem. Mo's toughness gave the Sixers something to think about and allowed Portland to take advantage of the quickness of Walton, Lionel Hollins, and Johnny Davis. The 76ers, in spite of their abundance of individual talent, seemed to have no team concept to speak of that year, and it proved to be their undoing. The Trail Blazers came back from an 0–2 deficit to win the NBA title.

The next year, 1978, the Bullets got their game on. Wes Unseld and Big E, Elvin Hayes, finally got their World Championship, winning over Seattle, coached by Lenny Wilkens. Later on, when I was out doing research for my shelved Jackie Robinson film project, Lenny told me when he was a kid in Brooklyn, about to go to Boys and Girls High, he delivered groceries after school. One day he delivered to a brownstone. The man who answered the door was Jackie Robinson. Lenny was shocked. He got a nice tip from Jackie. Lenny ran down the block, deliriously happy.

Lenny Wilkens and Seattle won the NBA title in 1979, behind a superior backcourt rotation, Gus Williams and Dennis Johnson and Downtown Freddie Brown. But something was happening. The Bullets' methodology—bang, bang inside—was almost painful to watch. Seattle was only slightly better. Something else was happening to the league during this time. It was way off Broadway now. The NBA championship series games were shown only on tape delay on network television, after the late local news. It may seem hard to believe now, but in the late 1970s and 1980, the NBA title game tipped off at 11:30 P.M. in the East, tape delay or live from a distant clime like Seattle. The games were shown after the fact, after the result was given on the late local news, when children, the ones who are idealistic about the game, should have been in bed. There were words written to the effect that the league was "too black," though I don't know when and where that might have gotten started. There was this malaise, and a lot of it had to do with teams from distant outposts with pound-the-ball themes winning the title. Media centers of New York, Los Angeles, and Chicago wrote it off as the decline and fall of pro hoop. There was dissipation in the land, therefore the league. This was personified, for me, by the career of David Thompson.

After David Stern became NBA commissioner on February 1, 1984, superstars like Jordan, Magic, Barkley, Bird, Patrick went to places like Chicago, Los Angeles, Philadelphia, Boston, and New York. It was convenient for focusing the marketing of and fostering of interest in the league. But back in the late 1970s, the commissioner was Lawrence O'Brien, who may not have understood certain marketing aspects and forces. The best teams were in the distant outposts, not a whole lot different from the original bases of Rochester, Syracuse, and Oshkosh. David Thompson ended up playing in the rival ABA, for Denver, until the league was merged into the NBA following the 1975–76 season. The ABA presence of players like Julius and David forced the merger. I don't think the NBA would've been receptive to adding the Nets, had they not agreed to trade Dr. J to an established NBA franchise, the Philadelphia 76ers. Denver was attractive because of David. During the next few years, people didn't get a chance to see Skywalker on television much. The general malaise of the late '70s overtook the NBA. The merger watered down the rosters like expansion. Dissipation wore you down, like accelerated age. In this tableau, David Thompson became the most wasted talent—in a marketing, creative, aesthetic sense—the NBA has ever had.

In 1978, David Thompson nearly won the NBA scoring title on the last day of the regular season. George Gervin, the celebrated Iceman of the San Antonio Spurs, was leading the league going into the final game of the season. David asked how many points he needed to win the title. Someone told him, "As many as you can get." His game would be first, at Cobo in Detroit. That evening the Spurs would play the Jazz, later in

New Orleans. The Nuggets were coached by Larry Brown that year, with Brown's old North Carolina teammate, Donnie Walsh, serving as general manager. Coach Brown said, "We've already got the division won. Let's see if we can get David the scoring title." David proceeded to put on the second greatest scoring exhibition in the history of pro hoop. He scored 50 points in the first half against the Detroit Pistons, matching for a half what Wilt did in 1962 against the Knicks. The Skywalker wound up with 73 for the game.

Down in New Orleans, Coach Doug Moe and Gervin's Spurs teammates were waiting for him in the hotel lobby. Moe said, "Ice, you need 59 to win the scoring title. We're gonna get it for you." Gervin said, "Hey, guys, whatever you think." For the first three minutes of the game, Ice couldn't score, 0-for-6. He wanted to just let it go. Like Denver, the Spurs were already in the playoffs. But Coach Moe said, "Keep shooting." The horn sounded. Ice didn't miss again for a while. He had 20 by the end of the first quarter, 53 by halftime. He'd outdone David for a half. With three minutes left in the third quarter, Ice came out. He'd scored 63 points in thirty-three minutes, and he won the NBA scoring title. Not since Wilt scored 100 had the NBA seen anything like that day. Later, when people asked Gervin who guarded him (a good defensive player, E. C. Coleman), Gervin said, "Casper the Friendly Ghost, 'cause I was going right through him." Few people saw either game, or even highlights; this predated ESPN. I told some Morehouse classmates, "You see this? David Thompson went for 73. And then Iceman got 63." I got some impressed grunts, but mostly quizzical looks: "Yeah, man, so? Dr. Stephens is about to drop the bomb."

Dr. Stephens was my English professor at Morehouse. She was hard on me, but she cared about me and we remain friends. She'd mark up my papers something awful. She reminded me of my mother. I would write my mother letters from Morehouse, and she would send them back to me marked in blood-red ink and then say, "How did I raise a semiliterate son?"

Like the man said, everybody is ignorant, only on different subjects. And at that, my mother had been given more reason to grieve over Chris. He had been kicked out of another high school.

The league had expanded even more with the absorption of ABA teams after the 1975–76 season and was beginning to become more watered down, each roster not as deep. The players were finding out about cocaine, having it brought to them on silver platters, I'm sure. David found out, to his regret, and he was never the same. After Donnie Walsh got him into rehab, David was held up for public ridicule. More would follow. It was a pathetic way to go out, the way the Terry Furlows, Chris Washburns, and Roy Tarpleys went out. They were highly publicized for doing so. The funny thing about it is that white talent was also wasted this way, only you never, ever read about it in the papers. The codes and lingo became different then. They were "addicted to beer" or "mentally exhausted" or "dependent on painkillers." It was no less of a waste to me, though.

As creative as David Thompson was in the air, Pete Maravich was on the floor, with the ball. Peter Press Maravich was an intuitive phenomenon. His father, Press, was coach at LSU by the time Pete went there in 1966, but Pete had been performing dribbling exhibitions at halftime during games since he was four years old. He was a dribbling and passing wizard. He was a willowy 6-5, looked like a stiff breeze would blow him over, wore dingy, floppy gray socks, and nobody could stop him. He averaged 44.5 a game one season at LSU and 24.2 during his ten years in the NBA. His game was lateral, horizontal, all about magic. One of my favorite moves was when he was in the middle of a three-on-one fast break. Sometimes he would circle his hand around the ball, and the defender had no way of knowing on which side the hand would stop to kick the pass. Pete could make you look bad. Master improvisationalist, white boy, usually meant unintuitive, not having played the game from an early age. Pistol Pete finished third to David Thompson and George Gervin for the scoring title in 1977–78. "The fact that Pete was there in New Orleans that night I hit 63—he didn't play, he was hurt, but he was there, that meant something inspirational to me," Gervin told me years later. In 1976–77, playing for his hometown New Orleans Jazz, Pete averaged 31.1. Used to kill Clyde, lay waste to him. Nothing predictable for Clyde to pick up and exploit on defense. Pete never had to use the same move twice. His last good years were '77 and '78. He finished in

Boston. Auerbach wanted to say he had Pistol for a while. That was the year the Jazz moved to Utah. Pete had faded badly, but he still averaged over 13 a game for the Celtics.

"The Pistol," said Frazier, shaking his head. "He was ahead of his time. Did a lot of creative things on the court. If he played today, he might be the most popular player in the league."

Pete died after playing a pickup game of basketball in Baton Rouge on January 5, 1988, at age forty-one. Heart seizure. There were murmurings of cocaine use. Len Bias, the number two pick of the 1986 draft, by the Celtics, died of a cocaine overdose the day after. Bias's death was a source of public hand-wringing and cluck-clucking, and rightfully so, with the cruelest cut coming from Larry Bird himself, who said if Bias used drugs, then he didn't feel sorry for him. But maybe Larry had been hurt. He had suggested the Celtics take Bias. Pistol Pete Maravich has a building named after him down in Baton Rouge now, on the campus of LSU, where the basketball team plays. So there is this unadmitted, cloaked double standard. The press buys any explanation about a young white player's bad behavior or demise, and his reputation and standing are secure. Elvis went out behind dope. Who cares? But if David Thompson does, he is banned from the pantheon of history and cultural memory, as if he never existed. David Thompson didn't make the list of the NBA's Fifty Greatest Players, announced in 1996. Pete Maravich did. Both of them should have made it.

Michael Jordan told me: *"Dr. J is who influenced my game. And David Thompson, when he was at North Carolina State."*

> > >

Slowly, the championship team of 1970 and 1973 was disbanded. I do not imagine it is possible to do this without bitterness.

> *Alfred "Butch" Beard . . . Luther "Ticky" Burden . . .*
> *Glen Gondrezick . . . Spencer Haywood . . . Herschel Lewis . . .*
> *Bob McAdoo . . . Tom McMillen . . . Lonnie Shelton . . .*
> *Jim McMillian . . .*

DeBusschere retired in 1974 after a twelve-year yeoman's career. He resurfaced in a few years as the Knicks' general manager. Barnett retired the same season, after fourteen years in the league. Reed retired the same season. When great players retire after winning a championship, they never do it the following year. They look for an encore. If they don't get it, they feel free to move on. Willis became the Knicks' coach in 1977, replacing Red. Frazier was traded to Cleveland. Willis might have felt as if he couldn't coach younger players with Walt around. Clyde took it hard. "I think, when Willis took over as coach, he had problems. With me out of the way it was his team. I was the last link to his playing days. Willis had taken me under his wing when I was young. When I was a rookie, he took me to Small's Paradise, in Harlem. He got me my first date, and we went to Small's. It was really jumping. They had go-go girls. Place was packed. They introduced Willis. He got a standing ovation. I couldn't close my mouth. They introduced me. A few people applauded. I thought, 'Boy, I wish I could become a star in New York, like this great big man, Willis Reed.'"

Now Frazier was traded. The thing that hurt him was that Willis was always the type who, if he had something to say, said it. Clyde got traded and no one told him. His agent was waiting for him when he got home, on Fifty-seventh Street. "I couldn't believe it," said Frazier. "At first I wanted to retire. I equated Cleveland with Siberia. But I went. It got my priorities in order. There was really nothing to do there, so I stayed in. I did my job, but other than that, I stayed in. I started reading these self-help books. And that was really the start of what got me into words."

Clyde is now a Knicks radio broadcaster, and Willis, after being replaced by Red Holzman after a couple of fruitless seasons, is now an executive with the New Jersey Nets. Cazzie Russell, after being traded for Jerry Lucas, played until 1978 with the Warriors, the Lakers, then a season in Chicago. Cazzie always did like the bright lights. But he loved the game more. Later on, he became one of the best coaches in the Continental Basketball Association, the CBA, the minor league reincarnation of the old hoop chitlin circuit. Phil Jackson also coached in that league, as did George Karl of Seattle. They both coached in the NBA finals in 1995–96. Despite his successes, Cazzie still has yet to make it back to the big league as a coach.

Bill Bradley retired after the 1977 season, entered politics, and was the junior senator, Democrat from New Jersey, for over a decade. It's kind of sad to me that he left politics, became disillusioned with power, because I thought he was going to be president of the United States one day. He had my vote. He understood what it takes, not so much because he went to Princeton or because he went to Oxford and was a Rhodes scholar or because he was a senator but, because he had played for the Knicks, he understood how to be part of the collective and had learned lessons about affirmative action and teamwork and chemistry and had lived and traveled with black teammates and seemed none the worse for wear. But it was not to be.

"I want to think through the next chapter of the American story—the need for economic transformation, the need for racial healing," Bradley told me. "Search for something that's deeper than the material in people's lives. Some people can't understand that, they can't compute that, and yet other people understand perfectly how giving up power is a form of power.

"I'm learning to use that power."

During the summer of 1977, as most of the old Knicks retired or got traded, I couldn't find a job. Not wanting to waste away before my time, I bought a Super 8 camera. That summer is distinct in my memory for at least two reasons—the great power blackout and the disco craze. Using my camera, I combined footage of people looting during the blackout with footage of people dancing. The big disco-craze dance that summer was called the Hustle. I named my first film *Last Hustle in Brooklyn*, and that was really my start as a filmmaker. The facilities we had in college were for Super 8. I learned under a great teacher, Dr. Herb Eichelberger. That got me started on my way. By my senior year I was set on the path. Film did something to me, for me, starting with looking through a viewfinder. I knew instinctively I had the vision for this line of work. I knew almost immediately that I would make films, and I knew that, once

I made them, I didn't want hundreds of people to see them. I wanted millions of people to see them. I think I got this from watching my father labor in obscurity. I too now had an art form—the same but different. I wanted to publicly express my craft—the same but different. That meant grab the people, shake them up—*make* them all pay attention.

In spite of my new interest, I still loved sports with a passion. I discovered there had never been a Morehouse intramural softball league. In my sophomore year, with nothing extracurricular to do in the springtime, since Morehouse is an all-male college, and since the Knicks were in the toilet, I organized an intramural softball league on campus. I was the commissioner, so I made the schedule, set the ground rules, ran things generally. I ran it like Judge Landis, with an iron fist. I also had my own franchise and elected myself captain of my own team; I'm the commissioner. I can do what I want. My team was called . . . the Yankees. Yes, the Yankees. At shortstop there was this one guy on our team, Jimmy Rhines, from Pittsburgh, and this guy was the most selfish bum ever. All he cared about was him. Whatever was best for him. He could play all right, but he would never consider hitting to right to move the runner along in a tight game, basic stuff like that. We had the same team for three years. After the first year I got rid of him. He tried to start a fight. General manager is a tough gig. He was a cancer on the club, just like the ex–New York Yankee Reuben Sierra, so he had to go.

So we were the Yankees, and every year our chief rival was the team representing the football players. The football players had a juggernaut. We would meet during the season, then usually lose to them for the championship. My senior year, we finally beat them. I have a scar in the shape of a star beneath my eye, which I got from playing softball during this time. It happened my senior year, a regular-season game against the football team. There was a play at the plate. Our shortstop, Gab Smith from Delaware, relayed the ball from the outfield. A guy named Booker Moore, starting free safety for the football team, was heading for home under a full head of steam. I had the smart idea of covering the plate from the pitcher's mound. Ball and Booker arrived at the same time. He was a solid 210 pounds. There was a collision. I remember seeing his forearm. It was what they call a bang-bang play. I'll say. I had a concussion and needed five stitches—but I held on to the ball. Was it worth it? No, but I wasn't going to get out of the way and just let them win, and that was the tying run that got tagged out. After going to the infirmary and vomiting, I returned in time to see us win in extra innings. Some football players were upset about Booker's play. Donald Edwards, our star linebacker, was two seconds off Booker's ass. Booker went on to become a preacher. He has a church in Indianapolis. Amen.

> *1979–80 . . . Toby Knight . . . Ray-Ray Williams . . .*
> *Hollis Copeland . . . Larry Demic . . . Mike "Stinger" Glenn . . .*
> *Michael Ray Richardson . . . Marvin "the Human Eraser"*
> *Webster . . .*

I guess the Toby Knights tried. But the Knicks were no good. And those weak trades. Mike Newlin, a long-range shooter who played in Houston for years. But he was through by the time the Knicks got him in '81. Paul Westphal, from USC, who was so good, very athletic with the Phoenix Suns for years, and helped them get to the finals in 1976, where the Celtics knocked them off. The Knicks also got him after he was all but finished. We got these guys when they were done. Kiki Vandeweghe. I was like "Come on, guys, what in the name do you guys think you're doing?" No question the Knicks management lost it before the players did. The players couldn't help getting old. But we weren't running a retirement home. It was during this period of abject futility, the late '70s and early '80s, that I first began to hear it: "the Niggerbockers." I don't know how that thing started, but it wasn't started by black people. "Niggerbockers." Not as complimentary as the Buffalo Germans, the Original Celtics, and those other monikers.

Upon graduation from Morehouse in May of 1979, I knew I still didn't have the necessary skills to become a filmmaker. I applied to the top three film schools: USC, UCLA, and NYU.

Now, to get into USC or UCLA, you had to get an astronomical score on the Graduate Record Examination. I did not get that score. Luckily for me, to get into NYU, you only had to submit a creative portfolio. I submitted some of my creative writing and some photographs I had taken. I got in. But I didn't really have confirmation at the time of Morehouse's graduation ceremonies; I still had not received word from NYU. The Morehouse graduation program listed everyone who graduated, what graduate schools they had been accepted into, what jobs they had taken, and the amount of their salaries. And next to my name, all it said was "Shelton Jackson Lee — Bachelor of Arts." No graduate school. No job offer. I was disheartened. You know, I was seeing Harvard Law School, Harvard Med School, Wharton, Northwestern, PaineWebber, Merrill Lynch, Chase Manhattan. And me? Nothing. To myself, I was saying, "All right, man. That's awright. One day. One day."

More than anything, I wanted something next to my name for my grandmother Zimmie. I wanted her to be proud of me—I already knew she was, but I wanted her to be able to make a fuss over my accomplishments. After all, she'd saved her pennies so I could get an education. I wanted to repay her. It motivated me. Because I already knew I was more than just hoping. I had already been told I'd been accepted into NYU, but the letter hadn't come. Until Morehouse got the letter, anything else was counterfeit. So there was nothing next to my name in the program.

Right after graduation I flew to L.A. I spent the summer in Los Angeles. I had an internship with Columbia Pictures. Each week was to be spent in a different department: marketing, editing, public relations, production. Columbia had a scholarship program, and I was lucky. Morehouse job placement found out about it, and I was on it like a hawk. At this time I wasn't closely following what happened between Magic and Bird in the NCAA title game; I saw the game and noticed that Magic was drafted by the Lakers that same summer, but I was too busy getting on with my chosen craft. In fact, the only time I followed box scores as religiously as I had when I was younger was in 1976, '77, and '78, when the Yankees of Reggie were rolling. In L.A. I steeped myself in the business of learning to be a filmmaker. At first I lived with the family of a friend of mine, Tracy Willard, out in Pasadena. Tracy had gone to Spelman. Her folks are good people, and they treated me like family, but it was too much of a commute from Pasadena to Burbank, two hours on that RTD bus, so I rented a run-down room in a fleabag motel on Sepulveda. Or maybe it was on La Cienega. I always got those L.A. streets with the Spanish names mixed up.

Then it was time to come home to New York that fall and matriculate at NYU. Historically, NYU lets in a big freshman class. Like USC and UCLA, it is a three-year graduate program. But at the end of the first year at NYU, they kick out half of the first-year class. You do three films in your first year, and that is how you are graded—on the films you make, not by written test. The faculty sits down and screens the film, and they decide your grade.

My third and most crucial student film that year was called *The Answer*. It wasn't about solving the matchup problem caused by 6-foot-9 Magic Johnson playing point, or Larry Bird swinging from both forward slots. Instead, it was about a black screenwriter hired to write and direct the $50 million remake of D. W. Griffith's *Birth of a Nation*—hired to do this by a major Hollywood studio. I used the most degrading scenes of black people from *Birth of a Nation* in my film. Somehow the faculty did not like this film. They felt I was defaming the father of cinema, or whatever. They wanted to kick me out. But they made a mistake. They had given me a teaching assistantship before the final grades came in. That first year, I had work study in the equipment room, and I worked very hard because I wanted it badly; this job would supplement my income to help get me through film school. I knew every nook, cranny, and function of that equipment room. When it followed, after the faculty screening of *The Answer*, that they wanted to toss me out on my ear, some gentle soul pointed out that they really couldn't kick me out because I'd been granted this position as a teaching assistant. So that's how I didn't get kicked out of NYU—because of a glitch.

Second and third year, that's when I met Ernest Dickerson, a graduate of the Howard University school of architecture, with a great eye. Photographer. We would collaborate for years, with Ernest as my cinematographer. He shot all my NYU stuff and all my films up to *Malcolm X*. One of my other classmates in film school was named Tony Drazen. Tony would later direct the film *Zebrahead*. Tony's father worked for an advertising agency and had season tickets to the Knicks games, second row, behind the basket, Eighth Avenue end. While at NYU, I would go to games with Tony and watch some truly bad teams, bad in an epic sense, and watch from up close, right behind the basket. Talk about warts and all. Made me pine for general admission. Tony was gracious enough to ask me to come along, and I appreciated that—if not the makeup of the Knicks' rosters.

Of course from 1980 through most of the decade, the league belonged to Earvin "Magic" Johnson of the Lakers and Larry Bird of the Celtics. I never liked the Celtics, we know that by now, but along through here—and we'll talk about why later—there was a turning point. Bird and Magic came into the league the same year. Seemed like they traded the NBA World Championship between them for the rest of the decade until Isiah Thomas and Detroit broke through. There was more to it than that, but the papers made it Magic vs. Larry, joined at the hip from then on. Magic and Bird, Bird and Magic. One black, one white. One blond. Even Magic or Bird might not have been able to take the Knicks to the World Championship during this time.

> 1980–82: *Reggie Carter . . . Bill Cartwright . . .*
> *Marc Iavaroni . . . Campy Russell . . . DeWayne Scales . . .*
> *Mike Woodson . . . Alex Bradley . . . Greg Cook . . .*

In the 1980 championship series, the Lakers faced the 76ers of Dr. J. Magic was a rookie. In the sixth and final game, he had one of those lights-out last-game performances that I had first seen mounted in the seventh game of the 1969–70 finals by Walt Frazier. Magic scored 42 points and had 16 assists, and the Lakers won the world title his rookie year—absolutely amazing—in spite of the fact that Kareem Abdul-Jabbar sat out the sixth and final game with an injured ankle.

But Magic didn't do it by himself. That night another former UCLA great, Jamaal Wilkes, scored 37 points himself. Silk, he was called, with good reason. One of the secrets to that team was Norm Nixon. Norm was considered the off-guard, the two-guard on offense, even though he was only 6-2. After he retired, Norm married actress-choreographer-director Debbie Allen. My grandmother taught Norm in Macon, Georgia, at Ballard Hudson Junior High School. He was in her art class. I'm telling you, it's too, too small a world. But that world was changing. A 6-foot-9 point guard was playing. It was thought Magic might change ball this way in some quarters, and it was hoped he would not in others. Magic played point, yet he was 6 feet 9. He had the handle, the vision, the awareness. Suddenly people went out looking for 6-9 point guards, which they never found. But size on the perimeter, started by Big O at 6-5, through Frazier, had gotten taller. No one yet has found any 6-foot-9 point guards. There was only one Magic. But eventually they did find Jordan, Pippen, Hardaway, and Grant Hill in the bushes, and they became the paradigm.

The Celtics won the NBA title in 1981 behind Bird. Magic missed the last shot of the Western Conference finals against Houston. People came down on him. Magic's Michigan State team had won the NCAA championship final over Bird's Indiana State team in 1979. Magic had won the NBA World Championship the next season. It was Bird's turn in the progression of play. The Celtics won the NBA in '81, '84, '86; the Lakers won in '80, '82, '85, '87, and '88. For Knicks fans, a broken record. For the league, a shot in the arm. Nobody said "too black" then. Some said Bird was the best. Some said Magic. I noticed a fervor, decided it was something I'd use one day.

Both men had outstanding teams around them. Bird played with three All-Stars around him: Kevin McHale, the 6-foot-11 power forward (Herman Munster look-alike) from Minnesota, with arms like an octopus and an unstoppable turnaround j; Robert Parish (now with the Bulls, the oldest player in the league—forty-three), the 7-0 center; Dennis Johnson, the ex–Seattle Sonic, who won the NBA title the same season Magic and Bird battled for the NCAA title. The Celtics ran players like Danny Ainge and Cornbread Maxwell in and out during their shared dynasty with the Lakers. They carried those like Jerry Sichting, and by the time Bill Walton came to Boston, his feet were a mess and he was nearly done.

That three-time World Champion team was Red Auerbach's coup de grâce. He always was a good horse trader, and his victims this time were the Golden State Warriors and an executive there named Scotty Stirling.

Red had already fleeced the Warriors out of number one pick for aging Jo Jo White back in early 1980. When the draft of that year came, Boston was up first, and available was a player, a smart young man with sensitive eyes and no great love of contact named Joe Barry Carroll, a 7-footer, out of Purdue. Auerbach said, "Hmm." Meanwhile, the Warriors had the young Robert Parish, who had a 32-point, 30-rebound game late during that season. Somehow Red Auerbach convinced the Warriors to send him Robert Parish, and he would give them the number one pick and the rights to draft Carroll. Red also got the Warriors to agree to throw in their pick in the first round, the third pick overall. And that turned out to be Kevin McHale. So for the rights to Joe Barry Carroll, a journeyman scorer—wonderful person, no Hall of Famer—Auerbach got two guys who made the NBA's Fifty Greatest Players list during the NBA's fiftieth anniversary season. Joe Barry Carroll. "Joe Barely Cares," as named by Peter Vecsey, the *New York Post* columnist. Say what you want about Vecsey, but he has amused at least one young brother during late-evening trips on the subway with his basketball column, "Hoop Du Jour."

Stirling, as penance for his misdeed, wound up, a few years later, running the Knicks. Oh, dear. That trade has to go down as one of the worst in the history of American team sports.

Like the Celtics of that era, the Lakers were loaded. Norm Nixon was a 17.5 scorer for the Lakers from 1978 until 1982, playing alongside Magic. The Lakers had Abdul-Jabbar, then in his mid to late thirties, and a rubbery, spectacular defender, a rookie the same year that Magic came in, a 6-6 player named Michael Cooper, who wore his white tube socks up to his kneecaps on those skinny melink legs. In 1980 they had Jamaal "Silk" (formerly Keith) Wilkes, who won two NCAA titles at UCLA with Walton and the NBA title in his rookie year with Golden State. Underrated. The Lakers had big Jim Chones and Bob McAdoo to specialize. Later in the decade, they replaced Nixon with Byron Scott, a 6-4 scorer they suffered with for a couple of seasons. For a while it seemed like Byron never made the big shot in the playoffs, but he ended up a reliable shooter. In 1982 they drafted a forward from North Carolina named James Worthy. Another of the NBA's Fifty Greatest. The Lakers added a Kurt Rambis or a Mychal Thompson here and there to help.

It all began one night in 1980, when the Lakers beat the Philadelphia 76ers at the Spectrum for the NBA title, Dr. J.'s Sixers—beat them with ball-changing play by Magic, who jumped center, but basically played no position. He played the Game. It was shown nationally on tape delay. Tipoff 11:30 P.M. Magic and Bird and the dynamic between them would soon change that.

Doc had come into the league in 1976 a legend, although his knees were already bothering him. He won the first slam-dunk competition— a holdover from the ABA, where Doc's take-off-from-the-free-throw-line dunk had taken all the air out of the gym in Denver in 1973. He was a great ambassador for the game. But bringing in Indiana's George McGinnis had not helped the Sixers win in the finals against Portland in 1977, and their resulting slogan—"We owe you one"— cut no ice with the Bullets in '78, the Sonics in '79, the Lakers in '80, the Celtics in '81, or the Lakers again in '82. In fact, the Sixers were seen as part of the late '70s malaise. Selfish gunners like Free, would-be space cadets like Chocolate Thunder. I felt bad for Doc.

Not for long, though. The Sixers got enterprising and brought in Moses Malone from Houston—another of the chosen Fifty Greatest NBA Players—and unloaded all their frustrations on the league, including the Knicks, in 1983. That Sixer team is truly an overlooked team. Now they had Answers. Moses was in the middle. They had the Boston Strangler, Andrew Toney, at two-guard; Steve Mix, Caldwell, and Bobby Jones were around for rebounds and defense, and Bobby, even at thirty-two, was still a good finisher on the break. And mostly they had Moses, Doc, and Chi-Chi. Maurice Cheeks was probably the most underrated point guard of this era. When he got ballplayer-old, of course the Knicks picked him up. But this was his last great year—he is still the NBA's all-time leader in steals with 2,310—and Magic couldn't guard him. In this series Doc had a great rocker-arm dunk on the fly against Michael Cooper. Coop, known as a skywalking shot-blocker, went up as Doc roared in from the left side, cupped the ball, and 360-ed his arm. Cooper was way up there, and as they flew past the rim, Cooper had to duck to avoid hitting his head on it, and after he ducked, here came Doc's follow-through.

Boom!

Doc also still makes the highlight reel for his up-and-under curlicue fly layup against Kareem and the Lakers, but that came in the 1980 series, when the Sixers lost. This dunk by the Doctor at the Spectrum made Kangaroo Kid, Billy Cunningham, leap out of his chair. Billy was coaching the Sixers. Philly stormed through the playoffs. Moses, who came to the ABA from a Virginia high school and was not the most articulate brother in the first place, had an answer when asked what it would take to win the NBA title before the 1982–83 playoffs began. Moses said, "Fo', fo', fo'," meaning the Sixers would sweep all three best-of-seven game series on the way to the title none of them had ever won. That they lost a game in the middle series hardly even seems to matter. The fusion group from Philadelphia called Pieces of a Dream recorded a tune, "Fo-Five-Fo," done to a rhythm similar to their classic, "Warm Weather," to commemorate what the Sixers had done.

I can still hear the P.A. announcer at the Spectrum, the late Dave Zinkoff: "And at fahwahd, from Massachusetts, numbah six, the Doctah, Julius Errrrrr-ving!"

No one deserved a ring more than the Doctor, Cheeks, Moses, Bobby, Caldwell, the Boston Strangler, the Celtic Killer, Andrew Toney. I liked Steve Mix—nice stroke. Bobby Jones. Stealthy at 6-9. White lightning. Anybody beating the Celtics I liked, but that team I liked for itself. The Doctor was finally in. Meanwhile the Knicks were stuck on stupid. Ray-Ray had talent, but acted like he had somewhere better to be, as did Michael Ray Richardson, who some called Sugar, but I never saw it. Sugar was not the Answer. As he himself said at the time, "The ship be sinking."

By 1984 things were starting to get better. The Knicks had gotten Bernard King, from Fort Greene, Brooklyn, in 1982. Went to Fort Hamilton High School. For me there is no argument that Bernard is the best offensive basketball player Brooklyn ever produced. At 6-5, with a pop-chest, a rump-roast high butt, 'Nard was nearly unstoppable, especially from the left side. He averaged 26.3 a game in 1983–84, and a monstrous 32.9 in 1984–85 to lead the league. Bernard was our only answer, but a damned good one—just not good enough to win the NBA title with the help provided. But Bernard gave out his share of box-score black eyes. Went for 50 on Boston in a playoff game in '84. Cornbread said, "I'd like to see the bitch score 50 again." Bernard did. Maxwell didn't ask for any more. 'Nard had the nastiest game face ever. He suffered a horrible knee injury March 23, 1985, at Kansas City. Not even 'Nard had gotten the Knicks over the hump.

If the Knicks weren't playing a seventh game of the NBA finals, then there were better things for me to do. Like make pictures.

Joe's Bed-Stuy Barbershop: We Cut Heads was my student-thesis film and signaled the close of my three-year education at NYU. *Joe's* was shot around Thanksgiving of 1981. I wanted to see different images of my people. Where better to start than in a barbershop, a social magnet. I finished it in 1982, then graduated. Wouldn't have done it without my grandmother Zimmie. She'd put me through NYU. By that I mean she also financed my films. You had to pay for the films you made. NYU gave you a couple of rolls, paid for processing. That was it. The cash had to come from somewhere. *Joe's* cost ten grand. Ten large was a lot of loot for a broke student back then.

Joe's won the students' academy award. I got an agent. Neither brought me work. I began working part-time at a small film distribution company, First Run Features, shipping and cleaning prints, running errands. Lived with Uncle Cliff and his family in Crown Heights, moved to a basement apartment on Adelphi Street in Fort Greene. I had no extras for nonessentials. Spaghettios was my diet. Saw four or five Knicks games. The Knicks were essential. I had two scripts in mind. One had hoop as part of its cultural motif. I'd even put a children's rhyme in my student-thesis film, *Joe's*. It went like this:

> *If your sneakers slip and slide,*
> *Get the ones with the star on the side*
> *Ask your moms to empty her purse*
> *And get the ones that say . . .*

SECOND QUARTER

Just Do It

The very first NBA draft lottery was held on July 15, 1985, and I was in front of the TV in the Harlem apartment of Cheryl Burr, my girlfriend at the time, as much as my attentions could be divided. The lottery had me riveted. Cheryl was not moved by it. But by having gone 24–58 the previous season, the Knicks now had a chance to hit this new lotto and win the rights to Patrick Ewing, a big-time 7-footer with large game, the best college player, who could eventually get us back to Broadway, to the heights of NBA World Championship—once we got him some help.

I felt as hopeful as Dave DeBusschere looked. He'd been the answer once. Now he was the Knicks' general manager, taking his seat with the other representatives of the seven NBA teams involved, trying not to look pressed. Historically the NBA team with the worst record automatically got the first pick. David Stern changed that at the end of the 1984–85 season, to keep teams from dumping games in pursuit of the worst record in order to get the draft rights to Ewing. He was that highly prized. The NBA team with that worst record was Golden State, represented at the lottery by Al Attles, Wilt's old teammate. As a head coach, Al won the NBA title with the Warriors in 1974–75. But now he looked like he'd been hit in the face with an ax handle as Stern drew the card of the team that would pick seventh, the bottom of the lottery.

"The Golden State Warriors."

"Spike, we need to talk," said Cheryl.

"Sorry 'bout that, Al, but hey . . . Hold up a minute, Cheryl."

As Stern read off picks number six, five, four, three, I locked in. Could this be happening? Could the Knicks be getting Patrick Ewing of Georgetown? Good things come in threes, they say. We were getting ready to shoot *She's Gotta Have It* the same month. Ernest Dickerson was my DP.

My father was scoring the film. I was glad to provide him an outlet wherein to utilize his gift, and he encouraged me to take control of my own game and run it. My father always said he was a good athlete. Other people did, too. He played sports down in Snow Hill, Alabama. A point guard on the basketball team, a quarterback on the football team, shortstop and second base on the baseball team, wasn't the most gifted athletically, but always was the sparkplug, the leader. He encouraged me to be the same way.

For *She's Gotta Have It*, I was directing and had a role. We had scrounged up the money to buy enough film. The prior winter I'd written the cozy script about the most universal thing in life. Not hoop. Other relationships. Basketball was part of the motif, though. The film was to be shot in Brooklyn. The character I would play was a young b-boy, bike messenger, named Mars Blackmon. He had a serious-serious "Basketball Jones." You remember the tune? "Basketball Jones, I got a Basketball Jones, I got a Basketball Jones . . . fo-or you. . . ."

I didn't know Mars's persona would be such a hook. I just knew Mars was a b-boy and thought a young urban black male at that time would be a fan of hoop. It seemed clear to me that Jordan was the next superstar, and that's why I chose him to be Mars's favorite, even though Mars was a big Knicks fan. Mars also loved Bernard King, but Mars was a purist and knew Jordan was the Man. We had to spend a portion of the film's initial $10,000 budget to buy two pairs of Air Jordans for Mars to wear; even when he's making love to Nola Darling, the central character, Mars doesn't take them off. All Nike agreed to give to us was a poster of Jordan, which hung on the wall of Mars's basement studio apartment—in real life, my place. We pleaded. We begged. No juice yet.

I was living on Adelphi Street in Brooklyn. There we would get a shot where Mars is on the phone with Nola; the poster is in the background. Jordan lifting off, life-size. Simple art direction, cheap stuff. You try to do the best job possible with what you have available. I didn't even know if we'd get through *She's Gotta Have It*, let alone that Island Pictures would put it into release as of August 7, 1986; or that it would be accepted into the Cannes Film festival; or that Jim Riswold and Bill

Davenport at Weiden & Kennedy, an advertising agency in Portland, Oregon, that had the Nike account, would later see *She's Gotta Have It;* or that they would then get the extraordinarily bright idea of pairing Mars Blackmon—a character only on the page and in my head as of July 15, 1985—with Michael Jordan in a long series of commercials for Nike Air Jordans. I had no way of foreseeing it all. I couldn't even foresee that the Knicks were about to get the rights to Patrick Ewing.

"Spike, we need to talk *now*," said Cheryl.

"One second . . ." I said. Every time Stern pulled up a card, the Knicks' logo wasn't on it, and the odds kept getting better.

"The second selection in the 1985 NBA draft lottery goes to . . . the Indiana Pa—"

On camera, knowing the Knicks had just gotten the draft rights to Patrick Ewing of Georgetown, DeBusschere pounded the table in front of him. Meanwhile, up in Harlem, I raised my hands in the air, raised 'em like I just didn't care—but I did. I'm jumping up and down, very happy, dreams of the NBA World Championship dancing in my head, and saying, "Ho-oh!"

"Spike, it's over between me and you," Cheryl said.

My hands came down. "What?" So it was that Cheryl Burr kicked me to the curb on the same day the Knicks got the rights to Ewing of Georgetown, the same month I shot *She's Gotta Have It.* Good things come in threes. I went home. Considered the error of my ways. Bit my lip. Picked up the phone. Punched the digits. Swallowed my pride. Time for commitment.

"New York Knickabockas," said the female voice on the other end.

"Yes, my name is Spike Lee, and I want to buy two season tickets," I said. I was told I had to come down to the Garden box office, which would open at eight o'clock the next morning, Tuesday. I was on line at 5:00 A.M. to buy tickets and I've had them ever since. I went from a high to a low moment, a funk it took me several months to get over. As the 1985–86 basketball season started, I still missed Cheryl. And a fine young thing she was, too. I had cast her as Ava in the film before she gave me the ax. I contemplated getting someone else, giving her the ax. We all know the big payback can be a mutha—but eventually I thought otherwise. So Cheryl played Ava, a dancer, a peripheral character in *She's Gotta Have It*. She kept her part. We remained friends.

To this day many people still feel that draft was rigged, that the NBA made sure the Knicks got Patrick. I think the great basketball God in the sky looked down and felt sorry for us long-suffering Knicks fans.

My first tickets were in the green seats, section 304, second promenade. Slowly I began to work my way down to the floor. Making films played a big role.

> > >

These were the historical factors that gave shape to Mars Blackmon's sensibility and persona, and added to the cultural backdrop of *She's Gotta Have It*:

In March of 1982, as freshman Patrick Ewing and Georgetown played freshman Michael Jordan and North Carolina for the national championship at the Superdome in New Orleans before a record crowd of 61,612 ticket holders, it seemed to me nearly every black kid in America had a Starter jacket or a cap or a jersey or a T-shirt with "Georgetown" on it. No doubt Mars would. A lot of white kids had them, too. Not to mention Georgetown alumni. You had a mix of kind of a street-smart savvy Mars Blackmon–type wearer of the jacket and a Middle America, wanting-to-be-down tip; then an elitist Newport Beach, Georgetown lawyer moneyed tip; all these people with the same jacket, the same hat, all for different interior reasons. I was there with them, too, observing the scene. Nowadays everybody wears every school, but in the '80s, Georgetown block lettering meant a lot in many ways. I surely identified with the way the Hoyas played for Coach John Thompson. The coach tolerated no nonsense, and his team was in order, on point, and people wanted to see a kind of discipline, but they wanted it legitimate—without the whip, the chair, the loud harangues intended to impress observers. Honest, well-intentioned discipline.

Being in New York, I found it intriguing to see how the local media would play up St. John's and the ways they would play off Georgetown. St. John's, in Queens, would be glorified, Coach Louie Carnesecca and the Chosen One, the golden white boy, at the time a 6-7 good kid who always played with the brothers, a kid with a serious stroke from Brooklyn named Chris Mullin. He was then pitted by the New York hype machine against the so-called thuggery of Georgetown. Chris could play, went to Xaverian High School, and I really don't blame him—he wasn't to blame, he had no control over what the spin doctors did—but it was still hard to take. This was the biggest basketball show in town at the time, and it was easy to inflame the passions of the locals. It worked, I'm saying. St. John's and Georgetown could sell out the Garden when the Knicks of this era couldn't.

I was at the Garden in January of 1985 for the game when St. John's and Georgetown were ranked number one and number two, the Sweater game, when Louie had on one of his famous ugly sweaters. Coach Thompson came out wearing a similar one under his jacket. Georgetown won that game. All through that time, whenever New York City produced a decent college-level local ballplayer, he would be overestimated for his age and level of game by the hacks, given a quickie hagiography by the New York hype machine, then pitted against Georgetown. Thrown to the lions. Or it would be upstate, Syracuse and its star of the moment designated in the heroic role. Pearl Washington of Syracuse vs. Patrick Ewing and Georgetown. Good vs. evil. The New York hype machine in effect. One year at the Big East tournament, egged on by a charged atmosphere, Pearl and Patrick had a near fight. Wouldn't call it a real fight. A near fight, almost came to blows. Pearl Washington—nicknamed for Earl Monroe, without anywhere near that level of game—felt the pressure. One of the New York papers said, "Pearl Washington pulled out a knife, and Patrick Ewing pulled out a gun." That's the way the scene was described. Maybe it was over my head. Anyway, Georgetown got a rep of being a bunch of black muggers, criminals, thugs, unintelligent illiterates; I think mostly it had to do with the fact Georgetown had a black coach, the team was mostly black, they were winning ball games, and they played aggressively, especially on defense. It was fortified by the fact that Coach Thompson would figuratively tell the hacks to kiss his black ass at the drop of a hat. He's a strong, authoritative man, and it's no secret that people, especially within the ranks of the majority media, have problems with strong black men, especially when they are as physically imposing as 6-foot-11 John Thompson.

So the New York hype machine would crank, set up Chris or Pearl or whoever as the next basketball savior of the planet—the end of it New York City holds up—and I would throw the paper down on the seat of the Brooklyn-bound D train in disgust.

And yet rarely was there a mention of how Coach Thompson came out of nowhere to keep the flame of big-time college hoop burning, taking a second-tier basketball program and turning it into an institution. Early on he did it with a concentration on defense, pressure defense, man-to-man, zone trap, full-court, 94 feet, end-to-end, get-in-that-ass defense, shot-blocker in back, some of this looking a lot like Wooden's old philosophy—"Be quick, but don't hurry"—and Russell and Auerbach's old Celtics. I liked to watch a pressing style. Georgetown's philosophy of defense first took over the college game and percolated up into the NBA when Ewing was drafted number one in 1985, a year after Jordan was drafted number three. Georgetown posed the problem: pressure D, shot-blocking. Jordan had the Answer in the 1982 NCAA title game—creative execution, in space.

Over the ensuing years, many college coaches made their reps by playing in the Georgetown style or by beating Georgetown's style. Coach Rick Pitino, a longtime assistant under Hubie Brown, made his bones in the 1987 NCAA tournament with a win over Georgetown at the Elite Eight, at Freedom Hall in Louisville. With that win, Pitino took Providence to the Final Four, again in New Orleans. In the 1987 NCAA semifinal against Syracuse, there was a big fight on the court, knuck city, although none of the players from Syracuse or Providence were later portrayed as part of thug life. It was seen as a boys-will-be-boys thing. Indiana and Bobby Knight won the NCAA title that year on a clutch baseline j by a kid named Keith Smart. As Smart's shot neared the basket, Knight blinked hard, one time, and when he opened his eyes, the nylon was dancing. I wonder if Coach thinks he wished it in. Nah. TV cameras showed celebrating Hoosiers. Mostly Knight hugging a guard named Steve Alford. I don't know what happened to Smart, but Coach Pitino went from Providence to coaching the Knicks for two seasons, playing a wide-open style I liked; then he moved to Kentucky, where his team became the 1996 NCAA champion, basically playing old Georgetown style: ten-man rotation, pressure D, wear you down in waves.

The University of Massachusetts beat Georgetown in the 1995–96 NCAA tournament for the right to go to the Final Four. The UMass coach, John Calipari, is now a rookie coach with the New Jersey Nets of the NBA. Pitino turned the job down and recommended his fellow *paisan.* So Georgetown was then and still is a primary character in the Game.

Coach Thompson, John Wooden of UCLA, Dean Smith of North Carolina, and Bobby Knight of Indiana came closest among college coaches to changing ball. Knight was the coach of the Olympic team that won the gold in L.A. in 1984. Jordan and Ewing were the stars. Knight cut Charles Barkley that year. John Thompson was coach of the 1988 Olympic team that won the bronze in Seoul. Danny Manning and David Robinson were the stars on *that* team. Nice players, but not special. Makes a difference. Larry Brown had coached Danny Manning and Kansas to the NCAA title in 1988. How Kansas beat Oklahoma that year is beyond me. One of those whole-is-greater-than-the-sum-of-the-parts deals. A decade before, Knight had also cut Larry Bird, at Indiana, in the mid-1970s. Coach Knight doesn't turn out a whole lot of pro players.

Georgetown played aggressive D. Indiana played aggressive D. Knight was more combative with the hacks and with the refs than Thompson was. Yet it was Georgetown that always got played off as a criminal element. Never heard that about Indiana. Georgetown won all through the 1980s with good defense, what many hacks said black players didn't play at the time in the NBA. So if you play good D and the scores go down, you're not a ballplayer, you're a thug. Coaches know you win with those kinds of thugs. Don't play great D, play good O, you're a showboat, not a team player. And you're just *totally* outrageous if you play tough D for Georgetown under "that man." You couldn't win with the hacks, not as a serious ballplayer, not in the columns written in the age of Reagan.

At Georgetown and before, while at Cambridge Rindge and Latin

High in greater Boston, Ewing always heard taunts about how he couldn't read, was a monkey, a prehistoric Neanderthal Man, Patrick Can't Read, all this. Between Patrick and Coach, they put the fear of God in a lot of people. Sports commentary and fan behavior went hand in hand. Georgetown won, so Georgetown was cheating, rough, whatever. When you have nowhere else to go, "the refs are cheatin'!" No fan has to be led far to go there. But there are bad calls, and then there's cheating. In the 1994–95 season, when Allen Iverson was a freshman, Coach Thompson took his team off the Spectrum court for several minutes after the Hoyas went to Philly to play Villanova. Coach Thompson did this because of an obtuse sign that was held up in the 'Nova student section. It said: "Allen Iverson: The Next O.J."

And really, that was not so very far from what some of the hacks wrote about Georgetown basketball. I'm not saying it was bigotry. But then I don't have to *say* it, do I?

> > >

So as North Carolina met Georgetown for the NCAA title in the spring of 1982, I was finishing up at NYU, crewing on a classmate's film. Besides the distraction of knowing such a great college ball game was on, the Academy Awards were also televised that night. For years both events, the Oscars and the NCAA finals, occurred on the same Monday night. I remember not being able to watch the game because we were working; most of the crew wanted to see the Oscars anyway. When you're in film school and not directing your own films, you're working on somebody else's. I was doing my job, going back and forth into a back room where a TV was on. I helped people switch from the Academy Awards to the NCAA final. One minute I'm watching Burt Lancaster get bleeped as a clip from Louis Malle's *Atlantic City* is shown. The winner for Best Actor—Henry Fonda, for *On Golden Pond*. The next minute I switched back to the game and Ewing was grabbing somebody's j. Ewing I knew of by then, and Thompson and Dean Smith, James Worthy, and Sam Perkins from Brooklyn. But, yo, who was the nice buster for Carolina climbing all over the boards? Never seen *him* before. Number 23. Somebody switched back to the Oscars. Why? *On Golden Pond* was supposedly a shoo-in for Best Picture. But *Reds, Atlantic City,* and *Chariots of Fire* were good films too.

Soon I was to get the NYU student academy award for my thesis film, *Joe's Bed-Stuy Barbershop,* starring my ace from mass-comm classes at Clark College, Monty Ross. I was also reading the sports sections in the papers, getting sick and tired of their portrayal of Georgetown led by Coach Thompson as thug life incarnate, like they were snatching chains from eighty-year-old white grandmothers and looking for a rumble. But Coach sailed through it with his head up, and his team, anchored by Ewing in the pivot, sailed through the NCAA bracket all the way to the national championship game.

The Big East conference had taken the place of the NBA at the time as far as what most fans of New York ballplayers followed. Hubie Brown was doing his number as coach of the Knicks. There wasn't a lot to get excited over but plenty to curse about. I imagined Hubie turned some brown ears blue back then. But *everybody* could get excited about St. John's and Georgetown. So Georgetown had gone from this place where your kid might go to law school if you were lucky and had money, to this Washington, D.C., citadel of doom. And it worked. Dramatically, it worked.

The Evil Empire of John Thompson and his imperial storm troopers won six of the first ten Big East tournament championships by scaring the other teams to death, according to the evaluations of the hacks. *Cheatin'!* They weren't supposed to *win.* They weren't supposed to be *disciplined* or play D. They were supposed to *entertain.* Make it interesting. Grin. Phi Slamma Jamma, something like that, then lose. Bear it. Go home and think about the error of their ways. Endeavor to persevere. The Georgetown Hoyas back then played like they'd rather win first, talk about the rest later. I had to like it.

The Big East tournament has always been held in the Garden, and the early '80s was the conference's heyday. Dave Gavitt, who went on to become general manager of the Celtics for a few years, helped start the Big East. John Thompson and Georgetown were the flagship team. Everything worked off that, in a marketing sense, a competitive sense, a can-we-get-a-better-rating sense. Teams measured themselves by how they did against Georgetown. During Ewing's four years at Georgetown, from '81 until '85, the Hoyas appeared in the NCAA title game three times. I'm not sure, but those may be three of the top ten Final Four weekends the NCAA ever put on.

In the 1982 NCAA finals, Georgetown met North Carolina and Coach Dean Smith, the man Coach Thompson had assisted at the 1976 Olympics, the man to whom he'd sent his first big-time college prospect and adopted son, Donald Washington, when Coach Thompson and Coach Mary Fenlon were still at St. Anthony's High in D.C. Neither Smith nor Thompson had won the national championship. No black man had ever been allowed to coach a team that could win the NCAA title. The drought could end for only one. And those teams they had that year! No wonder 61,612 fans showed up. North Carolina had Michael Jordan, Sam Perkins, and James Worthy on the floor at the same time. Georgetown had Ewing, Eric "Sleepy" Floyd, who could *really* see; the floor game was handled by a good 6-5 athlete named Eric Smith and a 6-5 New York ballplayer with all kinds of game, a sophomore named Fred Brown, from somewhere up in the Bronx.

That game was history-making, in a line of great NCAA title games. At the time the college game held interest for me, and I had company. After the Magic Johnson–Larry Bird game in 1979, the drama of NCAA finals seemed to increase, pick up the flow of the culture at large, which in turn was fed by hoop, until you had an action going on between the two. In 1980, Louisville beat UCLA in the NCAA title game. UCLA was coached by Larry Brown that year. He had a runt center, a 6-5 player named Mike Sanders. His scorer was Kiki Vandeweghe. That was just about it. That's when I knew Brown could coach, when he took that B squad to the NCAA finals. The whole-is-greater-than-the-sum-of-the-parts deal seemed to follow him around. He had a lot of New York in his game. I'd ask him about that one day. With only a few seconds left, and the small UCLA team hopelessly behind, Brown got down on bended knee, looked up at the young players who'd done a minor miracle just by getting to the final game, and just before he gave them the final strategy, he said: "Fellas, don't give up on me now. Something funny might happen!"

Well, something funny didn't happen then, but that was prophetic later, when Brown was coaching in the NBA playoffs for Indiana, in the '90s, against the Knicks.

The NCAA title was won in 1980 by Louisville, coached by a Wooden trainee, Denny Crum. They were called the Doctors of Dunk. The leader was a guard in the line of David Thompson named Darrell Griffith. They called him Dr. Dunkenstein. Great lift. George Clinton, musician and bandleader, was going around calling himself Dr. Funkenstein. His cuts, like "Flashlight," "Atomic Dog," "One Nation under a Groove," and "Night of the Thumpasaurus People," were set down to infectious rhythm tracks many of the rappers of today use generously. And huge corporations like McDonald's also use the tracks to advertise, in 1997. It was all in the centrifuge now, a synergy between basketball and popular culture, or counterculture. It was already hooked up by then. In 1981, Indiana won a second NCAA title under Coach Knight, this one over North Carolina, in Philly. The Hoosiers had won with a sophomore point who played as well as young Tiny. From the West Side of Chicago. Had handle on handle in handle. Isiah Thomas.

Now it was 1982, at the Superdome and on the set. Ewing, at Coach Thompson's behest, grabbed five of the Tar Heels' first six shots. Patrick grabbed everything, goaltending or not, to try to establish his presence. Later on, when I found out that Coach had played for the Celtics and had backed up Bill Russell for a couple of years, that explained why. The teams answered each other move for move, stop for stop, hoop for hoop, with Worthy's 28 points doing big damage, and the Hoyas relying on Ewing's j and D and the deep shooting of Sleepy Floyd.

There were sixteen lead changes in the game. It came down to the final possessions. Jordan swept in from the left and laid the ball up 13 feet off the floor, way over the box. He had to lay it that high to get it over Patrick. It dropped in the net for his thirteenth and fourteenth points. Carolina, 61–58. Patrick hit a j in the lane, 61–60, Carolina. Matt Doherty of Carolina missed the front end of a one-and-one. Floyd—a fine ballplayer who would later score 51 points in an NBA playoff game for Golden State—hit from in the lane to put the Hoyas up one, 62–61. Then, with thirty-two seconds left, Carolina called time out. In the team huddle, Coach Dean Smith diagrammed a play, then looked into the burning copper eyes of the freshman guard from Wilmington, North Carolina.

"Knock it down, Michael," Smith said.

Jordan did, from 18 feet away, on the left wing. With twelve seconds left, he lifted over the extended zone defense and buried the j. He was nothing but the truth. Carolina by one. That was when Jordan's legend began. Jordan has been beating defensive-minded Patrick Ewing–led teams ever since to get to the NBA finals—when he wasn't losing in his early NBA years to the Celtics, then the Pistons, until he and Patrick and the Bulls and Knicks matured, got their act together, as Bird, Magic, and Isiah retired. But at that moment, in 1982, nobody knew Michael was going to become what he is today. If people say they knew Mike was going to be Mike, they're lying.

I didn't see the final sequence. First I saw Warren Beatty pick up the Oscar for Best Director for *Reds,* and say, "It reflects more particular credit on the freedom of expression we have in our American society and the lack of censorship from the government or the people who put up the money." At just about the time of Fred Brown's gaffe, Hollywood was set on its collective ear as Loretta Young announced the Oscar for Best Picture. *Chariots of Fire.* A British film. One without the politically inflammatory content of *Reds. On Golden Pond* was left out in the cold too. The next day's *New York Post* headline would read: HOLLYWOOD FUMING OVER WIN BY *CHARIOTS OF FIRE. Chariots of Fire* producer David Puttnam said in accepting the award, "You are the most extraordinary, generous people on God's earth, not just the Academy, to whom we are thankful, but as a country to have taken what is an absolutely Cinderella picture and awarded it this and come to it in droves." By the time I could switch back to the game, it was over. Coach Thompson was patting a brooding Fred Brown's back behind the Georgetown bench, even though Brown had just cost Coach Thompson a chance at his version of the Oscar—the NCAA title. March madness, indeed.

This is what had happened: After Jordan's final shot, as the final seconds ticked away at the Superdome, Georgetown brought the ball up, in the person of Fred Brown. He had plenty of time, twelve seconds left, when he got the pill. Nine seconds left when he crossed half-court. He had the 6-5 Eric Smith out high on his right. Smith was not a shooter, but he was a tremendous athlete. Ewing was flashing up toward the high post. Sleepy Floyd sank down toward the corner. Worthy took a chance and flashed into the passing lane out high, to Brown's right. Smith cut to the basket, as he should have, and no one from Georgetown was out there with Worthy. Now the defense was all out of balance. All Brown had to do was penetrate a couple of steps and it's a five-on-four, drive, draw, drop, or dish, nine times out of ten the defense will have to collapse on Ewing. And Floyd had his feet together, spotted up and squared up outside. But with seven seconds left, Fred Brown inexplicably threw the ball back to Tar Heel Worthy, who was so shocked to get a pass from an opposing player that for a second he acted as if the ball was a water moccasin, but he quickly recovered, raced to the other end, and was fouled. And that was the ball game. People were stunned. It was an ill way for such a game to end.

What was curious about it was that Fred Brown usually played an immaculate floor game. His passing, defense, help, rebounding, were cold New York City. He'd been Player of the Year in the Big East as a freshman. Big hops, New York ballplayer, variety of inside moves, no deep j, but who needed one when you were as talented as Brown or Dean Meminger? But then Ewing came along, stealing thunder, and what was left was for Floyd. I don't know what was in Brown's mind. His thigh was wrapped, he'd strained a muscle, but for whatever reason he had not played the same kind of game against Carolina that he did against Louisville in the semifinals. I didn't see it live, but people who watched the game tell me Brown had something else on his mind. With 11:51 left and Georgetown up 49–45, Brown had the ball on a two-on-one break after a turnover. And he threw the ball directly into the hands of Carolina's Buzz Petersen, who got it to Worthy for a three-point dunk the other way. Georgetown up one instead of six. Another bad Brown pass, to Floyd in the corner, that Floyd couldn't handle. Then a Brown turnover while throwing a simple pass in the half-court set with the game tied at 56 with 6:04 left. Then the final gaffe with seven seconds left. These were not plays that Fred Brown the New York ballplayer made.

After the game, Michael Jordan was introduced to the American general public. TV commentator Billy Packer interviewed him and asked if the last shot came off a set play.

"Yes, sir, that was a set play," Michael said, respectfully but not obsequiously. Then he went on to briefly explain the options. Worthy praised the Hoya defense. Meanwhile, Coach Thompson was talking to Brown behind the Georgetown bench, patting him twice on the back, saying, "Don't worry about it, don't worry about it." As he spoke, Coach was looking up and away, looking at something distant, vague, with his lips curled at the corners. It was the best college game I'd almost seen, one of the best ever played, and it ended on this strange note.

I liked the way Coach handled himself, his players, and the Game. Plus the Knicks were terrible at the time. I still had my "Basketball Jones." Georgetown took care of it for me through here. Coach Thompson seemed to me, bottom line, to be a man who cared about his players. He seemed to be a strong black man. Any black person the mainstream media vilifies, I start to say, "Wait a minute." My antennae go up. I start to ask myself, "Why do they hate this guy so much? He must be doing something good here. He must be telling them to kiss my black behind, also."

> > >

In 1984, Georgetown was back in the NCAA Final Four again. I guess Coach was obsessed with winning the national championship, which no black man had ever done. Georgetown played Kentucky in the Saturday semifinals at the Kingdome in Seattle. I'd like to have a nickel for every eyeball on that game, for every Georgetown party held in living rooms and dormitories across the country. The Hoyas were down at halftime, 27–22, against a good Kentucky team, with a pro front line of 7-0 Sam Bowie, 6-11 Melvin Turpin, and 6-7 Kenny Walker, whom they called Sky Walker, but that sounded wrong—you know who that reminded me of: David Thompson. Walker was destined to be a number one pick of the Knicks. Nice guy, was the NBA slam-dunk champion one year, but not even a reasonable facsimile of the original Skywalker. Not even close.

In the second half, Ewing, guards Michael Jackson, Gene Smith, Horace Broadnax, and David Wingate, and forwards Reggie Williams and Michael Graham turned up the pressure D, denied good looks, got rebounds, held Kentucky without a field goal for nearly thirteen minutes. The Wildcats went 0-for-13, then 1-for-20. When Kentucky was 0-for-10 or something, Kentucky Coach Joe B. Hall inserted a guy from Louisville named Winston Bennett, kind of a hard 6-7 type, with a jheri-curl on top. Patrick immediately blocked his shot, and Bennett raked Patrick hard across his face and eyes on his follow-through. Slapped the crap out of him. This happens, when guys are getting beat. As the Hoyas raced the other way with the blocked shot, Ewing lay on the court. Billy Packer, commentating for CBS and reverting a bit, said, "This is notta gonna bea foul." It wasn't called a foul, it rarely is, but he had to know better. That should be an offensive foul, and a flagrant one, every day of the week, but it's the kind of subtlety that even referees miss, much less fans. Raking is retaliation when a play has been made against a guy who is finding himself being used. Patrick got up off the floor, tried to blink the pain away, and kept playing disciplined. Your average guy would have retaliated, understandably. But the stakes were too high to get caught up in rat bastards giving you the business when the refs were distracted by the flight of the ball. Play on. The 1984 title game came before the thirty-five-second shot clock in college hoop. Patrick and the Hoyas stifled Kentucky, showed themselves to be well drilled attacking a 1-3-1 zone defense, padded the lead, held the ball, forced Kentucky to play man-to-man defense, found the weak defender, beat him repeatedly to the basket, won going away, 53–40. Then Georgetown beat Houston and Olajuwon, and the more colorfully named Phi Slamma Jamma team, 84–75, in the NCAA finals Monday night. Coach had his Oscar.

Seemed to me nobody wanted that win more than Coach Thompson—and probably Fred Brown. People felt deeply about it across America because of how Georgetown was portrayed. Brown suffered a terrible knee injury after his gaffe in the 1982 NCAA title game. Freak thing. It was obvious his hops and lateral quickness were gone by the spring of 1984, his senior year. He wasn't going to play in the NBA. He's a successful businessman now. His senior year he played a smart floor game for Georgetown, heady ballplayer, but you can't drag a leg into the NBA. Can't do it. No way. Brown paid a price for throwing that ball away in 1982. The 1984 NCAA national championship was his redemption. Coach Thompson flung his arms wide and hugged Brown as Coach took him out of the game. Georgetown was number one. Just about everybody I knew felt good Georgetown won because people were disappointed with the strange way they'd lost to North Carolina in 1982. Still one of the most interesting plays in NCAA finals history. That 1982 NCAA final was the beginning of the ongoing legend of Michael Jordan.

It was also the beginning of the ongoing legend of Georgetown.

After Georgetown won the NCAA national championship in 1984, the NBA held its draft. It was a good draft. I was trying to get a feature made. I had suffered a major setback the previous summer when a project I had called *The Messenger* folded during preproduction. It was the story of a bike messenger and his family. Nothing spectacular. A small story. But *The Messenger* folded before it got off the ground. Nothing involving the Knicks, Georgetown, or any team made me feel like bawling. Losing *The Messenger* did. It was that important to me, somehow. I wasn't down long, though. I was setting up to write *She's Gotta Have It*. But *I* gotta keep up with the Knicks.

The first pick in 1984 was Olajuwon, of Nigeria and the University of Houston, to the Rockets. They already had a 7-4 center, Ralph Sampson, from Virginia, and would try the Twin Towers theory for a while, even made the NBA finals with it in 1986, but Boston smoked them as Sampson, trying to play out on the floor, trying to be multidimensional at 7-4, was reduced to flailing away as if trying to fight somebody. He was skinny; doesn't necessarily mean you won't be able to rebound in the big leagues, but if you are slender, you'd better be like rawhide, because they are going to bang you and see how you like it. Sampson did not like it—who does?—but he let it affect his game. Eventually Sampson faded from the NBA scene. Olajuwon was the Man. The rest is history—two NBA titles for Houston, one won while Jordan was on

Baseball was my first sport.

Young Spike and Chris,
ages four and three.

Third grade picture from
P.S. 29.

The Lees grow in Brooklyn. Spike, Joie, Chris,
and David on the stoop of 186 Warren Street in
Cobble Hill.

My parents cut their wedding cake.

Graduation from Morehouse College, 1979.

My beautiful bride, Tonya Lewis Lee.

Bill Lee with bass at the Newport Jazz Festival.

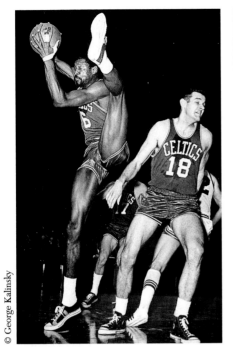

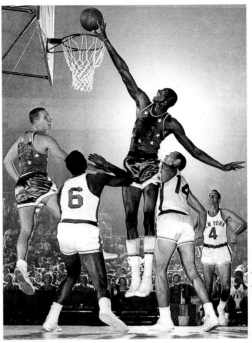

Bill Russell clears a rebound.

Wilt the Stilt dunks over Knicks in the old Garden.

Dick Barnett tries to drive past Sam Jones and Bill Russell of the hated Boston Celtics.

Willis hobbles onto court—game 7 versus the Lakers, 1970.

Red Holzman in huddle.

Dollar Bill.

© George Kalinsky

© George Kalinsky

© George Kalinsky

Clyde, my boyhood idol.

Willis on the subway.

Below: World Champions:
the 1969–70 Knicks.

Left: A U.S. senator.

© George Kalinsky

Walt shoots over Hondo.

60 Minutes' Ed Bradley with Dave, Clyde, and Riordan.

Cazzie Russell.

Jabbar's unstoppable skyhook.

Left: Fall Back Baby over the Big O.

Below: Coaching archrivals—Miami's Pat Riley guarded by Chicago's Phil Jackson.

© George Kalinsky

Black Jesus, Earl Monroe.

© George Kalinsky

Dean the Dream flies by Tiny Nate Archibald.

Top left: Mars Blackmon outside the Garden.

Top right: New York Knicks #1 lottery pick—
Patrick Ewing as DeBusschere smiles.

SPIKED!

Did Spike Lee's courtside taunts cost Knicks Game 5?

John Starks commits a flagrant foul against Scottie "Houdini" Pippen.

sabbatical. That's the one I think should have belonged to the Knicks. But that was still a decade away.

The second pick in the 1984 NBA draft belonged to Portland. Stu Inman, a Portland executive, sniffed, "We have a player like that," giving the reason why the Trail Blazers, based in Portland, Oregon, home base of Nike, would pass on the rights to put Michael Jordan in one of its uniforms. Boggles the mind now, don't it? The player Inman was talking about then was Clyde "the Glide" Drexler, Portland's two-guard who had played with Olajuwon at the University of Houston. Clyde was an outstanding ballplayer. He took Portland to two NBA finals, against Detroit in 1990, Chicago in 1992. And so, in the 1984 draft, Portland took the 7-0 Sam Bowie, from Lebanon, Pennsylvania, and the University of Kentucky, with the second pick. Sam was a fine athlete, a good guy, had game, but he was brittle, couldn't stay in one piece, broke bones in his lower leg any number of times. His base just couldn't take the stress. Michael Jordan fell to the third pick, to Chicago, to the giggly delight of Bulls coach Kevin Loughery, the ex-Bullet. How many nights did Portland management lie awake thinking about that later? Did they see visions of Drexler and Jordan in the same backcourt? How many nights did that vision dance in the head of Phil Knight, Nike CEO? How many NBA titles did they miss? Hindsight is 20-20, that's all you can say. In that same draft, Sam Perkins was picked fourth, by Dallas. Charles Barkley was picked fifth, by Philly. Otis Thorpe was picked ninth, by Kansas City–Sacramento. Kevin Willis was picked thirteenth, by Atlanta. John Stockton was taken eighteenth, by Utah. Not a bad draft. Especially for Chicago.

The Knicks had traded their pick to Indiana in a three-way deal that got them the rights to Ray Williams. Obviously we didn't have a Red Auerbach as general manager. Back to the drawing board and college hoops for the hacks, and me.

> > >

In the 1984–85 season, Ewing teamed with Michael Jackson, the Georgetown point guard, and Wingate and Williams, both of them from Baltimore's Dunbar High, where they played with Tyrone "Muggsey"

Bogues and Reggie Lewis. Lewis went on to play with the Celtics, became their captain and leading scorer—and then collapsed on the court one night in 1992. After medical examinations, he came back. The next time he collapsed, he didn't get up. He died on July 27, 1993, at twenty-seven—just coming into his prime. Heart ailment. This time the possibility of cocaine use was brought up; insurance companies have a way of trying to fleece black folks. Drug use was denied by Reggie's widow. They'd come a long way from Dunbar High. Fifteen years after playing there, Williams, Wingate, and Bogues are still in the NBA in 1996–97. Wingate is with the Seattle Sonics, one of the few players who can play the kind of D that makes Jordan work. Bogues, only 5 feet 3, has run point for Charlotte for years, although his body is beginning to betray him now. Four NBA starters on one high school team. The Dunbar Poets. One of the better team names, too.

In 1984–85, Coach Thompson had dropped forward Michael Graham from the team, and Graham had left school. He wasn't going to school anyway, and at Georgetown, Coach insists the players make that part of the scholarship-grant bargain available to themselves. I've got to like him for it. Graham thought he was better than he was. Coach dropped him on principle. Possibly cost himself another national championship by doing that, though maybe not, not the way Villanova shot in the NCAA championship game of 1985, held at Rupp Arena in Lexington, Kentucky.

Villanova shot 90 percent in the second half that night, missed only one shot in the second half, went 9 of 10—and still beat Georgetown by only two points, 66–64.

Georgetown and Patrick had a great four-year run of competition. Villanova's image was not much tarnished later when Gary McLain, point guard of that team, pretty much a slow player who got carried by his teammates, by 6-10 Eddie Pinckney from the Bronx in particular, came out in *Sports Illustrated* saying he'd been wired on cocaine the entire length of the NCAA tournament. Coach Rollie Massimino eventually left Villanova for Nevada–Las Vegas, although not over that, I don't think. Jerry Tarkanian had been run out of town. He's at Fresno State now, but he cast a long shadow in Vegas, so Massimino was eventually run out of town, too. Coach Thompson is still at Georgetown, still doing it the way he always did it, although I think age has made him mellower, and he is no longer obsessed with winning the national championship. He's supposed to be an educator first. He must also be a loyal friend, because he scheduled a road game against Massimino's new team, Cleveland State, for the 1996–97 season, and he didn't have to do that, not for a man who beat him out of the national championship.

Coach Thompson still will not let freshmen give interviews until after the Christmas holidays and runs a tight ship generally, with Coach Fenlon, Mary Fenlon, who supervises the players' academics. Trainer Lorry Michael, secretary Trina Bowman, Coach Ed Spriggs, Coach Mike Riley, Coach Craig Esherick—they've all been with Coach Thompson since then. Georgetown hasn't been to a Final Four since 1985, is no longer the power it once was, and people wear jackets of all schools now. But Coach Thompson is still in control over there off the Potomac. When you take a look at the NCAA rules and regulations, how ridiculous and probably unfair some of them are when it comes to dinners, phone calls, transportation, and know gunslingers out there in the media and within the coaching profession and the general public at large would love to drop a dime on the Georgetown program for some real or imagined malfeasance, then you don't wonder about why he does things the way he does. Scandals happen all the time in other places in college ball—even at places like UCLA. When you think about this, you can understand the control Coach Thompson demands—what the papers used to call Hoya paranoia. Whatever it was, it worked. And it beat Hoya stupidity.

Coach likes to say, "It's not paranoia if they're really after you."

I figured we'd get around to talking one day. It's a too, too small world.

> > >

So, anyway, that's how the persona of Mars Blackmon was formed. And now it's July 1985, Cheryl Burr has kicked me to the curb, the Knicks are about to go through another yawn-inducing Twin Towers experiment, this with Patrick Ewing and Bill Cartwright. Walking in the wilderness, big-time. Coach Hubie Brown was about to lead the Knicks to a 23–59 record for the 1985–86 season, with Bernard King out for the year with his surgical knee, destined never to play for the Knicks again. I've just gotten my two season tickets, in the green seats, Thirty-first Street side, second promenade, with no idea of how I'm going to cover this expense and the expense of making a movie, then rolling it out and finding a way to eat, too.

The story of *She's Gotta Have It* revolves around Nola Darling, a single black female in a love triangle. More a love pentagon. Inside it are Jamie Overstreet, straight-up guy; Greer Childs, narcissistic male model; Mars, b-boy bike messenger; and Opal Gilstrap, Nola's lesbian friend who is trying to get in them panties too. When Mars is introduced, we arranged tight shots of his cultural signifiers: an arrow part in his haircut, in the back of his head; a gold Mars neck chain; a Mars belt buckle; Air Jordans; a Georgetown tank top worn over a gray T-shirt. When Mars makes his appearance in Nola's apartment, he's wearing a New York Knicks jacket. Mine. When Mars makes love to Nola, she makes his foot shudder while it's still inside his untied Air Jordans.

Mars is in direct competition with Jamie and Greer. Jamie is the one Mars considers his most serious competition. Mars calls Nola late on the night of her birthday. She's in bed with Jamie.

> > >

MARS: Yo, happy birthday, Nola. It's me, Mars.
NOLA: Thank you, but I'm sleeping.
MARS: Sleeping? It's your birthday, Nola. Let me ride my bike over
    there, in five minutes we can celebrate . . .
NOLA: It is late. C'mon, call me in the morning. I'm really tired . . .
MARS: In the morning it won't be your birthday, Nola.
NOLA: It's not my birthday now, if you notice . . .
MARS: Nola.
NOLA: What?
MARS: Nola.
NOLA: What?
MARS: Nola.

NOLA: What?
MARS: Just let me smell it . . .
NOLA *(laughing):* You are ill . . .
MARS: Pleasebabypleasebabypleasebabybabybabyplease . . .
NOLA: Good night.
MARS: Good night?! Wait, wait, wait a minute. Is Jamie there?
(Nola hangs up.)
MARS *(pauses pensively, then to himself):* Fuck that girl, man. *(He punches digits in phone. The line is answered by a female voice.)*
VOICE OF ROXANNE *(offscreen):* Whatup?
MARS: Yo, Roxanne, whatup, I been thinkin' 'bout you.

Later Jamie composes a poem for Nola, who concludes reading it while in bed: "Made full by the warmth of your laughter. You have allowed and guided me into your heart gracefully. Timing, you say? Yes, timing. The eternal rhythm of natural love . . ."

Cut to Mars, in a Georgetown tank top, standing astride his bike near the cables of the Brooklyn Bridge.

MARS *(to camera, in pain):* Ah! Ah! That's the worst piece of shit I ever heard, and Nola fell for it, too! I don't want to badmouth the brother, but his poetry is not the answer! Jamie ain't got no rap. He's like ice cream on a summer day. Soft. Now if Nola had been righteous and correct the way she's supposed to have been, she would've recognized true love. Mine.

Later, it is Mars who is in bed with Nola, and Jamie who is calling late at night.

MARS *(o.s., to Nola):* Want me to answer it for you?
(Mars's foot, in his untied Air Jordans, kicks the phone off the hook.)

Mars is disdainful of the upwardly mobile Greer, who is equally disdainful of him and Jamie. They all meet at Nola's for Thanksgiving dinner and sit around the table, talking.

GREER: Thank God we have a lot to be thankful for.

MARS: Like what?

GREER: Well, our health and our careers.

MARS: Our careers? Greer, I haven't had a job in two years.

(Rapping): Fifty dollar sneakers and I gots no job

Tell me how to do it when times is hard.

MARS *(to Greer):* Who'd you vote for, Ronnie baby?

GREER *(to Nola):* Why do you always stick up for this . . . this . . .
    chain-snatcher?

MARS: Chain-snatcher? I didn't snatch this. I bought this. This is
    eighteen-karat gold. I did not snatch this. What do you know?
    You're a Celtic fan.

Even though Mars has knocked Jamie's poetry, he has no resentment
against him.

MARS: Jamie, let's settle this between you and me, once and for all,
    man to man.

GREER: What about me?

MARS: What about you? You ain't down, so chill.

NOLA *(to herself):* I don't believe you. . . . I don't believe this.

MARS: This is a quarter, right? Heads, tails, call it in the air, you gonna
    call it, right?

JAMIE: Right.

MARS: In the air, right?

JAMIE: Yeah, Mars . . . You can't live without a head.

MARS: Tails, you lose. Nola, will you tell these two gentlemen it's time
    to go?

NOLA *(to herself):* My fate decided by the flip of a coin.

Later Mars and Jamie sit on a park bench and discuss their problem:
their competition for Nola's affections. Mars finds a way to extend the
olive branch. I wanted to come up with common ground between them,
where they would have a comfort zone, something that would not continue the rift caused by their pursuit of Nola, because their conflict was

that they were trying to get into the good graces of this woman. In order not to escalate matters, something had to be found to cut down on the static resulting from rivalry. What would be the common thing both could talk about, agree upon? Basketball. Outside of Nola, that was the common thread.

MARS (*in Georgetown tank top*): Nola's about as dependable as a
    ripped diaphragm.
JAMIE: Hey, wait, hold it, watch your mouth.
MARS: Man, making a date with her, it's fifty-fifty she shows at all. Last
    year I had two tickets to a playoff game, Knicks against the
    Celtics, I asked if she wanted to go, she said okay, you know I
    waited outside the Garden for the first goddamn two quarters and
    she never showed. And guess what?
JAMIE: What?
MARS: Bernard King scored 35 points.
JAMIE: Oh, I remember that game. Bernard was pitching a bitch.
MARS: You remember that game? 'Nard was serving the whole Celtic
    squad, he even jammed on Bird's ugly mug, a vicious, death-
    defying Brooklyn Bridge, high-flying 360 slam dunk!
JAMIE: Wait a minute, man. The white boy is bad and you got to give
    him credit. Larry Bird is the best player in the NBA.
MARS: The best?!
JAMIE: He's the best in the NBA!
MARS: The best!?
JAMIE: The best.
MARS: He's the *ugliest* motherfucker in the NBA, that's what he is.

At that point, we had Pamm Jackson, a coproducer on the film, walk through the shot. And both Mars and Jamie take a pause for the cause and watch her. Then they continue.

JAMIE: That's too bad, man. [Nola] never made a move like that on
    me.
MARS: You know how you got over? You're taller than me, it's 'cause

you're taller than me, you're six feet, I'm kinda small. That's why
Nola dogged me. . . . I'm tired of talking about Nola Darling. The
sister was bogus, 24-7-365 . . . I'm booking. Call me sometime . . .
we'll go to a game. You gonna leave me hanging? Call me . . . you
gonna call me?

I wasn't ready for the explosion of laughter after Mars's line about
Larry Bird. I heard it each time I saw the film with an audience. I think
what made this line funny was the off-truth of it—it was a funny expression of a legitimate feeling; it fit Mars and the emotion he felt and his
means of expression—or lack thereof. So I got lucky. I thought it was
kind of funny, and you hope other people laugh, but when you're doing
that kind of humorous stuff, you never know whether the audience is
going to think it funny also—whether or not it's universal. There've been
instances where I thought I had lines that were hilarious, but people
didn't get it, so you never know. At the time I didn't have any experience
with mass audiences. This was my first feature film.

Black people were tired of hearing how Larry Bird was the greatest
basketball player ever. Bird this, Bird that: Bird himself, to his credit,
never tried to tread on it, even though he was a great player. Mars was
articulating a frustration about the accomplishments of black folks, how
they are denied their due all over. When one of my heroes, Muhammad
Ali, came onto the scene in the 1960s and was beating everybody, he was
Cassius Clay, the handsome loudmouth who made good and beat the big
bad Bear, Sonny Liston, Floyd Patterson, and anybody else they put in
front of him. So a "computer fight" was "arranged." Ali vs. the long-
retired Rocky Marciano.

No need to say who won the "computer fight." Whose computer
was it?

Then in 1976, after Ali had beaten George Foreman in Kinshasa,
Zaire, in 1974, and then beat Joe Frazier for the second time in Manila
in 1975, *Rocky* won the Academy Award for Best Picture and Best Original Screenplay. The movie was written by and starred Sylvester Stallone
in the title role, with a former Oakland Raider football player named
Carl Weathers in the role of Apollo Creed, the Muhammad Ali figure.

[128]

Rocky was a Joe Frazier figure, from Philadelphia like Joe, who trained by working over sides of beef in a meat locker with his fists, just as Smokin' Joe had done in his early days before he became the first man to get a decision over Ali, in March of 1971 at the Garden. But, for drama's sake, Rocky was white, and of course, he beats Apollo Creed for the heavyweight championship. Any time black people start to dominate a sport you're going to have a movie where it's reversed. The number one case is *Rocky*. If Apollo Creed had been portrayed as white, that movie would have bombed. The fact is, Creed represented not just a man, Ali, but every would-be egomaniac, loud-talking, flashy, overpaid black athlete; every nigger, not just in boxing, but all these nigger athletes who are taking over sports. The reaction was pretty amazing. I saw *Rocky* in a theater where I was one of few black patrons, and when Rocky started to beat up Creed, there was a strange feeling coming up from the audience. People weren't cheering because an underdog was beating the champion. It was deeper than that. White masses finally had a hero in boxing again, even if it was only a movie, beating an uppity, loudmouthed, flamboyant nigger, the way Floyd Patterson had not been able to do against Ali. That's why they have to keep making sequels, because who knows when there will be another white heavyweight champion in boxing for real? Have you seen Pete McNeely? *Rocky* won the Oscar and has become a cottage industry unto itself with all the sequels. Young boys would come up and ask Ali and other black heavyweight contenders, like big Earnie Shavers, "Think you can beat Rocky?" Shavers tried out for the part of Clubber Lang in *Rocky III*, but made the mistake of hooking one into Stallone's ribs, just because he'd been asked by Sly to make it look authentic. Sly went into the bathroom for a little while after that punch, then sent word out: Earnie could go. The part went to a less authentic puncher and a much, much smaller man, but a better growler—Mr. T. He gave great *grrrr!* Very Kong-like.

So if you can't beat 'em—make it up.

The Mets unveiled a phenom in 1984, a quiet pitcher who was very nearly unhittable named Dwight Gooden. He happened to be black. A couple of years later, *Sports Illustrated,* which is known far and wide as the Bible of sports, published a famous article about a phenom the Mets were bringing up, a pitcher who went to an Ivy League college, played the French horn, studied Eastern mysticism, and oh-by-the-way had this unhittable, almost invisible fastball, 140 miles an hour. Siddhartha Finch, they named him. Then later, after the Mets had gotten many calls about it, it came out that the story was an April Fool's Day joke. There was no such pitcher. I had never heard of such a prank before. Here I thought it was journalism. People in Brooklyn and Queens were very upset. They thought Finch was real.

Then, in 1982, Rickey Henderson of the Oakland A's baseball club set a single-season stolen base record of 130. *Sports Illustrated* came out with another article, this one stating that the stolen base record wasn't important, and that the stolen base itself wasn't important, using all these statistics to "prove" it. You're telling me advancing a base without benefit of a hit or an out is not important? Ask a good manager like Joe Torre of the Yankees or Felipe Alou of Montreal who he'd rather have on first, down 2–1 in a World Series Game, bottom of the ninth, two out. Jackie Robinson or Cecil Fielder? Please. It's not a question.

And then, after the Lakers won the NBA world title in 1985 or 1987, *SI* ran yet another sour-grapes article and retouched photos to accompany it showing Bird in a Laker uniform and Magic Johnson in a Celtic uniform. That article stated, in a most convincing way, that because of the way they played, Bird would make a great Laker, while Magic would be a trash Celtic. This was the environment in which Mars uttered his line of frustration. This is what he had lived with in his recreational entertainment. You can imagine what evaluations were like in business and the arts.

But Bird was real too, now. When you average 24.3 points, 10 rebounds, and 6.3 assists per game over thirteen years, with three league MVP awards and, most convincingly, three NBA world titles, you really don't need anybody's validation. Bird was one of the best, and there were nights when he *was* the best, on those nights when he was experienced but still relatively young, zoned, locked in. But when Jamie says Larry Bird is the best player in the NBA, and Mars reacts the way he does, there was this cathartic laughter. This was the age of Reagan, when Mars spoke that line. When you try to destroy a people, what you get is destroyed people who aren't dead yet. Hoop was one thing that could not be taken away. Game. Manhood. I don't care who, if you ask any black man if he "got game," he'll say, "I got game." If he doesn't mean in basketball, he means with the honeys. Trust me. Watch any group of middle-aged brothers hooping at a playground or a YMCA, you'll see what I mean. Arguing over possessions, foul calls, and violations like they're getting paid, or married. Upset. Manhood thing. At that point in history to say "Larry Bird is the greatest player in the NBA" or "Bird is the greatest ballplayer in history" was dichotomous.

My mother's admonition about raising a semiliterate son has always stayed with me. Maybe that's one reason why the lead passage of Zora Neale Hurston's novel, *Their Eyes Were Watching God*, crawls over black at the start of *She's Gotta Have It*. Her favorite writer was James Baldwin—who, with Arnold Perl, wrote the original version of what became the script for *Malcolm X*. And she had made me read Charles Dickens. His famous lead paragraph from *A Tale of Two Cities* is what I would have used to describe and illustrate the dichotomy and the situation around the public perception of Larry Bird, and Mars's line on him:

> *It was the best of times, it was the worst of times, it was the age of wisdom, it was the age of foolishness, it was the epoch of belief, it was the epoch of incredulity, it was the season of Light, it was the season of Darkness, it was the spring of hope, it was the winter of despair, we had everything before us, we had nothing before us, we were all going direct to Heaven, we were all going direct the other way—in short, the period was so far like the present.*

My brothers and my sister and I had always been steeped in the arts. My mother took me and Chris to see Broadway plays and musicals when we were children. Joie is an actress, writer, and can still today pick out tunes on the bass violin. David is a still photographer and has shot on the sets of most of my films. Cinque is a filmmaker and an actor, having appeared in films like Jim Jarmusch's *Mystery Train*. The Lees have a good club as far as the arts are concerned. I moved quickly, had good visual retention, was not very big but saw things in a big way. Film was natural for me. Chris was different. The art form Chris tried, graffiti, was deemed socially unacceptable, and even physically risky. Michael Stewart, a graffiti artist, was killed, the life choked out of him by New York's Finest, and this fact was part of the shaping of my later film, *Do The Right Thing.*

Basketball was larger than life to me and I was particular about its mythology. On the one hand, we were living in this time of backlash against the gains of the civil rights movement, this take-back period of Reagan, hearing Larry Bird was one of the greatest ballplayers who ever lived, and there were nights and days during this time, especially during the Boston Celtics' World Championship seasons of 1980–81, 1983–84, and 1985–86, when he *was* the best in the NBA. But his stats weren't as overwhelming as Chamberlain's, Jerry Rice's in pro football, Hank Aaron's or Babe Ruth's in baseball, Wayne Gretzky's in hockey, Jack Nicklaus's in golf. I hadn't yet gotten around to comparing Bird to Chamberlain, Russell, Big O, Frazier, Pearl, David, Pistol Pete, or West. I was still trying to figure out if Bird was better than Havlicek. I thought maybe I could tell by figuring out which one I hated the most. And I hated them because they were Celtics.

If Bird had been a Knick, I would have loved him—probably loved him more than I'd loved either Bradley or DeBusschere if Bird could've taken the Knicks to three NBA titles, like he did for Boston. But in the end it didn't matter what I thought or what the hacks wrote. Bird made his own statements out on the wood. And now, today, if you go back to that same playground, that same Y, and watch another group of brothers hooping, and you see a white boy is running with them, and playing good ball, too; taking people, sticking the deep j, on the boards, hooping hard, and if he ain't trying to hear the trash that's being talked, igging the brothers when they ask what he's doing out there, just keeps on playing his game, busting people right and left, especially busting the one talking the most, then you will hear those brothers call that white boy by this name:

"Larry Bird. Yo Bird Man. You runnin' with me next, or what?"

> > >

When Isiah Thomas threw away the inbounds pass and Larry Bird stole it and passed to Dennis Johnson for the layup that won a pivotal playoff game and Eastern Conference final series between the Detroit Pistons and the Celtics in 1987, I wanted to jump through the TV and choke Isiah. It was after that game that Dennis Rodman and then Isiah made comments about Bird, while in the frustration of losing. Petulant Rodman said that if Bird was black, he'd be just another good ballplayer, and not Larry Legend. Dennis was bitter because he had just been beaten. When the press went to Isiah with this, Isiah laughed it off, and then said it *was* taken for granted that he came out of his mother's womb dribbling a basketball, like he never had to practice religiously, like only white players have a strong work ethic. That only white players played with intelligence. I knew what he meant, but he must have been called in on the carpet by David Stern, because one of the most complete spin jobs ever done was in place the next day. I believe had Isiah *not* cleaned that up, he would not be in the position he is today, as a minority shareholder and general manager of an NBA expansion team, the Toronto Raptors. They remember those transgressions. So, in retrospect, he made the right move, but what he originally said still is true nonetheless.

Here is where I had to give Bird credit and dap. He never tried to enter the conversation about any black-and-white issue, even though the press was on him, and I'm sure they were pushing that stuff and it would have been easy for him to portray himself as a victim. It would've played. Or he could have done what some black people do—question whether they should have their job, question their own abilities. Bird was not giving any legitimacy to that mess because he was concentrating on what he had to do. Because it wasn't Larry Bird who was insisting Larry Bird was the greatest basketball player who ever lived after the Celtics dusted Houston for the NBA title in 1986. The hacks—it was obvious what they were doing. Mythology of their own. Kevin McHale was not getting the press he should've been getting. Dennis Johnson, they never would have won without him. Robert Parish never got his due. But Bird never tried to ride that wave. He was all about ball, trying to win. It wasn't about marketing or mythology. It was about trying to get the easiest shot, the last W. Beat Magic. Beat the Lakers. Win. He regarded the rest as garbage and trash. Which it was.

After *She's Gotta Have It* came out on August 7, 1986, I was sitting in the Garden for a game against the Celtics, and at one particular point, during a time-out or something, Bird was on the bench resting, and Danny Ainge was sitting next to him. I was sitting in the good seats at the time, had called in to the Knicks' front office and had gotten 'em, close to where my seats are now. I saw Ainge elbow Bird and point at me. Larry said something to him—something unpleasant, by their looks. There were several times after that when we met, Bird and I, when we'd see each other. He wouldn't say one word, but give me a mean-assed look. I'm sure he heard about that scene, being called "the ugliest motherfucker in the NBA."

Just watching him told you a lot about Bird the ballplayer. What was frustrating in trying to watch the game was the chatter of the TV and radio announcers: "hardest-working ballplayer who ever lived," "most intelligent and intuitive ballplayer who ever lived." I know it was great for Celtics fans to have a great player, but there is no statistical basis for work ethic or court sense. It wasn't like Bird was standing alone in his era, the way Jordan does now, with no basis for comparison. Bird and Magic were right there together, doing about the same things, but in different ways, trying to beat each other, and, really, coming out fairly even. At the time they were the best thing that had come along. But they had always been together. Hard to imagine one without the other. That's really the reason why black folks laughed at that line in *She's Gotta Have It*. It had nothing to do with how Larry Bird looked. Well, maybe a little bit. No, it had to do with Magic, Kareem Abdul-Jabbar, and Michael Jordan also being there. It told how black people are made to be invisible. And they were fed up, hearing it 24-7. People's complaints about the portrayal of black athletes eventually had their effect among the non-hacks. You have to be careful about those intelligence assessments now.

> > >

No way did I know *She's Gotta Have It* would blow up like it did, but it happened. Out of the clear blue, I got a call from Jim Riswold, a creative director at Weiden & Kennedy, a Portland-based ad agency that had the Nike account. Jim later came up with concepts for Nike, like Mr. [David] Robinson's Neighborhood and the Bo [Jackson] Knows campaign. What got him off was this: he wanted to pair Mars with Michael Jordan. Jim saw *She's Gotta Have It*, and when he saw the tight shot of Mars's feet in untied Air Jordans shuddering orgasmically, a light went on in his head. Before you could say Spike Lee, they'd have scripts and storyboards. He asked me to look them over. It would be a national campaign. Would I play Mars Blackmon and direct the spots?

Well, it made all kinds of sense to me. Mars Blackmon came into being the year the Air Jordan shoe came out. We shot it with Mars wearing a pair of original Air Jordans, those red and black ones. Mars had those big fat shoelaces in the Jordans, and his gold nameplate—it wasn't really gold, we couldn't afford gold, it was brass. These two men at the advertising agency, Riswold and his producer, Bill Davenport, saw the movie and went to their bosses with the idea of pairing Mars and Michael. Nike bit, and then they approached Michael. Jordan had no idea who I was at the time, had not seen the movie, and could have easily decided to say, nah, let's get a hotshot Madison Avenue director, but he gave me a break. If Michael had said he wanted the next man instead, that would have been it for me, but Jordan decided to give a young brother a chance. I'm still in his debt for saying yes. We ended up being the talent in a series of Nike spots I directed starring Michael Jordan. Jordan didn't see *She's Gotta Have It* until after we started doing the commercials together. In one of the early ones, Nola Darling (actress Tracy Camilla Johns) appeared with Michael and me. Word filtered back that Michael's lovely wife, Juanita, was not enchanted by that particular spot, didn't like it too tough, and it was quickly pulled.

Jim wrote the scripts and I directed the spots and it worked. Some say Mars helped Jordan pierce the culture at large. I think Mars and Michael helped each other in that way. I truly believe those commercials, going to Knicks games, having the best seats in the house, have given me more visibility than I got from being a filmmaker. It wasn't my astuteness. It was an accident. I had no idea at the time what would happen to Michael. He was thrilling to watch, and was the only one with his own shoe. What I'm saying is that I had no idea that these two guys up in Portland, Oregon, would see the movie and put two and two together and make it a national advertising campaign. I happened to get pegged to go with this fellow who turned out to be one of history's greatest athletes ever and did these commercials with him for six years in a row, and we were, like, joined at the hip for a little while there. Even now, to an extent. In 1995, when the Bulls and Jordan embarked on that 72–10 NBA World Championship season, there was a three-year-old on the thoroughbred futurities circuit named Mars Blackman (check out that difference in spelling) that won several races.

In the wake of those commercial spots, I began my own relationship with Nike. And with each film I became more visible, combining making films—*School Daze* was released in 1988—with the fact I was doing commercials with Jordan for the best basketball sneaker ever made.

As I got more and more visibility, every year the Knicks upgraded my seats. And charged me more—not *just* me, but the prices kept rising. They weren't giving me a discount, but I wasn't asking for one. I wanted to be down on the floor. Whenever there was a big game, VIP seats on the floor of the Garden were given to celebrities back during this time. So for the Lakers or Bulls, I'd call up John Cirillo, now a vice president for the Garden, and he would hook me up. The Garden finally got hip and decided, we can sell these seats, why give 'em away? Once I found that out, I was faxing the Garden, saying, "If you do sell these seats, please put me on the list." They did. Those are the seats I have now.

I first met Jordan at a Knicks game in the Garden. He had already agreed to do the spot with me, but we hadn't shot it yet. Later, in the working environment of being the director and playing a role in commercials in which he was the star, he was immediately friendly, but in a challenging kind of way. Listening, paying attention, but distant somehow. He met me, and first thing he said was "Spike Lee." Like "Okay, Spike Lee, show me what you got."

He hadn't done very many commercials at the time. At first he was stiff, but he was a quick study and was a real pro before long. Audiences have always loved Michael Jordan. The camera, too. He has a twinkle in his eye that you can't quite figure out; he's intriguing, mysterious, yet has a warm personality that always comes through. That's why he became a big spokesperson for all these corporate images—Nike, General Mills, Hanes. In one Nike spot we did, Mars Blackmon has his arms wrapped around the rim, holding on to it, calmly talking about Michael and Air Jordans. Then the camera pulls back and you see the only way Mars is grabbing the rim is because he's standing on Jordan's shoulders. Then Jordan walks away, leaving Mars dangling from the rim. Then Mars says, "Money, Money, you just gonna leave me hanging?" In one take, Michael turned back, lifted, and slam-dunked the ball hard, right in my grille. Couldn't help but shield my eyes. I was saying, "Money, that's cold." I was laughing, but having Jordan cram on you isn't always funny.

That was the take we decided to use.

The Nike Air Jordan was released in March of 1985 and sold $130 million worth in its first year. By September of 1986, while *She's Gotta Have It* was in release, over 2 million pairs had been sold. By late 1987 the Mars Blackmon–Michael Jordan spots began airing. Later on, for initial airing during the 1991 All-Star game in Charlotte, we shot an Air Jordan commercial with Little Richard playing a genie who grants Mars one wish. Mars doesn't want money. He can't drive, so he doesn't want a car, either. Oh, snap! Then Little Richard does his thing, and suddenly Michael Jordan is wearing Mars Blackmon's bike-messenger ensemble. Mars then says in voice-over, as Jordan mouths the words, "Look, Mom, I can fly!"

"Look, Mom, I can fly!"

In October of my sophomore year at Morehouse, I received a call in Atlanta. The most terrible news. I was told, "Your mother is dying." She had been saying she didn't feel very well and had checked herself into Brooklyn Hospital for a physical examination.

The doctor had kept her. She had cancer of the liver.

On my way back to Brooklyn, I thought only about my mother. I was her first of five children. She didn't have any siblings; she was an only child. My grandmother Zimmie later told me that she had actually wanted six children and she "missed it by one." I was heavily nurtured even long before I can remember. I was built to last. My mother and I got along great. She was hard on me, rightfully so, because she knew I had to be pushed. I could be lazy. I can say for sure if my mother hadn't pushed me like she did, I wouldn't be a filmmaker today. My father's approach was "Gem, leave them kids alone, they'll be all right." Especially he would defend Chris. My mother would say, "What?" Our mother thought exposure was everything. Museums, libraries, theater, the cinema, concerts—that steady diet had been crammed down our throats since I was five and Chris was three. She was a woman of arts and letters, and she tried to steep her children in them. My mother was ahead of her time, visionary. That's where I get it from, what little of it I might have. She was one of the first women I know to wear braids, beads, African floral print dresses; first to buy a brownstone, long before gentrification. She carried the emotional baggage of the times of my youth for us, her children.

Once, on a warm spring day in April, Chris and I were outside playing on the stoop of 180 Warren Street. Suddenly we heard this woman's voice. It seemed to come from blocks away. "They killed him!" the woman screamed. "They killed him!" The voice got closer. I looked at Chris and said, "Hey, that sounds like . . . Mommy!" My mother was on our street now, doubling over in pain. "What's wrong, Mommy? What's wrong?" I asked. Dr. Martin Luther King Jr. had been assassinated in Memphis. When John F. Kennedy was assassinated back in 1963, I had been in my first grade classroom at P.S. 29, and over the loudspeaker we were told to put our heads on our desks and pray. My mother did not ask us to pray now. But I'm sure she did. She took us inside and, one by one, held us close.

My mother was amused by my preoccupation with sports. "You're too little to play pro ball," she said. "Let's go see *The King and I*. How about that?"

One thing she recognized very early about me was that I was not a good loser. I hated to lose. Very competitive. She understood how much sports meant to me, which is why she let me miss three school days to see the Mets win the World Series. She wasn't always so understanding. On school nights she wanted me to do my homework and turn off that idiot box, as she called it.

"Is that TV on?"

"No!"

She knew better. She would sneak upstairs, bust us, and tan some royal hide.

One of the things that happens in families is that parents take different roles when they raise children. My father's approach was hands-off. Mr. Freedom: "Best way to raise kids is to let them make the choices." Ultimately the other parent—in this case, my mother—is going to be the bad cop, the one left to be the disciplinarian. Believe me she had to do that or we would've run amok. She was the one who said, "Get your lesson, get to bed, go to sleep, do your homework, speak grammatically correct English, do your chores, don't eat candy or ice cream before dinner, eat the vegetables, give the TV a break." She was the one who squashed all those questionable things children want to do all the time. Now, we could say to my father, "Uh, Daddy, can we jump off the Brooklyn Bridge?" Our father would say, "Yeah, go 'head, have a good time!" and would stay hunched over his scattered sheets of musical composition. And Chris might have done it, too. We loved both our parents. Our outward display of love was shown more to our father than to our mother, I think, and that was because we knew our father would let us do whatever we were going to do. He loved us. She raised us.

I thought of this as I returned to Brooklyn. I saw my mother lying in the hospital bed. I'd never seen her like this. I didn't want her to suffer. I didn't want her to die. I didn't know what to do or think. I was told she was near death. But she clung to life tenaciously. Five days. Ten days. Then it was like Maybe she won't die. I was very hopeful of that. My father told me to go on back down to Morehouse, I was missing too much school. I didn't want to leave. I felt if I left, something bad would happen. Then I started to think, "Act normal and things will be normal. Things will be like they were." So, very reluctantly, I went back to Atlanta, back down to Morehouse, where Dr. Martin Luther King had also gone to school; his class had graduated two years ahead of my father's.

"They killed him!"

"Mommy? Mommy!"

I called Brooklyn the next day. Aunt Nancy, my uncle Cliff's wife, answered the phone. "Spike, when are you coming back?"

"Why? Why? No . . . no . . . has something happened?" I said.

"Child, has nobody told you?" she asked. She sighed deeply. And I knew, before she said it. I knew, but I didn't want to know. "Your mother passed."

I think those are the worst words a human being can ever hear.

At the funeral, I felt I couldn't cry. I had to be the one to bow up. I was the eldest. So I had to be strong, for Chris, David, and Cinque. I didn't know what to do about my sister. Joie was lost in her own world. My mother was her model and comfort in a house full of men and boys. Later Joie told me it wasn't until after she and Cinque wrote an original screenplay draft called *Hot Peas and Butter,* which I revised and shot as *Crooklyn* in 1993, that her catharsis was complete, behind her. Only then did she feel that she had finally come to terms with Mommy's premature death. It was a great loss for all of us, the five Lee children. I think of my mother all the time. My mother—her ways, her passions, her demands, her precision—how she shaped and molded her children.

I saved all the letters my mother wrote to me while I was away at Morehouse. I take them out and read them whenever I miss her. She had a sense of humor, could make you laugh, and at the same time, she would constantly stay on me—on my "narrow, rusty behind," as she might call it on days when it wasn't in gear. She did this service for all her children. She pushed all of us to do our best. Lord knows we needed that push. One day I proudly showed her my report card—85 in every subject. I was happy. Mommy looked at me and said, "That's good . . . but you have to do better next time. Get some 90s, like some of your white classmates. To be successful you have to be much better than they will be—not just as good. It's not fair, but that's the way it is." She didn't live to see my successes. My grandmother Zimmie, my mother's mother, is a spiritual person. She told me God sacrificed my mother so I might do what I did, that she never really left me. And it is true: I did not pick up a Super 8 camera to shoot *Last Hustle in Brooklyn* until after she died.

> > >

In the Nike commercials, Mars Blackmon began as Michael's comic foil—losing Nola to Jordan in one ad, left hanging on the rim in another. Then they became more compatriots; even though Mars was Michael's biggest fan, they became buddies. This came across to the viewer as Jordan's accessibility. We did one spot where Mars asks if Jordan's lift comes from his baggy shorts or his no-socks look. We did a spot where other NBA players went to Michael Jordan Flight School, where they learned to play golf, stick out their tongues, upgrade their hang time, and, in short, be like Mike. Later, it would be suggested the ads were exploitive of "inner-city youth."

I believe the ads for Air Jordans that we shot were not aimed primarily at inner-city kids. Even today the most hard-core Bad Boy and Death Row rap albums sell best out in the suburbs. And NHL hockey jerseys and Timberland boots sell best in the inner city. So it's not all cut-and-dried. I thought Nike was tapping into the authentic black basketball cultural motif more than trying to get an exclusively or predominantly black clientele. This began negative publicity for Nike, Mike, and me. Community activists said Michael Jordan and Spike Lee were the opiate of the masses.

Michael Jordan was no hypocrite. He was the furthest thing from it. Jordan is as true to his craft as anyone I ever met. He hasn't squandered his God-given abilities. I began to see that clearly as I watched him play in the early years when the Bulls were struggling, couldn't get past the Celtics, then the Pistons, and when we talked during the breaks while shooting the commercials, I began to see that nobody has a greater work ethic or a higher level of commitment to his craft than Jordan does to what he called "the game of basketball." Nobody says anything much about that love, though. Even if the man has talent, it's Michael's heart, work ethic, conditioning, mental approach, and will that breaks their backs, puts him above everybody else. The man never gets tired. He's getting older, maybe he can't sustain it as long now, but for years he was the best-conditioned athlete I'd ever seen. To ask him to become the Reverend Jackson on the side seemed a bit much. I know Jordan, and know that he's a thinking man's man, so he has no doubt considered all of this. He's not oblivious.

Sometimes African-Americans are too quick to look for a savior, somebody to lead us out of the wilderness. It's understandable, with Martin and Malcolm being assassinated long ago now, but Michael Jordan, Michael Johnson, and Tiger Woods are athletes; Michael Jackson, Eddie Murphy, and Oprah Winfrey are entertainers. The things we ask them to do, they might not be equipped to do in the same way a Martin Luther King Jr. was. There's a world of difference between being a celebrity or being a leader on a professional ball club and leading an entire race of people. Can they do more? Probably yes. Can *I* do more? Yes. Any one of us should answer that question the same way. But no athlete or entertainer is going to stop young brothers from killing each other, no matter what. The makeover on environmentally induced self-hatred must be done from inside.

Over the years, I've had many conversations with Mike, and he's told me what he thinks about hoop. That's what he *knows*. And I've seen where it comes from—his dominance, I mean. He understands what he's doing. He's not just out there. He understands it, and more, he understands his competition, especially their weaknesses. Once, we had dinner at his restaurant in Chicago, after one of the Bulls' routine thrashings of the Knicks. Oakley was there, and Juanita, Mike's wife. Michael went over the competition for that year, 1992–93, and finally brushed them all off with a regal "There's nothing out there to threaten us this year." I said, "Mike, can no one on this planet even challenge you?" It was Juanita who looked askance and slowly shook her head. No.

I think back about that knowing shake of Juanita's head and reflect on what it meant. Who would know him better? My mind goes back to the conversation Mike and I had in his Range Rover: What challenge was there for him then, for the coming season?

> > >

Well, winning back-to-back championships is tougher than anything because you've got to sustain, and stave off complacency," Jordan said. *"I mean, it's relatively easy to just sit on your laurels. You've got players who never experience this, then they've got to try and experience it twice. They lose some of that edge. You lose that hunger, and then it's up to the* veterans who have gone through it many times, know what it is to fail, to kind of refresh these young players about just why we are playing—that, hey, we still have got something that we can win here.

"Right now, Luc [Longley] and [Toni] Kukoc, if they keep their game together . . . because they are still learning the game, and there is so much they need to learn about the game. I mean, when you talk about European basketball, they think they are on our level now. But they've got so much to learn about the game, and sometimes they are not willing to take the time. It gets frustrating, you know, and it's crucial for our team. Those two components, Luc Longley and Kukoc, are very important components for our team. If they come out and keep learning the game like we know how to play the game, then that makes us better. But if they want to come sometimes, once every four or five games, with these long periods of no productivity, then that really doesn't help much. And that frustrates you, as a leader, and I'm pretty sure it frustrates Phil Jackson. We know what this organization is about now—winning. And they can't afford not to work on the court. I don't mind if we lose, if we put forth the effort. But if we're not putting forth the effort and we're getting our asses whipped, then that's when I lose my temper."

"So what do they say when you curse them out, Mike?"

"Nothing. They are very smart men. Luc is good at this. He knows the game some now. A lot of times he'll make a mistake and he'll say, 'My fault, my fault, my fault.' Well, don't say it again, now. We know damn well it's your fault. So don't say that again. Don't be so smart about the game that you become dumb about it. You know everything, but yet you can't go out there and execute. Now, that tells me you're book-smart but street-dumb. You've got to go out there and play the game and play it with the intention of playing it with your head first, not with your skills first.

"Spike, in this game, what separates the good and the great players is how they apply their skills in certain situations. And that is all mental.

"Right now, Luc and Toni don't always have the mental capacity to deal with this every game. Somehow they've got to obtain that, or else we can't be successful. They get psyched up for the good teams. It's the ones they don't respect that cause problems. I was guilty of that when I was *younger. I've been in situations where I've played against a player, and you just don't give him any inkling of respect, and the next thing you know, you get burned. It happened to me a few years ago, when I played against a kid out of Louisville, named LaBradford Smith. He was with the Bullets. Not really on my level. Came in and gave me 35 points. I had to respect myself and the game, really, the next time, and show him. And now . . . well . . . he's not in the league now."*

"What about Damon Stoudamire, in that overtime game in Toronto, an expansion team, when they won against you guys, on a humble last [1995–96] season?"

" . . . He's tough, Spike."

"Yeah?"

"He's tough. He's nice."

"Did you hold him that day?"

"I was guarding him."

"How many did he score that day?"

"I think he scored like . . . 28 points."

"He scored more than that, Mike."

"No, he didn't. At most, 28. He didn't drop 30 on me, now. And you're talking about a guy who's in a whole different position than me, and he's a little point guard and I'm a two-guard, and I'm trying to guard him and he was the quickest guy in the league at the time."

"Then how are you going to hold Allen Iverson? Allen's faster than him!"

"Yeah, and as of today he's shooting less than 44 percent from the field. Now he may be shooting less than that. It ain't a matter of who can score, Spike. I mean, if they can't guard you, for their size—who is he going to guard at the other end?"

"So . . . okay, Mike, who do you like to beat? Who are the teams you can build hate against? Would that be any individual players? Would that be the Knicks? Detroit? The Celtics?"

"Nope. Cleveland."

"But . . . you've always killed them, Mike."

"Yeah, I have. And that's one reason why. I've always liked playing at Cleveland and doing well there because, number one, they seemed to be

the best competition when I first came into the league, so when you're going to play your best, you're playing against the best, which at the time was the Celtics, Detroit, and in terms of rudeness and just despicable actions, Cleveland."

"More than the Detroit Pistons? The Bad Boys who broke your heart and won two NBA titles when you were younger and Scottie wasn't ready to step up yet? Had those headaches?"

"Hey, leave my man Scottie alone, now, Spike. Leave my man alone. You all have had a lot of headaches in New York, you know."

I laughed. "That's true. Not Boston, not New York, not Detroit, with Isiah and Dumars?"

"Cleveland," Michael says flatly.

"Because of the fans, the players, or what?"

"The fans. Not the players, the players are very respectful. It's the fans. They are very loyal to their Cavaliers, and I respect that, and they had a good team then—under Lenny Wilkens is when I'm talking about. I respect fans cheering, but not to the point where you root against some people physically. I mean, I got hurt—I almost got hurt—in one game in Cleveland, and they were cheering. They were cheering me being hurt, instead of being concerned. They saw the game as being bigger than someone's well-being. And I took that personally."

"What would you say about the fans in Madison Square Garden?"

"Very loyal, but they know the game of basketball. Very respectful."

"Would you say they are the most knowledgeable fans in the NBA?"

"Chicago . . . New York.

"One and two?"

"One and two. You can flip a coin. But I really like playing in New York."

"Yeah, I can tell."

"I think really New York would get the edge in knowledge because of the origination of the modern game of basketball, the way I see it. All the great talent and players that came out of New York. Chicago has had some great players as well, but I mean, when you talk about big-time basketball, you always think of Madison Square Garden."

"You've saved some of your best performances for the Knicks. Of course, no one can ever forget when you gave the Knicks that double nickel, 55 points, when you came out of retirement. What was that, your . . ."

"Fifth game back. I know I made you feel bad, didn't I?"

"The 55 points, I was happy for that. What killed me was the pass, the assist at the end, when you passed underneath to Wennington for a gimme. That's what killed me. We lost."

"I know. The game-winning basket. That's the one that counts. I know you would've loved more than anything to see me shoot and miss, because that accomplishes two things. I would've scored 55 points in a major game, with your team coming out on top."

"How much longer are you going to play?"

"I'll probably just take it year by year. As long as we win championships, I'll keep playing. If we don't win and I see the team start to break up, then I'm pretty sure management is going to take a different direction. Then it's time for me to move on."

"And then what will you do with the rest of your life? Play golf?"

"Relax. Do whatever it is a black man can think about. Right now my biggest goal is to win another championship and do it playing the same caliber basketball that I've been playing thus far. People are looking at me now through a microscope, seeing little discrepancies in my game, to say I've lost a step here or there. No matter what they say, as long as I'm still beating double-teams, I haven't lost that much. I think my skill level is still there, right up there with some of the best, if not the best, and I'm pretty sure they are going to look at my stats to determine that, so I want to make sure that I can continue to play consistently and put the same numbers I put up years before, and wind up with the championship back in the city of Chicago. Right?"

"Right. I mean, no!" Michael laughs. Mind games. "Mike, c'mon now—how many more years do you think you are going to play?"

"Probably just take it year by year."

> > >

John Thompson and Georgetown might not have invented defense, but they damn sure made it popular. Four Georgetown players were on the Eastern Conference NBA All-Star team in the year of our Lord 1997. From that I took it that D did not necessarily have to be accompanied by a slow style. D led to fast breaks, gave you more easy opportunities. The old Celtics played that way. UCLA under Wooden did, too. The difference—one difference—between Jordan, Bird, and Magic was that Jordan played great individual man-to-man defense and could play D up in vertical space as well. Bird and Magic played on the floor, in one-man zones, edged into the passing lanes, but Jordan could shut an opponent down, steal any point guard's dribble, block any shot. Jordan thought defense first. Several times, though not as often as he should have been, he was named NBA Defensive Player of the Year. In the '60s and '70s in the NBA, it was about outscoring your matchup. Now Jordan is always telling me who can't play the other end. He knew the points would come. The stops were more important. The stops win the championships. How many times had I seen Mike come out of nowhere in the last minute, coming on a double-down, switching off his man without giving any prior indication, rising to swat Patrick's potential game-winning j out of the air, 12 feet off the ground, grabbing or altering Patrick's shot from behind, while his eyes narrowed and his tongue hung out? How many times had I gotten excited by a new Knick on the roster or a rookie in the league, only to have Jordan's eyes begin to glow as he asked me: *"But, Spike, tell me this—who is he going to guard?"*

One thing I've never asked Jordan: What is his favorite basketball film? Guess he'd say *Space Jam,* the flat-as-a-pancake Warner Brothers movie starring Michael, costarring L.J., Patrick, Barkley, Shawn Bradley, along with Bill Murray, which premiered in November 1996. It was a cartoon combining actors, ballplayers, and animation characters like Bugs Bunny and Daffy Duck, kind of like *Who Framed Roger Rabbit?* *Space Jam* made $29 million its first weekend, ended up grossing $88 million, domestic walkup. *Who Framed Roger Rabbit?* did $11 million in its first weekend and grossed $150 million. If Mike had to pick his second favorite basketball film, what would he choose?

Here's a list:

The Absent-Minded Professor (1961): Fred MacMurray. This black-and-white movie is a bite on a more original picture, *It Happens*

Every Spring, starring Ray Milland, about a mild-mannered college professor who discovers a chemical substance he can rub on a baseball and have the ball avoid solid objects—like baseball bats—which gives him better stuff than John Smoltz and a major league contract. In this one, the college discovers a chemical formula that turns sneakers into minitrampolines. The college ballplayers, all of them white—this was a Hollywood movie from back in the day—are soon jumping around like so many Phoenix Gorillas. Only for the lonely.

Go, Man, Go! (1954): Sidney Poitier, Marques Haynes. A riff on the founding of the Globetrotters, one of the first if not the first to use the actual ballplayers. Directed by the great cinematographer James Wong Howe.

Drive, He Said (1972): This movie was a statement against the Vietnam War, and for Jack Nicholson's love of hoop. Two college roommates, one representing Nicholson, are at odds over what is important—protesting to end the war or playing basketball. One roommate disses the other for caring about basketball, just a silly game, while the other tries to show him the beauty in it. Bruce Dern plays a gung-ho coach. Nicholson's directorial debut. Don't know if directing is his forte, but he does know the game.

One on One (1977): Robby Benson, G. D. Spradlin. Small-town high school hotshot comes to big-time college—UCLA, it signifies—finds out he's a pawn. I ain't buying it from word go. Robby Benson? Wonder Bread Robby Benson? Hell fucking no. Benson's character gets busted up, which is realistic. He cowrote the script. He tells the head coach that the coach is not going to take his scholarship away, which isn't realistic. Gotta like G. D. Spradlin. Gives a great cold fish, and he's had more coaching jobs than Larry Brown.

The Fish That Saved Pittsburgh (1979): Julius Erving. A kid who's into astrology gets only Pisceans to play for a local pro five in Pittsburgh. Doc's vehicle. Doc is sincere, but this isn't even *The Greatest,* the 1975 film starring Muhammad Ali. Doc was kind of stiff. Ali had a ball.

Cornbread, Earl and Me (1975): I liked this one. I have a one-sheet for it hanging in the offices of 40 Acres and a Mule Filmworks in Brooklyn. The late Rosalind Cash was one of my favorites. Silk Wilkes, the ex–UCLA Bruin, Golden State Warrior, and Laker, played the title role. Paul Winfield was also in it. This was the film debut of Lawrence Fishburne, who starred in *School Daze*. During the shooting of *School Daze*, we'd tease Fish by crying, "They shot Cornbread, they shot Cornbread," his signature line from the film, one giving you the gist of the narrative as well.

Hoosiers (1986): Gene Hackman, Barbara Hershey, Dennis Hopper. In some ways, *Hoosiers* is similar to *Rocky*, although better made, containing much better performances. At the time, the NBA was becoming rife with black players, while Georgetown had been establishing a dominating presence in the fabric of the college game, so what do you do? You fill a nostalgic need with a fantasy, turn back the clock to a much simpler time, a time . . . when "nigras knew" their place. It helps if the story is good. This one was taken from real life. Indiana high school basketball in the 1950s, when a state championship was won by a tiny small-town lily-white high school. They had to do it as a period piece because it's not going to happen in contemporary life unless the state is Utah, Wyoming, or Montana. So reconstitute history as mythology. *Chariots of Fire* was similar in intention and effect. They are usually warmly embraced, these pictures about how wonderful and fine it was when, basically, niggers weren't around. I agree, but "niggers" come in all races. Tell me when, in America, *black folks* weren't around? Exactly when was that? And there's been an honorable black basketball player or Olympian or two down through history, with stories that deserve to be told and told well. When Indiana won the national championship in 1987, right around the time *Hoosiers* was released, you knew with your own eyes the brothers were out there working, sweating, rebounding, hitting the game-winning j for Coach Knight's team. But not in Hollywood, the land of I Wish. It was ironic—for all of the team-play talk, in this film the game is won when the coach, the so-called keeper of the flame, runs a clear out, and lets its star go one-on-one, and he breaks the defender down off the dribble, then hits the game-winning j. Even with all the baggage, Gene Hackman was great in this. He usually is, come to think of it.

Fast Break (1979): Gabe Kaplan, Bernard King. Gabe Kaplan resembles Franco Harris, former Pittsburgh Steeler running back. Mars Blackmon always did love 'Nard's game. Not a *total* loss.

Sunset Park (1996): Rhea Pearlman, as a basketball coach with the acid tongue and the heart of gold at an inner-city high school in Brooklyn? What happened? Couldn't get Michelle Pfeiffer?

Cooley High (1975): Glynn Turman, Lawrence Hilton-Jacobs. One of the classics, directed by Michael Schultz. I've seen this film a hundred times, used it for one of the film classes I taught at Harvard. A simple story, but the acting, direction, and Motown score are flawless.

Celtic Pride (1996): Dan Ackroyd, Damon Wayans. Two fanatical Celtic fans kidnap a star player (Damon Wayans) of the Utah Jazz (read Karl Malone). Damon is a talent, but the roles he does? Either he has bad taste in material or his agents are giving him the wrong material. *Celtic Pride* is worse than the current edition of the real Celtics and, in the argot of the blue seats, they stank. Or, if you speak Ebonics, they be stank.

The Basketball Diaries (1995): Leonardo DiCaprio. Good book by Jim Carroll, but the realization is poor, basketball is lame. I can take Leonardo down low myself.

Blue Chips (1994): Nick Nolte, Alfre Woodard, Shaquille O'Neal, Penny Hardaway. The director, Billy Friedkin, has made great films like *The Exorcist* and *The French Connection*. *Blue Chips* wasn't one of them. The script, by Ron Shelton, was dated by the time they got around to filming it. Seemed based on UCLA and the sugar daddy backer of that program, Sam Gilbert. One thing bothered me about the dialogue. From the scene where Shaq's character is talking to the coach, the Nick Nolte character, and he refers to the coach's wife as a bitch—that bitch is something-or-other. Nolte's character doesn't even say anything to him. That bothered me. No athlete is going to call a coach's wife a bitch to his face, and no coach is going to allow an athlete to do it, especially not in college. That was pathological. You could tell a white screenwriter wrote that. Nolte is good, and so is Alfre Woodard, playing the mother of a prized recruit (Penny Hardaway). Alfre later played the character based on my mother in *Crooklyn*. *Blue Chips* possibly was made because Shaq and Penny were available for plum roles.

Documentary-style basketball scenes, college players, and a few pros played staged scrimmages, but it was missing something.

White Men Can't Jump (1992): Woody Harrelson, Wesley Snipes, Rosie Perez. Ron Shelton who wrote *Blue Chips* also wrote this. I thought his first baseball movie, *Bull Durham,* was an excellent film, the best thing he's ever done by far. I wasn't as taken with *Cobb.* This particular movie made money. I don't think it was popular because it was such a revealing story, I thought it was okay as far as the basketball was concerned. It was rudimentary. Wesley Snipes and Woody Harrelson have a magnetism that came across, and they should be commended for making it somewhat believable—I know they worked hard on the basketball skills—but it wasn't engaging to me.

Above the Rim (1994): Leon, Tupac Shakur. Tupac has an allure that's hard to deny, but this was formulaic, the same old refrain. Basketball, O basketball, save me from the horrors and the pitfalls of the streets! Junkies and whores and dope dealers, oh, my! Coach Thompson has a brief cameo. He called earlier and asked me to read the script and see if he should do it. I told him he'd be better off passing. The opening scene of a rooftop one-on-one game where a guy falls to his death while trying to slap the backboard is a device, a confusing one. Miss and go splat on the street, young brother? This accident gives Leon's character a reason to hit bottom. He was why the brother died while playing ball. It also gives him interior motivation to save the life of the next young scrub, uh, superstar, the son of a woman who becomes his love interest.

If I see another eight-foot goal . . .

The Air Up There (1994): Kevin Bacon. I refused to see this. I thought the one-sheet, the poster for the film, was racist—like some African tribesman is just going to pick up a basketball and be Hakeem Olajuwon. They had already used that joke once in *Airplane!* and in a headache-inducing scene from *Bonfire of the Vanities,* showing the black citizenry protesting outside a hotel start speed-passing basketballs, like they're all on the Globetrotters. Okay, it's funny in *Airplane!* The second time, it's lame. To base a film on it seems desperate. Rosalind Swedlin, who produced this, also produced *Clockers.* When I went to meet her for the first time, she had the one-sheet for *The Air Up There* hanging in her office. I said to myself, "Oh, boy, here we go." I didn't have a bad experience with her, but I knew, looking at the one-sheet, this was not something I needed to see. It would upset me. Before leaving the meeting, I asked her about the one-sheet. She said she had shown it to several black people, and they had all liked it. I never could bring myself to see this movie.

Forget Paris (1995): Billy Crystal, Debra Winger. Billy Crystal, the star and the director of this, is a sports buff, and a longtime acquaintance of Kareem Abdul-Jabbar. Billy plays an NBA ref, and from there it goes into a love story that clanks. If it was a story about a ref, then it should have been a story about a ref, about what it is to run up and down with these large, swift athletes night after night, having what is, I believe, the toughest refereeing job in sports. And these guys die young. The drama, the physical aspects, being on the road, the other refs your only friends, the moments of doubt or fear or displacement, being called every kind of sunovabitch no matter what you call, then having these—what are they called?—epiphanies, when you have the best view in the house. A *romantic comedy* about such a creature? What audience would buy it? Not me.

Eddie (1996): Whoopi Goldberg, Frank Langella. Good concept gone bad. John Salley, the Brooklynite ex–Detroit Piston, ex–Chicago Bull, and Dwayne Schintzius weren't all that bad in this. The ballplayers gave better performances than the actors. Disney asked me to make a cameo appearance. I said, "Thanks, but no." Whoopi, coach of the Knicks? No love lost. Bullshit movie.

Hoop Dreams (1994): Arthur Agee Jr., William Gates. Documentary. Affecting, poignant, exhilarating, leveling, and down by law. Two filmmakers out of Chicago named Steve James and Peter Gilbert stayed on two fourteen-year-olds—one a chosen star, the other a big maybe—all the way from ninth grade until after their final games in high school. Totally believably honest because it was real life. You can't make it up. Even if you did, Hollywood would never buy it. They'd say, nah, it's unbelievable, this could never happen, we don't care for the subject matter, focus groups don't connect with it, blah—blah-blah-blah. But it happened. I met the filmmakers and the two young players, Arthur and

William, and their families. I'm glad this was made. I was surprised to see I had a cameo in it, while giving a speech to the young high school stars at one of the Nike basketball camps. One of the best films ever made about basketball, the culture, the lies and deceit. How thousands and even millions of young African-American males chase the pipe dream of playing in the NBA.

Rebound (1996): Don Cheadle, Eriq La Salle, James Earl Jones, Forest Whitaker. This HBO production worked because of the performance of Don Cheadle, who is also great in *Devil in a Blue Dress*, in the role of Mouse. The brother can *act*. As Earl "Goat" Manigault, the playground legend from Harlem, Cheadle reels off a performance describing an authentic character arc not usually seen so sharply. The story is too familiar, but his performance gives it a range, depth, and focus that previous ghetto-claims-its-own sports stories lack. Again, it is difficult if not impossible to stage authentic basketball sequences, especially on those eight-foot goals. Hard to resist putting yourself in the hoop scenes, as director Eriq La Salle did. He threw a between-the-legs pass that was funny without trying to be. Eriq may have been asked to appear in it by HBO for commercial purposes. He's a star of the hit NBC show, *ER*. But it doesn't lend to the authenticity of the hoop scenes. All in all, the film worked, and there is Cheadle, although he did look a little long in the tooth to play the Goat in high school.

The problem with most sports movies is twofold. The first difficulty is the story, the hold of the narrative; the second has to do with the re-creation of the sport, as it relates to scale. The best sports film yet made is *Raging Bull* (1980), with Robert De Niro as the core character, Jake La Motta. Number one, it's not just a sports film, it is a great story. Number two, the scale is correct. The boxing scenes are staged atmospherically, lots of slow-mo. Martin Scorsese, the master, displaying his many and considerable skills. De Niro did a magnificent job, adding 60 pounds to his frame—the production was shut down so Bob could stuff his face with tons of pasta to play the older, embittered La Motta. It isn't as hard to physically re-create a middleweight boxer with a plodding style as it is a high-flying Skywalker. A 160-pound man is a 160-pound man. But in the boxing scenes in *Raging Bull*, La Motta's foil, Sugar Ray

Robinson, *is* Sugar Ray Robinson. That's who he resembles. He is an actor giving the effect of the real Sugar Ray Robinson. So you buy it. Martin didn't get Ray Leonard to try to play Sugar Ray Robinson. He would've only looked like Sugar Ray Leonard trying to look like Sugar Ray Robinson. Scorsese found a reasonable facsimile of Robinson, had him in the conked hairstyle of Robinson, with the graceful movement of Robinson, as much as could be manufactured. It paid off in believability.

It's unfair to compare a made-for-cable production with a feature release, but in *Rebound*, for example, the scale is off immediately when they are playing on eight-foot goals. Then, to have current NBAers Joe Smith as Connie Hawkins, and Kevin Garnett as Wilt Chamberlain . . . In the first place, they look nothing like them. That's Kevin Garnett of the Minnesota Timberwolves, not Wilt Chamberlain. He had the height to scale. Nothing else. The actor who plays Alcindor has the correct physical resemblance, but on the court the scale of the basket and of those around him makes him look maybe 6-6. Alcindor, at 7-2, towered over everyone. And to have somebody playing Earl Monroe who looks nothing like Earl Monroe, then having him *dunking—that* is inauthentic. If he's not moving with stiff-legged steps, knock-kneed, working two spin moves with a look-away pass or a nasty lay, then it's not Pearl. Earl never dunked. And cutaways to the star bounding off an unseen trampoline to dunk like some Kung Fu or Ninja guy flying through the air or to show a shot going through a net, then cut back to a player saying, "Yeah!" so you can't see the full range and effect of motion—they don't work. Of all the sports, basketball is the most difficult to re-create, so that's one reason why there have been so few satisfying basketball movies.

Basketball has been used effectively in scenes, though, in movies that were not really about basketball. In *The Great Santini* (1979), Robert Duvall is the Marine drill sergeant of a father playing one-on-one with his son, and they are talking to each other—manhood thing—and the son wins the game, much to the delight of the mother and the daughter—similar to a real-life scene from *Hoop Dreams*—and then Duvall's character takes umbrage, demands another game, even goes so far as to go off on his wife and daughter when they try to intervene and say the boy won fair and square. Great stuff. Duvall bouncing the ball off the head of his son (Michael O'Keefe). O'Keefe's best performance; he then gave up his season tickets to the Knicks games, moved to L.A., and married singer Bonnie Raitt—guess he didn't love the Knicks.

In *One Flew Over the Cuckoo's Nest* (1975), Jack Nicholson chewed up the scenery while playing a sane man, R. P. McMurphy, occupying a ward with mentally ill patients, organizing a basketball game among them, picking the mute Chief for his team. Chief is seemingly oblivious. McMurphy's entreaties to Chief to use his height and size in the playing of the game, and Chief's recognition and participation and then revelry in the game—that's good drama, fine setup for later events.

There were times, in the first three years after I got season tickets, that I was glad that first the league and then ITT/Cablevision/Paramount and the executives they hired to run the Knicks were not juggling chain saws instead of running the Knicks. That would have been ugly. As ugly as some of those teams played. Hubie Brown coached Patrick's first three years. DeBusschere was general manager for only a hot minute during the 1985–86 season. And then the aforementioned Scotty Stirling was brought in on January 3, 1986; the league brought him in, he had been a vice president of operations for the NBA. The Knicks bumbled to a 23–59 mark. The next season, 1986–87, lived in infamy too, a 24–58 record. Then ITT/Cablevision came in, and Richard Evans was appointed president and chief executive officer of Madison Square Garden Corporation in January of 1987. Evans made two hires. One of them was good.

I had my original seats in the green section for three seasons. It was after *Do The Right Thing* in 1989 that I got moved down to the next level. Into the red. Not the floor yet. I had my eye on the floor. A film producer, David Picker, was sharing some great seats with Harry Belafonte; those seats were in the loge, one level up from the floor, and so for particular games I would buy those seats from him. I did that for another year or so. Then the Knicks started having this VIP row, so if you were some kind of celebrity, an actor, a filmmaker, or hot—Paramount, you know—you could call the Garden a couple of days beforehand and maybe get seats.

So I began to do that. I still had my season tickets, but for the big games I'd call and get the VIP seats.

Eventually I got those seats as my season tickets. It was at the time we'd done *Jungle Fever* and *Malcolm X* and were developing *Crooklyn*. Originally the seats cost $500. Then it went up to $1,000. And then they raise the price even more during the playoffs. I told the *Daily News*, "I guess at these prices the Knicks are gonna win the championship. If I pay $2,000 a game and the Knicks suck, now *that* would be something." And all during this time, I watched the slow, painful ascension of Patrick Ewing. When I had watched Patrick Ewing at Georgetown, I knew that was someone who was a warrior, who would do anything possible to win. A lot of people questioned his offensive game at Georgetown. Mostly all he had to do was block shots and play defense. But Patrick turned out to be one of the best shooting centers ever, probably second best to Bob McAdoo when he was burning up the scoring column in the '70s with the Buffalo Braves, back when Tommy Heinsohn, a former Celtic and Celtic coach, had said, "The bleep never misses." Patrick could get hot, too. A lot of people say your center shouldn't be shooting shots that far away from the basket, but I think Patrick's offense really surprised a lot of people. But he suffered during those early years. A point guard like Mark Jackson or Allen Iverson can come into the league and have an impact immediately because he has the ball. Centers are dependent on the people around them getting them the ball. Add to that the learning process that goes along with being an NBA rookie. It's so far above college-level hoop that it's ridiculous. Yet I don't think the young players realize this. The realization was harsh for all rookies, including Patrick. We suffered with him. The Knicks were terrible. St. John's and Georgetown sold out the Garden much quicker than the Knicks. The Twin Towers experiment bombed. Neither Cartwright nor Ewing could step out on the floor and guard a forward. They were both centers. Bad blend.

After two years of frustration, the Knicks finally made the moves they hoped were the answer. Evans brought in Al Bianchi on July 8, 1987 as vice president and general manager. And then Rick Pitino was brought on to coach, on July 13, 1987. I loved that move. The second one, I'm saying. And then, after Pitino improved the Knicks' record to 38–44 in the 1987–88 season, the Knicks traded Cartwright to the Chicago Bulls for power forward Charles Oakley on the eve of the June 1988 NBA draft. The Knicks made one of their best trades ever when they got Oak. Cartwright turned out good for Chicago. He was a center on three of their teams that won championships, and I think it helped the Bulls when they played the Knicks in later years in the playoffs, because they now had a 7-footer who could lean on Patrick and who also knew his moves. In the end, it would always be Jordan flying in and making the play on Patrick. Cartwright never stopped Ewing alone. But Patrick could never solve Mr. Bill either, especially looking over his shoulder for Jordan. We weren't going to outscore Jordan and Pippen, so we were looking at center to be the spot where we could outperform them, but over the years, Cartwright, with help and those infamous flailing elbows, was able to neutralize, as much as you can, a player like Ewing.

As I said, Richard Evans hired Al Bianchi as general manager and Rick Pitino as coach in 1987. And the Pitino half of the equation worked. The Bianchi half . . . *eh.*

Coach Pitino thought the problem was management hiring general managers and coaches without making sure they were on the same page. Pitino and Bianchi got along fine off the court, according to Pitino. But on the court they had different philosophies. And the style Coach Pitino wanted to play was proven, in a line from Russell's Celtics through UCLA through Georgetown. It's a winning philosophy, rather than one owned or invented by anybody else. Full-court trapping defense, shot-blocker in back, running game, ten-man rotation, wear them down in waves, and now Pitino added the icing: shoot the three at the slightest provocation. "With the three-pointer, the whole theory of the game changes," Bill Bradley had told me. "Now you've got one-on-one pick-and-roll basketball, if you don't make it to the basket with some athletic move, throw it 30 feet out and some guy pumps a 30-footer. It could have added a couple of years to my career, but I still don't like it. I prefer the old way, where you tried to get the easiest shot possible."

The three-pointer was the brave new world. Pitino embraced it. I liked watching him work. He was emotional, seemed unable to help it. Then we got Oakley. Then in Pitino's second season, 1988–89, the

Knicks won the Atlantic Division. I was ecstatic, because their success was mirrored by my own with *Do The Right Thing*.

I didn't expect the veritable firestorm of criticism that I received for that film. I expected it to be noticed, discussed, I wanted it to have an impact, but I didn't expect to be asked why I was so angry, or asked to make a choice between Martin Luther King and Malcolm X, or asked, so many times, why the Mookie character, played by myself, would throw a garbage can through the window of an establishment where he worked. No critic asked me about the death of Radio Raheem, however, the choke-hold that was based on Michael Stewart's real-life murder. People didn't even seem to get their own assumption of the priority of white-owned property over black human life. So many white people asked if I was choosing between Martin Luther King Jr. and Malcolm X, or who did I agree with, Buggin' Out or Sal the pizzeria owner? I didn't make *Do The Right Thing* to make anybody agree or disagree. I made it to provoke thought, chronicle life. I don't make pretensions about being an artist, but I make big pretensions about trying. It seemed like finally the Knicks were back on that wavelength, too. They played a pressing style, in your face, and they kept dropping those bombs from deep. *Do The Right Thing* did the same thing.

The story of *Do The Right Thing* concerns a pizzeria owner, an Italian-American patriarch (Danny Aiello) who, along with his two sons (John Turturro and Richard Edson), runs a pizza parlor in the Brooklyn neighborhood of Bedford-Stuyvesant, what is now a black neighborhood. One of the neighborhood guys, Buggin' Out, has an inspiration one day, having to do with the photos that adorn the walls of Sal's Famous Pizzeria—all photos of Italian-American icons. Buggin' Out (Giancarlo Esposito) then lobbies for photos of prominent African-Americans to be displayed on the wall of fame. My character, Mookie, a pizza delivery boy, is caught between escalating forces, along with his friend Radio Raheem (Bill Nunn). In the film we had a scene where a character played by John Savage goes up into his brownstone after running his bike over Buggin' Out's brand-new pristine Air Jordans. John's character wore a Celtic jersey. Number 33, Bird's number, but of course. When Buggin' Out agitates a crowd, Savage says, "I'm from Brooklyn."

Lots of talent sprang out of this film. Rosie Perez, Samuel L. Jackson, Martin Lawrence, the late Robin Harris. Aiello, Turturro, Edson, and Nunn were all great.

During the 1988–89 season, *Do The Right Thing* hit hard. It began at the 1989 Cannes Film Festival. Jane Fonda gave away the Palme d'Or, announcing the winner. Steven Soderbergh, for his debut film *sex, lies and videotape.* The buzz was that German director Wim Wenders was against *Do The Right Thing* because Mookie wasn't a "heroic figure." In truth, film is an elitist industry. I was quoted as saying, "What's so heroic about a fucking pervert who interviews women about their sex lives on TV?" Take away the expletive, I still feel the same way. Sally Field was a judge at Cannes, and afterward she told me, "I'm so sorry. I fought for your movie till the end, and I'd do it again."

Things went pretty much the same way back in the States. Joe Klein, in *New York* magazine (the same Joe Klein who later wrote *Primary Colors* as Anonymous and publicly denied having written it for a year), said my film was "irresponsible" and predicted race riots would break out at every venue. I was asked by *USA Today* why there was no depiction of drug use in *Do The Right Thing.* I replied that nobody asked that question about *Rain Man,* or *Working Girl.* Reaction was everywhere— from *Nightline* to *Oprah* to *Newsweek*—"This movie is dynamite under every seat," wrote Jack Kroll. *The New Yorker*'s Terrence Rafferty said the film "[wound up] bullying the audience—shouting to us rather than speaking to us." There is more than one way into the consciousness. The preferred approach for someone like me, I think, was exemplified by that year's *Driving Miss Daisy.* People flocked to it—especially considering the alternative of *Do The Right Thing.* You can get into the strangest places reviewing films, let alone making them. How much reaction to *Do The Right Thing, Driving Miss Daisy,* and *sex, lies and videotape* had to do with the clarity of the work, the evocation, the realization of the script, and how much had to do with the acceptability of the director's vision, the acceptability of the material itself? Questions that remain unanswered were asked again by *Do The Right Thing.*

One thing about it: the film grabbed attention. Black filmgoers were defended by Brent Staples in the *New York Times,* who wrote that they were not what some fearful whites thought: "[A] conspiratorial mass out beyond the perimeter, waiting for the drumbeat that will cue their rampage." One critic, Abiola Sinclair of the *Amsterdam News,* wrote that Joe Klein didn't come off very well on *Oprah,* "trying to defend his position, amid guffaws and poo-poos from the largely white audience. He looked like the jerk he is." That was Abiola who said that, although for once I was in total agreement with her. Nobody was laughing and talking and tinkling their glasses through my set. I had made them listen, if not shut up.

Not a year later, on March 26, 1990, Kim Basinger got up at the Oscars and said the best film of 1989, *Do The Right Thing,* wasn't even nominated for Best Picture: "We have five great films here," she said, "and they are great for one reason: they tell the truth. But there is one film missing from the list that deserves to be honored because, ironically, it might tell the biggest truth of all. And that's *Do The Right Thing.*" That was brave, because she caught hell for that interjection on my behalf. I sent her a note thanking her after she sat down. I'd attended the ceremonies at the Dorothy Chandler Pavilion because Danny Aiello was nominated for Best Supporting Actor as Sal. I appreciated what Kim Basinger did, and because of that, I was glad I went.

The Knicks were 52–30 in the 1988–89 season. In the 1989 playoffs, we beat the Sixers three straight. Mark Jackson led some Knicks with a broom in sweeping the Spectrum court after the last game of the Knicks' three-game sweep over Philly, rubbing it in to Charles Barkley. I knew it could come back to haunt us.

We played Chicago in the Eastern Conference semis. This was the beginning of Jordan's playoff parties at Knick expense. Led by him, the Bulls took a 3–1 lead in the best-of-seven. In the fourth game, at drafty old Chicago Stadium, Jordan warmed us up with a 47-point, 11-rebound game. I just sat there. How could he do this to me? He looked over as if to say, How can I not?

The scene shifted back to the Garden. Ewing's 32 helped us get a 121–114 win. But Michael closed us out in Chicago three days later, dropping 40 as the Bulls won, 113–111. They went on to the Eastern finals, where the Jordan Rules—Detroit's double-teaming—stopped the Bulls cold. The Pistons, long bridesmaids, went on to win the NBA title over L.A.

And then, just like that, Pitino was gone to Kentucky. Stu Jackson, one of his assistants, took over the next season and went 45–37. In the playoffs that year, in a best-of-five series with the Celtics, the Knicks fell behind 0–2. But we came back and won three straight, taking the series at Boston Garden in the fifth and final game. I thought about Red Holzman's raised fist when we won the seventh game at Boston Garden back in 1973. Patrick was a man in there, on his game, averaging 34.5 points and 15 rebounds in the three wins. Now the Garden was rolling again. But the Detroit Pistons were waiting, and they routed us in five games on their way to back-to-back NBA titles.

The 1988–89 group was probably one of my favorite Knicks teams. Those Knicks averaged 117 points per game, and that's when the NBA three-point line was back farther than it is now. Who knows what would have happened if Coach Pitino and his philosophy had stayed in place? But Pitino and Bianchi clashed over philosophy. Those philosophies were embodied in the play of the two Knicks point guards, Mark Jackson and Rod Strickland.

Jackson and Strickland, New York ballplayers, were an embarrassment of riches to have at point guard. Nice problem to have. I remember when K.J.—Kevin Johnson of the Phoenix Suns—and Mark Price were both young players in Cleveland, in 1987–88. Lenny Wilkens and Wayne Embry, Big O's old teammate in Cincinnati, then general manager at Cleveland, traded K.J. Something similar happened to the Knicks. The two point guards couldn't coexist. They were both pure point guards—neither one could swing to two-guard. To me, there was playing time for both to play. Minutes are important. You can't show what you've got without minutes. Bradley put it this way: "I'd say my relationship with Red Holzman was that of a boy to a father who rationed out what was important, which was playing time." You can't help the team without minutes. You can't get stats without minutes. You don't exist without minutes. If you don't show what you've got in those same minutes, then the team won't do so hot. Bradley says, "It sounds so simple—play team ball. But what happens is, guys' egos get out of control, and they make the mistake of thinking they're going to get a big contract if they average 20 or 18 points a game as opposed to 15 points a game. But if you win the championship averaging 15 points a game, you're going to get a contract as if you scored 18 a game, and the damage you do to the team in trying to score 18 points a game, if you're a 15-points-a-game scorer, is in the end self-destructive."

Mark Jackson came to the Knicks as the eighteenth pick of the 1987 draft. Number 18 is low in the draft. You rarely find starters, let alone longtime starters, down that low in the college draft. There aren't that many college players who can stick in the NBA, period. What, maybe ten a year that are worth having, but that's down the road. At best, two or three can step in right away and play minutes for a contender. Mark was one of them. Coach Pitino gave him the rock, and he won Rookie of the Year and the next season played in the NBA All-Star Game. Mark's a great guy, fine personality, from Bishop Loughlin High, Fort Greene, Brooklyn, raised in Queens. Nobody could solve Mark's change of pace on offense when he came in. He would lull you, go by you, and he made great decisions with the ball. He's intelligent, competitive, like most New York guards. He wasn't the fastest, or the greatest on defense, couldn't always stay in front of the other team's point guard. But we had Patrick back there cleaning up mistakes, grabbing all garbage.

I guess Mark's status was threatened by the arrival of Strickland, the nineteenth pick of the next year's draft, in 1988, out of DePaul. Strickland was from Harry Truman High up in the Bronx. He came in a year after Jackson did, on the heels of Mark's Rookie of the Year honors. Pitino wanted Strickland. Bianchi didn't. Strickland had an I-should-be-starting attitude, that kind of junk, right away, and even though you watched him and said to yourself, "Strickland has to play. He has to play," I wish he'd been more patient. Like Dream was. But it was a different era. The players were becoming different. The fans and the atmosphere in the Garden were becoming different. Even I was different, in a way. I was making a movie each year, making nice money, too. I always prided myself on being an entrepreneur. I spent my childhood watching my father being a struggling artist. But with the Knicks, I felt I had no choice but to pay $1,000 apiece for two seats. In his own way, Strickland had no choice either. Dream didn't outplay Frazier and Monroe in those practices back in 1972. But I heard Strick outplayed Mark in practices as soon as he arrived, outplayed him often enough for Mark to feel threatened. Instead of "This guy can help us," it was "This guy is after my job" in Mark's case, and "This guy is not better than me" in Rod's case. If we asked them again, knowing what they now know after gypsying around the league for the last seven or eight years, they might regret things they did and said, because their asses would still be here in New York and they would own the city.

One of them had to go. They both ended up leaving. Strickland went first, to San Antonio. Later, Mark was sent to the L.A. Clippers in the deal that brought in the 6-10 forward Charles Smith. We'd had an abundance of riches at point guard—Oakley was here, Ewing was here. Pitino had wanted the kind of players who would run, play up-tempo, apply pressure D all over the floor, trap, and shoot the deep j, not conducive to Mark Jackson's pace and skills. So in the end Bianchi the genius traded Strickland, and Pitino was gone, replaced as Knicks coach by Stu Jackson, then general manager, now coach in Vancouver.

If they—Strickland and Jackson—had adopted the attitude of Dean Meminger, we'd have veterans at the point, and maybe, just maybe, we'd have had a better shot at the Bulls over the years. We'll never know. Mark is in Denver, in a rebuilding situation with the Nuggets. Strick is in Washington, running point for the Bullets—one reason why Jordan told me not to sleep them is because of Strick. He's thirty. I think maybe he shoots too much for a point, a lot of crazy—and creative—shots. He has to get C. Web and Juwan Howard off first.

I always did like Mark Jackson's personality and his offensive game. Defensively is where we had the problem with Mark, but I think we could've found a way to live with it. I don't know about that little airplane wing–body shake he does whenever he makes a play, but I guess you do what you feel out there. But Mark couldn't stop the ball from going to the hole off the dribble. That was always his Achilles heel—he's slow for an NBA guard and has trouble defending the basket. But he made great decisions—the best decision-maker we had since Clyde Frazier. Sometimes Clyde watches the Knicks today and you can see the pain creasing his face when a Knick guard makes a poor passing decision or takes an out-of-context shot. Coaching would help. But after Pitino and Stu Jackson and John McLeod, the Knicks' coaching position looked like it had become the revolving door at Bloomingdale's. And it was costing the Knicks on the court.

Oughta let me coach the team now. I nearly faxed 'em that. But I'd wait and see. "So many Knicks off those championship teams went into coaching," says Frazier. "Look at it: Phil, Cazzie, Bibby, Dean, Willis, even DeBusschere for a while. You would think the club might have tried one of them, like Phil or Cazzie." There were periods, before Pitino came and after he left, when the papers said John Thompson might come in. Larry Brown had already been interviewed.

But neither would be the next Knicks' coach.

I got to know John Thompson better through Patrick Ewing, then Ralph Wiley. At the time *Do The Right Thing* came out, Ralph was working with the coach on a project and had done an article about Ewing for *Sports Illustrated* when Patrick was at Georgetown. Between becoming friendly with Patrick, and *Do The Right Thing* being out, and the Ralph connection—that's how I met the coach. I was one of the fellows when Georgetown came to play St. John's, after Patrick came into the NBA. I'd go to the locker room and talk, and I occasionally went to D.C. to a Georgetown game.

I didn't know Coach Thompson while Ewing was at Georgetown. I met him after Alonzo Mourning came there. I also have a cousin, Malcolm Lee, who went to Georgetown and was an equipment manager for the men's basketball team. Coach has always been supportive, even when we don't see eye to eye. After he saw *Do The Right Thing*, he told me he agreed with Sal, owner of Sal's Famous Pizzeria, played by Danny Aiello, who'd said, for all intents and purposes, you niggers can kiss my Sicilian ass, get your own damn place. In many ways, Coach Thompson's thinking is very conservative, but that's all right. It was after *Do The*

Right Thing that he became interested in what I was doing with film. I think that the honesty and integrity of the effort is what attracts people to my films; to them it's not about whether they agree or disagree with the content. Coach likes to tell the story of how he made sure to tell me how much he agreed with Sal; it was Sal's shop, Sal decides what goes on the walls, not customers like Buggin' Out, get it? Coach was really talking about his own shop at Georgetown. The customer is always supposed to be right. Not in this case, Coach said. He said the brothers have to own their own before complaining.

If you sit down and talk to John Thompson, you might deem his philosophy reactionary. Nike was having trouble with its corporate image at the time, and I was becoming part of the market forces that are out there. One of the commercials I'd done in character as Mars Blackmon for Air Jordans had caused the Reverend Jesse Jackson to stir. It's the one where Mars is speaking idiomatically—"Yo, Holmes, yo, Holmes, these sneakers be housing"—and the Reverend Jackson said that made it manifest that the sneakers were being targeted to black male inner-city youth. There had been incidents, especially early, when youngsters had been beaten up and had their Jordans taken off their feet, and there were reports that some had even been killed for their Nikes. You can't brush that kind of stuff off, like some lint from your shoulder. Those charges and the realities of day-to-day living make you pause and think. At the same time, several local hacks, including one from that bastion of diversity known as the *New York Post,* Phil Mushnick, used this as an opportunity to lambaste me, saying, "Do the right thing, Spike, you're helping kill children." Like he cared.

The Reverend Jackson and one of his lieutenants, the Reverend Tyrone Crider, and Operation PUSH became involved. The Reverend Jackson called for a boycott of Nike products. At that time, Coach Thompson and I met with the Reverend Crider, who had been running Operation PUSH. Tyrone and I had been classmates at Morehouse, so it is funny how things go around and come around. The rotation is always true. Too small world. I talked to Coach Thompson about it. He said he had listened intently to the Reverend Jackson, but in the end, Coach said, "I told him I understood, but, Spike, I wasn't going to drink the

Kool-Aid." This was a reference to that People's Temple Guyana cult massacre, led by Jim Jones, where his followers committed mass suicide by drinking a punch laced with lethal poison. It was morbid humor, but it was funny. Laugh or die. I laughed. A little while later, Coach became a member of the board of directors of Nike. Phil Knight, the CEO of Nike—we've become friends over the years, he's a nice guy, if a strange guy; revels in being an outcast, a rebel, the underdog—expressed genuine concern. The sticking point was that Nike knew changes had to be made, but still did not want to be dictated to by the Reverend Crider. Coach and I flew to Chicago to meet the reverend. We both agreed with his cause; we thought his tactics were a little heavy-handed. Coach and I told the Reverend Crider what to do, step by step. It was Coach, Jordan, and I who had the ear of Knight. The Reverend Crider didn't want to hear that noise, and the thing blew up for a while.

Coach and I would talk often. I'd call him up and ask him about what he was trying to do with his program—just two brothers talking sports, talk about how the press was on him, how the press was on me, how he had his favorites and I had mine, things like that. *New York* and *Time* magazine never failed to give me grief, and he said the same was true with him about some newspapers and magazines, but that nobody cared what was written. I doubted that.

I miss the old Georgetown style. I asked Coach why he didn't play a 94-foot, pressing, ten-man rotation in the '90s. I didn't get it at all. Coach Pitino had the Knicks playing a similar style when he was in New York. Then he went to Kentucky playing that style. So I asked Coach Thompson why he'd given it up. How come you don't press anymore, Coach? How come you go deep on the bench? He said, "I don't have the players, Spike." For a while I don't think he minded not having the players. Sometimes having the players means having the problems.

Coach Thompson played with the Boston Celtics for two years in the mid-60s, backing up Russell, and once broke Wilt Chamberlain's nose with an elbow, although Coach is quick to point out that it was an accident. Later, while in D.C. shooting Coach Thompson for a piece I did for HBO's *Real Sports,* I went and talked to Red Auerbach. Took a crew to Red's D.C. apartment and spent the day. He knew I was a Knicks fan, but in spite of that he was nice, fun to be around. I found out that it grieved him when Thompson was vilified, how people had the wrong idea. Red was willing to speak for the record about what type of person he thinks Coach is. So behind Coach I had to reevaluate my hatred of the Celtics. Maybe. Enough to be able to appreciate the good Celtic, one I'd soon meet. But the Celtics were still on my list, and hopefully on the list of the Knicks' coach for 1991–92. Even without John Thompson, Lenny Wilkens, or Larry Brown coaching, I felt we were back in the hunt, and I was all up in the house. But who would direct the Knicks?

THIRD QUARTER

In da House

S ome people have tried to compare me to Jack Nicholson as a hoop fan, him with the Lakers, me with the Knicks. Jack has been courtside for mad runs over many years.

Other than that, more than anything to do with me, Jack made going to the Fabulous Forum fashionable, politic for Hollywood stars to get into the NBA in L.A. Jack's a true fan, a buff, loves the Game, grew up in Joisey, played in high school. He's serious about his game, even invading the Boston Garden during the playoffs in the '80s. With Jack courtside, Showtime was rolling at the Forum in Inglewood, while the Knicks were going through ownership, coaching, and personnel changes. Systematically I was moving down from the green seats to the yellow, to the red, then down to the floor, while seeing Jack hold up four fingers on TV, indicating the hoped-for sweep, grinning wickedly right in Boston Garden. Nobody formed a mob and tried to string him up. I wouldn't be so lucky later, at Market Square Arena in Indianapolis, in '94 and '95. Fans of the Pistons at the Pontiac Silverdome received and wore paper Jack Nicholson masks when the Lakers faced the Pistons in the NBA finals. Jack's run came back when the Lakers were changing ball, winning five rings in eight years, 1980 through 1988. The Pistons took over for a couple of seasons, until M.J. finally got enough help, in 1990–91. It's pretty much been Mike's league since. If the current Lakers win or lose, Jack's not that upset. He's not going to live and die with them. Nor should he. I know he doesn't have to pay for his seats, so he's got the big edge on me there.

Denzel Washington, another great actor: he hoops, and hoops hard. Native New Yorker, Mount Vernon, home of the Williamses, Gus and Ray-Ray, and the McCrays, Rodney and Scooter. Denzel says he played one year at Fordham before grabbing the rim of the proscenium arch. Starred in *Mo' Better Blues,* nominated for *Malcolm X,* won an Oscar for

Glory, has been outstanding in many other roles. During the shooting of *Mo' Better Blues,* Denzel almost broke his ankle playing basketball. After that, ball was banned. We've worked together, gone to the run together, been in the best seats in the house together, but he's been in Cali for too long—the Lakers are his team. I don't know when my brother went wrong.

> > >

Like me, Woody Allen is a true-blue Knick fan. Big games, little games, he's usually there. He and his beloved sit opposite Tonya and me at the Garden; they sit behind the scorer's table. When the game is over and we head out, or while waiting for the elevator in the bowels of the Garden, we may say "Good game" or "Bad game" to each other sometimes, as the case may be.

Unlike me, Woody is quiet there. I don't recall him leaving his seat during a game (except when he leaves early to beat the crowd). That's how he watches the run. Like an analyst. Undemonstrative. I couldn't do it. So we acknowledge our loyalties, if not our methodology. The Game is deep inside our cultural makeup. We have some things in common—hoop, cinema, and Brooklyn, of course. Woody grew up over in Flatbush. He is a writer and a filmmaker, in that order, he might say; I may be just the opposite. Opposites can react. I wanted to find out more. So I looked Woody up, over at his cutting room.

"In Flatbush? *Sure* I played," he said. "I played punchball, stickball, boxball, stoopball, all the Spaldeen ball games, two-hand touch, two-man basketball, three-man basketball, and baseball. I was a very good athlete. For a while I wanted to pursue a career in baseball. I played second base for the 70th Precinct Police Athletic League team. I was a good ballplayer. I played all the time, night and day. That's all we ever thought about then. Mostly it was baseball. Then when I got to be sixteen or seventeen, I started writing. Drifted into that. I was a Giants fan. Right in the heart of Brooklyn."

So I was on the money about sports and Brooklyn being somewhat synonymous—but a *Giants* fan? In Flatbush? That was an extreme polarity, inside New York City. Woody Allen is provincial about Manhattan, as reflected in his work; and I am provincial about Brooklyn in mine. Maybe one's fandom was part of it—maybe the start of it. Sensibilities must start somewhere.

"Woody . . . you could probably *walk* to Ebbets Field from where you grew up."

"You could," he said. "It was a *long* walk, but you could walk, sure."

"So explain to me how you came to be a Giants fan, growing up in Brooklyn."

"I don't know how it happened. I was just taken with the Giants, I'd say starting from 1946 on, I was a Giants fan."

"Even with Duke Snider, Campanella, Jackie Robinson, Pee Wee Reese . . ."

"I was of the Willie Mays, Bobby Thomson school."

"They didn't come until later, though, '51."

"Right, right. In '46 they didn't have anybody. In '46 there was a good Dodger team, and a great Cardinal team."

"So . . . being a Giants fan, you must remember the shot heard 'round the world, in '51."

"Yeah. I was a delivery boy for a Wall Street stationery firm. I used to lug stationery, you know, bottles of ink—cases of ink, actually—and cartons of stationery up to these Wall Street firms. I was on the street that day. I had a good bet on that game. I had gotten tremendous odds. I had taken the Giants just on a lark when they were 18½ games out or something. I couldn't pass up the odds. Then they started closing the gap. I was standing near a newsstand at a corner. Must have been a hundred people around me listening to the radio, and when [Thomson] hit it, we just exploded. We went crazy. That was the single greatest moment probably in sports in my lifetime."

Well, that's enough of that, for a Brooklyn fan. On to common and level ground.

"So how long have you been a Knicks season ticket holder?"

"I've been a Knicks season ticket holder since 1968."

"Sixty-eight?"

"When the new Garden opened. I used to go to the old Garden when I was growing up, but I never had season tickets. I asked Howard Cosell if he could get me season tickets for the Knicks and he said, 'Absolutely, no problem,' and he did. Way up in the balcony. I thought he was, you know . . . because he was so *calm:* 'Oh, sure, don't worry. I'll take care of you.' He had been in my movie, been very nice to me, sweet guy. The seats . . . I can't tell you. When I would say to people, 'Howard Cosell got me these seats,' they couldn't believe it. 'Howard Cosell got you *these*? Up *here*?' I asked if he could upgrade me. He said he'd got me the best he could.

"So Diane Keaton and I used to go to all the games. We would never miss a game. Even if they were playing a last-place team, we went automatically, because you would see some great basketball. That team was so much fun to watch. Such a joy to see Dick Barnett and DeBusschere and Frazier, particularly; then, of course, Monroe. It was so much fun to see them that Diane and I simply never missed a game—if they were playing the last-place team, it didn't matter to us. We went automatically. . . . Now I don't feel the same way today. The Knicks are not as entertaining. Now, if I was a Chicago fan, a Houston fan, I'd probably be seeing every game."

"Going down through the years, who was your favorite Knicks player?" I asked.

"Earl Monroe and Walt Frazier were my two favorite Knicks players," Woody said. "Of course I appreciated Earl beginning when he was in Baltimore. They were the two most exciting Knicks, and the two great Knicks players. I always felt the Knicks never got over the curse—like the Ancient Mariner and the albatross—of trading Walt Frazier. It was a mistake. An emotional mistake. When a player like that is so New York, both in his life and his style . . . but to watch Earl Monroe, he was a poet, he was an artist. . . . There was a game I saw where Earl never missed a shot. Something like twelve of twelve from the floor. Frazier was just amazing. He was so confident and so in control when he played, the fans got the impression he could take the ball whenever he wanted to, and of course he couldn't, but the fans got the *impression* he had that much control. When his skills started to diminish a little and he couldn't do it whenever he wanted, they got annoyed, they got pissed off, that he wasn't in as much command as they had fantasized. So I heard him booed. So as far as being booed, I think Patrick Ewing is right and the fans are wrong. Because first off, people are always criticizing Patrick for not being the most complete ballplayer in the league. That's all bullshit. First of all, he's a great player, a Hall of Fame player. He's been the franchise for twelve years. Without Patrick, they would have been languishing in last or next-to-last place. They've never surrounded him with a great team. If he had played on other teams with other personnel, he would've won championships without any question. . . . I was there the night they booed Walt Frazier at the Garden, and I couldn't believe that either, because these people do miraculous things for them night after night, if not year after year, and then they do something wrong, miss a couple of foul shots, have a bad game or two, and when they need the support, they don't get it. So I'm firmly with Patrick Ewing on that one. But Walt Frazier . . . he was miraculous.

"I think Frazier is the great Knick of all time."

Bingo. Complete agreement. But at the same time, there was something special in Woody Allen that was reserved only for Earl the Pearl. Earl's game always did have that way with people. Black Jesus from North Philly. It wasn't an ignorant, flippant nickname. It was not haphazard.

Earl Monroe's game had drawn Woody in, too.

"My favorite Knicks team was the team with Earl Monroe and Walt Frazier, the [1972–73] second championship team. Only because of the casting. It's like casting. Only the addition of Earl Monroe—it's like casting Marlon Brando in a part. The guy was so great. But they were not better than the first championship team. Dick Barnett was certainly a sensational basketball player."

"Why do you love basketball? And you do love the game, don't you?"

"I love the game because I think it's the one sport where the personal expression of the individual ballplayer comes across the best. Each individual guy's style is so clear and pronounced. It's so individually expressive, there is no similarity between Magic Johnson and Isiah Thomas and Walt Frazier. Each one of these guys is an artist. It's so individually expressive, so that's great."

"Okay, now, what do you *dislike* about basketball?"

"I don't mind the money for the players, because I think they certainly deserve that. I don't like the extra expansion, because it's hard to get enough great players to do that."

"So you're not showing up for Vancouver?"

"It waters it down, exactly—and I don't like the rough game that the Knicks were playing into a couple years ago."

"With Pat Riley?"

"Yeah, only because it's not as much fun to watch. So you get a couple of bruisers out there and they foul and they hit hard and you know, who cares? That's not, that's never what the game, you know, that's not what you liked when you saw Julius Erving or Michael Jordan. You do that as a last resort, when you have no other skills going for you and the only thing you can do is hit hard. Not much fun to watch that. It's more fun to watch the finesse players."

"Can you tell me some of your most memorable games you can recall from your numerous years as a season ticket holder?"

"Yeah, I've seen some great ones. Of course, the famous great one, where they were playing the Milwaukee Bucks . . ."

"When they were down by eighteen."

"Yeah, and they came back in the last quarter. That was a fabulous game. Nineteen straight points. The game that Willis Reed came walking out. Everybody thinks that's his game, but it was really Frazier's game. When Willis was hurt in that series, I felt that it wasn't going to make a huge difference, and that it would've been worse if Frazier was hurt, because he was the guy they couldn't live without. But Willis, I felt, they could live without; he was great, but they would somehow adjust, but they would not have been able to survive without Frazier. He was unbelievable. And there were many games when I'd be going home and the announcer would be saying, 'Walt Frazier had 34 points, 15 assists, 12 rebounds. . . .' That was great to watch. And Michael Jordan's 55-point game was great to watch."

"Do you think Michael's on the level of a Picasso or a Louis Armstrong?"

"Michael is the great artist of the game, definitely. The most exciting players I've seen play are Michael, Magic Johnson, Walt Frazier, Earl

Monroe, and Isiah Thomas. And Julius Erving. Michael seems to be the best of those super, super players. When he first came up, I thought it was all press hype. As the years went by, I realized, 'Michael never disappoints.' It wasn't like you go into the Garden and then come out saying, 'Gee, I caught a bad Michael Jordan night.' There are so few bad Michael Jordan evenings. He just never disappoints. Michael is a great, great poet with the basketball. . . .

"Of basketball, I think—and I'm sure you do too, Spike—I think of it in the same terms as jazz. It's the spontaneous creation of something. That's what makes the game great and so much fun to watch. You give Michael Jordan the ball, or Earl Monroe the ball, and they create for you. It's a strict improvisation they are doing. This kid Iverson has it now. He's an exciting ballplayer. It has a real jazz feeling, because they're making it up as they go along. That's what is so great. You're seeing a very individual style that you can mistake for no one else's. When you see Julius Erving play, or Walt Frazier play, it's a style you don't mistake for anyone else's. It's the same when you hear piano being played and it's Bud Powell or Thelonious Monk or Horace Silver."

I'd heard Woody shot at least one basketball scene he never used.

"Yes, I had a terrific scene I had to cut from *Annie Hall.* We shot a sequence with a team of intellectuals and philosophers versus the Knicks. We shot it after the last game of that [1972–73] season; shot it with Earl Monroe, Butch Beard, Phil Jackson. It never made the picture, but it was quite funny to see these intellectuals—Kierkegaard, Nietzsche, myself—people who were basically cerebral and couldn't do anything until they had thought it to death. No spontaneity at all. Everything had to be debated. And of course the Knicks were effortless. Everything they did was completely spontaneous. So I've done a number of basketball things over the years because whenever I think of going to the Garden I think of basketball. I changed it once to a hockey game in *Manhattan Murder Mystery,* just to get a little bit of variation, but basically, when I think of the Garden, I think of basketball.

"I had a few basketball scenes. I had one in *Mighty Aphrodite. . . .* That was the one where the strong-arm guy wants to beat my brains out—I'm playing a sportswriter—and I give him tickets to the Knicks games, I get him season tickets, I get them to upgrade his seats, and [in return] he doesn't beat the shit out of me."

"Have you ever thought about doing a purely sports film?"

"No . . . although many years ago, when I first started in the business, a guy came to me with a script, or an idea, that I thought would make a funny film. It was about a very religious rabbi who suddenly discovered he was a brilliant field goal kicker, could just kick three points from 65 yards out, and the team wanted him. I believe the thing was called *The Kicking Rabbi.* I went on and made *Bananas* instead, but that was the only sports film I ever contemplated. Funny concept."

"What do you think is the best sports film ever made? *Raging Bull?*"

"The greatest sports film ever made? I don't think of *Raging Bull* as a spor— Well, I guess it is a sports film. It probably is the best sports film ever made, although it's not my favorite film of Marty's. That is *Goodfellas.* I think it was better than *Raging Bull. Raging Bull* probably is the best sports film, because it was made by a master, and the other ones are all . . . pathetic. I mean, they're all equal to *The Glenn Miller Story.*"

"Have you ever had to schedule your shoots around the Knicks' schedule?" I asked.

"Oh, I do that all the time. I'm sure you do."

"Then we are in company. I get heat for that. Tell me how you do it."

"I get heat for it, too, but I do it all the time. You have to know that in filmmaking, the companies, everybody thinks the priority has to be the clock. I never thought that. I always think the most important thing is your life. To me I would never ever miss a basketball game I wanted to see for shooting. I just wouldn't do it. So I schedule around it. I go home early. I knock off early all the time because it's too important. I'd never miss a game I wanted to see for work.

"I don't know if it's going to be Chicago this year. I think it probably will be, but I don't know. I don't think the Knicks are going."

"You don't think so?"

"No, I don't think so."

"You don't think they can beat Chicago this year? Chicago is showing signs—"

"I think the Knicks are going to have trouble with Seattle, with Utah, with Houston."

"But they have to beat Chicago first, to play one of them. . . . So, Woody, what is it you get from going to the games? Is it just something that adds enjoyment to your life? Is it an escape?"

"For me, it's pure pleasure. The burden of entertainment is on them. I don't have to think. If I go to a movie, I think, 'Oh, God, this guy's movie is so great and mine is so terrible,' or 'Gee, he did that wrong,' or, you know, I'm not in the same business so I have no connection. Here I can go, and it's just pure pleasure. It's a joy to watch, just a joy."

"You ever emote at a game?"

"I don't emote. You do. Once in a while I catch you over there and you're deeply— I'm just watching, I'm thrilled inside, but you're *high-fiving* them and *badgering* the other guys . . . that was hilarious, when the city blamed you for our loss."

Uh, I hadn't quite gotten around to re-creating and reflecting on that just yet, Woody. . . .

"A lot of people want my seats," he said. "The same with you, I'm sure. So how'd you feel when they upped the price?"

"I was not happy at all. Think it was louder with the championship teams than it is today?"

"Yeah, I certainly thought the old Garden—maybe it was the acoustics—but it seemed more frantic, more frenetic. I agree with you. The whole lower section, not just courtside, but the whole lower section . . . I'm paying 600 bucks a game for four seats."

"I'm paying two grand for two."

"Right, but you're sitting right there."

"But still, you've got great seats also. . . . I don't want to pay it, but if I don't, somebody will."

"Somebody who'll come in from a corporation and pay it."

"Just have to put it in your will and pass it down. Hope to be able to cover," I answered.

"Right. A guy sitting not far from me who had a pair of season tickets offered them. He wanted $100,000 for the privilege of buying the seats. He got a hundred grand, and then you buy the seats. You still had to buy the seats. For the privilege of buying the seats, he gets a hundred grand."

"He got it?"

"He got it? Yeah, he got it."

"Who's your all-time favorite athlete?"

"I guess Willie Mays or Sugar Ray Robinson. One of the two. Well, these two guys, like Michael Jordan, like Earl Monroe, they're both great poets. When you watched Willie Mays play baseball, it wasn't like watching anybody else play baseball. That was a style that was sensational, and he was so electrifying every time he came up, every time he was on base, every time a ball was hit in the outfield, there was a *moment* when you waited for him to do something, and so many times he did it. It's so hard to do that in baseball. It's a more mechanical thing. And Sugar Ray Robinson was the dream of my childhood."

"Did you ever see him fight?"

"I never saw him fight live—I was too young—just on television. But I knew him. I had dinner at his house. I got to meet him. I had never seen anything like that. He was like a quantum leap forward from the other fighters. I loved boxing. Later, I flew places to see fights. If I was working in Florida and there was a fight in New York, I would cancel that night in the hotel and make up an excuse to fly to New York or Vegas to see a fight. I had seen fighters growing up quite a bit, but when I saw Ray, I mean—I'd never seen anything like that. He so dominated the sport. It was like Michael Jordan. He was *so* superior to everybody. *So* superior. I mean, the speed, the hand speed—everything you wanted in a fighter. He was a finisher, he could hit with either hand. He was just . . . it wasn't just that he had the mechanics down pat, he had that extra star quality. . . ."

"If you hadn't become a filmmaker, would you have wanted to play major league baseball?"

"If I could have been an athlete, if I could've had any athlete's ability, I would have wanted to have Sugar Ray Robinson's."

"So you'd have been a boxer?"

"Yes, if I could have been a boxer as good as him. But when he talked about it, he used to say, 'God, it was a tough life, and it was ugly, and it was a mean way to live, a hard way to live.' But I would've rather had his ability than Willie Mays's or Michael Jordan's."

"So, then, Woody . . . you have a killer instinct?"

"*I* don't have a killer instinct. But *he* did. And, you know, he wasn't that way as a kid. He wasn't a street fighter or a bully or anything like that. I heard that from him, and I heard the same thing about Ray Leonard. They were not tough in the sense of picking fights like Jake La Motta, yet they were great fighters. Sugar Ray Robinson, of course, is in a class by himself."

"All right, then."

> > >

John McEnroe is a fan. Don't know if he has his seats down from me anymore, but he knows the game and was a great athlete himself of course. Ed Bradley of *60 Minutes* knows ball. Matt Dillon is in the house when he isn't shooting. Tom Brokaw only comes to the big games. When I went to suburban Detroit, to the Palace, for the seventh game of the Eastern Conference finals of 1989–90 when the Bad Boys ground Jordan down and Scottie had a headache, the Reverend Jackson was there. The Bulls lost by seven. Michael was gassed and inconsolable afterward. The American sporting public heard him say the Bulls "had to get better." He was hurt. The Reverend Jackson went to the Bulls' locker room. So did I. I'd heard Jerry West once said nobody could re-create the mood of a losing locker room of a good team that's given its all and lost. That feeling—nobody could capture it, West said. I told Mike he'd played a great game. I saw his father. I thought about mine.

"Spike, I just want to see a good game. . . ."

By the beginning of the 1991–92 season, the Garden wasn't a bad place to be once again. Cheering could be heard again. *Jungle Fever* had been released. I had taken on the biggest work-related challenge in my life, making *Malcolm X.* And whenever I went to the Garden run, people still would shout: "Spike, do da right thing, Spike! And tell it to da Knicks, will ya?"

Coaching *is* like directing. As a director-producer, you're really more like a general manager. You're assembling this team to do this project.

I'm not just talking about the actors in front of the camera but also the talent behind the camera. It's like a draft, or a season, every film—you see who's out there, and you move pieces around, you have to deal with agents, somebody costs too much, well, you have your own salary cap too, you can't exceed the budget. So you might not get your first-choice player, but you have another couple of people in mind, and a lot of times they end up being better people for your project or for that role. A perfect example: Robert De Niro was my hands-down first choice to portray Sal in *Do The Right Thing*. But he is such a big star that his largeness would have detracted from the film, which was an ensemble piece. So as it turned out, Danny Aiello was perfect for Sal. That's how you try to gain chemistry. It's difficult. It's all about working together, and if you put together people who can't stand each other—it's hard enough to make a movie without going through a lot of personal bickering and ego trips. Then you have the other side. In *School Daze,* we had cooperation because most of the actors were unknown, in their first film, many of them; they were *very* cooperative, there was jostling for lines. Equate minutes in basketball with lines in movies. Everybody is bucking for lines. Like ball hogs in basketball, in film there are similar animals; they are called camera hogs.

Like a good basketball team, or any good sports team, the good casts have a mixture of seasoned grizzled veterans and youth. I try to cast my films that way. If you only cast established people all the time, a lot of times those veterans are locked into one way of thinking; they've been doing the same thing for twenty years, and they don't want to try anything different—are not as apt to take chances. But if you go totally the other way to the fullest extreme, then you have youth and the total inexperience that goes with it. They're ready to try something new, but don't know a lot of the basics, so you end up taking all your time teaching when you should be shooting. To get the proper blend, youth and experience—it's a challenge to achieve each time, for every project.

In coaching, just as in directing, you need to meld individual talents into a cohesive whole, an ensemble. The best coaches in the NBA are the ones with the best players. The best NBA coaches are Phil Jackson of the Bulls, who has proven he can coach talent—temperamental talent in some cases, like Scottie Pippen and Dennis Rodman, veteran talent in others. With experience comes attitude. Phil has shown he can get the talented players to see his logic. Lenny Wilkens of Brooklyn, in Atlanta, Larry Brown of Indiana, Mike Fratello from Joisey, in Cleveland, he's good, too. Lenny has a style. Give him a solid point guard—Gus Williams in Seattle, Mark Price and Kevin Johnson in Cleveland, Mookie Blaylock in Atlanta—and Lenny can work the rest of it out. He's won more games than any coach in NBA history, and the NBA title in '79 in Seattle. Speaks for itself. Larry Brown is smooth, has to be challenged by a situation. Reminds me of Bill Walsh in football. Near genius. Never had great personnel to work with in the NBA, like Pat Riley in L.A. or Phil Jackson, now in Chicago, but has still done very well everywhere he goes. Fratello went from coaching a talented Atlanta team featuring Dominique Wilkins to the NBC-TV booth, to the Cleveland Cavaliers, where he flourished, showed he could thrive with not lesser talents but more one-dimensional talents. Gotta like Fratello. Jerry Sloan, the ex-Bull, year in and year out, keeps Utah deep in the playoffs and doesn't bellyache when they finally lose.

Dick Motta in Denver and Bill Fitch with the L.A. Clippers are older than dirt, but once the game is in your blood, it's in there. Still, there are many brothers who have never gotten a single chance to coach in the league despite paying dues—guys like Cazzie Russell never got one chance. So I don't see how they can recycle these same guys all the time, like they do in the NBA, the NFL, and major league baseball. Motta and Fitch both have NBA titles in their coaching past. They should be retired by now. K. C. Jones, who played with Russell at the University of San Francisco back in the '50s, on the Celtic teams in the '60s, later coached the Celtics to two championships, even got the Bullets to the Finals; K.C. wasn't in coaching for a while, but now he's back on the Celtics' bench as an assistant. He could get the job done, obviously. He proved it. Please add former great Dennis Johnson to that list. Rudy Tomjanovich, Rudy T., he held the reins loose and the Houston Rockets have won two NBA titles with him at the helm.

Rudy T. has a couple of excellent assistant coaches; Rudy coached hard, he and Larry Smith, formerly a fierce rebounder with the Rockets, before that with the Golden State Warriors, and Bill Berry, a former college head coach. Bill's son, Ricky Berry, was a 6-8 flexible perimeter player, part of the avant-garde, with all kinds of potential, drafted number eighteen, one ahead of Rod Strickland, in the June 1988 draft. For all I know, Ricky Berry might have been a Knick if Sacramento had been caught missing. But in only his second year in the league, he committed suicide over a love gone sour in Sacramento, where he was on the roster of the Kings. So talent alone is not enough; even talent and work ethic is not enough. There is also will. The will to keep trying, the will to keep living and trying. Ricky's father, Bill, who had been Ricky's coach at San Jose State, gave himself up to the Game after that and helped coach the Houston Rockets to NBA titles under Rudy T.

Chuck Daly was a great coach before he left the bench once his Detroit Piston World Championship team was broken up by age, and by the Bulls and Michael Jordan in 1991. Under Daly, Detroit won two NBA titles, in 1988–89 and 1989–90. Daly coached the original Dream Team at the Barcelona Olympics in 1992.

And then there's Pat Riley, once of the Lakers and, as of the 1991–92 season, the new coach of the Knicks. When Riley got to the Garden I felt he was a great coach. We'd gotten over. He had the rings to prove it— coach of the Showtime Lakers. Over his four years with the Knicks, pacing in front of the bench across the court from me, I started to think he believed he was more important than the organization—that he *was* the organization.

But he took us all the way. Almost.

Toward the end of Riley's run with the Knicks—he resigned in 1995— I came to think that Pat was too much of a dictator. Every coach has belief in his or her system, but the game is about adapting, making adjustments, making changes. His ego was getting in the way.

In the beginning I thought Pat was flexible and could adjust, and that spoke well for him. With the Lakers, he had a fluid, running, offensive-minded, fast-breaking team led by Magic Johnson, Kareem, Worthy, Michael Cooper, Byron Scott. When he came to the Knicks it was obvious that the Knicks could not win in a fluid game against Chicago, Scottie Pippen, and Michael Jordan. So he became defensive-minded, stressed banging, grinding it out.

To me it seemed as if he had no choice. When Riley came in, in 1991–92, he had the following roster.

The rookie point guard Greg Anthony had run point for the University of Nevada–Las Vegas NCAA champions in 1990 and was a self-described Young Republican who often played like the boxer Coach Jerry Tarkanian said he could have been. He was a gamer, he came to play—he was the only Knick who ever went to a great former player like Walt Frazier for advice, but he seemed to punch at the ball when he handled it. That was okay at first—Mark Jackson was still there to run the offense—until he was sent to the Clippers for Charles Smith.

John Starks was coming into his third year. Gerald Wilkins was a good athlete; the only problem with 6-4 Gerald was that he wasn't his older brother, Dominique. Him I'd like to have seen in a Knicks uniform in his prime. Gerald, Billy Ripken, younger brother of Cal, Albert King of Fort Greene, behind his brother Bernard; they convinced me that younger brothers may be better off in another line of work in the long run, especially if the shadow of the older brother is long.

For 1991–92, the Knicks had Kiki Vandeweghe, in his eleventh year, on the roster, by now virtually useless; a one-year wonder named Jarvis Basnight; a guy who looked good in the lobby named Brian Quinnet; and our three heavy bangers: Anthony Mason, an ex-CBA'er, 6-7 and a hard 250, and a little crazy—that doesn't always hurt; dependable Oakley, 6-9 and 245; and Xavier "X-Man" McDaniel, 6-7 and 205 but played heavier. Ewing was in the middle, backed up by Tim McCormick and Patrick Eddie. There was nothing flexible, no one who could really swing from big forward, 4, to small forward, 3, or from small forward, 3, to big guard, 2. The interesting part about what Riley had to work with when he came to New York from L.A. was the quick realization that nothing resembling a Magic Johnson, a Michael Cooper, a Silk Wilkes, or a James Worthy was on this Knicks roster. Certainly no one with any hope of checking Jordan or Pippen, straight up. The closest we could come was Starks. Riley immediately took John under his wing.

The Knicks went 51–31 in Riley's first year, 1991–92. The Knicks went 60–22 in 1992–93. During this time a tension developed between Riley and Bulls coach Phil Jackson. The Knicks were the Bulls' great nemesis in the playoffs in those years. Jockeying for position, Phil said the rough, slow style the Knicks played was "not basketball." Riley vehemently disagreed. The Knicks were the team that gave the Bulls the most trouble in '91, '92, and '93. And today the Bulls may look different, may even be more efficient, and some parts have changed: the rebounding machine, cross-dressing, RuPaul-kissing, nuts-kicking psycho Rodman at power forward instead of Horace Grant; the Australian Alp, Luc Longley, at center rather than Cartwright. But they're still the Bulls.

"I think if you look at the Bulls, they've got Michael Jordan, so on one level you've got a whole different world there," Bill Bradley had said to me, "because he's better than anybody who played on those old Knicks teams. I think. Yeah, I think he is. I know he is. But people play roles on that team, they know what they're supposed to do, and that's not a coincidence. That's because Phil played on the Knicks teams. He was my roommate for two years. He brought the Bulls to Capitol Hill after they won it one of those years, and I took them down on the Senate floor. You know Phil likes to take them on excursions. When he was a Knick, Phil knew his role. I knew my role. Everybody knew their roles. Why don't [other teams] know it now? Beats me. It has to do with maturity. I remember asking Oscar Robertson, 'What do you think of Michael?' Must have been Michael's fourth or fifth year, I think around '87 or '88. Oscar said, 'He's a great player, but he has yet to realize that the truly great player makes the worst player on his team good.' He realizes that now, and has for the last several years. You've got to have a coach who can get that across, but more importantly, you've got to have peer pressure on the guy who wants to do it all on his own, so he can recognize he's not part of the program."

Phil Jackson told me, "One of the things I learned from Red Holzman is that the biggest thing about basketball is the chemistry between people. It's not particularly that you have the best talent. You don't always have to have the best players on the floor, but you have to have people really understand each other and the roles they have to play. And the other thing is that defense has to be the priority, because no one has the ball on defense. You're playing without the basketball, and that's when everybody can give of themselves and be unselfish."

I was hitting and missing as far as going to games was concerned in the 1991–92 season. We were shooting *Malcolm X,* and I was being taxed and tested mentally, physically, and spiritually. We finished shooting in Africa, in Egypt (which is in Africa, for those who may suffer confusion about world geography) and in South Africa, where I met and filmed incoming president Nelson Mandela. It was the biggest film I'd attempted. I'd always worked on smaller canvases. This was big. In December of '91, the film's bond company, Completion Bond Company, sent certified letters to the film's editors and fired them. Not to be beat, I fired off calls to many people I had met and who had supported me and my efforts, and these people, including the ballplayers, they rode to the rescue like the Massachusetts 54th. It meant a lot for *Malcolm X* to be done right, for the mythology to be well told. And people responded that way; Michael Jordan and Magic Johnson helped financially, as did Peggy Cooper-Cafritz, Janet Jackson, the artist formerly known as Prince, Bill Cosby, Oprah Winfrey, Tracy Chapman. Face, bond company. Team ball over here. It was touch-and-go for a while, financially, emotionally. People picked me up. When I was down and out, they took me in. Those were the hardest phone calls I've made. It was no coincidence that two of the very first people to cover my back were Michael Jordan and Magic Johnson.

Meanwhile, the Knicks were showing their mettle too, as was Riley. I was going back and forth with them—enthralled by the Knicks, who were on their way to that 51–31 regular season record, then challenged and stretched thin by the workload and financial realities of *Malcolm X;* disappointed by any Knick loss, then exhilarated by the dailies from *Malcolm X;* talking hardball with Denzel at meal breaks, watching him as he got into character, doing my swan song with Ernest Dickerson. The shoot took 120 days, into January.

In the spring of '92, I was asked to present the Oscar for Best Documentary with John Singleton at the Academy Awards ceremonies at the

Dorothy Chandler Pavilion in Los Angeles. The Bulls were invading the Garden on the night after the Oscars. And then, on the very next day after that, on April Fool's Day, a priority screening of the work print of *Malcolm X* was scheduled for the big cheeses at Warner Brothers, Bob Daly and Terry Semel, back out in Burbank. And on top of all that, the dentist was kicking my teeth in. But I presented the Oscar with John, then flew back cross-country and saw the Bulls beat the Knicks, 96–90, in front of 19,763 fans at the Garden. I was on the floor, having a ball. Despite Ewing's 31 points and 18 boards, we got two-timed. Jordan looked at me, shook his head, and dropped 36 points. Pippen led all rebounders with 18. The following morning I caught the first thing smoking from JFK, shot back out to L.A., got in a limo headed to the Warner Brothers lot. We screened the four-hour rough cut, went back and forth about pacing, what should stay, what could go. I got positive feedback for the most part and continued editing, preparing for a November release.

We met the Bulls in the playoffs that year, 1992. In game seven, Jordan had to come to Scottie Pippen's defense against Xavier McDaniel. I believe X-Man had stolen Pippen's heart in that series. X had him terrified. Finally, Money had to get in X's face and tell him he'd have to deal with him if he didn't stop harassing Pippen. That's when Scottie was experiencing another one of those Excedrin headaches. The Bulls and Jordan rose on us without even thinking hard, wiped us out in a romp. They had to figure out how to beat Detroit, and once they finally did, it was over. Now we had to go to school on them, learn how to beat them. And something like a mini-feud began occurring between me and Scottie Pippen.

Of players I've had run-ins with—from Rick Mahorn, who (inadvertently, I hope) threw a ball at me that broke my glasses during warmups while my head was turned one night, to Reggie Miller—I didn't feel they were at all mean-spirited. I think the mean-spirited stuff happened from Pippen. We know about the series against Detroit in 1989–90, when he took off because he had a headache—and I'm not doubting he had one; Kareem used to have monster migraines in June, when the Lakers were battling the Celtics; Russell used to throw up before every big game. Scottie is a great, great player, who also has a history of pulling Houdinis, disappearing in the crunch. During one playoff game in 1992–93, Knicks vs. Bulls, we were in old Chicago Stadium. I was in the front row. Scottie did a nasty dunk over Patrick, who fell backward and was lying on the floor. Scottie stood there, straddling him, standing up. It's a basic manhood move you see a lot in ball now. I would be kicking my way up, if it was me down there. Don't be dangling your gonies over me, you mother . . . It looked a little like that old shot of Ali standing over the fallen Liston in their second fight. I jumped up out of my seat and screamed at referee Jake O'Donnell. "He's taunting him, Jake! You can't allow that! Tech, tech!" Jake would have called it anyway. I just wanted to remind him. Scottie walked over to me and said, "Sit the fuck down, Spike."

Scottie's been one of the two or three best players in the league for a few years now. Michael shaped Scottie in his image as a player and did wonders with him. Yes, he did—but the thing was, when Mike wasn't there, when he retired for the season of 1993–94, and for most of 1994–95, Scottie reverted in crunch time. On the one hand, when Michael was there, Scottie was crying about his headaches or how he's tired of being Mike's caddy—he actually once said during Mike's sabbatical that the Bulls were a better team without him. Michael leaves to play baseball and all the burden is on Scottie and what does he do? He benches himself for the last shot in a playoff game five against the Knicks, in 1993–94, against Phil Jackson's orders, because Jackson had designed the last play to go not to Pippen but to Toni Kukoc—who ended up hitting the shot with Pip sulking on the bench. Of course it was complicated at the time. Scottie was having serious problems with Kukoc getting twice the money he was getting, and Kukoc's $3.9 million was even more than the $3 million a year Michael had been getting. I definitely understand the part about him being upset at Bulls G.M. Jerry Krause and owner Jerry Reinsdorf for giving all the money to the unproven white boy from Croatia, but that can't affect what you do on the court. And even today, at $2.25 million a year, Pippen is one of the bargains in the NBA. He is not stealing money. But he stole it that day. In the heat of an intense playoff game with his team's arch rivals, with Michael Jordan now gone and the issue left up to him, Pippen didn't want to be a decoy for Kukoc, and as Phil Jackson diagrams the play for the game-winning shot in the huddle, Scottie says, "Fuck you, Phil," and like a baby goes and sits at the end of the bench.

I had to ask Phil about this.

"I don't know if that's ever going to be something people will forget about Scottie Pippen," Jackson told me. "As great a player as he is, there's always going to be the stigma that he sat out the last second and a half of a ball game. But you know, I had to make a choice. Scottie was either going to facilitate the play, and if he didn't want to do it, we'd have to go without him. And I knew his frustration. I understood what he was dealing with, but I knew that he owed his team an apology also, after the ball game, because of what had gone on. He was a leader, and he let his team down because of his own personal interest in the ball game."

Now, I'm not in the NBA, but even when we were kids growing up in Brooklyn, nobody pulled anything like "If I'm not playing, I'm taking my ball and going home," because anybody like that would have had to run home to keep from getting his ass beat. And if you had decided to go off on your own under Red Holzman, you wouldn't have to worry about benching yourself. You sat down. And if you pouted when you sat down, you stayed down. There are guys who would kill to be in your position, to be able to play for the Chicago Bulls, and because the coach doesn't call your number, thinks it's better to throw them a curve and set up a 6-11 guy who can shoot and in fact made the game-winning shot with you not out there, then you don't want to play? Because you ain't the Man? What in hell is that? It's not championship-level basketball, which is, basically, the collective realization that no one player can be as good as all five can be collectively. But it has to be a collective realization. If one of the five doesn't realize it, the composition is ruined, and the goal is eventually missed. I don't care what he does from now until he retires, that is gonna stay with Scottie. And that definitely shows something is missing. Be a good decoy on the play and hopefully everyone will think you're going to take the shot, and they may put two men on you, and Kukoc will get a good look at the winning shot. Isn't that the most important thing? If he doesn't make it, you can howl like a banshee after the game and call Phil Jackson seventeen kinds of fool. What Scottie did was put himself in front of the team. In the stunned Bulls locker room after the game, Bill Cartwright, with tears in his eyes, asked Scottie, "How could you do this to us?"

The Bulls tried to trade Scottie after that. Even up for Shawn Kemp. Seattle pulled out at the last second. Scottie added insult to injury in the same 1994 series when, in the final game, Hue Hollins called a foul against Pip on the three-point shot by Hubert Davis. Hubert hit the three free throws and we went on to the NBA finals against Houston. The Bulls still hate to see Hue: "Oh, God, no, we got Hue tonight?!" Personally, I like him. Anybody who has the stomach to make calls against the team (Chicago) and the players (Jordan, Pippen) who get all the calls is a friend of mine.

> > >

I *really* like to talk to the refs. I have trouble remembering their names, keeping them all straight, but they're fun to talk to. In a line going back to Mendy Rudolph, Darrell Garretson, Earl Strom, up through Jake O'Donnell, now with the likes of Joey Crawford, Dick Bavetta, Hugh Evans, Hue Hollins, Jess Kersey, Danny Crawford, Ed T. Rush, Ron Nunn, Mike Mathis, Steve Javie, Bill Oakes, Garretson's son, Ronnie, the whole lot. They do talk back to me, you know. I may yell, "How can you call that?" They might say, "Don't ask if you don't know." I'm ready for one of them to say, "If you don't know, you better ax somebody."

During one game, a ref made a call, offensive zone, some crazy call. I said, "Whoever heard of that?" He said, "I've gotta call it once a year, and this is it."

And they do mess up. They'll miss one. And sometimes you get a makeup call.

There was one game during the time, a Knicks-Pacers playoff war. It was late in the game, the Pacers had the ball, and the ref thought they called time out. The Knicks double-teamed, had one of the Pacers trapped, but, incredibly, Steve Javie called time out for him, I guess out of a sudden pity. The Knicks were apoplectic.

Very quickly, Javie called the ball boy over: "Bring that towel here. Wipe up this wet spot."

I was apoplectic now. "But there's no wet spot on the floor! There is no wet spot on the floor." All on television and everything. I was scream- ing, "You made a mistake. There is no wet spot here!"

He just calmly told the ball boy, "Wipe that up."

"Wipe what up? This floor is as dry as a bone. What are you talking about?"

He looked at me, smiled, and said, "Easy, easy."

He knew what he was doing. And it was really smart on his part, an experienced ref's move. He was thinking on his feet. He called time out in a critical part of a crucial game when no time had been called. "Why don't you just admit it?" I hollered. He was like, Play on.

I find them amazing, the refs. Growing up you think that refs and umpires are robots. But they're human. They make mistakes. They have vendettas. Jake O'Donnell was famous for one he carried against Clyde Drexler. One NBA ref, Derrick Stafford, graduated from Morehouse in the same class with me. It's always good to see one of the brothers do well. I'm also on him if he makes a bad call. The guy who is a real pain to me is Ronnie Garretson. His father, Darrell, is the NBA supervisor of referees. He was a longtime ref himself, never quite as good as the late Earl Strom, or O'Donnell. His son is like the warden's son. He has a chip on his shoulder, and he is probably one of the least-admired refs in the league. He's the one that Nick Van Exel sent flying last year. No one should ever touch a ref, but with Ronnie, I almost understood Nick.

When Riley took over the Knicks, he had his picture taken with Red Holzman for the cover of the Knicks' press guide. A return to the thrilling championship days of yesteryear with Riles. His Hairness. Riley had won four rings coaching the Showtime Lakers. The Knicks—and the Bulls—posed a different problem. We had a strong team—physical, not the quickest group ever put together—with Ewing, Oak, and Mase inside. We didn't have flexible, so-called athletic players. We didn't have anybody but Mase who could really play three, and match up with Pippen at all. But once Jordan was gone, even for a minute, we were the ones who got in there, and you have to credit Riley. He cut a striking figure on the sideline, Armani-ed down, and very intense, and he had a look—I had heard that the *Chinatown* screenwriter Robert Towne wanted Riley to take a costarring role in *Tequila Sunrise*, but Riley wisely turned it down. Coaching was more his act.

Riley led us to some good times, highest level. Three times he got us to a seventh game against the Bulls in the playoffs. But, unfortunately for the Knicks and Riley and me, and Lenny Wilkens in Cleveland, and Larry Brown in Indiana, and every other team, coach, and fan in the NBA outside of Chicago, Jordan was now ascendant, and the Bulls were hard to beat one game, let alone four out of seven. Chicago won the three straight NBA world titles by beating the Lakers and Magic in five in '91, the Portland Trail Blazers and Clyde Drexler in six in '92, and the Phoenix Suns and Charles Barkley in six in '93. I was happy for Mike but remained a Knicks fan to the core. I was upset when Charles Smith— he's pumping-pumping-pumping—could not get a winning shot up and down or a foul call against the Bulls in game five in '93. I had to calm down later when John Starks told me, "He didn't get fouled." But nobody played the Chicago Bulls tougher than the Knicks did. Nobody else could even force them to seven games. The Knicks did, three times. Jeff Van Gundy, an assistant coach under Riley, later told me, "If this was about playing them close, then we had the perfect team. But if it's about beating them, we never proved we could get over that hump."

Despite his rigidity, Riley is a great coach. Others say he's better at assessing talent. Eventually Riley left New York after the 1994–95 season for a sweet deal in Miami, where he has part ownership of the club and *final* say in personnel matters—in other words, he's God. The Knicks, in their infinite wisdom, brought in Don Nelson. Nellie had gotten himself a rep coaching Milwaukee and Sid Moncrief back in the '80s, even though they never so much as made an Eastern Conference final in Nellie's time. Nellie lasted, oh, about five minutes. Van Gundy, the thirty-three-year-old protégé of Riley's, took over as head coach on March 8, 1996. Van Gundy led the Knicks to a 47–35 record during the 1995–96 season and was brought back to coach the 1996–97 edition of my hometown team. I like Jeff. Whether he has the experience, cojones, and cunning to coach players who are as old as he is, give us a chance against Chicago in 1996–97—all that has yet to be seen. The Knicks made a big investment in new players. With experience comes attitude, but a coach can handle attitude if he knows what he's doing. I'm hoping Van Gundy turns out as well as Riley did. But when I asked Jordan to assess NBA coaches for 1996–97, this is what he told me:

"I'm sorry, Spike, Van Gundy is not even included. Throw Van Gundy out of the conversation. He's thirty-four years old. He hasn't really done anything yet. You can't compare him to a Phil Jackson and a Pat Riley. Van Gundy is taking over for Pat Riley. He was a Pat Riley clone for a long time. Now. Whatever Phil and Pat have against each other, it is a matter of philosophy to a certain extent. And some of it comes from how you leverage to get the certain calls from the referees—position your team to win. That's what a good coach is all about.

"I mean, I don't think Pat and Phil like each other, just for the sake of their business. There has been so much different leveraging along the way, it's kind of burned the bridge a little bit. But you also got to realize—Phil has always taught a certain way, he plays a certain style of basketball, and he's not changed. Pat changed. Now he wants his teams to be all physical, knock people down. He never stressed that with the Lakers when he won."

"Yeah, but look who he had, though. Worthy, Magic, Kareem, Byron," I say.

"That's my point. So, I mean, not to take anything away, what made him a great coach? Now you tell me that. He hasn't taken another team to any kind of championship at any level."

"Well, he took the Knicks to the NBA finals."

"Yeah? So what? How many teams have done that? Rick Adelman did that with Clyde in Portland. Are you telling me he's a great coach? George Karl did that with Shawn in Seattle. Brian Hill did that with Shaq and Penny in Orlando. Is he a great coach? All right, then."

> > >

You look at things through your own eyes. Most of us don't have the gift of being in someone else's shoes, looking at other people's lives from their perspective, to see why they see things the way *they* do, and maybe that's unfortunate. Maybe I do identify with pesky point guards playing the passing lanes, snatching the ball from the big men's hands, dodging elbows. Those guys are more like me. I hope I'm not limited to seeing the Game from that one point of view. . . .

It was Denzel Washington on the line one day in the fall of 1991. He asked me if I had heard yet. Heard what? Heard about Magic, he said. What about Magic? It was Denzel who called me and said Magic was about to announce he was HIV positive, carrying the AIDS virus, and would retire from basketball, effective immediately. Why did Denzel call me? It was a call being made all across America. We had worked together. We had gotten to know each other that way, and then there was the common element of ball and having game. You couldn't hold this in, walk around with it. It was between the brothers. You had to ask your brother, Is this real? What is happening? Help me out here, brother. Help me understand. Help me get past this. So Denzel called me and said, "Spike, guess what?"

"What."

"Magic has the AIDS virus."

I just whistled, real low. I couldn't believe it. I said, "D, are you sure? This is me, Spike. Are you sure?"

Later that same day, November 7, the announcement was made.

Magic never changed. Just this past school year, he called me and said, "Spike, I'm going to be in New York, and I want you to pick a high school for me to go and talk to the young people."

I said, "Just give me a date, Magic. Let's just go across the street to Brooklyn Tech."

Several weeks later he spent two hours just talking to the kids, at a special assembly that they held. Those kids were asking some rough questions, but he answered them all truthfully. He's got courage. I know some people would have committed suicide rather than face the world admitting they were HIV positive, facing the fact that it might blow up into AIDS.

It's funny how things work out, because athletes who weren't being careful about their sexual habits were careful for like a month after Magic's announcement, but then they just forgot about it, blocked it out of their minds, maybe said, "Hey, Magic looks fine to me," went back to doing whatever they were doing. And for NBA stars, there is a whole lot available for them to do in that particular arena. Nearly anything they can think of, probably, and stuff they hadn't. Now I don't know if you can say today's athletes are any more careful now than before Magic came out. But it's not just the athletes—unprotected sex is on the rise in the gay population too. I guess some people don't give a damn anymore, gonna go out and have some fun. Makes no sense to me.

After Magic made his announcement, he came back for both the 1992 All-Star Game, and then the 1992 Olympic team, the first U.S. basketball team to feature NBA players—the Dream Team. And there were some problems with that. Karl Malone was on the Dream Team. They had a training period where they played several exhibition games before they went over to Spain, and Karl didn't say anything. Then when Magic decided he wanted to play, if allowed, and was allowed, Karl said, Oh, hell, no, I'd rather you not—or words to that effect. If he felt that way, while I respect it, he should have said so earlier, but maybe he thought it was more than the Olympics, that Magic was going to come back and play in the regular season, which Magic eventually did do, three seasons later.

I hope Magic stays retired now. You know, people think only of coke, heroin, and nicotine as drugs, but fame can be a drug too. The roar of the crowd, being the focus can be a drug. Being in the spotlight 24-7 can be a drug. Some people become junkies for it; they can't go cold turkey because they have withdrawal symptoms. Magic is a good friend, and I'm just being honest. I feel that if Jordan had not come back late in the 1994–95 season, Magic would have stayed retired. Seeing Mike come back and do what he did, at that level, Magic couldn't help but wonder and then believe that he could do it too. I remember the emotional 1992 All-Star Game, held at the O-rena in Orlando, when Magic came back, and then at the end of the game, he took on Isiah and Michael, and then hit a three-pointer on the last shot of the All-Star Game, as the West won, 153–113. That should have been the last shot Magic ever took in the NBA. I know he thinks he took Jordan then, but if you asked Michael, he would tell you that on his last defensive stand against Magic

Johnson in that All-Star Game, he didn't bear down. He took one for Magic that time.

Magic came back during the 1995–96 season to the Lakers and people got all het up. I think Magic is more than a player to Jerry West, the Lakers' general manager, and to Dr. Jerry Buss, the principal owner. I think he's family to them, and sometimes it's hard to tell somebody in your family things that they don't want to hear. But the other players on the Laker team were just that—players. I don't know if anybody on the team welcomed Magic like family. I heard things weren't all peachy-keen between Magic and Nick Van Exel. The team chemistry was messed up because they had Magic at strong forward, but he didn't choose to play strong forward. He wanted to play up top, but then where do you put Nicky? To Del Harris, it probably made no difference if he was strong or not, how are you going to tell an icon like Magic what to do? It was rough. Magic has a great wife, Cookie, and children, his businesses are thriving. His theater complex at the foot of Baldwin Hills is one of the biggest grossers in the United States, and he just opened another in Atlanta, so he has things to occupy his time favorably. What I admire about Magic is that he's one of the few athletes with an acute business sense and he is always thinking along those lines. More athletes, black and white, can learn how to use the game, after the Game has gotten all it can from them.

In the summer of 1992, after the Knicks went 51–31, bum-rushed the Pistons in five games, before going the limit with the Bulls in the Eastern Conference semifinals when Jordan lit us up for 42 at Chicago Stadium, I was fortunate enough to go to Barcelona as a guest of NBC for the Summer Olympics. There weren't enough hotels for the crush of people in Spain, so the Olympic organizing committee brought in these luxury-liner cruise ships and docked them in port, right on the blue waters of the Mediterranean, and that was where I stayed.

I checked in, walked down the gangplank of the ocean liner, and soon was checking out all the angles on the architecture from the cobblestones of Barcelona—hangin' with the Castilians. I found out where the

Dream Team was staying, at a posh hotel, separate from the Olympic Village. They had so many guards in and around that place you wouldn't believe it. There was also a big stink about the fact that the Dream Team was staying apart from the rest of the Olympians.

So I went up to the hotel, went in, to the closed door of a private dining room, and boldly said, "I'm here to see Magic, I'm here to see Patrick, I'm here to see Charles Barkley. I'm here to see Michael Jordan," and the guard finally said, "All'dright, all'dright!" and he let me up in there. The players were eating dinner together at the time, so I went from table to table, and I was happy that most of them seemed pleased or at least surprised to see me. "What's up, Spike? Whatup?"

Then I saw Bird. He was sitting with Malone, off to one side, at a table. A couple of years before this, Karl had been going around with an FBI baseball cap on, and I really assumed he was oblivious to the politics of this and so I faxed him a note, trying to give him the background and history of the FBI in relation to Dr. King, Malcolm X, and countless others, and offered that he should think twice before wearing that hat. By wearing that hat while doing interviews that would be seen the world over—that was not smart. Karl was really promoting it. J. Edgar Hoover and his FBI were no friend to African-Americans, no friend to the civil rights movement. *Mississippi Burning* did not get it right—frankly, that film was a lie. So I wrote to Karl: "Karl, if you only knew, you wouldn't wear that hat. . . ."

Karl faxed me back saying, "I collect hats, nobody in the world tells me what to do, I can wear any damn hat I want to." And he had a couple of points there in his favor, too.

We already know my history with Larry Bird.

So anyway, there both of them were, at one table. But you know me, I'm going to say hello, so I walked over. They looked up and they were not smiling. I just said, "How are you, Larry? You, Karl? My name's Spike. Glad to see you." They spoke back, I said good luck, meant it, and that was that. I went on to the next table.

Karl Malone is a great ballplayer. By the time of the next Olympics in Atlanta, in 1996, I saw him again. Same situation. Different location. Again, I was "What's up, Karl?"

This time Karl was much more engaging: "What's up, Spike?"

So I said, "We made some serious moves, Karl. The Knicks are going for it."

Karl said, "Yeah, but how did you get around that salary cap? Come on, Spike, they need to check out that salary cap situation in New York."

I said, "Look, Karl, the league needs a winner in New York."

"You know, you're right, Spike," Karl admitted.

Back in Barcelona, later the same evening that I stormed the dining hall of the Dream Team, I sat up and watched Magic, Barkley, and Jordan play cards all night long in the lounge. I don't know what game they were playing—I'm not a cards guy. Might have been poker, but whatever it was, the cards were being slapped down with force and they were calling each other names not meant for all ears. I learned then that "bitches" and "hoes" can come in all genders. They called each other more names and talked more noise than they ever do out on the court. I just sat there and listened and laughed and had myself the best time. As for the card games, I don't know who won the most. They all won some, they all lost some. But for me, it was the greatest feeling. Nobody else was there, and they felt comfortable enough to have me there and didn't change at all. It was like I *wasn't* there, just three brothers playing cards, signifying, selling wolf tickets—your mama this, your game is weak that, what about this dunk I did in your face—all the while slamming cards down on the table. Barkley got beat up the most verbally, because he hadn't won any rings—he had no comeback for that. I wished I could have videotaped this scene, but they never would have let me do it, and even if I had, the camera being there would have changed their behavior.

Barkley had been traded to Phoenix from Philly. The Suns would make the NBA finals against the Bulls and Jordan at the end of the upcoming season, where they would go out in six tough games. The Bulls won it on Phoenix's home court in game six. And Phoenix had a shot at the game too. Dan Majerle had a good look from the right baseline at the end of the game, but he thought about Jordan and pulled the string on the shot, and it was off; John Paxson hit the game-clincher in the Bulls' first two NBA title-winning games, because the good defense is not going to let Jordan beat it in the clutch; it is going to trap and double him, and then rotate, and the Bulls will swing the ball, and the last man down gets the good look. And the defense forces that to be Paxson, or, before him, Craig Hodges, or after Hodges and Paxson, Kukoc, Steve Kerr.

At that time, the summer of '92 in Barcelona, Magic had won his five rings and was now fighting another battle. Jordan let them know that it was his time now. That was Mike's attitude the whole time. Yeah, Magic, you were great, and I feel for you, Charles, but you *do* know I'm the one in charge now. Pharaonic. And they tried to give him some back, but you know, now that I think back on it, I think Michael was the most convincing one, even at the time.

Charles Barkley has to be the funniest and craziest player in the league. Whatever he thinks, he says. Not all of it is intelligent, but it's honest. During the Olympics, the United States played Angola, and Charles elbowed an Angolan player—actually it was mostly show, not nearly as bad as the media played it, probably scared the Angolan player more than anything. Asked why he did it, Charles snapped, "Well, he might have pulled a spear on me." The first thing I thought was Mr. Barkley had seen one too many *Tarzan* movies, thought all Africans were ignorant savages in grass skirts with bones through their noses, but then I thought that maybe I was not giving Charles enough credit for his satirical slant. It was either that or a totally ignorant statement, but I gotta admit, I laughed when I heard it, so maybe Charles knows what he's doing.

I didn't get back to the cruise ship until the first streaks of dawn began to run a fast break across the sea. Little did any of us know that by that same time next year it would be Jordan, the winner of three straight NBA titles by then, who would be retiring from the Game, suffering a tragedy of his own, the seemingly senseless murder of his father.

I had known basketball was going global just by watching who was coming into the NBA. Longley from Australia. Schrempf from Germany, who played like he didn't know how good he really was, like some brilliant white sax player jamming a set with the brothers, with great talent, but not wanting to intrude. All he was missing was Bird's mentality.

Dino Radja, Vlade Divac, Kukoc, the late Drazen Petrovic, Sasha Danilovic, all from the former Yugoslavia; Dikembe Mutombo from Zaire and Hakeem Olajuwon from Nigeria; and Oscar Schmidt of Brazil. I knew basketball was a world game when I went to Barcelona. And Magic was getting more hype over there than Jordan was. *Ma-gic! Ma-gic!* The world knew them all. One player had his picture taken during the game while the ball was in motion; he gestured for his friend to take a picture with him with the ball, and Magic guarding him. None of the people expected the United States to lose; it was more like they were going to the Louvre of hoop, to see the way the great artists painted. It was fun seeing Charles Barkley walk down the streets. He was one of the few who went outside the hotel and just walked around. Magic and Michael couldn't have done that. They would have been immobilized, mobbed by the crush of people. But Barkley would walk down the piazza at night, totally at ease. Sir Charles has a lot of politician in him, but, despite his stated wishes, he won't win the governor's seat in his home state of Alabama.

One night in Barcelona, *Sports Illustrated* gave a party, and I went and found John Havlicek was there. I ended up spending a good two or three hours with Hondo. I'm not going to lie. I used to hate him. I hated him because I hated the Celtics. But then I found out Havlicek was really a beautiful person—warm, engaging, outgoing, very talkative, intelligent. We talked about all kinds of things—basketball, movies, the Knicks, the Celtics, Michael Jordan. I learned a lot in talking to the man. He plays a lot of golf now, and fishes. I could tell that the competitive fire in him is not fully banked, probably never will be. Sometimes he plays golf up on Martha's Vineyard. My summer place on the island is on the eighteenth hole, so I told him the next time I saw him playing golf, I would join him. Not that I play. I just liked John a lot, after hating him from afar all those years. Some people probably say the same about me. At the end of a game, if you were a Knicks fan, you did not want to see Havlicek with the rock. With the game on the line you did not want him and Cowens working the two-game. You didn't want West of the Lakers to have it, either. Both made many killer shots against the Knicks, stabbing me all up in my heart.

But respecting Havlicek doesn't change the way I feel about Boston. Having Boston win was galling. Historically, African-Americans know how hard it is on black people in Boston. That bus being turned over with black children in it during the busing protests up there, it's still etched in the psyches of many African-Americans who are old enough to remember that. And they were very late in baseball, the Boston Red Sox nearly got to the '60s without black players until they signed Pumpsie Green right at 1960—last team in the major leagues not to have any African-American players. And this was the team that gave Jackie Robinson a fake tryout at Fenway Park in 1945—until somebody yelled, "Get that nigger off the field." So the Celtics and the Red Sox, in playing to their fan base—it's amazing how they could try to have so many white players. I don't know if that's real or not—the selling of the Green—it just seemed like the Celtics went out of their way to get the white boys. I mean went *all* out of their way. Not all of them could play. I had special dislike for Havlicek, Bird, Cowens, McHale, and Ainge because I knew they could hurt us. But I didn't care for Larry Siegfried, all-time hatchet man Jim Luscatoff, Bailey Howell, Don Nelson, Henry Finkel, Brad Lohaus, Fred Roberts, Jerry Sichting, Greg Kite. I thought I'd have a heart attack later, seeing Lohaus and Kite in Knicks uniforms. M. L. Carr, the towel-waving head cheerleader during his playing days—how did *he* get the job as general manager and coach of the Celtics? Hope they keep him around for twenty years. He must really have the white folks fooled.

At the same time, even with this history, meeting Havlicek was like this breath of fresh air. He was open and honest, with no little tinge of rancor. He didn't ask me, "Why are you so angry?" That is a typical greeting, especially pertaining to my films. Usually I don't respond anymore to such inquiries. Earlier in my career I sometimes wanted to ask back, "When you look at my films, is that all you can see? Anger? Nothing else? Nothing else at all?" But now usually I say nothing. With Hondo Havlicek, he was just very open, easygoing—confident, as if to say he had no problem with himself, therefore he had no problem with me.

> > >

Filming *Malcolm X* took us to three continents. The film was released after the NBA regular season started. I'd never gotten such press for a movie. *Esquire* ran a cover article with the dubious title "Spike Lee Hates Your Cracker Ass," with my arms folded into a skull-and-crossbones effect, which is one of the all-time misrepresentative manipulations, and it depressed me for days on end. *Malcolm X* hit theaters at the same time as *Home Alone II, The Bodyguard,* and Francis Coppola's *Bram Stoker's Dracula.* Once you put together a body of work, people like to ask what is your favorite film. If you ask a parent, which is your favorite child, the parent cannot choose. Well, at least not on the record. Similarly, I love all ten of the films I've made. I love them all the same. Proud of them all. But some have been more fully realized, closer to what we set out to see. The realization of the idea from page to screen was probably more accomplished in *Do The Right Thing* and *Malcolm X.*

While *Malcolm X* was hitting the screen, the Knicks were hitting, too. It was a productive season for us all. The Knicks went 60–22 in 1992–93, with Ewing averaging 24.2 a game, Starks, 17.5, Charles Smith 12.4, Mason 10.3, and Rolando Blackman, a tall scoring guard from Grady High in Brooklyn, whom we'd gotten from Dallas late in his career, averaging 9.7 points, even though he was thirty-four. Doc Rivers, the point guard, averaged 7.8. It wasn't quite the beautiful breakdown we'd had in 1969–70. If you stopped Ewing and Starks, you could stop the Knicks, but Riley had the rotation down and most nights they played well. The Knicks won 39 of their last 47 games, 24 of the last 28, 9 of the last 10, and the last 5 in a row going into the playoffs. Riley had them running liked a well-oiled machine.

The playoffs of 1992–93 began. I had a new seatmate, whom I will return to in one moment. We played Indiana, best three out of five. Reggie Miller had 32 in game one, 36 in game three, and 33 in game four. He gave Starks the blues. But we had them well in hand. The Charlotte Hornets were next on our list, and we crushed them four games to one. Alonzo Mourning had hit a clutch jumper from the top of the key to win their first and only playoff series against the aging Celtics, and then they faced us. Alonzo, small for a center at 6-9, cannot be questioned on effort. The Hornets won a double-overtime game in Charlotte. Other than that—not on our level.

Ewing averaged 31 points a game, and they were dismissed in five.

Now came the Bulls and Jordan. We jumped on 'em. To the surprise of nearly everyone, we jumped on 'em right away. The first two games were at the Garden, and we won both, and that was as near as I've come to the hoop heaven of '70 or '73 in all the years since. Starks was great in game one, with 25 points, and he helped hold Jordan to 27. That's some holding, right there. The Knicks won, 98–90. Then two nights later we won again, 96–91, as Ewing had 26 and Oakley controlled the boards with 16. We had them. Starks was playing out of mind. Couldn't have played any better. That was the warning sign that everyone—including me—ignored in our bliss. Jordan hadn't played his best.

I was courtside in Chicago for games three and four. Now they jumped on us in game three. The Bulls were the two-time defending champion and their pride had been stung badly. Phil was jockeying with the media and the refs. That was the game we should have gone for, but Chicago was too good to think about sweeping—hard enough to think of a way to beat them, to take one more game than they take off you. Starks couldn't maintain. You have games like that. Like game six in 1973. You can't keep playing way over your head every single night. So the Bulls won that game in the first few minutes and coasted to a 103–83 win.

Game four was Jordan's showcase. Starks had 24 points, played well for a mortal man. Jordan was Jordan; he scored 54. The Bulls won 105–95. Then we came back to the Garden for game five. There is a period in a high-level game between relatively evenly matched opponents, when everyone is playing at optimum, championship level, where the point differential that is being maintained is true. You can watch a team maintaining a 3-, 5-, or 7-point lead for long stretches, down to one, back to three, up to five, back to three—and that point differential is really the differential between the teams. This is what happened in game five. The Bulls stayed one and three and five points out of our reach, and won 97–94. Jordan had 29. Patrick Ewing had 33 and gave it his all. The key play was when 6-10 Charles Smith had an offensive rebound right under the basket, at the Seventh Avenue end, and then he pump-faked, pump-faked, pump-faked, and Pippen waited patiently and then blocked his shot. Starks averaged 15.2 for the series, while Jordan averaged 32.2 for the series. Hard to overcome. They closed us out at home in Chicago on June 4, 96–88, with me sitting there. That was when Scottie Pippen and I had words.

It was the third straight year that we had lost to the Bulls in the play-offs, the fourth time in the last five seasons. We played them until June this time. They went on to beat the Suns in six games for the NBA title. Jordan and the Bulls were three-time defending champions, and now they were in a league with Russell's Celtics and Mikan's Lakers. Nobody else had won three in a row. Then everything seemed to happen at once. Michael asked Phil Jackson if there was anything more in the game he could do. Phil had to think about that one. He said, "No, not really." Bad move, Phil. And so, incredibly, Jordan retired from basketball. The murder of his father had a lot to do with it, that and being constantly in the limelight. He can't go out in public without being mobbed. Not once he'd won his third ring. There were allegations about gambling. His father had been murdered. Even the High Pharaoh needs a getaway now and then.

It was still shocking, and all any fan could talk about. First you were sad to see Jordan go, and then you were glad if you were the fan of a contender, because now you had a chance.

I shot a Nike commercial with Jordan and baseball greats Stan Musial, Willie Mays, Ken Griffey Jr., and Bill Buckner. They all said, "He's trying," as Michael runs around on the baseball field. The owner of the Chicago Bulls, Jerry Reinsdorf, also owns the Chicago White Sox of the American League. Michael had taken swings in a White Sox uniform and hit the ball hard in exhibitions before games at Comiskey Park. And there is no greater anonymity than that of a minor league baseball player. So he switched sports. Really, it was incredible, baseball being what it is, another game of skill, but completely different skills from basketball, for the most part, yet Michael took it on and tried to sink into whatever level of anonymity he could enjoy.

Meanwhile, my sister and brother had brought me the makings of *Crooklyn.* I also know what it's like to lose a parent. But I had long ago dealt with the grief of my loss. And so we set about the beginnings of making that film, and I waited on the upcoming basketball season with high hopes in a number of different areas. It was an exciting time to be a Knicks fan. I had my seats on the floor—best seats in the house. With Jordan retired, the Knicks had a real shot. We won sixty games the previous regular season, not to be taken lightly. Jordan did us in six games again, but it was a war. Now Michael was gone from the scene for the 1993–94 season. Grant Hill my ass. It would take him years to get there, if he could. It was our turn. Patrick's turn. But he needed more help than Jordan did. We had it set out for him. With Riley, Mason, Patrick, Oakley, Starks, and Derek Harper, the point guard we'd gotten from Dallas, we had a shot. Jordan had denied us. We'd gone 60–22, then put three arrows in him in the playoffs, along with the mental burden of the gambling stories and veiled accusations just as we took them on in the playoffs. And still he rose. And still he stood. And still he denied us. What a ballplayer. But now he was gone. Now we could win the NBA title, just like back in the day, in 1969–70, when we were for one moment great.

But on the rare occasion when I walked into the Garden up top, where the box office is, I noticed the pillars with nameplates of the greats of the past—Cousy, Oscar, Mikan, Ali, but there was something different about the place, and it wasn't just my age. Something was changed now, something beyond the seat colors. No longer were they of a rainbow shade, cascading down in all those colors. Now there were only two colors. Turquoise high, purple low. Now it was just expensive and more expensive. I didn't see many young people like I had been at the games. I thought about that. These were getting to be desperate times for a lot of people, and I'm not talking about crack and heroin addicts. People were having trouble making ends meet in general. And it was almost like I was representing the working class at courtside. I was a kid from the blue seats who had gotten a break and who now sat courtside. Money changes everything.

The two greatest Knicks fans are Fred Klein and Stan Asofsky. They have sat side by side, season ticket holders since 1959 back in the old Garden. "The flavor, the aroma came out of the marquee. You had Nedick's and the Murphy bar across the street. We always met before the game under the marquee. In the old Garden I felt every sound, every texture. The new Garden is too businesslike, it's too preppy, it's too tweedy. The old Garden was immersed in the freshness and the flourishing of what I call New York City basketball," remembers Stan Asofsky. His partner Fred Klein adds, "The fans in the old Garden were more knowledgeable. Today it's more of a corporate rich-crap thing. I'm not partial to these fans; they're fair-weather fans. The minute they go bad, most of the people you'll never see again. I also think 90 percent of this is money. People want to be seen here, so they come."

Down through the years, since my childhood in Brooklyn, through the last dozen years, since I got season tickets to the Knicks, I've taken many different people to the games. Earl Smith, my high school buddy, was one of the regulars. Earl knew hoop talent and I knew Earl. Later, when I began the 40 Acres Basketball Camp in Brooklyn, I saw Earl would be the perfect person to oversee it. You have to go to the run with somebody, best case scenario. That's why I had gotten two season tickets in the first place. What's the use in seeing something amazing if you can't turn to somebody you like, respect, care about, and say, "Did you see that? Do you believe it?"

> > >

I met Tonya Lewis in late September of 1992, in Washington, D.C., during the Congressional Black Caucus's annual legislative weekend. We were at the Washington Hilton Hotel, attending their dinner. As fate would have it, both of us got up from our tables to freshen up and, in my case, to relieve the burden on my kidneys. If I hadn't had to answer the call at that moment, we might have never met. Later, Tonya told me that she decided to go to the event at the last instant. She attended the dinner with her sister Tracey, and as Tonya got up from the table, Tracey said, "Hey, Tonya, go bump into Spike Lee." Tonya laughed it off, but somehow we intersected in the middle of the room. She says my mouth dropped open. I don't remember that, but I was taken aback by her drop-dead beauty. Blazing red hair, and freckles too. At first, I thought she was a waitress because she had on a black-and-white outfit, but I quickly regained my senses—or some of them.

"Hello."

"Hello."

Hellooooo.

That was it until the end of the evening. As I was leaving, going down the escalator, only thinking of her, she appeared again, going up the escalator. We shared a big smile. When I reached the bottom, I did a quick about-face and raced back up to find her. Took a while, but I tracked her down. Tonya says I started doing a jig on one leg. I don't remember that, either. What I recall is blabbing questions like "Are you married?" and "Do you have a boyfriend?" When Tonya answered no to both, well, maybe I did start to dance a little bit then. I asked for her number and promised I'd call her. At the time, she was working as a lawyer at a D.C. firm. She'd gone to Sarah Lawrence and to the University of Virginia Law School. I called her the very next morning and asked her when she was coming to New York. Next thing I know, I'm taking her to the run.

I took Tonya to a game as soon as the 1992–93 season started. She was excited. She had seen me courtside on TV but never had the great opportunity to see the Knicks play at the Garden, especially not from this close. Where my seats are located is where the guys take the ball out on certain side inbounds plays. Big sweaty poo-butts, all up in ya face. I had never noticed ambivalence about their proximity in me before. So we'd go to the game and I would tell Tonya, "I'll be calm tonight, I'm on good behavior." Five minutes later I'm jumping up and down and Tonya looks at me, looking like "You're going crazy!" But it was a bad call, baby, c'mon, I had to say something.

"*I do.*" I said it, she said it, we said it, exchanging vows at the Riverside Church in Harlem on October 3, 1993, with Tonya standing beside me. There were plenty of witnesses, too. Denzel was there, Patrick Ewing, Coach Thompson, and maybe a couple or three hundred more invitees. The Boys Choir of Harlem and Stevie Wonder sang. It was a very big wedding. Bunches of folks. Looking over at Tonya, I saw immediately why I said I do. I had stumbled upon this intelligent, conscious, beautiful soul mate. Tonya possesses all the right qualities. When I later found out she liked sports, especially basketball, well, then of course I had to marry her. Now we were one.

My friends were happy for me—some were sad, although for selfish motives. They knew they wouldn't be going to games with me anymore. That seat was now taken. That seat was now Tonya's. Until this day, she is convinced that I was ready to get married, that I was of the mind-set, that I was on the prowl. It's not true. I was enjoying dating. She just hit me like a ton of bricks. Tonya also says I never proposed properly to her. She says all I said was "When are we getting married?" and said it very quickly too. Now on that, she is telling the truth. Frankly, I was scared to death and could hardly get the words out. Why was I scared? I was terrified she would say, "*Hell* no!" Or even worse, laugh at me. So therefore my proposal was unromantic. Unlike my maternal grandfather's proposal. Richard Jackson Shelton, for whom I am named. Here's how my grandmother Zimmie recalls the first time they met.

"Well, Spike, your grandfather was a senior at Morehouse College, and I was a freshman at Spelman College. The occasion was a play in Howe Chapel on Spelman's campus.

"We were all standing, Spelman women and Morehouse men, standing on the stairway waiting for the doors to open so we could get in before the play started. I felt someone pulling on my dress. And of course I didn't pay any attention to it, because I just thought we were all standing there waiting to get in, and then when my dress was pulled again, I said, 'We all want to get in there—you can wait just like the rest of us!' The third time, I turned around and looked, very vexed. 'Are you trying to speak to me?' I said.

"'Yes,' your grandfather replied. 'What's your name?'

"I said, 'Does it make any difference to you?'

"He said, 'Yes, it makes a difference to me, because I've been looking for you for two thousand years, and I'm going to marry you.'

"Spike, I was *so* embarrassed. Who was this crazy man? I had never seen him before in my life. We got married right after I graduated."

> > >

In 1992–93, the Knicks were good. But in 1993–94 they were inspirational. Getting to the NBA finals in the 1993–94 season, in the late spring of 1994, was no walk in the park, despite the absence of Jordan.

Michael was out of ball, and it looked to me as if it would come down to teams led by mature superstars who'd been, for lack of a better word, bridesmaids behind Michael, after he paid his dues against the Celtics (I remember when he scored 63 in a playoff game at Boston Garden in '87 and Larry Bird had said he wasn't a human being but "God disguised as Michael Jordan"), and then against the Pistons of Thomas, Dumars, Rodman, John Salley, and Vinnie Johnson from Brooklyn. Michael had been in control, winning the World Championship three straight years and blowing up further at the 1992 Olympics. But now Michael was chasing a curve with a baseball bat somewhere down in the bush leagues, and it came down now to Hakeem Olajuwon in Houston, Charles Barkley in Phoenix, Patrick Ewing in New York, and Reggie Miller in Indiana. I liked our chances.

The Knicks met the Pacers in the Eastern Conference finals of the 1993–94 playoffs. I was feeling great. It was, like, fate. Jordan was retired. The job was simple. We had beaten the Bulls in seven games when Pippen fouled Hubie Davis on a three-point try. As the clock went to 00:00, I ran to midcourt, jumping up and down. Tonya says I was a maniac. Maybe I was for a minute there. The mighty Bulls were dead and gone and outta here. Of course, some people said it wasn't the same without Jordan, but I couldn't help who they put in front of us. Now the job was to beat Indiana. Then beat whoever came out of the West—it looked like it would be Phoenix at the time, after the Suns and Barkley won the first two games of the Western Conference finals on the road at the Summit in Houston. And after we beat Indiana and then Phoenix, we'd be in there. Tonya was pregnant with Satchel. Her birth would make it complete. Everything was lined up perfectly.

Indiana's Larry Brown is a great coach; by now that has been established. Besides his college credentials, he had coached the Carolina Cougars of the ABA to a 104–64 record in two seasons, 1973 and 1974. Then he coached the Denver Nuggets to a strikingly excellent 241–124 combined record in five years, in David Thompson's heyday. Then, in 1981–82, he went 44–38 with the New Jersey Nets. That is hard to do. Coach Brown's teams won 55 games one year and 56 the next in San Antonio, in David Robinson's youth, in 1989–90 and 1990–91. Brown coached the lowly L.A. Clippers, going 41–41 in 1992–93, and was actually 64–53 overall as the Clippers' coach—the only coach ever to leave the Clippers with a winning percentage over .500. All this before landing in Indiana for the 1993–94 season. But he was bringing in a team I thought we should beat.

The Pacers' star was a willowy 6-7 shooter named Reggie Miller, out of UCLA. Had been in the league seven years at the time. Reggie couldn't dominate the boards like Barkley, or on D like Jordan. But Reggie Miller could score with anybody. This we found out.

The series was tied at two games apiece going into game five at the Garden. At that time, we were starting Oakley and 6-10 Charles Smith up front, Patrick in the middle, and Derek Harper and Starks at guard, bringing Mase, Hubert Davis, and Greg Anthony off the bench, and sometimes Herb Williams. It was a solid eight-man rotation, defensive-minded. Ro Blackman was not in the rotation, but still on the roster, had been one of the best scorers in the league. He was 6-6. He'd lost a step but hadn't lost his stroke. The stroke is the last thing to go. Calvin Murphy is somewhere demonstrating his free throw proficiency or dropping j's in his street clothes even as we speak, probably. But Pat preferred to play fresh, younger legs. Riley seemed to have all the ducks in a row. It seemed to me many fans in the Garden might as well have been at Tavern on the Green or Elaine's. It was now the chichi thing to do—go see the Knicks and be seen.

"It becomes prohibitive, the ticket prices," said Bill Bradley. "The people that come to the arena now are like a studio audience; they are going to be part of the show."

We jumped on them, 28–16 in the first quarter and led at halftime, 43–35. Starks and Hubert Davis were doing a good job on Miller, and Patrick was on that day—10 of 15 from the field, 29 points. This was the swing game, game five. At the beginning of the fourth quarter, the Knicks led, 70–58, and there was no way for the Pacers to come back, not against our defense. I began to get on Reggie, just a little, like a normal fan, as blue-seaters can be called. It gave him something else to concentrate on, and quite by accident, I found myself to be too correct.

Reggie Miller's fourth quarter started with the Pacers putting a team of center LaSalle Thompson, forward Dale Davis, a monster on D and the boards, a nonentity named Kenny Williams, a backup point guard, not a starter but a New York ballplayer named Vern Fleming.

The quarter started with Reggie hitting a three-point j over Hubert. It wasn't Hubert's fault. It seemed as if Reggie had let fly as soon as he crossed half-court. All net. Knicks by nine.

At this time I was still having fun. I shouted to the Knicks guards to touch him, find Reggie, stay up on him. Stay up on him and make him put it on the floor. He wasn't going to beat us by driving to the basket. At this point I was unconcerned, especially with Riley sending in Starks to replace Hubert Davis. There was no way for Reggie to beat us all. With 10:23 left, the Pacers ran Reggie off some screens and he caught and turned and fired all in one motion, from 24 feet away. *Rip.* Uh-oh. He was getting warm: 72–64, Knicks. I turned to Tonya and said, "Are we in trouble here?" Greg Anthony is a good athlete, good defensive player, but until this time he had not shown much O. He was in the game now, made a steal, and then threw the ball away. I shot up out of my seat, said not a word. Coach Brown shot up off the Pacers' bench at the same time, screaming instructions. Miller mid-range j: 72–68. Riley got Harper and Charles Smith back in there. It made no difference. Miller, off a creative set designed by Brown to get him free, Starks struggling through the screen, the screen is moving! Moving screen! Neither Joe Crawford nor Jack Madden paid me any attention. Reggie from the corner. *Swish:* 72–70.

"He got hot," Starks told me later. "Hubert was on him at the beginning of the quarter, and then all of a sudden he exploded, he went off. I couldn't believe it, because I was in his face the majority of the time. When a player gets hot in this league . . ."

Ewing lost the ball. Workman hit two free throws to tie the game at 72, Thompson made a steal, Reggie on a breakaway, pulled up a good 3 feet behind the 3-point arc. He let fly, then turned and looked directly in my face as the ball split the net. His third 3-pointer of the period, with 7:40 left in the game, made it 75–72, Indiana. With every shot after that, Reggie was looking at me, going, "Yeah! Yeah!" I got caught up. I yelled back. And the Garden fans and everybody in a national TV audience saw. It was like Reggie was playing me as well as the Knicks. He pointed at me. He gestured. I pointed back at him. His nostrils flared. "Let's get on this guy!" I screamed.

Larry Brown was calm as the Pacers gathered around him. He seemed to be having fun. This was not his first group out there, except Davis and Reggie, but they were on a roll, so he broke his rotation and let them stay. Offensively, the game was in Reggie's hands now, and that's where Brown wanted it. It was their only way. The Knicks defense was impenetrable, but Reggie didn't have to penetrate. He could bomb from deep. Reggie had made a 12-point Knicks lead evaporate in a scant four minutes and twenty seconds. The Knicks came back out, but now Reggie was unconscious, zoned, locked in, and I was in the middle of his bombsight. At 6:59, another 3 from deep, off a triple-screen. Reggie came back down the court pointing at his chest, with a De Niroesque scowl leveled directly at me. I stood straight up. "Get *up* on this guy, willya! Come *on*!" At 5:52, Reggie hit his fifth 3-pointer of the fourth quarter on a pass from Dale Davis and a screen from Thompson, giving Indiana an 8-point lead, 81–73, and as Riley called a twenty-second time-out, Reggie gestured at me as he sauntered back to the Indiana bench.

You could have fried an egg on my forehead. Marv Albert, by now the national announcer for NBC, was saying on the air that I was not part of the game and that I "should realize that." Marv, you're from Brooklyn too. What, you want me to just sit here? At 500 bananas a pop? What on earth did I have to do with Reggie setting an NBA playoff record with five 3-pointers in a quarter? And there was still 5:52 left! I was into it now, exhorting the Knicks to come back and make Reggie pay. The Knicks did claw back into it, scoring the next 6 to cut the lead to 2.

But as soon as the defense's eyes left Reggie Miller, there he was again, getting a good look at it, from 19 feet away, all net, barely even disturbing the net, with 2:45 left. Then, as Oakley stepped out to try to double Reggie on the next trip, Dale Davis went backdoor for a pillar-crashing lob-slam that seemed to be right on top of my head. Reggie hit two free throws with 2:25 left, making it 87–79. The Pacers played the passing lanes, doubled Patrick at every turn, and the Knicks tried to force it in there to him and were unsuccessful at it, and we were reduced to fouling. Workman hit two free throws with 42.5 seconds left, and then a triumphant Reggie hit two more free throws after a hard foul by Oakley with 21.1 seconds left, giving Indiana a 10-point lead, 93–83. After Oakley fouled, Reggie's eyes found mine. And all eyes at the Garden followed his. They knew where he was looking. Reggie gesticulated. I gesticulated back. There was nothing to be done—not by me. I might as well have been catatonic as Patrick hit a meaningless three with 2.3 seconds left.

Then it was over, and Reggie Miller, Larry Brown, and the rest of them were running off the floor, through the dark square passageway. The Knicks had lost. Miller scored 25 fourth-quarter points—*the twelve-minute equivalent of a 100-point game,* including a playoff record five threes, to give Indiana a game five win over the Knicks at the Garden, putting the Pacers up three games to two, with the chance to close us out two days later at Market Square Arena in Indy.

"I've seen guys go off, have big quarters, but not under those circumstances," Larry Brown would tell me later. "A game that was that important to a franchise, against a superior defensive team like the Knicks were then and, most importantly, Spike, with the people we had on the floor at the time. LaSalle Thompson was at center. He'd been injured and had barely played that whole year. He was no offensive threat at all. We had Kenny Williams out there, and also Heywoode Workman for defense. And I never saw anything like it. I just sat there and became a spectator."

Did Coach Brown notice that I was dying over there? "I was too busy coaching," he said. "I didn't realize it until I saw you bury your head at the end. Everybody blamed you, Spike. And it was good to see somebody else get blamed for a change."

Reggie had snatched my heart out of body, then capped on me on top of that. Marv Albert said I had to realize I was not part of the game. Reggie made me part of it, then left me lying there. Until the next game. Game six, two days away, on Friday, at Market Square Arena in Indianapolis. If anything was left of me by then after the scavengers finished picking at me. "Spike Lee lost the game, he got Reggie pissed off."

Those were the words of Madison Square Garden President Bob Gutkowski. "Spike definitely said something that set him off. I'm not sure what it was, but Reggie sure took us on a ride after that," said Indiana Pacer Antonio Davis. "Sometimes [Spike Lee] opens his mouth a little too much and gets the other guys going. Tonight was one of those nights," added Reggie Miller.

Reggie had played it—and me—like a Stradivarius. He stared at me and gave the choke sign, his hand around his throat, then moved his hands to his privates. That's when it got ugly up in there. He was like a rabid dog and had to be restrained by his teammates. He ran off the court yelling, "Chokers! Chokers!" He had finished with 39 points, several disrespectful gestures. And he also should have sent out some nice Christmas cards to the refs that year. I don't know if I've ever been so inconsolable on the one hand, livid on the other, that Reggie had brought me into it and then done what he did. I took it personally. It was heat of battle. At the time it was hard not to take it personally. He focused on me. It was between the brothers. Later, he apologized. It can happen, between teammates—or brothers. Oakley and Starks are always going at it, and it seems they are always yelling at each other on the court. Yet Starks waves it off. "Oh, naw, that's going to happen in a family, especially when you're trying to accomplish something together," he says.

At other times, this byplay is fun, like two years before, whenever Michael Jordan hit a couple of shots, he looked at me and said, "Uh-oh, I'm getting warm, Spike. Uh-oh, I'm getting hot now." Or when he starts hitting shots and then he looks over and I turn and look the other way. All that makes the game more exciting. I remember the last good year Mark Price, the Cleveland point guard, had. He was having a terrible game. They were warming up for the second half; I'm reading the stat sheet. Loud. "Mark Price. Two-for-ten, five turnovers." He came over, started to laugh. Hmm, Mark, do we have a chill tonight? Are we coming down with something? In that third quarter, he must have hit five deep bombs in a row, one of them right in front of me. The ball went in with a rip of nylon, and just as it did, he turned and pulled my baseball cap down over my eyes. That stuff is good-natured. The only times I thought it wasn't were the times involving Scottie and the Reggie thing. I know it intensifies in the playoffs.

On our way home from game five, things were sort of quiet between Tonya and me. Then she said, "He fed off you, that's what happened. He used your energy." She was perfunctory. Wasn't a scolding or anything. We can have our debates. She likes to go to the ball games, and that is important to me, that she would, maybe in the way that it is important to a man for a woman to like his brothers, or at least be able to tolerate them. Or at least get along. A man does want that to happen. I know she would rather be ringside at a World Championship title fight in boxing, even though she doesn't care for Mike Tyson. To put it her way, she has "issues" with Tyson. I don't care how many times I say Tyson, she has "issues" with him. At the same time, she would go to the mat with me quick over Tupac Shakur. I don't care how many times she might say that Tupac was misunderstood, I had "issues" with him. But what could I say now? Reggie probably had used me. But I was just being me. Reggie brought the playground to the Garden, and I was in his way. I was mad. I took it personally. Later on, somebody tried to tell me he didn't even know Tonya was there. It was between him and me. I had put myself in that position by being the kind of fan I am, by getting the best seats in the house. I was right there. It was another sellout of the Garden. Nobody went home happy. I didn't. Tonya said there'd be another game another day. I didn't say there was no way I'd miss it. But then, I didn't have to say it. She already knew. At the same time, Pat Riley was telling the press, "There was a massive thud of everybody jumping off the bandwagon. There will be the same resounding thud of everybody jumping back on."

I remember a lifetime I lived in the hours between game five at the Garden on June 1 and game six in Indianapolis on June 3, 1994—the game following the one when Reggie went off with 25 in 12, the equivalent of a 100-point game. For twelve minutes Reggie was up there with Wilt and Skywalker. That's what we were facing in game six. I couldn't wait. I couldn't wait for a chance to wipe the previous game off the books—or at least take it out of my short-term memory.

I wouldn't have missed it. What choice did I have? I was getting killed over the airwaves and in the papers. People blamed me for us getting torched—like I called for Miller time. The sports highlight reels showed more of me than of Larry Brown. First Reggie was talking noise, and then him dropping five 3-point bombs on the Knicks in the fourth quarter, looking for me, at me, jaw-jacking after each of the last three. People took up where he left off afterward, dissing me on the radio shows—WFAN and everywhere else. I never got so much negative hype for making a film—not even for *Do The Right Thing*. Everybody was now saying the Knicks were dead and I was the one who did them. "Reggie is the king of talk," Antonio Davis said. "Tell Spike thanks."

Me, of all people. I had made not one substitution, not one call, didn't fail to fight through one pick, didn't give up one good look, didn't call or fail to call one time-out or make one sub. I did my heckling, yes, I did, but all things considered, I'm not the late Leon the Barber in Detroit or Robin Ficker, the leather-lunged madman down in Washington at the Bullets games. I mean, it wasn't personal. It just so happened you could see me. I was down there. And they said it was *my* bad. Joie called me and wanted to know what I'd done; she said total strangers were stopping her in the street, yelling at her, saying, "Tell your &#!@* brother to stay home! He made the Knicks lose!" I called a friend who knows some ball and doesn't live in New York, because New Yorkers were looking the other way while I was being figuratively mugged—if they weren't blaming me for making myself available to be mugged. Outside of New York I was reassured that Reggie couldn't stay that hot. The Knicks would be sure to touch him now, and still could win. I couldn't give up the gate. I wasn't pulling a Pippen. I'd be at Market Square Arena.

I went out to La Guardia airport very early on Friday morning to get a flight to Indy. I'm at the airport, having my morning tea, picking up the papers, and—*bam!*—there I am again, bigger than hell, on the front page of the *Daily News*, the *New York Post*, and *Newsday*.

Headline in the New York *Daily News*, my hometown paper, Friday, June 3, 1994:

THANKS A LOT, SPIKE!
Outraged Fans Say Lee's Taunts Help Pacers
Beat Knicks

Headline in the *New York Post,* my hometown scourge, Friday, June 3, 1994:

SPIKED!
Did Spike Lee's Court Side Taunts Cost Knicks
Game Five?

Ditto *Newsday.*

In twelve short minutes, by the NBA game clock, I had gone from being known as the Knicks' biggest fan to being a well-meaning lunatic, like Colonel Kurtz from *Apocalypse Now.*

The horror . . . the horror . . .

Three of the four dailies in New York were blaming me for the loss, in style. I had to look around to see if anybody noticed. It appeared they did. The mayor, Rudy Giuliani, defended me in the *Daily News*: "I think Spike Lee plays a positive role for the Knicks. I think it's a shame he's being scapegoated. The Knicks lost the other night because they were outplayed by the Pacers." The *New York Daily News* ran a telephone poll that asked: "If the Knicks and Pacers meet in Game 7 Sunday night, should Spike Lee be allowed to sit courtside at Madison Square Garden?" Some asshole stockbroker told the *New York Post,* "Spike Lee should stick to making bad movies and shouldn't get involved with anything going on on the court."

I boarded the plane. Everybody asked me about the Knicks and Reggie Miller. Some people eyed me—could have been idle curiosity, but it seemed like suspicion. People who didn't care about basketball were asking what I did and exactly why did I do it. It was a relief to go to Indiana, so I thought. I got off the plane in Indianapolis and there were four or five TV news crews, cameras rolling. I'm just coming to see the run. They were loving it, the vultures. Busting out in an angelic afterglow.

I'm the catch of the day. Broiled Spike on a bed of wild sound bites. If I could've only found out who the rat bastard was who tipped off the press . . .

"Where are you staying, Spike?"

Like I'm going to tell them that.

This one reporter wouldn't stop asking, so I said, "I'm staying at the governor's mansion."

"East wing or west wing?" the reporter shot back.

"The slave quarters," I replied. This ain't good, I'm thinking. What a lovely sport; be a fan, make Ten Most Wanted.

Now, I never heard about Jack Nicholson going through anything like this.

I picked up an Indianapolis paper and got no relief. The *Indianapolis News* had called my office before I left and asked how I felt about 16,000-plus fans having the opportunity to wear my face as a mask. I said it was all right by me, if they could stand it, but I surely didn't want anybody getting their Klan card revoked on account of my black face. So they were waiting.

The *Indianapolis News*, Friday, June 3, 1994:

DON'T LET THE SPIRIT DIE

Actor Spike Lee's antics in New York inspired Pacers star, Reggie Miller, to score 39 points in leading his team to victory in Game Five in the NBA semifinals Wednesday night. To keep that spirit alive, here is a cut-out face mask of Lee for all Pacer fans to wear to tonight's game at Market Square Arena. Cut it out, glue it to stiff cardboard, find appropriate string or rubber band and have fun.

"Oh, yeah," I thought, "a real laff riot."

〉 〉 〉

This wasn't my first mission to Indiana. I had already given a lecture at the University of Indiana at Bloomington. This was after Coach Knight had been shown in a publicity photo while "playfully" whipping Calbert Chaney on his behind. Chaney was an All-America player, now a so-so guard with the Bullets. Something about that image infuriated me. Maybe Chaney's uneasy smile. Corporal punishment from parent to child is one thing. Whipping-the-chattel had to go. I came out onstage at the auditorium at IU with a whip and a chair. People got it. People laughed.

Before game six, I went directly from the airport to the Plainfield, Indiana, correctional facility where Mike Tyson was housed and visited with him. Like Jordan, he had also been born in Cumberland Hospital on Myrtle Avenue in Fort Greene, Brooklyn. He was contained, had been doing a lot of reading. I wondered if that would make him less inclined toward prizefighting. He didn't think so. We talked, laughed, though it saddened me to see him locked up. During my visit, the cons and guards taunted Tyson and me, saying the Knicks would be put out of their misery that evening by Reggie Miller. Before game one, I was asked to be on a live news feedback to Indianapolis with Reggie. At the end of the interview we made a bet. If the Knicks lost, I had to cast Reggie's wife, actress Marita Stavrou, in my next film. If the Knicks won, Reggie would have to visit Tyson.

I met up with my pal Al, at 300 East Market Street in Indy, for game six. Al Palagonia is a stockbroker from Brooklyn, East New York, and grew up in Queens. I had met him in Chicago, the year before, during the 1993 playoffs, at game four. The Knicks had come out onto the floor at old Chicago Stadium and I was in a seat in the eighth row or something, but that wasn't going to put me in check; when the Knicks came out, I was waving my towel and the crowd was booing with all it had. I looked down and saw this guy, a *paisan*, looking at me with this quizzical gaze. He had his palms up. "Whaddaya doin' way up there?" he said. Immediately, just by idiom, inflection, stance, look, and demeanor, I knew he was from N'Yock. I'm normally reticent with strangers. Not unfriendly. Just reticent. I warmed to this guy immediately. He reminded me of this guy Botz that I grew up with in Cobble Hill. Just by his manner, the look on his face.

"What'cha doin' way up there?"

Al gave me his card, said give him a call; when I came to Chicago for games, he had front row seats. And he could get front row in places like Indiana, he said. I called Al, he got back to me, and we agreed—he'd help me get into some games and if I could, I'd get him a seat on the rare occasion when he didn't know somebody. We ended up being at several games together, not only game six at Indy in 1993–94 when the Knicks were down 3–2 but also game six in 1994–95, same scenario, Knicks down 3–2, going to Indy. We'd jet out together for that one. But this time, 1993–94, it was the Eastern Conference finals, and the winner would go to the NBA finals.

"I was proud of you for showing up, Spike," Larry Brown said to me, "showing that you cared about your team. For the Knicks to come back like they did after that game Reggie had against 'em was a heck of an accomplishment."

Starks played as if possessed. He'll always hold a place in my brotherhood because he did not leave me hanging. If the Pacers had beaten the Knicks, I would have been the most mocked man in both Indiana and New York state history (at least for that summer), and I wanted no part of that. John hit five out of six 3-pointers. He was zoned. The Knicks never trailed. They never let the crowd get into it. Starks helped hold Reggie to 8 of 21 shooting. It was the D that did it for us. Indiana didn't score a point over the final 2:06 of the ball game. And later Pat Riley even gave me credit, saying the crowd had concentrated on me so much, it freed up the Knicks from the crowd's focus.

At the final buzzer, Starks ran across the court and gave me dap— three big times. People in New York told me that's how NBC ended its telecast, with John and me. Al and I needed security to get out of there. It was a completely hostile crowd, didn't seem to be that far away from actual violence, and I kid you not. So we were looking for our people after the game, me and Al—trying to get out of there. Now I know why teams used to winning on the road hit the winning shot and then run off the court. No sense being caught up. But the limo wasn't where it was supposed to be. Then we got chased. A crowd of about fifteen or twenty guys, looking none too pleased, stared at us, then started our way. At first they were walking, then walking faster, and then I heard one or more of them say, "Git 'em!" And that was when Al and I started moving pretty much in earnest. So we ran back to the rear of the arena, where the locker rooms are, and ducked into a room.

"Get me security!" I said. And somebody did. We finally got to the car.

Al hoisted his eyebrows. "I've seen the Indianapolis 500, Spike, and it ain't worth dying over," said Al.

We got back to the hotel and there we were on the local TV news—not the game, but us getting chased. They had filmed us being chased—the camera crew was running right along with us, it looked like. People were running and screaming. It was scary-looking. But somehow we got out of Market Square Arena with our lives. Only a fool would do that kind of thing twice.

A fool—or a Knicks fan.

I should have known Coach Brown would have the Pacers up for game seven at the Garden, on June 5, 1994. The place was packed to overflowing. Tonya was right there with me. I looked at her, and she looked back at me in a way that said, "Well. Go ahead." So I did.

That was Patrick Ewing's game. After nine years in the league, having the thorn of Michael Jordan in his ass, the Thorn of Thorns, Patrick did not want to let it get away. The Pacers had Dale Davis inside. Dale is a man in there. Rik Smits, the 7-4 Dutchman, was a scorer. Defense and rebounding win the rings. Reggie Miller, closely watched, made seven of seventeen field goals and scored only 17 points. But here came a championship veteran, Byron Scott, the ex-Laker, who had been through so many wars, with the Celtics in Boston Garden, with the Pistons at the Palace. He knew what the air was like in a situation like that. He knew how to breathe. He hit six out of seven field goal tries, each one a dagger in my chest, and scored 17 points himself off the bench. Byron had helped win Riley those rings in L.A. Now Pat looked like he wanted to choke him.

"I really believe players set the standard in this league, when you have competitive tough guys," Coach Brown told me later. "Your kids with talent are great, but you've gotta have guys who are pros, who've been through hard times, tough times. Guys who know what it is."

And that was the way Larry Brown coached it, and he played it almost perfectly. The Pacers led by 12 points, 65–53, with 4:39 left in the third quarter, but the Knicks went on a run and trailed by only four, 71–67, after three.

"It's going to be all right," said Tonya coolly. "They're going to be just fine."

"Fine? We're down four! Somebody get on old-ass Byron Scott!"

Harper stroked a three. The game was tied. The Knick D wore heavy on the Pacers. Larry Brown was down there working it. But so was Riley. The Knicks somehow got the lead up to five at 85–80, but Brown went to his defensive lineup and they got the stops and crept back, point by precious point. Less than a minute left now. The players were weary. I saw the healed gashes, the scars left by fingernails all along Ewing's arms, his face, throat, and arms coated with a fuzzy layer of sweat. His chest was heaving. He was exhausted. But against a front line of Dale and Antonio Davis, and 7-4 Rik Smits and Derrick McKey, Patrick had been a lion. At the time, he'd scored 22 points, grabbed 22 rebounds, with 7 assists, and 5 blocked shots. It was the best total game a Knick had played so deep in the playoffs since Clyde had gone off in game seven in 1970.

But the Pacers were right there. They would not go away. I looked down at Larry Brown as the Pacers called time out with less than a minute to play. . . .

Don't give up on me now. . . .

With thirty-four seconds left in the game and the Knicks leading by a tenuous point, 89–88, the Pacers ran their play. The collective realization was there. Heywoode Workman spun off left, Miller popped around as a decoy, and Dale Davis feinted a screen and cut hard and at an angle toward the hoop. Oakley was there, but Davis had a half-step. Workman fed him perfectly, and the big man scored the goal. Pacers, 90–89. Larry Brown applauded. Pat Riley called time.

If I could preserve moments, I would preserve that one. The anticipation of the crowd, the feeling of something great imminent, something dreaded coming, the uncertainty, the performance at the highest level. I wonder if Jordan was watching or if he was just out somewhere shagging flies. The Knicks came back and set up. Time. Brown adjusted the D. The Knicks inbounded. I felt Tonya's hand, then got down on both knees, summoning my mystics. Starks had the ball, out high right. He took Reggie off the dribble—John can *play*— right to the hole. The defense collapsed like so many falling redwoods. John made a great athletic move, a spontaneous, original move designed not to look good but to do precisely what it did: somehow Starks got the ball through all those strong, leaping bodies, by Dale and Antonio Davis, and up on the rack. It's not going, I thought, and it didn't. But it was in play. The ball bounced high off the iron. Two relatively small brown hands appeared out of the sea of limbs. The Pacers' big men had to contest John's shot. And now, as they began to descend, two hands extended toward the ceiling of the Garden. The small hands of Patrick Ewing. He played the carom perfectly and slammed it through the rim with all the force his weary body could muster. "Big Fella . . . he was there to save me," said Starks.

The Knicks led, 91–90, with 26.9 seconds left.

Ever been inside during a tornado? My body involuntarily rocked back as I stood, and my arms shot into the air. I bent backward with the joy of it. But it still wasn't over. It's never over, I think. Brown called another play during a time-out. Reggie this time, from 20 feet away, for all the marbles. But just as Unseld had done to Bradley years before, Oakley this time anticipated the play, the move, and the shot and went flying out at Reggie, and it was just enough, just enough to make Reggie miss, the ball bouncing harmlessly away, off groping Indiana fingers. Starks was flagrantly fouled by Reggie and hit both shots. The Knicks still had the ball due to the flagrant foul, so Starks was fouled again, made one, and the Knicks were home free, 94–90. As the clock expired, the Garden stood cheering as one, and Patrick stood in the middle of the court with his arms up. I don't know how he got 'em up, as hard as he'd played. Harper, Starks, Oakley, Mason, they all celebrated, and well they should have. It was probably the most gratifying Knicks game I'd witnessed since game seven of the finals in 1970. They were the Eastern Conference champions, and nobody but the Bulls had been able to say that in the decade of the '90s. I felt like I'd played forty-eight minutes myself. I was toast, physically and emotionally. Reggie Miller walked up to me and Tonya, we hugged, he apologized, and we walked off. As we left, Tonya said, "See, I told you."

I put my arm around her shoulders. "Yeah. Yeah, you did at that."

> > >

VIP 1994 NBA Finals tickets, Knicks vs. Rockets
Gate 54, court 28, row AA, seat 9
Ticket price $550. $508.08, plus $41.98 tax

I called up a friend who knows some ball, talking about the Knicks winning the NBA title. "They can," he said, "but, you know, there's nothing Patrick can do with Olajuwon."

But without Patrick, we never would have gotten there.

The series had played out this way: Houston won game one at the Summit, 85–78. I sort of expected that. We were emotionally drained, and the game was just three days after we'd given it all to beat Indiana. I was there, unbothered by the loss. Game two was key. If we could win that, then under the format we were playing, the next three games would be at the Garden, and we could run the table on them there. The Knicks won game two, 91–83, behind Derek Harper's 18 points, including 4 of 6 from deep. Patrick had 16 points, 13 rebounds, 6 blocked shots. Hakeem was a big problem for us—for anybody. With Michael gone, there was no player in the league better than Hakeem Olajuwon at this particular time. He had 28 in the first Houston win, and 25 in the loss. But if he was all they had, we'd beat them. We shouldn't let them out of the Garden.

Game three was crucial. Sam Cassell was a problem for us the entire series. He was a second-rotation guard for Houston. He had an odd change of pace, kind of like Mark Jackson, and he could really see from deep. He hit a three with 32 seconds left, after the Knicks D collapsed on Olajuwon and Hakeem kicked it out to Cassell for the open three. The Knick defense chose Cassell to take the shot and, give him credit, he knocked it down. "Old boy hit that shot on us," says Starks, shaking his head. "That was when the series got away." Now Houston was up,

2–1. The Knicks won the next two games, 91–82 and 91–84, the latter being the O.J. game. NBC cut into the broadcast of the game to show O.J. in his Bronco making a break for it. And a lot of people out there were saying, "Get back to the game, willya?" The series went back to Houston for the final two games. We should never have let it get to that, or even to a seventh game.

Game six was critical—where the Knicks should have put them away. The Rockets had us where they wanted us. They were beating us soundly. They had a 15-point lead. And then John Starks went off in the fourth quarter. Tonya and I made the trip. The pride Pat Riley had in John was obvious during and after that game. Starks took over, scored 16 points in the fourth quarter. He was hitting bombs from everywhere. Even the Rockets' guards—Kenny Smith, Vernon Maxwell, and Cassell—seemed to be in awe of what he was doing.

"Game six was key. I hugged everybody before we came out on the floor and said, 'This is our game right here,'" said Starks. "That's why I had such a great fourth quarter. I wanted to take them out right then and there."

Houston led by 9 with nine minutes left. John was unconscious. Could do no wrong. Starks's three with 1:17 left got us to within two, 84–82. Then Mase came up big with a layup that made it 86–84; then Mase ripped off the rebound of a Kenny Smith miss. We had the last shot. A three would win it. A two would do. The Rockets knew who the men were. Starks and Patrick. Two-man game. Pick-and-roll. Patrick picked for Starks and rolled out beyond the arc. Patrick is a good jump-shooter. John was locked in. Hakeem gambled and flew at John's shot attempt. If John had changed and passed to Patrick, the big man had a wide-open look. But John shot, and Olajuwon blocked it, and the Rockets held on, 86–84. "I don't know if Patrick was open or not. I didn't see him. I was going for the win. If I had it to do over, I probably wouldn't call Patrick up for that pick," says Starks. "I would've just gone one-on-one, rose for a three to win the game."

John had been in the zone then. But he couldn't get it back for game seven.

"We had a plan of getting away between games six and seven," he says. "For whatever reason, they changed it. Stuck in Houston. As a player you don't want to always think about the game. I couldn't stop. I couldn't sleep. The night before game seven, I was up the whole night. I was ready to play. It kind of hurt me, waiting. Not making excuses. Coming into the game I was thinking, No matter how I feel, we're going to kick the crap out of Houston tonight."

Ro Blackman could have helped the Knicks at two-guard in game seven down in Houston. Maybe even Hubert. It just wasn't Starks's night that night. And Riley never adjusted.

"In game six, we had every opportunity," Derek Harper told me. "In game seven, John wasn't able to hit the big shot in that game . . . I don't know if I should comment."

John Starks shot 2-for-18 from the field, and that was that. You can't make that up against a team with a player like Olajuwon. Harper played his heart out, scored 23 points, and was the best guard on the floor. In game six, Starks had been the best guard on the floor. Patrick had 17 and 10 boards. Oakley had 14 boards. But you can't recover from that kind of bad shooting percentage from a guy taking 18 shots. Pat stayed with Starks a little too long. John was his guy. Starks made the All-Star team under Riley that season. Starks was Riley's favorite, everybody knew it; Starks was his project, someone he rescued, molded like clay, his creation. It doesn't matter in the end. If he's shooting 2-for-12, then he ain't gonna get a chance to shoot 2-for-18 and I don't care if we're identical twins. Not in the seventh game of the finals. I don't think that would have been wrong, I don't think that would have been abandoning John. He starts, he's a part of the team, he helped get us to the NBA finals, but he didn't carry the Knicks to the finals all alone that year, so it's not like you're tanking if you sit him down. I don't know if Mr. Riley has ever conceded that he might have made a wrong move there.

"I didn't know I was off during the game," says Starks. "I still felt like I would make the next shot. My teammates said, 'Keep shooting it.'"

"Well, I don't remember telling him to keep on shooting, first of all," says Harper. "If he didn't realize he was cold, then I think John really needs to see the team doctor. He really needs to be examined if he didn't know he was cold, because I think he missed eleven in a row. And with that, you just have to try and do something different. I was really, really, hoping that Ro got a chance to come in and play. But he didn't get his opportunity, and that's the way it is sometimes."

Honestly, Harper and Blackman had been teammates in the backcourt for years in Dallas, but I have to agree with Harper here. Van Gundy, assisting under Riley at the time, disagrees: "I remember specifically Pat asking in the fourth quarter, should we go with somebody else," says Van Gundy. "And in his mind I think he already knew his answer, but he just wanted to see if . . . and to this day I agree with the decision he made, agree wholeheartedly."

"[Riley] felt like he had to stay with John. You make a change and a guy like Ro comes in and does well, it raises questions as to why the guy wasn't getting chances in the first place," Harper said. "Puts a coach in a difficult situation, I think, when he has to make a call like that. But Ro was a seven-time All-Star, the kind of person who's always prepared himself to play. There's no doubt in my mind, personally, that Ro would have been able to come in and give us something. Hit a basket here, make a play there. And that's all we needed at the time."

"John can miss forever, and then make big plays. We felt he had a chance to do something on the defensive end, too. [Ro] had injuries and was never healthy with us. It wasn't the Rolando of the heyday in Dallas," Van Gundy says.

Starks missed three 3-point tries in the final minute. Hakeem had 25 points and 10 boards, and Mad Max Maxwell killed us with 21 points. You never knew who it was going to be for Houston, other than Hakeem. Kenny Smith, Maxwell, Carl Herrera, and Cassell took turns on us.

On June 22, 1994, Houston won its first NBA title, 90–84, over the New York Knicks. It was the lowest point total for seven games between two teams in the playoffs in NBA history. And that was because of the great D that was played, by both teams. You can't blame John Starks totally for the fact that the Knicks lost to the Houston Rockets those seven emotion-filled games. Where was Riley in game seven? John had to come out. He reached his ceiling in game six. The Knicks outscored Houston in total, 608–603. I was at every game. The

Knicks played three game sevens in the playoffs. They'd won the first two. I've got to give Hakeem, Sam Cassell, Kenny Smith, Robert Horry, Otis Thorpe, Larry Smith, Mario Elie, Bill Berry, and Rudy T. credit, too. But I believe the Knicks should have won that NBA title. Up three games to two, going back for two in Houston. Game six was there for us to take.

After the seventh game, I went into the locker room to try to find John Starks. I couldn't find him. He was ghost. I thought about what Jerry West once said: Nobody could capture it.

Starks was taking refuge in the shower. Sitting there, flesh on tile. He didn't come out for a long time. I went into the Houston locker room; they poured champagne all over me and gave me grief. I congratulated them all. But for me the drama was in the other locker room. I went back.

"I was in the shower for probably an hour," Starks said. "Tears were coming out of my eyes. Rolling. I couldn't stop them. I was trying to collect myself, letting the water run over me. I was heartbroken. The way we worked—the struggles we put in—for me to come up all of a sudden with a b.s. game like that—I let a lot of people down, not just my teammates but the city of New York, the fans that have been supporting me for so many years. It *hurt*. We kind of let one get away. And that spilled out of me. Then . . . I just had to try and collect myself. Get up. Try again."

The 1994–95 season. An old married man. Father. Satchel was born December 2, 1994, our first child, a girl, named after the oft-quoted Hall of Fame pitcher of the Kansas City Monarchs and the Cleveland Indians. I went out and bought an autographed ball and an 8-by-10 photo of the great pitcher for Satchel's nursery. Got myself two ball partners now. *Clockers* made. It was a film that studied some aspects of the retail commercial drug trade in Brooklyn, the dynamics of the relationships between the police detectives and the "clockers," the low-level sellers, and their suppliers. It was also about the dynamics of a family— a relationship between brothers.

And in the NBA, Michael Jordan had come back, and toward the end of that season, he came in and dropped 55 points on the Knicks. Then the Bulls played the Orlando Magic—Shaq and Penny—in the Eastern Conference semifinals. In the other Eastern Conference semifinal playoff bracket, the Knicks were set to play Larry Brown and the Pacers again.

Game one. We settled into our seats at the Garden. Oakley came out, tossed me the ball, and the run was on. I eyed Reggie Miller. He eyed me back. This time wouldn't be like last year. This time the Pacers had Mark Jackson. We were basically the same. We had come within one shot of winning the NBA title the year before. Why change? Greg Anthony was getting more minutes. Indiana was up by two after one period, 29–27. New York scorched them with a 32-point second quarter. The Garden was rocking, and I was up and down like a jack-in-the-box. Tonya was next to me. The Pacers led by 3 entering the fourth quarter.

Greg Anthony played the best game I ever saw him play in the play-offs. A 3-pointer by the Young Republican who could have been a boxer, from deep in the left corner, tied the game at 80–80 to begin the final period of play. The Garden began bubbling and boiling with noise. Then Anthony hit a driving layup to tie it at 84 with 7:22 left. I was all off into it by now. Couldn't help it. It's my nature. I was throwing fists, up out of my seat, my arms extended. Maybe I should've been sitting with my legs crossed like I was at the opera, but that's not me, not where I come from. Rik Smits was hurting us inside. He kept drawing fouls, making free throws. He'd end up with 34 points. But we ended up with seven men in double figures, five starters, plus Mase and Anthony. We did everything we had to do in that fourth quarter. So did Indiana. It was nip and tuck. Ewing hit a 15-footer to give us the lead, 89–88. Mark Jackson threw a bad pass, and Starks made him pay on the other end. *Slam!* Knicks by three, 91–88. Immediately, Larry Brown called time. On the next Knick possession, Miller played a lane and made a steal and Smits hit from the baseline. Now Anthony again, on a kickout from Patrick, for threeeee . . . *Yesss!* Knicks by four, 94–90 with 2:58 left in the game. The Garden was on fire, the house was on fire, I was on fire. . . .

We began to methodically cash in our free throws. Oakley made two.

Mason made two, while Reggie—amazingly, for him, against the Knicks, at the Garden—actually missed one of four free throws in that span. We let him know about it when he missed, too. The Knicks were banging him. First Starks fouled him, then Patrick. Patrick hit two free throws to make it 99–95 with 1:40 left. Nobody was giving up easy looks, nobody was giving up layups—especially not to Reggie.

In all those years, watching Willis crash to the floor in game five at the Garden in 1970, then from the green seats, then the gag-me teams, even watching from underneath the Eighth Avenue basket with Tony Drazen, it was now that I really noticed the ferocity of the battle of the titans that goes on beneath the NBA boards in a playoff elimination game. It ain't for the weak-minded or the faint of heart. One look at Dale Davis tells you that. Mark Jackson wheeled into the lane, but his shot was blocked by Anthony. Ewing's shot was then blocked by D. Davis. What beasts the Davis boys were down low. What D! Reggie hit a spinner. So did Mase. Knicks by four with 34.4 seconds left. Just take care of the rock. Just put it on ice. This might have been the time to bring back Derek Harper, for ball control's sake, but Anthony had played so well. He'd played so damn well. Now he got fouled. When he hit two free throws with 18.7 seconds left, giving the Knicks a 105–99 lead, it looked like ball game, and Greg Anthony was the new Knick hero. He'd made three of four from downtown, four of six from the field, and was a perfect four-of-four from the line, with two assists, in twenty minutes. Fifteen points is a lot of points in a tough, defensive playoff game. And he'd played quick, rock-hard, airtight D.

Larry Brown called time after the second of Anthony's free throws was good, with 18.7 left. Anthony held his hands high as the Garden erupted, blew kisses to his wife, Crystal, accepted all accolades. I was up too, but my eyes were cut toward the Indiana huddle. Brown was working. He smiled as he spoke. He smiled! He and Reggie had done it before—but, nah, this one was bagged. I looked at Coach Brown. I could not believe it. He actually seemed to be enjoying this.

Something funny might happen. . . .

The Pacers ran a quick inbounds that shaped Reggie up immediately for a shot. Anthony was there, but he wasn't really on him. Didn't want to foul Reggie, give up three free throws while the clock was stopped. So the shot was there, 24 feet away, and Reggie didn't miss.

Knicks, 105–102, with 14.1 seconds left.

Why Mason had to be the one to take the ball out, I don't know. He was behind the end line on the Eighth Avenue end of the court. The Pacers denied all over the backcourt. If Mason had only thrown the ball all the way downcourt, down to the other end, at least it would have been away from our own basket. Mason looked as Anthony feverishly zigzagged to get free. And then Mason threw it in, just as Anthony lost his balance. Reggie got a shove in on him, shoved him right to the court. "Yeah, he did," said Starks. "He pushed him. And Mase was already leaning in."

Mason ended up throwing the ball almost directly to Reggie while Anthony stumbled to the floor. Reggie calmly stepped back behind the arc—nearly right in my lap—and let fly. All net. He knew as soon as he let it go. With 13.3 seconds left, the score was tied. People have said it was amazing the Pacers came from six down with 18.7 seconds to play. Well, for the Pacers, 18.7 seconds was kind of extravagant. The score was now tied and there were still 13.3 seconds left in the game. The Pacers had come from 6 points down to tie the game in exactly 5.4 seconds.

"Down six, eighteen seconds left. I had no idea we could win that game. And I never think a game's over," Brown told me later. "It happened so quickly. With thirteen seconds left, it was tied."

The Knicks were shellshocked. So was I. Sam Mitchell fouled Starks. As Starks went to the line, Brown sent in Heywoode Workman for Mark Jackson. Speed. "C'mon, John," I said under my breath. "One time. One time, John. We can't go out today. Not like this. You can't let Reggie do this to us again."

Starks missed both. "My mind was still in the other end. I still had a chance to put us up by two. But I was thinking, 'What just happened?'"

With 7.5 seconds left, Mason fouled Reggie Miller, off Workman's drive, draw and dish to Miller. Two free throws. Put 'em in the book. Pacers, 107–105. We didn't even get up another shot. Anthony threw it away. Reggie gave us the choke sign on his way out.

"I was worried about what people might make of Reggie saying that

['Chokers! CHOKERS!'], when I knew we all had respect for the Knicks, a team that had made it to the NBA finals, a team that had beaten us the year before in the playoffs," Larry Brown told me later. "Yeah, I said something to Reggie about it later. But I didn't say anything about it immediately. Knowing him, looking back on it, I shouldn't have said anything about it at all. He's emotional, like I am, and sometimes he doesn't mean a lot of the things he says."

I went back to Market Square Arena for game six, the same scenario as the year before, down 3–2. Met up with Earl, my cousin Malcolm Lee, and my pal Al, and flew in. The Knicks were down three games to two, once again a game away from elimination, Reggie Miller and I had become a cause célèbre, and I was beginning to develop a definite distrust of some residents of Indiana. We had front row seats for game six. One of these wild fans was sitting next to me, wearing billboards, a hard hat—you know the type, every town has one. The game went on, and the Knicks established distance—three points, five points, three points, five points, seven points. I was cheering. The crowd at Market Square was restless. Couldn't get into the game. They'd been taken out of the game. The Knicks never trailed. At halftime I noticed the wild fan sitting next to me had been kicked out. And then the Indiana team owner's son, one Mr. David Simon, sits down. Al is sitting on one side of me, Troy Aikman of the Dallas Cowboys is on the other side, and then David Simon sits down right next to me. As the second half moved along, this putz gets crazy. Much crazier than that wild fan he replaced. Market Square Arena is almost hermetically sealed, and the noise level gets high, and then they play a recording of Formula One car engines gunning and cars roaring by, signifying the Indianapolis 500; it can be disorienting. I'm willing to offer David Simon that excuse for the things he started doing. He starts calling me "Jew-hater" and an anti-Semite, saying these things. He's throwing paper at me, making believe he's throwing a punch. The cops had already kicked Earl out for cheering the Knicks. The security guards just looked at me. Later one guy whispered, "He's the boss's son, Spike. What am I gonna do?"

Do your job, and get this guy off me.

But security wouldn't help me with the owner's son. So naturally this Renaissance man, David Simon, is going to want to impress Troy Aikman, not to mention his daddy. He had set the tone, and then the lunatic fringe patriot movement took over. This was not very funny or to be studied as sociology while it was happening. While it was happening I remember thinking I could not believe it was happening. I'm busy watching the run and here's this guy trying to make points with the crowd and Troy.

The Knicks pulled away in the third quarter. Starks and Harper hit 3-point bombs to cap a 10–0 run and we were up 69–56. Patrick had 25 points and 15 boards. Starks had another 3-point backbreaker with the clock running down, making it 84–76 with 3:04 left. Starks was lighting them up again. Every time he launched a three, I stood straight up as the rock spun true. *Yesss!* "I loved it," said Starks. "It was great to go into that environment and then play the way we did. To see you up in there—I heard what they were calling you—and to play that way; that game will linger in my mind the rest of my life." The Knicks never trailed. Reggie hit only 12, as the Knick D suffocated him. The closest the Pacers got was 79–76, and then the Knicks pulled away to eight on Starks's deep j. The owner's son is going nuts, the 16,529 are going nuts, we don't know where Earl is, since he got ejected from the building, and he can't miss our chartered flight back to the airfield at Teterboro, New Jersey. And we thought, after our last experience, some of these rednecks will try and lynch Earl for sure.

My pal Al is looking at me as if "How in the hell are we gonna get out of here with our lives if we win?" I'm worried about the last two minutes, and Reggie Miller. But the Knicks applied good D, shot 50 percent from downtown, and won with relative ease, 92–82.

We were set up as perfectly as the Celtics had been in game six against the Knicks back in 1973. But I didn't put it together that way then. I was happy. But David Simon wasn't happy. And I wasn't happy about him, either. If the Knicks had lost, we wouldn't have had any problem after the game. But now our problems were just starting. The Pacer fans didn't take too well to their team losing, forcing the series to seven games, with game seven back in the Garden. They knew what losing this game had meant to the franchise. But there was a game still to be played. Both teams had won on the road in the series. In some ways home court advantage is highly overrated in pro ball. It's much more important to the media and to the fans than it is to the players.

On the way back to the airport, the radio in the limo was on, and the announcer and his call-in guests were crying in twangs on the call-in shows: "How'd he ever get them seats in the first place? Spahke Lee? Why it's a dis-grace!" Well, I hadn't meant any harm, and they could have the seats back, now that the game was over.

So the Knicks won game six at Market Square, déjà vu all over again, as Yogi said, 92–82, actually really subdued the Pacers, as Patrick had 25 points and 15 boards. We were going back to the Garden for game seven. It was over. I was looking forward to the Bulls again. Only this time Indiana did not cooperate. Neither did Orlando. The Pacers won a nail-biter over the Knicks in game seven at the Garden, 97–95. Miller scored 29. Starks hit a three with 32 seconds left to get us within two. Patrick had a shot to tie the game, a good-enough look in the lane, a shot that was virtually uncontested, a rare shot against Indiana. It hit the back iron and bounced out.

"We played a good game," said Starks. "It came down to the last shot. Patrick did the correct thing by driving, going to the basket. Shot just didn't fall. He thought he was too far away from the basket to dunk. Looking at it, he probably was. If his knees had been healthy, he probably would have dunked it. But he had been there for me, I should've been there for him."

The Pacers went to the Eastern Conference finals. And that was the last game Pat Riley ever coached for the Knicks. The Pacers, having spent their shells, were beaten by Penny, Shaq, and the Magic for the right to go to the finals, where Orlando was then swept by Houston. No way they should have been swept. Riley wouldn't have been swept—not with Shaq and Penny. Larry Brown definitely wouldn't have been swept. Larry had run onto the court after the Magic beat the Pacers, and as much as he must have been hurting, he congratulated Shaq and Penny.

Houston was back-to-back NBA champion.

That was the year I became convinced about Coach Larry Brown.

I asked Larry if he ever thought about coaching the Knicks.

"I tried, once," he said. "They asked me to come in in the middle of the season, and I couldn't. That's when they hired Bob Hill as interim coach, in '86. Then I got interviewed before they hired Pitino. I talked to this guy Evans, head of the Garden at the time. While they were interviewing me, they were on the phone talking to other people, so I didn't feel like I was way up there on their list. But I want to win a championship, Spike. If you say you would like to coach someplace, that means you have to replace somebody. I don't want to get into that. I'd always dreamed about being the Knicks coach." It was then I found out that Larry Brown was a New York ballplayer. Grew up on Long Island, played much ball as a kid in Brooklyn. "I grew up in Brooklyn, might as well say," he said. "I used to play all the time down at the Brownsville Boys Club. That's why I love city kids. They go to the goal, they know how to play, and they have a toughness." He went to school at North Carolina when Doug Moe was a star and Frank McGuire was the coach. A scandal hit and then Dean Smith came in. Billy C., the Kangaroo Kid, was a sophomore when Brown and Walsh were seniors. Brown and Walsh had been together almost ever since.

I still remember Larry Brown taking every edge, milking every second, Brown as much as Miller who did us in, while Knicks guard Greg Anthony blew kisses to his wife, thinking the game was over, in the spring of '95. All Mase has to do is throw the ball to the other end of the court. Both times Mase kept trying to force the inbounds pass to Greg Anthony. That game one, when they scored 6 points in five seconds. Coach Brown told me later, "I was equally as proud of my team for coming back from having lost a game six at home for the second straight year to you guys, and having a chance to win game seven. I was proud both years. Yeah, I looked at you, Spike. I like you. You remember the no-call, when Patrick fouled Dale on that dunk in '94?"

Hunh?

The Rockets were good in 1994–95. I don't know if they were *that* good. Orlando's Nick Anderson missed four free throws in a row in the final minute of game one, when any two free throws would have iced the game for Orlando. And it wasn't just that he missed the free throws. They weren't even close, not even in the cylinder, with crazy rotation, four bricks. You could see it on his face. The pressure got to him. Four straight missed free throws, and Orlando just appled up after that. And it also seemed to me that Orlando made no adjustments in any game after that. They kept trying to use Dennis Scott, when it was obvious he could guard no one out there. No trouble staying up on him and taking away his 3-point bomb. The Magic were out-coached. Shaq was deferential to Hakeem, the Rockets became NBA champions. Back-to-back.

In 1993–94 the Knicks had gone 57–25, won the Eastern Conference championship and came within a foot of winning the NBA title. In Riley's last season, 1994–95, the Knicks went 55–27 and didn't make it to the Eastern Conference finals, and the fact that the Bulls didn't either was no solace at all. No, 1993–94, that had been the best chance, that was it, that was the year, and I think it was Riley's inflexibility in the seventh game of the NBA finals that year that may have cost the Knicks that title, while Michael was out on sabbatical. Of course, after the next season, Riley left New York of his own volition. We weren't promising enough for him. He didn't have all the say-so. He doesn't have that problem coaching (and owning) down in Miami, because he sort of is the organization down there. Billy Cunningham from Brooklyn was part of the original ownership of the Miami Heat when the franchise came into the league along with Orlando. Then Billy got out, sold his end, made a killing doing so, and now Riley is all up in the house down there.

By the time Pat Riley left, after the 1994–95 season, the Knicks had a roster of Anthony, soon to be gone to expansion Vancouver; Starks; Doc Rivers, who replaced the traded Jackson; Hubert Davis, a shooter; Derek Harper, a point to run the club we'd gotten from Dallas; Monte Williams; and Doug Christie, who had some flexibility but never had the talent or experience to run with the Bulls; and we still had the rhinos, the big boys up front: Mason, Oakley, Ewing, 6-10 Charles Smith, and Herb Williams. There was still no real flexibility. The problem always came down to who would take Pippen, who could guard Jordan, who would check Kukoc.

Luckily the Knicks didn't have to play Chicago every night. In between the seasons of 1991–92 and 1994–95, under Pat Riley, the

Knicks went 223–105 and won two Atlantic Division titles and one Eastern Conference championship. The only thing that evaded him— and us—was the thing that I wanted most: another NBA World Championship.

> > >

Michael Jordan never worked so hard in his life, probably, as he did in the off-season before the 1995–96 season. The Bulls had lost to the Magic after Jordan made a critical turnover on offense, losing the ball to Nick Anderson on a move to the middle.

"That was a bad year," Jordan told me. "I was unprepared for basketball. I thought I could live off my reputation and the Game proved me wrong. The Game taught me a lesson. It wasn't Orlando that taught me, or New York. The Game taught me the lesson. You can't leave and think you can come back and dominate this game. I will be physically and mentally prepared from now on. I promised myself that. I mean, if I do that, and things don't go my way, then I can respect that. I will say, Hey, somebody got the best of me. It was the Game itself that humbled me, Spike."

There is something of a difference in the attitude of the players about the Game. I remember what happened between Rod Strickland, Mark Jackson, and the Knicks, and I remember what happened when we had Frazier and Monroe, when Dean Meminger and Henry Bibby came in as rookies. Players back then were much less selfish than the guys now, because now there's so much more money to be made, and the more points you score, the bigger the endorsements, the bigger the shoe deal, the bigger the playing contract, just like Bill Bradley said. So I feel people really wanted to win more back then than they do now, and that's a by-product not just of the basketball players but of society as well. It's just more about "me" and "getting paid" nowadays.

Whatever its merits might be, that philosophy doesn't make for winning basketball.

It's also a much different Garden crowd. The whole financial landscape has changed. The average working stiffs who bleed orange and blue are not really able to afford season tickets. If they are not sold out.

What I pay now for one game was the price of a season ticket back when I was in junior high school.

Okay, stealing money. Jordan, at $30,140,000—Bulls in the bargain store. Definitely not stealing money. The thing about Michael is, he's never been, probably never could be, paid what he's worth. I guess his people tried to rationalize—look how much he'll make in endorsements—but he's worth every penny of that 30. Shawn Bradley, $5.13 million—stealing money. I guess being 7-6 and white pays a dividend, but he's still a stiff and he's stealing money. David Falk worked them over really good on that one. Dennis Scott, $3.5 mil—stealing money. He needed Shaq a lot more than Shaq needed him. One dimensional, but he was Shaq's boy. Danny Ferry, $4.6 million—stealing mo' money. Mookie Blaylock at $2.8 mil is underpaid and underrated. Always liked him. Glen Rice, $4 mil—great deal for Charlotte. Jim McIlvane in Seattle, at $3 mil for blocking shots—stealing money. Shawn Kemp, getting $3.3 mil—bargain basement. Calbert Chaney, at $3.2, is very lucky—stealing money. Penny, at $6.65—flea-market steal for the Magic. Derrick Coleman at $6.7—grand theft. Scottie Pippen, at $2.25 mil—grand theft by the Bulls. I could go on, but I won't. People get what the market (and they) will bear.

Okay, one more. Reggie Miller, at $11.2—fair and square. I like Reggie as a person, and I like him as a player. We'll probably be linked together for life now. I can't speak for him, but every time I'm out and about, people ask me, How's Reggie Miller doing? How's your friend Reggie? You and Reggie get along? You guys really dislike each other that much? Reggie still your boy? Was Reggie ever your boy? Wonder if he gets similar questions. When he did his book, I wrote the foreword. He's sort of a funny ballplayer to rate because he has superstar status, yet you have to run him off a couple of bumps to get him open. When I learned Larry Brown had said in all honesty that he had the most unlikely superstar in the league, Reggie heard about it and didn't like it very much. I thought, Not good for Coach Brown to say, but reality. I'd find out more about it when we went to Indiana to shoot a Nike commercial with Reggie in November of 1996. Reggie doesn't look tremendously athletic, but he's got all kinds of heart, has a quick release on his shot, and unlimited range. The Knicks can testify. Reggie told me that he wanted to come to New York, but Dave Checketts didn't want him. Reggie wanted to come. He says he would've come for the same money they gave Allan Houston, but the Knicks needed youth.

In the summer of 1995, Michael Jordan killed himself to get back in basketball shape after Nick Anderson stole that ball from him and Orlando beat the Bulls in Jordan's return. Probably one of the few times Jordan felt embarrassed. He didn't blow it off. He went to work. It paid off, because in 1995–96, the Chicago Bulls went 72–10 in the regular season, a new NBA record, eclipsing the 1972 Lakers' mark. The Knicks beat Cleveland in the first round of the '96 playoffs, under Van Gundy, who replaced the disaster hire, Don Nelson, halfway through the season. The Knicks played Chicago in the second round, and I am still miffed about the two walking calls made by Bill Oakes against the Knicks in the last minute of game four, when a victory could have sent the series back to Chicago tied at two games each. But the fact remains that we offered no resistance as compared to the past, didn't have the goods to beat 'em. The Knicks won one game off the Bulls. And Scottie Pippen and I went at it again. I missed two great games at the Garden because I was at the Cannes Film Festival with *Girl 6*. We saw the games via a satellite feed shown at the American pavilion. The film critic Roger Ebert and I went and watched and traded barbs throughout. The Pavilion was packed, and fairly evenly divided between Knicks and Bulls fans. I was dying, cursing the schedule-makers for the conflict. Woody wouldn't have missed those games. I flew from Nice to Paris to New York to Chicago to get back in time for game five at Chicago. The Knicks tried, played the Bulls tough, but we had no offense. As the clock ticked down, Scottie started talking serious smack to me. He hadn't said anything the whole game; now that both game and series were over, he starts talking out of the side of his neck. The Knicks played hard but had limited weapons, a thin arsenal.

Then Orlando got swept again, by Chicago this time. In the finals, Seattle was on the way to being swept before Coach George Karl changed his rotation and the Bulls lost concentration after going up 3–0, and Gary Payton got over the hype. Rain Man was no joke. When Jordan said, *"Shawn Kemp can play the game of basketball,"* I knew Kemp had finally arrived. I can't recall Jordan saying that about anybody else. In the end, the Chicago Bulls won another NBA title.

After the Knicks lost, I was morose. Somebody asked if I thought I'd ever win an Academy Award. Not a good one to ask me in the springtime of a desultory year for the Knicks. "Yeah—the next time the Knicks win the NBA title," I said. Then the Knicks made moves, dropping Harper, who can still play. Hubert Davis was sent to Toronto for a number one pick. We drafted John Wallace—Tonya likes his game—Walter McCarty, and Dontae Jones, and they may help us win one day if they can develop a collective understanding that five can always beat one if they play like one. Then we brought in L.J. and Allan Houston and Chris Childs for the current season.

As the season began, I put out my tenth film, *Get On the Bus.* The film is about a diverse group of African-American men from Los Angeles who ride a chartered bus to the Million Man March in Washington, D.C., in 1995. The film was made with the backing of fifteen prominent African-American investors from the worlds of business, entertainment, and sports, including myself: the others are Larkin Arnold, Jheryl Busby, Johnnie Cochran, Lemuel Daniels, Danny Glover, Calvin Grigsby, Robert Guillaume, Robert Johnson, Olden Lee, Wesley Snipes, Reggie Bythewood, Reuben Cannon, Will Smith, and ex-Knick Charles Smith.

I hoped the Knicks bus was heading to the finals. I remember what Michael told me about the teams, coaches, what it takes to win. Maybe he was trying to get inside my head. But maybe he was telling me the God's honest.

We'd soon see.

FOURTH QUARTER

Dropping the Bomb

It seems like a simple enough thing to do. Anybody can walk out on a deserted court and pick up a 12-inch ball and put it through an 18-inch netted hoop suspended 10 feet off the floor. Put the sphere through the circle. Anybody can do it. Put it up there soft two or three times, and it will go. The difference comes in when you *need* to do it, consistently, under extreme duress, while being watched. If somebody or five somebodies are trying to stop you from putting the same ball into the same hoop—somebody with hops, somebody quick, strong, tall, cunning, a combination, then putting the ball in the hole becomes the guts of the Game. And then it's not so simple. It gets complex. It takes skill, hard-won over many years. Sometimes it takes more than that. Exhibited skill at such a popular activity will fill up a window. And there are twenty-four hours in a day, and many windows to fill every hour in this brave new world of cable television, cyberspace, Blockbuster video stores, cineplexes, multiplexes, and shiny new skybox-laden downtown arenas.

> > >

Division One college basketball players should be paid. Stipend. Trust fund. Work-study. Whatever you want to call it. No doubt in my mind that they should be salaried.

They are not stupid. They are not blind to the big picture. They see everybody is salaried, from the coach to the school to the conference and its employees, to the concierge and the desk help in the hotels, to the bus driver, to the airline pilot, to the commentators in network blazers, to TV producers and technicians, to sneaker manufacturers, to the sneaker reps—everybody under the sun making a good living off the annual contesting of these college games—but if one of the actual *participants* in these televised-for-profit events gets so much as a quarter, *he's* crooked. Nice hustle if you can get it. Young people glom the hypocrisy. Selling jerseys of collegians at sporting goods stores. Selling their likeness on football and basketball cards. Everybody grabbing a buck. These are the only performers I know who are featured on prime-time television and don't get paid—unless you're counting *Cops, America's Most Wanted,* or *America's Funniest Home Videos,* and even they get a little something kicked out, don't they?

The whole thing is a racket. At the same time, when they don't get a stipend, where are the ends going to come from? Don't tell me about the value of a scholarship when many if not most coaches don't leave room or time, don't encourage the players to study. John Thompson, Dean Smith, John Chaney, Rick Pitino—and these are the good guys, as far as I'm concerned—make money from sneaker companies, from Nike, Reebok, Adidas, Fila, and Converse. But so-called student athletes are out there busting their butts getting little or nothing. I won't say nothing because in the end it's on them to get an education, an education that costs tens of thousands of dollars. They have an opportunity to get an education. That should not be belittled. People also have to live day-to-day. Some have families in need; some have children. They see everybody getting paid. That's what the unscrupulous prey upon, slipping them money or dry goods or, as Coach Thompson says, "a sausage sandwich," to obligate them for when they become professionals in the NBA, *if* they ever become NBA material. The kid is compromised once he takes the cash. They learn this is the way the world works. Under the table. Maybe it's true. But it *shouldn't* work that way. And that's one of the things college is supposed to teach you.

If it was me at age eighteen, I would have taken money, too. Can't adopt a holier-than-thou attitude now that I'm relatively comfortable—act like I don't know. And there could be a chance I would have ended up screwed also. Gotten greased for getting greased. But somewhere along the line, be it a greedy relative or an unscrupulous coach or a slimeball agent, the system demands that a young person become a hypocrite along with it—duplicitous, unethical. But the whole thing is unethical to begin with. People have to live. People got to eat. You can say, "It's wrong," but if your stomach is growling, it's going to win a philosophical debate with your conscience.

The young kid players know what the coaches are getting, right down to high school level now. Deliver me that kid and you'll get that job, I'll carry your nephew on scholarship, whatever. The young kid players know what the schools and conferences and the NCAA get if they get into the tournament, to say nothing of if they get to the Final Four. They can look up and see all the people in the stands. They see the ESPN highlights. They are on the highlights just like the players in the NBA, and just as often. They know what the TV deals are, who's got the loot. They know somebody's got it and it's not them. If I'd been a young Division One athlete and I needed money, I might have taken it from somebody, knowing there could be repercussions if I got found out, but also knowing if I don't have *any* money, then there are more immediate repercussions that take precedence. I don't expect things to change because some young people have problems. Won't hear many violins over that. The NCAA should put in a trust fund to be drawn from, but it won't. If it did, some pin money would be less tempting for the young men. They could better resist crooks, shysters, bad agents, flimflam artists, gamblers, and leeches who prey on them only because of this imbalance of cash. If they knew it was being put aside for them, they could have the fortitude to say "I'm not taking money from you, fool." Until then, it's going to be the same thing rising.

I've gone to many colleges on speaking engagements, including the Universities of Indiana and Kentucky. Lots of basketball history at Kentucky. I went there a few years ago. I was invited to speak to the student body. They gave me several dates to choose from. I said, "Send me the basketball schedule." If I was going to speak there, I wanted to see a game in the process. So it was that Kentucky was playing on a Saturday afternoon when I went down. I let Coach Pitino know I was coming. He was great about it. I spoke on the Lexington campus on Friday night. The lecture was to begin at 8:00 P.M., but was delayed: there had been a death threat against me. I've had several when I've gone to speak at colleges. Another came once when I went to the University of Georgia at Athens. When I went out onstage at Kentucky, I talked about why I thought films like *Do The Right Thing* and *Malcolm X* were important. I also talked about how for years nobody black was allowed to play ball at Kentucky, and the myth of Adolph Rupp.

'Coach Pitino didn't miss a beat. He let me come to the shoot-around, and on Saturday he let me eat the pre-game meal with the team. I was in the locker room with the 'Cats before the game, at halftime, and after. He let me sit on the bench. I was sorry he'd left the Knicks for Kentucky. We could've won it all with Coach Pitino. I loved the way he'd had the Knicks playing back in 1988 and 1989. I like that type of team. Pressure D, deep rotation, traps, bombs away.

Kentucky played Tennessee in that game. Allan Houston was playing for Tennessee, under his father, Wade, who was the coach while Allan was there. The family is from Louisville. Kentucky has more of a winning tradition in basketball than Tennessee. At halftime, Coach Pitino— well, he was cursing them out left and right, but like Coach Thompson, you can tell he was teaching with it. But, yes, he's a yeller and a screamer, too.

Whoever he yelled at had a great second half. Kentucky won with ease, led by All-American Jamal Mashburn.

It was odd: Kentucky's winning basketball tradition is long held, started by the Man in the Brown Suit, Rupp. I don't think Rupp ever wanted to coach a black player in his life. Not because he couldn't have. He didn't want to. He's the Obi-Wan Kenobi of Kentucky basketball. You can see where I might react. But, history being what it's like, Kentucky was one of the teams, along with Houston, that Georgetown beat in the Final Four in 1984, when John Thompson became Obi-Wan at Georgetown. Then, when Villanova played a perfect game and beat Georgetown for the national championship in 1985, that game was held at Rupp Arena in Lexington. It was almost like nobody can get too arrogant about ball around here, all right? And then to realize that Coach Thompson was once a Celtic and that Coach Pitino came to New York, then Kentucky playing Georgetown style, UCLA style, Celtic style, winning style—it was clear to me that it's all one thing.

> > >

With Earl "the Pearl" Monroe *(left)* and Dean "the Dream" Meminger.

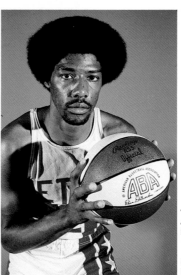

Dr. J., Julius Erving from Roosevelt, New York.

Charles Oakley and the Knicks present me with a jersey on my thirty-ninth birthday.

My nemesis, Reggie Miller; we hug after the Knicks win game 7 of the 1994 Eastern Conference Finals.

Satchel Lee attends her first Knicks game, on Tonya's lap.

With Woody Allen.

With Tonya and Denzel Washington.

With Bruce Hornsby and Branford Marsalis.

Jack Nicholson in the Garden.

With the Reverend Jesse Jackson.

Ray Amati

With Bill Cosby and Michael Douglas.

© George Kalinsky

The artist formerly known as Prince and his wife, Mayte. The Knicks murdered the Bulls that night by 30 points.

© George Kalinsky

With Madonna.

You can always tell when Chicago, oops, I mean Michael, is in town.
The front row here includes Itzhak Perlman, Jerry Seinfeld, Rob Reiner,
Connie Chung, and Maury Povich.

Money talks to Samuel L. Jackson and myself.

The greatest ever, but he must be stopped. The Knicks *will* beat Chicago.

I consider John Chaney a friend. I was introduced to him by Bill Cosby in 1988, the year Temple was ranked number one most of the year, basically playing only five men, 31–0 before they were finally beaten in the NCAA tournament by North Carolina. I went down to Temple to watch them play UMass in 1994–95, senior year of Eddie Jones, now def with the Lakers, and Aaron McKie, who played up in Portland. They were playing arch-rival UMass, coached then by John Calipari. The first time they played that season, UMass beat Temple at Amherst. During Coach Calipari's press conference afterward, he must have intimated something that enraged Coach Chaney, who had to be restrained. It looked as if he wanted to give Coach Calipari a Philly ass-whipping.

I made it a point to be at Temple for the rematch. That game was like a heavyweight fight. The game started at eight. By six o'clock, McGonigle Hall, the gymnasium on the Temple campus in Philly, was packed to the rafters. The atmosphere was incredible. What was most memorable to me was what occurred afterward. Coach Chaney had been accommodating and let me come into the locker room at halftime and after the game. He told me, "You just stay with the team, Spike, and see whatever is there to see. You're at home."

Temple lost in the final seconds. I went into the locker room. It was very still. The air was thick. Thick with the warmth of heated bodies. Thick with emotion. And dead quiet. People had their heads in their hands. People were crying. You could feel their dismay, but you could not be as sharp about the feeling as they were; if asked what the feeling was, it would be hard to try and describe it. You could best describe it as indescribable. I don't know if you can reproduce that, capture it. Jerry West might be right. To send or take somebody there, into the losing locker room of a good team that has worked its hardest, given all it has, and still lost the game in the end. No one can capture that kind of emotional crucifixion from outside, because you have to know the people involved, you have to have seen them work in practice, have gone through their late-night cramps, their disappointments, their small victories. You have to be a Coach John Chaney or one of his assistants, or maybe one of the parents, roommates, friends, even instructors or tutors, to understand what it is the players on a good team that lost are feeling. It is about as far from acting as humans get. They have given so much to the Game, and in a time of loss, seemingly great loss, they begin, however briefly, to question their own worth, their own existence. Why am I here? You're here to try. Be assured only of that. Times like this begin to make the facts of life painfully obvious to young people. At McGonigle there was a pained atmosphere of realization. Time slowed down. Nobody said anything. Nobody moved toward the showers. The different looks of anguish, pain, heartache, actual physical pain, great weariness, reflection. All of it was there. And then Coach Chaney stood in the middle of them and said, "Remember how this feels. . . . Okay . . . Tomorrow morning, six-thirty."

The most interesting stuff about sports is what happens in places like that losing locker room at McGonigle Hall, or in that halftime locker room at Kentucky or the pre-game locker room at Georgetown. Everybody can see what happens out on the baseball diamond, on the gridiron, on the court, but in those locker rooms, when the coaches are yelling and cursing and the players are questioning and encouraging and ignoring each other, and when they either do or don't commit to the purpose, and when it works out, or doesn't, that is real life and what needs to be put on film.

I have no preference for college ball over the NBA or vice versa. I just want to see a good, competitive game, at whatever level. I can watch a high school game, if it's a good game. If it's competitive, teams are evenly matched, then you have a story. That's what I enjoy—competition, the story. I think that's what makes sports great. Competitive games and stories can be found on every level, be it *Hoosiers* or *Hoop Dreams* or one not done yet. It doesn't matter what level. We all know the college game isn't what the NBA is, but I enjoy watching both. Always have.

Once, in Pat Riley's first year with the Knicks, I did a story on him for *Interview* magazine. Riley had played at Kentucky under Adolph Rupp. During the course of the discussion, I questioned him about Adolph Rupp, about him being a staunch segregationist. I said, "Pat, ever notice that there were no black players on your team?"

Pat said, "Spike, when I was at Kentucky, pretty much the whole

Southeastern Conference was all-white. I'm speaking now only in looking back, because at that time, I was probably naive to it. It had to do
with racism at that time, and the thought processes of a lot of the black
players in high schools in the South on where they would go to college,
and whether colleges in the SEC would recruit them—it just wasn't
done. It wasn't so much whether or not Adolph Rupp was a segregationist. The real breakthrough was when we got beat in the finals by Texas
Western [in 1966], by a team that started five blacks. The perception
was that these guys were city, street players. But the point guard Bobby
Joe Hill, Dave "Big Daddy" Lattin, Willie Worsley, Orsten Artis, Harry
Flournoy—these were great players. And they just kicked the hell out of
us. When that happened, the whole attitude changed. . . . I can remember Bob McAdoo telling me in 1984, 'That game affected me as a black
player in the South, because now maybe it was okay for me to go to college at North Carolina [which McAdoo did] or wherever.'"

That was all fine and good, but I wanted to get back to Rupp.

"Spike, he was a great man," said Riley. "He was a staunch disciplinarian. He was a military type of coach. Everything was 'Yes, sir' and
'No, sir.' I mean, there was just an ultimate respect you had for him
because he was a great leader and a great teacher. He was a hard man,
you know. But he had the biggest influence on me because of how organized he was, and how repetitive he was in his drills."

And that was it. Riley didn't see what I saw, which was fine also.
Despite Riley's opinion, none of the Texas Western players went pro,
except Big Daddy, who was up for a cup of coffee. The Kentucky team
had three pros on it—Louie Dampier, Riley, Dan Issel was coming in
later that year. So it had been a better collective effort from Texas Western. They had just played the game better that day, more as one, and as
organized as Rupp was, Don Haskins must have been better that day.

College basketball has changed since then. A school would be hard
pressed to win in Division One without trying to recruit African-
American scholarship players. Coach Riley didn't want to talk about
how it was, he wasn't touching that with a ten-foot pole. But sometimes
you have to talk about the unpleasant aspects, so maybe you can
become more aware of them, and, if you want to, you can work them

out. Great coaches like Adolph Rupp at Kentucky and Bear Bryant at Alabama tried to avoid a changing world. But it was too big—even for these giants.

C O N E Y   I S L A N D

You want to hear about the Marburys? If you do, we have to run it down a certain way, because it's that kind of story. You want to talk Marburys, you gotta talk first about Donald, the father. Donald would agree, I'm sure. Donald would be, like, "Yo, start with me." It was a joke on Coney Island, Brooklyn, where ball rules, where the Marburys came up. They said, "Donald Marbury has Division One sperm. All his sons played Division One." Donald didn't mind the joke.

There were five brothers in all, at least that I know about. There might have been more. There probably were more. There was Eric, Donald, Norman, Stephon, Zacky. Three brothers before Stef—that's what everybody called Stephon. Stef's not even the youngest. The youngest is Zacky. He's a junior at Abraham Lincoln High, right today, in 1997, and already Zacky thinks he's better than Stef. Snap, this whole Marbury thing is going right on into the two thousands, know what I'm sayin'? Donald runs it. He's the mayor of Coney Island. The mother's name is Mabel. She's real nice. Good people. Everybody likes Mabel, but Donald, he's the mayor.

Coney Island, if you look at how small it is, it's a wonder it puts out so many ballplayers, and then if you look at what's there, it's no wonder to it. It's probably no more than twenty blocks long and three blocks wide. Besides Stef and his brothers, you got Mo Brown, who played at St. John's. You got plenty more. It's all sixteen-story projects. But they're not like projects if you live there. Then it's home. Red elevator, green elevator, blue elevator—that's one building. During the summer your project plays against the other buildings. So you got about forty teams out on Coney Island and all they do is play against each other, sunrise to midnight, break for food, if you got it. Got enough game, somebody will feed you. And then when you go off Coney Island, you know how good you are. Never stop to think it's 'cause you play so much.

What else was out there on Coney Island? It's always been that way, so that's the way it is—boardwalk, Nathan's, Wonder Wheel, beach, basketball, projects. That's all you got. Basketball is all the work that's available in Coney Island. Twenty hard blocks by three short ones, that's it. There's lights on the courts, so you can play all night. So that's what they do. All night. If we go out there right now, they're playing. O'Dwyer. That's not the name of the park; that's the name of the projects: O'Dwyer Gardens. Then you have the three blocks—Mermaid, Neptune, and Surf. Coney Island is only three blocks wide. Then there's a train station. And on every project you got courts. So you got nothing else, but the train out of there. You go along 23rd Street, 25th Street, 27th Street, 28th Street, 29th Street, 31st Street, 32nd Street, all up and down Coney Island, the whole twenty or thirty blocks, and there are all those projects, and all of them have all those courts, and they be out there hooping hard, and you can call it what you want and call me what you want for calling them out like this, but this is the only way to tell it like it is—it's basketball 24-7-365.

Okay. You've got Keyser Park. Fifteen courts right there. Then you've got Cornell Houses, that's another fifteen courts. You've got Sea Rise, more courts. So all you do is play basketball. If you don't play, you'd better be playing some football. If you're not an athlete, you ain't getting no rap, don't no girls want to have anything to do with you. Unless you're a gangster. So you play ball. That's what you do. That's how you get props. You're good, and everybody knows it. That's all anybody ever asks anywhere, ain't it? You know the guy is good. That's what everybody is trying to get across. This guy can play. That's what Stef had. He had the stuff to be the Man. Early.

Lincoln High is over on Ocean Parkway. Then you've got Grady High. Grady is right down the street. In the last six years or so, Grady and Lincoln always battled for the championship. And Grady's players, where do they come from? Coney Island. So between Grady and Lincoln— that's all ball, right there. Lincoln is always stocked with Coney Island ballplayers. Lincoln always has a good team. There's probably been a Marbury on the Lincoln High varsity for the last, what, twenty years or so. If there wasn't a Marbury brother on the team, there was a cousin.

See, you had the Marburys and you had the McEaddys. That's Mabel's side. Mabel is their mother, right? Her name was McEaddy before she hooked up with Donald. Mabel's whachacallit, maiden name, is McEaddy. I may have met a McEaddy under 6 feet 2, but I don't remember it. They all could ball, too. Come to think of it, all of the McEaddys are like 6-6, minimum, seems like, and they all played for Lincoln. One plays for Robeson High now. Maybe it was like Division One eggs and Division One sperm put together. They were all groomed for basketball.

Eric, the oldest, was the best offensive player out of all of them, Donald's sons. He played at the University of Georgia back in the late '70s, early '80s. Yeah, I believe Eric was around for all'a'lat. Donald—Donald Jr.—he was crazy at first, back when he was young, maybe because he came behind Eric and it was already a tradition by then, or maybe it was because Eric didn't make it, so then Don knew he had to. Don probably had the best all-around game of all of Donald's sons. Don played at the University of Texas. I don't know what he did while he was down there, but for a while they said he could never go back to Texas. Don had played juco—junior college. He was like a basketball nomad. He went to every school.

Eric, he had a bunch of game, back in the day. Eric could've made it.

When Eric was in high school, it all started, the legend. Now the coach at Lincoln was a good coach, and Eric wasn't starting. He was *playing*, but he wasn't *starting*. He was in, like, the ninth grade, know what I'm sayin'? The coach told Donald, "I got seniors, I'm going to try and get them scholarships. Eric's a freshman. He's got three years after this, Mr. Marbury."

Donald said, "My son's s'posed to be starting. I don't care who you got. He ain't starting?" He told Eric, "Give the man his uniform back. You quit." Two weeks later, back on the team. When Eric was down at Georgia, they say both Donald and Mabel went down there and cursed out Coach Hugh Durham 'cause Eric wasn't starting. Finishing, that was going to be the problem.

'Zay, that's their cousin, the Marburys. He was only about 5-7. But he could play. Coney Island, yo. He was playing in summer tournaments, won a slam contest at City College, even though he was 5-7. He won even though he missed his first two out of three dunks. His last one was just that nasty. He got a scholarship, to Arkansas or somewhere down there. The day before he leaves he's in a stickup, a cab, driver gets shot and dies, 'Zay is still in jail today. He's Donald's nephew. He's Donald's brother's sister's child or something like that. But I mean, in Brooklyn, when I say the name Marbury, it tells a story right there. They been out there for years. Now I heard Donald used to be a great athalete. Used to run track. You know how you hear these rumors, who knows where they come from, but they out there, and they say when Donald was younger, the cops were chasing him one night on Coney Island. They say he ran in a straight line, right down Mermaid Avenue. The cops were doing 120 miles an hour in their cruiser and couldn't catch him on the straight-away, and so he got away, which was proper, 'cause he hadn't done nothing in the first place. These rumors out of the way, it's pretty safe to say he used to run track. Donald Marbury.

So it was Eric, Donald Jr., Norman, Stef, and now Zacky. They've got one more round in the chamber. Zacky's 'bout 6-4 and 220. But he already thinks he's a star. All of them think they're stars. I didn't like Zacky's attitude when he was on the team with Stef. He thought he was Stef. I mean, with Norman, Earl used to say, let's go play, and Norman was like "I can beat Mark Jackson right now. Why should I go work out with you?" That's the attitude.

Eric helped put Georgia basketball on the map, playing for Hugh Durham. When Eric went to Georgia, he played more his freshman year than his sophomore year, after Durham got to know him better. Not that Durham was no day at the beach, not by no means. He was in business. I think Durham had told him, "Eric, you need to transfer." Eric, he might have known it was true, but his philosophy seems to be Go opposite. So they say he said, "I ain't going nowhere."

I heard one time, Georgia played a game at the Garden and was down one to somebody, in the finals of some tournament. Eric, because he was at home, had something to prove. He was playing the best game he ever had for Georgia, and Eric had played some nice games, especially as a freshman down there. When Eric was at Georgia, he'd come back to

Coney Island and bring his teammates with him. The Marburys' place was kind of small, and they had all them boys, but Mabel, the type of woman she is, you don't tell her no, especially about her cooking. She's like everybody's mother rolled into one. Eric brought Unique home—Unique, that's Dominique Wilkins. He played with Eric for a minute down there at Georgia. Eric brought Terry Fair home, Jeff Thomas, all those ballplayers he met and played with down in Georgia, every type of player, he brought them all home and they all stayed at the Marburys' so they could play with Eric on Coney Island and see what real ball was like. They ate their meals over there. Mabel set it out for them. They lived on the second floor of their building. They used to live up on the twelfth floor, but then a couple of apartments on two that were joined came to be had. Then they moved down to the second floor and they are still there today. If they ain't, somebody named Marbury or McEaddy is there, I don't care if Stef bought ten houses and five condominiums, they've got to come back. I hear Mabel still works at the community center, day care, Thirty-fifth Street, on Coney Island. Ever since I first heard of her, she's been working. Whether she keeps on now that Stef is in the league, making big bank, now that the dream finally came true, only time'll tell. Only thing she ever said was "Buy me some house plants and I'm happy, boys." She just wants her boys to be happy. I think that's all it is.

Georgia even made the Final Four with Eric. But at the same time, Eric let it go to his head somewhat. He had to be the one. And so he pulled some shit in a game at that tournament at the Garden that day. Georgia down one, calls time with eight seconds left, and Durham says, "Eric, take the last shot." Figuring Eric is at home, wants to do good, can't nobody stop him anyway.

Eric supposedly told Durham, "I ain't letting you win *nothing.*" And then Eric takes the rock, dribbles through everybody upcourt, loses his man with a great move, pogos for the uncontested jumper, pogos over everybody for the game-winner—and then he comes down with the ball. He never shot it. Traveling. True story, they say, but it's hearsay to me 'cause I wasn't there. They say Eric was like You jerked me, I'll jerk you. That's what did Eric. That summer he came home and all he did was get high. Didn't want to ball no more. Eric could play. The change of environment and Durham took it out of him. Went up over everybody and came down with the ball. Never heard of nothing like it. Didn't shoot it because Durham had shamed him, taken his honor.

Then you've got Don.

Seems like after Eric left, Don had to fill some big shoes. When Don came through, he was smart. Don didn't have a big guy when he was at Lincoln. There was a big guy named Riddick, 6-6, had game, he had just come out to Coney Island. Don saw him play, hung out with him all summer, convinced him to leave a Catholic school, where he had tuition help, and transfer over to Lincoln, Public School Athletic League. So now they had a big man to go with a Marbury. So Lincoln went to the championship that year. Don went down to Texas. Don scored 50 points in one game down 'nere. Then I don't know what happened, they caught him with something, or whatever, and they kicked him out of school and he didn't get drafted. I don't know when else a tenth-leading scorer in the nation don't get drafted, 'doe. A Marbury, too? Don made amends, he went back to Texas for two years, and I think he even got his degree down there. Now he's teaching. Yeah, he's still up here. Teaching in Coney Island. Damn, they have to come back. They've got to come back.

You know, it becomes perpetual. At first it was like We'll get out of the projects as soon as Eric makes it. When Eric didn't make it, well, kick Eric to the curb. Now Don is the Man and we going! We out! As soon as Don makes it, we gone! Don was like the tenth-leading scorer in the nation, so it was like We're in there! If Don doesn't make it to the NBA, or when he didn't, it was like Ah, what's going on? Everybody blind?

By then people in Brooklyn almost felt sorry for Norman. Some did, anyway. People felt sorry for him because Norman was the one with the least game, but still all the hopes then went to Norman, after Eric, after Don. I went to see Norman play one night with my boy Earl. Earl's like "You got to see the next Marbury." Norman had a poor game. I'm looking at Earl like "Earl, thought you knew talent." Earl looks back like "He's a Marbury. You gotta see the whole set."

They were all guards, the Marburys.

But the thing with Norman, people say he wasn't as good as the others, but then again, Norman was the only one of the brothers who made All-City three years in a row, I don't know if it was because he was good or because he was a Marbury. But even Stef didn't do that.

Stef was tracked perfect. When he went to Lincoln, they went to the championship in his freshman year, but if you look at that team, the whole team was Division One. I could have played in the backcourt on that team. Stef did what he had to do. Give the rock to the old dudes, don't let nobody take it from you. And he did do that. Lincoln won the championship, and since he was a Marbury—We're *baaaack*. The year after that, he got hurt. His junior year, they just lost. He didn't have the same kind of help. His senior year, he wanted it, plus he had some help, so they went to the championship again. Good timing on that. Yeah, perfect timing.

Stef kind of redeemed Donald. Stef kind of redeemed Earl, too, once I saw him. Stef kind of redeemed Brooklyn. Stef was so obvious. Game on top of game. But then Eric had been obvious. Don had been obvious. Norman had been . . . Norman. Something always seemed to happen to the Marburys. Something always seemed to get in the way of the game. I mean, sometimes that can happen. People can get off into that Section 8 mentality, you know, and once you do that, it's hard to get out. Something good can happen, a knight in shining armor can come on through the door, people can end up in a ten-room house with eight bathrooms, a refrigerator and a freezer and a pantry stocked with grub, way out in the suburbs, and they'll still be sleeping five to a room, four bedrooms empty, talking about they can't sleep because there's not enough noise, talking about the good old days on Coney Island or in Bed-Stuy, West Side Chicago, Compton, or wherever it might be; talking 'bout how it ain't right, so they can't sleep. Oh, it can happen. The Marburys are the best, but all of them ain't gonna make it off Coney Island because . . . well, they just ain't. But we can always hope and pray.

On the day of the June 1996 NBA draft, there were so many different kinds of Marburys up in there that it was almost a family reunion. When Stef got picked third in the whole draft, right after Iverson and Marcus

Camby—all that pressure was released. You could see it on Stef's face. Deliverance. Redemption-Marburys. He declared hardship after just one year at Georgia Tech, but it wouldn't be official, the Marburys wouldn't be in there, until Stef got picked and Stef got signed. Then, when he got picked third, third in the whole draft, you could see the relief flooding his face. All the Marburys gave each other pounds, and Donald, he's laughing. And then Stef got interviewed on TV, and he just broke down. I've seen guys cry because they lose a game, or cry because they're happy, but Stef was outright weeping, couldn't hold it back an inch. It was more than being happy.

"It's the happiest day of my life. It just feels . . . I've just been under so much . . . you just don't know!" Then he broke down and just started bawling. Dog, Stef almost had *me* crying.

Actually he may have wanted to stay in school and be the Man. But I mean he was getting it from everywhere: No, you got to go, Stef. It could have been me, Stef. So you got to go and show 'em for me. Yeah. His brothers were telling him that. So he just knew that it was too much pressure on him at that age and ever since he was in the sixth grade he was hearing it, you know: Stef's going to be the one who's going to the NBA and get us all out of here. Stef's going to the NBA. He was groomed for the NBA. You know, they took him out of Coney Island early and let him play with all those outside teams. In the summers from his sophomore year of high school on, he was probably with Yo Riverside more than he was with his parents. He even went to Europe once. Went to Hawaii. They made sure everybody had a little investment in him. Seemed like all investors were at the draft. Somebody else said they noticed. Said they saw twenty people there with Stef. Earl said, "Twenty? More like forty-five." Had cousins coming out of the wood-work. I mean, Junior's had already named a cheesecake after him; they already had Stephon Marbury cheesecake on the menu. So you tell me. Does he eat at Junior's? Dunno. But I know they had the press confer-ence over there when he announced he was leaving Georgia Tech and making himself what they call available for the 1996 NBA draft. Yeah, I'm "available" too, then. Stef can bomb. I know Bobby Cremins, the coach at Georgia Tech, he must not have loved it. As much time as he'd spent in Coney Island over the three years before that. So at Junior's, it was like Coney Island was there.

So what Stef has to watch out for now, in the NBA, ain't so much other players, but leeches. He has got to get rid of the leeches. Buy me this, get me that. See, they got used to doing it like that when Stef was being recruited, because he was—is—the gravy train.

So they were like We're gonna be rich. We got it like that now. Some of his brothers said that. Eric said that. When Stephon was a freshman at Georgia Tech, they played Georgetown at the Garden. So I went on over there to see. Of course all the Marburys went. Stef is a freshman, matched up against Allen Iverson. Now, we're not talking about matching up with just anybody. This is Allen we're talking 'bout. So Allen gets off. Stef does some things, but you can tell he's under a ton of pressure, playing at home, in front of his people, at the Garden, and playing against Georgetown for the first and only time, and being a freshman and matching up with the best point guard since Isiah Thomas—maybe better than that. Allen was a sophomore, but it don't make no never mind, Allen is Allen. Allen did what Allen does. Once, Stef rose up for his j, and Allen hit the penthouse button on his lifters and got all on top of Stef's j. Just pinned it, right into Stef's hand and came down to the floor with the ball and Stef. Just snuffed him out like a candle. And then Allen patted Stef on the butt, kind of something like Jordan would do, and said, like, You gonna get your game on one day, Stef. Somethin' like that. Georgetown won.

After the game, Eric goes off on Stef, right there, right up in the Garden, right in front of everybody. I can't see how he was fronting, either; I mean, he meant it. Eric goes over to Stef and actually curses him out, just because he couldn't do nothing with Allen Iverson. Say, man, that's Allen you talking 'bout! Can't nobody do nothing with him! We can go all over the country and not find nobody who can do nothing with Allen. Ain't nobody around here *asking* to get dogged. But Eric was out there hollering at Stef in front of everybody, "What's wrong with you? Hunh? He ain't shit! He ain't shit! How you gonna let him do that to you! You're a Marbury! You understand me? You're a Marbury! What's wrong wit you? Hunh? Hunh?"

No wonder that boy cried on draft day, man.

I was there. Earl was there. Georgia Tech's coach, Bobby Cremins, he didn't say nothing to Eric. What was he gonna say? What could he say? You'd have to know Eric. Was it loud? Was it public? Was it. Eric's that type of guy. You'd have to know Eric.

But Donald, the father, he's the Man, the mayor. Don worked at a community center out on Coney Island, and there's always stuff going on, and Don wasn't involved, but whoever was doing it had to run it by him because he's Giuliani, he's got the boys, and everybody knew one of them was going to make it, and that meant they all made it, that meant Coney Island was something, so everybody ran their stuff by Donald. But the head of the Parks Department came after them, and they had this meeting one day, and so they were going back and forth, and Don looked up and said, "Do you know who I am?" Now that's getting to be the Word among all kinds of players—especially when they've screwed up and are looking for a window to get out of. When Michael Irvin, that fake Jerry Rice of the Dallas Cowboys, when he got caught in that suite at that hotel in Dallas with those quote-unquote lady friends of his or, as they describe themselves, "self-employed models," and a piece of crack the size of the Brooklyn Bridge, first thing out of his mouth was "Do'you know who I am?" Yeah, Michael Irvin, I do b'lieve they do know who you are. Why do you think they're celebrating down at the precinct? And when my man Juwan Howard got stopped on a D.U.I. down in D.C., first thing out of his mouth, "Do you know who I am?" Yeah, they know. All the better. Juwan got better sense. He had signed a big contract, and Juwan got pressure on him now. Who can he trust now? Nobody. His grandmother, who raised him in Chicago, died. Juwan, he'll be all right, though. Because he's smart and got good home training.

Donald, the father of the Marburys of Coney Island, wasn't a ballplayer, never been a pro, and before Stef, never had a son who had been a pro, at least not in the NBA, and here he comes now with "Do you know who I am? If I give the word, you won't be leaving here." So the meeting's over. Guy from the Parks Department was gone before you could say "Stef."

What does Donald do now? What he always did, I guess: my son is

Eric, my son is Don, my son is Norman, my son is Stephon, my son is Zacky. You can borrow favors with that collateral around Coney Island. My son's gonna take care of you. Don used to work construction in the summers, but wintertime, construction is out, and he was always hustling. Being a rolling stone. Andrew is from another woman, but he couldn't ball so they don't count him. If you could play, Don would claim you. If you can't play, then you're not a Marbury. At sixteen, a Marbury starts jumping. I mean up there. Eric was the best offensive player, and if he couldn't dribble great, so what? Once he gets the ball beneath the foul line, forget it, he's going over you. Don could take you off the dribble— more complete game. Stef's game is probably patterned after Don's. Don't know whose game Norman's was patterned after. Norman was good, but he might have been lazy. Zacky was with Norman. He can play. He can play off his name. He does very well at the camps. Of course, when you tell people you're a Marbury, it has an effect, I don't care where you are, I don't care how far you are from Coney Island.

It was good that Stef got picked up by the Minnesota Timberwolves—good so he could get away from the leeches, but it was mostly good because they had this big boy there named Kevin Garnett. Stef took notes from Don. Find yourself a big man. A big man and a Marbury, you're set. That's what they have up in Minnesota now, a big man and a Marbury. They should be golden.

Stef told Milwaukee, "I don't want to play for you." So Milwaukee drafted him number three and then traded him to Minnesota, for the number five pick, Ray Allen, and what they call considerations. So right there you tell a kid, Well, you can do whatever you want. Now we all know a superstar can do that. Michael Jordan, Isiah, Magic, Patrick Ewing—if the coach crosses them in their prime, the coach is gone. Same thing with a player who crosses them or doesn't fit the game they feel like they need to play to win it all. But busters like that, they are saying who will or won't win the NBA title—that's how good they are, what gives them that power. John Elway did the same thing in NFL football. Sent Dan Reeves to New York after Reeves picked that bum QB—what was his name, Maddox?—with a first-round pick when he was in Denver. Ain't saying Elway fired Reeves. Just go to the owner and say, "Mr. Owner, it's obvious you're going in another direction, since you took a college sophomore quarterback with a first-round pick, with Pickens right there to be had, while I need some receivers. Ain't had no receivers since I got here, so here's a list of four teams I'd like to be traded to. Hope you and Coach Reeves and your new quarterback will be happy."

Now the team owner, he's a smart man, so he tells John to come in and close the door. Next thing you know, Reeves is coaching the New York Giants. Magic, same thing in L.A. with Paul Westhead, when he wanted to slow it down. That's how Pat Riley got in there in the first place. Isiah said on the down low he'd rather have Mark Aguirre posting up low than Adrian Dantley on a clear out, facing. There it is. And Michael Jordan just about handpicked Phil Jackson. Word is Ewing stamped the trade sending Mason to Charlotte for Larry Johnson. So it ain't like it's unusual. But it is unusual for a nineteen-year-old to be able to say, I'm telling the NBA where I'm gonna play. Takes a Marbury for that. A Marbury wouldn't think there was anything strange in that at all. Stef asked to be excused because there's so many Marburys, too many to take care of, they're that type of family. So it's always going to be more. Eric has three kids now. Don has two or three kids. Stef has a daughter. And then, like I said, there's a bunch of cousins. I mean a whole bunch of cousins. You could go to a Lincoln High game, and I'm not exaggerating, 45 to 55 percent of the crowd would be Marburys, or related somehow. And the other 45 to 55 percent are on the bandwagon with them. In all of Brooklyn, all of Coney Island, there's nothing like them.

Donald Senior was so large that if he gave the okay, if Donald said you could play, you could play. If Donald said you could stay, you could stay. He ran it. Now, I never saw Donald Senior play outright himself, but Eric's uncle, Donald Senior's brother, he played. Donald was always coaching. He would tell you what you gotta do if you wanna be good, like a Marbury. And then, being that his sons could play so well, it seemed to make it be that he knew what he was talking about.

Some flashy guy took Stef under his wing back when he was at Lincoln. It must have been run by Donald. Took him and made sure he played for all the teams he sponsored and gave him a car. Stef got in trouble with that car. The guy came in and said, "Well, it's my car." This was just as Stef was going to Georgia Tech. Guy said, "It's mine, but I let him drive it." Stef kept a roll on him. Furnished the apartment. I don't know who furnished it, but with all the agents and would-be agents and coaches and assistant coaches coming by all the time, wanting to meet with Stef, Stef was like Well, can't let nobody come to my house; I ain't got no furniture. Next week—new living room set. I don't know where it came from. But it came. Everybody was milking it.

Stef's the Man now. He's barely twenty. Hope his body holds up. Hope his mind's strong. He's blowed up all over the East Coast, big billboards hooked up on Thirty-fourth Street in Manhattan and everything. And One sneakers. First Down gear. Could Stef and Garnett change ball? Hard to do. Harder than winning the NBA title, changing ball. I asked Larry Brown about it. He was cautious.

"Allen Iverson has unbelievable athletic ability and talent, but I thought Stephon Marbury was more comfortable as a true point guard. I just wish Stephon's family would leave him alone."

Stephon Xzavior Marbury, the hope of the Marbury clan, the bright light of Coney Island, Brooklyn, Abraham Lincoln High School, the Minnesota Timberwolves, and the NBA. This young man has had pressure on him from an early age, and when that comes from within, from your own people, your own blood—that's some different kind of shit to be dealing with right there. Your average person way out in the suburbs would crumple up under all that. Despite this weight, this burden, this Marbury will handle it. He will overcome. Stephon will save his peeps from the streets. He is the savior, minus the *x* and the *z*, but with an *s*, like Superman, like Stef.

CHANGE THE GAME

Who changed ball, changed the way the Game was played?

Hank Luisetti, an Italian-American *paisan* and a student at Stanford, changed ball, they say. In the 1937 NIT Tournament, instead of shooting the de rigueur two-handed set shot, he jumped up before he shot, then extended his arms before releasing at the tips of the fingers on one hand. He was the first jump-shooter. The first history knows about. In his line are Jerry West, Sam Jones of the old Celtics, Sweet Lou Hudson, Downtown Freddie Brown, Byron Scott, Reggie Miller, and countless others. An innovation became a basic. You need more now. Now a player doesn't want to be known as "just another jump-shooter." Jump shots can be denied by defenders in airspace.

George Mikan changed ball. Great size, at 6-11½, plus agility, inside. Complete physical dominance of the opposition, from a great height. Wilt, then Kareem, and now Shaq are of that tradition. Wilt especially. Individually dominant. Nobody of his era to compare him to in size and strength. Mikan, Wilt, Kareem, Shaq now. Wilt scored 100 points in one game—a record that may never be broken. One thing is for certain: it won't be broken by a good team, unless they are just trying to do that. Whatever Mikan decided to do, that's what he did, too. Whatever Wilt decided to do, he did. Wilt led the league in assists one year, led the league in rebounding, led it in scoring.

Bill Russell changed ball. He fostered the blocked shot as a weapon, both physically and psychologically. He would block a shot, then maybe not block it the next time, but feint the block and play the passing lane or angle. The shooter would think about the last time Russell grabbed his shot, and would alter his own shot. "If I was going to pick one player to begin a franchise, I'd pick Bill Russell," Bradley said. "I think he's the ultimate winner, and he's also the big man. Maybe that shows my age. Russell controlled the game with his mind. Wilt tried to control the game with his body. Russell would do enough with his body to be able to control the game with his mind. It was uncanny. He was intimidating, and he forced people to change [their shots]. Blocked my shot? Sure. Absolutely. Not a unique distinction." Russell brought in psychological warfare. In his line in that way are Magic, Bird, Olajuwon, and Jordan. In Russell's shot-blocking line: Caldwell Jones, Nate Thurmond, Bill Walton, Olajuwon, Ewing, Alonzo Mourning, Dikembe Mutombo, and young Tim Duncan. Billy Cunningham from Erasmus High recalls when the 76ers finally broke through in '67, after nine years of Celtic dominance, in the meaningless final seconds of the last game of the Eastern finals, a game the Sixers had clinched, as forward

Luke Jackson dribbled in for a meaningless layup—Russell ran him down, trying to block the shot. "He would not accept defeat," Cunningham said. Russell could be ornery, too. When we shot *Crooklyn,* there was a clip we needed for the old Knicks. It was an ABC game; ABC used to carry the league back in the day, Chris Schenkel and Bill Russell commentating. Bill would not give us the permission to use his voice. He said I came up to him one day and asked, "Bill, how could you play for the Celtics?" Now, I never said this. That's a crazy statement. I never formally met the man, but until this day he's mad about that. We tried to talk to him, but he sent word through his reps that he wasn't interested.

Russell has the reputation of being eccentric—and the ultimate winner. Russell was not the best play-by-play or color announcer, nor was he a great coach or general manager, but often the great ones are not. They don't have the same patience with mortal men. Russell once thought Pervis "Never Nervous" Ellison of Louisville would be in his line, drafted him when Russ was the general manager of the Kings in Sacramento, but it didn't work out. But he has a very interesting theory: he says there are usually twelve great players in the league at any given time. That was not enough, even in a fourteen-team league, for each team to have one. Now it's a twenty-eight-team league. Russell's genius on D started a push in vogue in the NBA now, always been in vogue on winning teams.

"The system has hurt, too. With this 1, 2, 3, 4, and 5 thinking, it's an era of specialization," says Frazier. "Many of these guys aren't basketball players. Not really, Spike. They're great athletes impersonating basketball players. Take a Dennis Rodman. He can't shoot and he can't pass and he is a weak dribbler. But you can win with him, on a certain kind of team. In this league, he's a star. Is he a better basketball player than Gus Johnson, Dave DeBusschere, Chet Walker, Elgin Baylor?" Clyde's eyebrows go up, like they did when he made a steal.

Oscar Robertson changed ball. He was a 6-5 guard and could do everything, perform all functions, from the guard position. "Oscar's thing was 'Why should I take the twelve-footer when I can get the eight-footer on you?' Earl Monroe was like that too," said Bradley. In Oscar's line were Walt Frazier, Dennis Johnson, Joe Dumars. The Big O brought multidimensional size to the perimeter. Whenever I see older ballplayers from the league, I ask them, "Who's the greatest player ever?" The people who don't say Michael Jordan, they say Oscar Robertson. By the time I actually saw him play he was at the end of the line, feeding Kareem in the post with Milwaukee, and Frazier was better by then. But I've heard it I don't know how many times: "Oscar was the Man." He was big and strong, playing the Game from outside in, instead of from inside out.

Kareem Abdul-Jabbar changed ball. His skyhook was the first *shot* that demanded a defensive double-team, forcing the defensive rotations that are commonplace today. He always seemed to be such a very conscientious brother. Someone who listened to jazz, who was well-read, well versed, so you could tell his parents had given him exposure to many things besides basketball. They did not raise some dumb jock. Great player. Great heart. A winner. After *She's Gotta Have It* came out, he invited Monty Ross and me out to his home in L.A., and we sat around and chatted, not about basketball but about our business. At the time he was involved enough to have optioned Wallace Terry's book, *Bloods,* about the experiences of African-American soldiers in Vietnam. The option must have lapsed, because years later in 1995, the Hughes Brothers used one of the stories from that book as the basis for their film *Dead Presidents.* The fans at the Garden were always hard on Abdul-Jabbar. I really think this used to hurt Kareem to his heart. Usually, even if you're on the opposing team, if you're originally from New York, most of the time Garden fans will give you a hand, but Knick fans were always hard on Kareem.

Earl Monroe and Pete Maravich changed ball. They brought *functional* showmanship. Marques Haynes of the Globetrotters could have done it twenty years earlier, but he went from Langston U., in Oklahoma, straight to the Globetrotters, after Langston beat them one night. As people have pointed out before me, Pearl always spun toward the basket. Pete had magical ball handling designed to get the ball in the hole—not just eye candy. They outwitted and outskilled defenders more than they out-quicked, out-jumped, or out-muscled them—but fooled them going to the goal. In some ways, Magic Johnson, Isiah Thomas, and Allen Iverson are of their tradition.

David Thompson changed ball. He brought the ability to bring a variety of functions in the third dimension—airspace—to the perimeter, to guard play. Jordan is his heir. Possibly Iverson. "I called him David the Giant-Killer," says George Gervin, the former scoring champion and All-Star of the San Antonio Spurs, the Iceman, often the foil of David and Maravich. "He had the greatest first step. And once he went up—he was 6-4, but he could jump out of the gym. He had the type of hops where he could go up and *throw* the ball down into the basket—never even touching the rim. His pull-up j was unstoppable. He got such *height*. Could not defend it."

Julius Erving changed ball. He was *explosive* in airspace, creative in swooping to the hoop, making the dunk accessible, a means of inspirational self-expression. Connie Hawkins and Elgin Baylor were his progenitors. His heirs were Dominique Wilkins, Shawn Kemp, Jordan, Pippen, Grant Hill, and a lot of wanna-bes. Dr. J. I remember a special that ran on TV: *The Doctor Makes a House Call.* The doctor would operate on people out there. Cut 'em all up.

Magic Johnson and Larry Bird together changed ball. They brought more size than Oscar and Clyde to multidimensional play. And they rebounded better. And they took responsibility and mental control of a game. They were tall, 6-9; skilled in all offensive ball functions, particularly passing; comfortable on the perimeter; saw all the possible horizontal angles. This formerly was a little man's game, then a 6-4 or 6-5 man's game. Magic and Bird raised the bar higher. Bird was a forward-forward, Magic was a center–point guard. Really, they didn't have positions, per se. They just played. They changed ball in the manner Oscar did, only taller; they did everything, played anywhere, except they could not defend in 3-D—laterally and up in airspace. Magic *needed* to be in the arena, but he couldn't play forever. Athletes can't play forever. Except in our memories. Time goes on, generation to generation, the players come and the players go. We all grow old, even our gods—the athletes. Bradley said it best for them: "What I miss most is the feeling that you get when you can see something happening two passes down and you start it and it happens, the moment occurs, and you're in a different place. The magic of it. I miss the feeling I had twice in my life, knowing I was part of a team that was the best in the world. I miss the camaraderie of the team, a team that executes, that executes in a way that is as much choreography as it is sport. I miss the improvisation within the context of structure. Where everybody knows what the play is, but everybody also knows, if you see an opening, take it, and if you score, terrific, and if you don't, your ass is . . . I think sports is perhaps the only place you can get it. I think as you leave sports, it's a memory, and the key is to keep the memory of it alive. Find a way to do that."

He also said athletes were by nature disciplined, had to be, to train themselves to become world-class. They have to learn to be disciplined in their non-athletic lives.

Frazier is a great example of this, to me. "I had too much pride," Frazier says, speaking of when he began in broadcasting, after retiring with Cleveland. "I just started working. I knew the Game, of course. But expressing that to people in terms they can understand and might enjoy—that was something else again. Every Sunday I'd get the *New York Times,* and I had my dictionary, and I'd go straight to the Arts and Leisure section, where they would critique plays. That's where I got 'dazzling,' 'riveting,' 'mesmerizing,' 'astounding'—the first descriptive words I incorporated. I had a book. I wrote words down in it. Soon I had five books filled with words. Then ten. Then twelve. I studied them— where they would be appropriate. I grew to love it. My girlfriend at the time was an English major. I'd run them by her. Finally she said, 'You're starting to get to me.'

"Finally I didn't have to look certain words up at all anymore. I found I knew them. It's like people. The more you see them, the more you know them. My vocabulary grew by an astounding percentage. I'd had to make a transition. See, New York fans are so knowledgeable. I was saying 'fast break,' they were saying 'transition.' I was saying 'passing,' and they were saying 'dishing.' So that's how I started. I added 'swishing' to their 'dishing,' 'shaking' to their 'baking,' wheeling and dealing. Watch Magic Johnson—man, this guy isn't just dribbling, he's gyrating, vibrating, he's a sneaker-squealer double-dealer. . . . For example, Spike, the

Knicks tonight were dreadful, hapless, pathetic, inexplicable, comatose, disoriented, stupefied, stagnant, lethargic. . . . I ran out of words to describe them." I had spoken to Clyde after a blowout Knicks loss to Pat Riley's Miami Heat. Some might like Clyde's delivery, some might not. The point is, he applied the same discipline to his new career as he had to his old. You can imagine how multidimensional he was in basketball.

Magic has done the transference—certainly he has in business—and I know I'll always have, like Clyde, the memory of him charging down the middle of a three-on-two break as the rat-tat-tat of Chick Hearn described the yo-yo-dribble, the look-away hook pass, and showtime, baby. . . .

Michael Jordan changed ball, brought Scottie Pippen, then Grant Hill, and particularly now Penny Hardaway along with him. Jordan was multidimensional with size on the perimeter, *and* multidimensional up in space, in the air, *and* explosive in airspace, *and* saw all the horizontal creative passing angles, *with* the added shot-blocking and psychological warfare edge of a Bill Russell. He had all of the components, and brought them all to both ends, offense and defense. Jordan is now the top of the line. And there will always be only one Michael Jordan. You should really watch him carefully. I doubt we'll see anything like him again. We may see something different, something like Allen Iverson, or some kid getting his third grade picture taken right now in Brooklyn or North Carolina or anywhere. But as of 1997, five Michael Jordans would beat five of any other ballplayer who ever lived, or probably ever will live, in their prime. It would be fun to watch five Jordans play against five Chamberlains, five Magics, five Birds, five Havliceks, five Russells, five Tinys, five Wests, five Isiahs, five Oscars, five Davids, five Pistol Petes . . . even five Walt Fraziers. The Jordans would win most of those. Also, the Jordans would show you things you'd never thought about before. He's convinced me enough times.

Michael Jordan is one of the greatest athletes who ever lived in any sport in any era, and all of us are fortunate that we saw him play, because the greats are like that—spectacularly individual. Singular in approach. There will never be another one truly like him. I can't say I saw Babe Ruth, Jack Johnson, Ty Cobb, Joe Louis, Jim Thorpe, Josh Gibson,

Sugar Ray Robinson, Ben Hogan, Cool Papa Bell, the Herculean guys, but now we are in the midst of one of the greatest athletes ever and we're able to see this gentleman perform, so even now we still don't fully appreciate how great Jordan is, and we won't even begin to know what he is in the context of American history until years from now.

I consider Jordan an artist. Not all athletes are. Not all make it to that level. Jordan is like John Coltrane, Louis Armstrong, Duke Ellington, Miles Davis, Ella Fitzgerald, James Baldwin, Toni Morrison, Romare Bearden, Paul Robeson, Jean-Michel Basquiat, James Van Der Zee, Jacob Lawrence, Elizabeth Catlett. When we speak of African-American artists, I think we now have to include Michael Jordan, and Muhammad Ali would be up in there, too.

"The guy I respect the most, and I've got to talk about him: Michael Jordan," says George Gervin. "He's making over 50 million a year, and he still has the desire and pride to be the best."

"Jordan thrives on having a challenge," says Derek Harper. "When you win the way he's won, it becomes more of a challenge to continue. A lot of teams are better than they've been in the past. But Michael and his confidence and ability will be able to come through again. Without a doubt, he's that much better than everybody in the league. That much better. You'd better believe it. No hype at all, man. I take my hat off to Mike and what he's been able to do as a basketball player."

The nature of basketball, the Game, is so that you can put an individual stamp on it, and that's what the African-American has done to and in the Game.

And I think maybe we can begin to include the black woman, because people like Sheryl Swoopes and Lisa Leslie and Dawn Staley have made inroads and brought a beauty and aesthetic to the playing of the woman's game also. The United States won the Olympic gold in 1996 in Atlanta, but there wasn't as much distance between them and the next team, the distance was not as great as between the Dream Team and the rest of the world, so there wasn't any tension in those games because the United States was going to win. That wasn't the case with the women's Dream Team; you weren't sure, you wouldn't bet the house. But they did win, every bit as convincingly as the men. But if you notice, the

American women had the baggy unis, just like the American men. The Australian women's team played in those one-piece Spandex hookups. That looked like next level to me. I asked Lisa, Sheryl, and Dawn to wear that one-piece uniform. They all hated it.

You see, how you play and how you look as you play depends on who you are and where you come from. The same thing with playing any instrument. I don't want to sound like we're the greatest people on this earth, but we are indeed people on this earth, and there's something to be recognized, something unique that African-Americans bring cultur-ally to music, to dance, to sports, to literature, to photography—whatever the medium is. This creativity shows in this game, basketball. It is harder to do in football. You might dance after you catch a touchdown or when you make a sack, but I'm talking about within the actual playing of the game. Basketball allows improvisation, and black folks have changed the game. Look at old footage and photos of the NBA of the two-hand set shot and that type stuff. It was bland. Bland, boring, and non-black also. It's like a cultural imprint being left on something. Like the way the Brazilians play soccer—not only the way they play soccer, the way the Brazilians *cheer* for their soccer team. They don't play like anybody else, either. It's because of their culture; that affects how they see the game and how they play, and I'd have to say it's the same for African-Americans in basketball. That's not to say that one way is good and another way is not. It's just different. For me, basketball shows what we as a people can do if the environment allows us to put our stamp of definition and cre-ativity on it. Everybody has an instrument, but it's how you play, you know; it's the same thing with sports—we've been able to do our part, certainly, put our creativity to work, put our spin on, and this is one area where we've really been able to express ourselves in a variety of ways. If you can argue that the Game isn't the better for it, then you're better than I am. The Game has been improved beyond any imagination.

I don't think this is a black-white thing, but nowadays guys make a whole lot of money and there's very few players out there whose fans really believe they want to win anymore. Michael Jordan wants to, whether it's in Ping-Pong, bid whist, pitching pennies, or whatever. But I bring up the question to a lot of athletes today, black and white, whether they have the will to win. Everybody wants to win on Saturday afternoon or Sunday afternoon when the game begins and the cheerleaders are out there and everybody tunes in. But the games are won in the preparation—are they willing to do what it takes to win before the game ever starts? Seems like some of them just are making so much money that they don't care. But they can just as often be vilified in the media for caring too much. So the media portrayal is one thing. But not playing hard, that's almost criminal. Not caring is criminal. Not trying to be the best ballplayer you can be is criminal.

"That pride and desire to be the best, to keep improving," Gervin told me. "Many guys don't have it anymore. I don't know if it's upbringing—it's gotta be upbringing to some degree. The things I was taught when I was young—morals, principles, spirituality—I wonder sometimes do our young people have any of those values, if they are holding on to their humanity, not becoming objects. A guy really has to come to the understanding of what is important to him, Spike.

"All basketball players have an Achilles heel—they want to play, and they want to play well—but some of them are getting this money, and I'm happy that they are, but some of them aren't working, and I ain't saying working for the money. I'm saying working to be better. Work on your hook shot. Work on your going left and right. We had a guy named Abdul-Jabbar who shot a hook for twenty years. Nobody does it today. These guys today don't know who he is, who Oscar Robertson is. They go back to Dr. J, that's it. I don't see 'em going back no further. That's where my stuff came from—Hawk, Dr. J. I tried to emulate Doc, then add my own, come up with something original. You had to watch somebody coming up. You need that—a pattern, a model. You gotta come out here and work. You've got to bust your butt. You've got to come to practice, and come ready to work. This is what I did to be successful. Hard to motivate a guy who doesn't want to work. They're glad they've got the good job, reached the goal, can rest on their laurels, getting a good check, and will take everything else that goes along with it . . . but sometimes, when you take that word 'struggle' out from in front of you, then it's easy for a guy to quit getting better. You get that big check, the struggle is gone, and then you've got all that in front of you—fine women, all that you can see. And you don't know—even *she's* got a plan!"

To be a professional athlete and not care if you win or lose—to me, that's sacrilegious. Why? Because the artistic innovations—to say nothing of the drama—come within the context of winning the game. That's the picture that's being painted. That is the canvas. Sometimes it takes creativity to accomplish it. How do I do this in order to score or to stop the other guy? No one may have ever seen it before, what I'm about to do. I don't know, but this is what I had to do in that moment to make it happen, to take another step toward winning the game. Not looking good. Winning.

I don't think Charlie Parker said, "Let me think of something now that nobody else has done, so people can say, 'Ooo.'" It was between him and the instrument, him and the music. Artists don't approach it that other way. They play what they feel. It was something inside of them. That's the way Michael Jordan plays. Same thing with Ali. Creative self-expression by mental control of human muscularity. That's what it all is, really, all the arts. You have guys who manufacture it. That's where I would put a Deion Sanders, he has a definite goal of marketing himself, to make his services more valuable. And it has worked for him, that sizzle, that flash. It's more like a marketing thing with him, though Deion is truly a great athlete and might have had to do what he did in order to be paid commensurately with his talents. Dennis Rodman, too. What can I do to make myself stand out? But it is not within the context of the game. And I wonder if sometimes you start to believe your own hype, your own game. A choreographed dance here. Changing your hair color in pastels. Full-body tattoos. Mascara. Marrying yourself. Wearing wedding gowns. That has nothing to do with playing or winning the game or artistry. Distinguish myself from the rest. That's just manufactured expression, that's all marketing and promotion, and it's hollow. No one else ever had the instrument that Michael Jordan has. He has the total game, the total flawless package, and he's the best promoted and most marketable athlete since Babe Ruth.

Michael has great will, too. In a competitive sense, and probably an

artistic sense too, that's what gets him over. Forget about his great athletic abilities. What I most admire about him is his will to win. It is
unparalleled. He just refuses to lose and a lot of times these guys are
evenly matched physically. It's a matter of who wants to win it more and
who can exercise his will within the context and confines of the problem
at hand. The guy with the biggest heart won't give up, just keeps on
coming and he makes the other guy quit. Muhammad Ali's *will* beat Joe
Frazier in Manila in 1975. Jordan does the same thing. He makes the
opponent believe as he believes, that if it keeps on going long enough,
he is going to prevail because it is predestined, so he demoralizes the
other guy, takes his spirit, and eventually makes him quit. Hesitate.
Takes his heart. Makes him doubt. And that is all it takes against Jordan.
It happened to Dan Majerle in the NBA finals, Phoenix vs. Chicago, in
1993. I don't think Dan has been the same since. He had a shot in game
six, a good shot at the end that would have sent the series to game seven.
He was open, right baseline. He went up, and you could see him looking
around, breaking form, thinking of Michael Jordan—where is he, I
know he's here—and he pulled the string, missed. That was it.

"Last year in the playoffs, Jordan came over and started talking to one
of our players at the time, Willie Anderson, at halftime," Jeff Van Gundy
told me after the 1996–97 season started. "And I said, 'Willie, get the
fuck away from him.' Because he's a con man. He doesn't give a shit
about one person in that other locker room. I don't care what he says
about it. He cares about one thing, and that is winning. And I respect
him for that. And he uses everything he can to his advantage . . . uses his
movie to bring them in, like he really befriends them. He knows exactly
who he's bringing in, and he knows who he's trying to get—to soften up
a little bit. He uses everything in his power."

Coach Van Gundy told me this and then must have thought about it
later and become so enamored of the view that he repeated it before the
Knicks played the Bulls for the first time this season, on January 21,
1997. The results were interesting, and we'll go over them shortly. But
for now let us allow him to finish his thought: "I think [Jordan] is con-
sumed with winning and I really admire him for that, because so much
of this league is now about 'me' and the stats and all that . . . if every-

body was perfect, they'd all be Jordan. It's like with Patrick. Every time he's put up to be graded . . . it all comes out: 'He's not Jordan.' Well, you know what, Spike? He's not. And neither are the other 326 players in the league, or whatever it is."

Not to be the old Yankee Yogi Berra and say that 90 percent of the game is half mental, but that is not so far off. Take a Jerry West. What can you say about the tenacity of this man's mentality? Won the Olympic gold medal in Rome with Oscar, when West was known as "Zeke from Cabin Creek," as in West Virginia. Goes to the Olympics. Sees Oscar. No doubt thinks, "Damn." West dunked during those Olympics in Rome. Then he had the fortitude not to quit, even after all those losses in the finals to the Celtics in the 1960s, to the Knicks in 1970 and 1973, losing all those times as Boston and the Knicks won championships, being in that losing locker room after the last game, time after time, averaging 30-plus points the whole time, hitting 62-footers and losing, for Christ's sake, then finally winning a ring in 1972. Fourteen broken noses. One ring. Now he's one of the best executives in basketball, been with the Lakers through the Showtime run of the 1980s, and today. West never knew. He'd get it all on the back end. But he had the fortitude. He had the fortitude to keep showing up. That's mentally tough.

Now a few young players are on the horizon as Jordan is at his apex.

The person who first told me about Allen Iverson was Bruce Hornsby, who is a Virginian. He said, "Spike, you have got to see this young man." I'd heard similar comments before, but Bruce was very enthusiastic. I'd met Bruce through Branford Marsalis. Bruce is a big sports buff. He met Branford when they were playing together on the Grateful Dead tour. Bruce told me about Iverson, then later about this incident at a bowling alley where some teenagers and adults got into a dustup, and the upshot was, Allen was accused of throwing a chair that hit a woman and injured her. Allen denied it. He' been Virginia Player of the Year in football and basketball two years running—quarterback in football, a guard like nobody had seen in hoop. Bruce talked more about Iverson's talents as a quarterback, raved how Iverson was special, and anybody who saw him would see it too. Somebody must have known something, because the next thing I hear, Iverson is in jail.

I wanted to go and visit him in jail. He had gotten a lengthy sentence behind the alleged chair-throwing incident. What it really was—any fool could see this—is that this young man was immensely talented, with a great future promising equally immense wealth, and he was black, and that combination still doesn't sit well in some quarters in Virginia. Even though the governor of the state at that time was L. Douglas Wilder, a black man. However it began—with jealousy in Allen's group, or from another group escalating in a free-for-all—it ended with Allen absorbing this undue penal hit, five to ten for felonious assault with attempt to maim, or something equally bogus. They said he hit somebody, threw a chair, and the judge threw the book at him.

So did I. I sent him a copy of *The Autobiography of Malcolm X*, to keep him inspired while he was in the slammer. Later he thanked me for it.

The next year Wilder pardoned Iverson. His mother had gone to John Thompson, and Coach stepped in and laid down the law, his law, and Iverson went to Georgetown. I had no idea that's how it would turn out when I sent Allen the book. Once I saw Allen—the Truth. He looked unguardable. His first game was against Arkansas. Coach Nolan Richardson's defending NCAA national champions won the game, but as Coach Richardson said, "We put traps on him nobody gets out of, and he got out of them with ease. That young man is way past quick. He's special."

I watched him over the next two years. I went when G'town beat St. John's at the Garden in his freshman year—when the hype machine pitted Iverson against Felipe Lopez. Georgetown lost to North Carolina in the tournament that year—to Jerry Stackhouse and Rasheed Wallace. Allen played nervous in the first half, but then scored twenty in the second. Even though it was too late, the crowd gave him a standing O when he left the floor. In his sophomore year, I went to the Garden when Georgetown played Georgia Tech and Stef at the Garden. Too much Allen.

During the 1995–96 season, Georgetown played Memphis. Allen was Allen. In the first five minutes of the game, Coach Larry Finch tried four different guards on him. Allen left them all standing there or had them going the other way. After the game, Coach Thompson gave his usual press conference. Somebody asked if Coach was concerned about Iverson; sure, he had talent, but didn't he lack discipline? "What you are calling discipline might in fact be physical limitation," Coach said. "For it's one thing to bring the ball out and run the offense if you know you can't beat your man. That's not discipline so much as limitation. It's another thing to know you can take your man and go to the goal and probably score, but you bring it back out anyway, because the coach tells you to, in order to run the offense. That's a different kind of discipline. I'll tell you what, in a couple of games we ended up losing, I wish I *had* let him go."

The room got quiet. For a press conference. "Let me ask you," said Coach Thompson. "Have you *ever* seen a guard with that kind of athletic ability?" An unsettled mood came over the five or six reporters. Sure they had. Hadn't they? After I saw Allen play, I knew what Coach meant.

Iverson declared hardship after Georgetown was eliminated by UMass in the Great Eight round of the 1996 NCAA tournament. He was the first pick in the June NBA draft, by the Philadelphia 76ers— which made the Sixers' day. They already had Jerry Stackhouse.

Allen Iverson of the Philadelphia 76ers scored 30 points in his first NBA game. In his second game, the Sixers came into Air's Crib, when the Bulls lifted a fourth NBA championship banner to the rafters. The season before, Stackhouse, then Philadelphia's rookie two-guard, was dropping 30s on people, and said the league wasn't as hard as he thought it was. Michael took umbrage. Went for 50 on Stack. Now on Iverson's first trip in, after the Bulls established the welcome-to-the-NBA blowout, Scottie Pippen heckled Iverson. Said he couldn't guard nobody. That's the insult now: *"You can't guard me, boy. You can't guard nobody out here."* The answer is to find a way to guard him. Or get off with your own O and say, "You can't stop me, either." Michael came over, I guess to mediate. Michael told Iverson not to worry, there'd be other nights, whatever he told him. It was between the brothers. Iverson told Michael Jordan to get away from him. At first, that might seem to be asking for it. But when playing Jordan, you can't let him inside your head.

More Coach Van Gundy on Jordan: "There is almost a need by the players to have Jordan like them. And he uses that unbelievably, he strokes them, and then he sucks off of them."

In his first game against the Knicks, Iverson had 35. He fouled out both Charlie Ward and fill-in Scott Brooks. When Chris Childs recovered from a hairline fracture of a bone in his leg, Childs was back for the next game against Philly. Now we'd see. This time Iverson scored 25 points, with 9 rebounds and 9 assists. The Sixers won both games.

In this way, Stef and Iverson are alike. They both will have a hard time leaving their past behind, because their past will always be personified by people they carry with them, out of guilt, out of misguided loyalty, out of naive youth. Stef and Allen are two of those rare ones with a chance to change ball. But I don't know if they can do it by themselves. No one can. Stef can do it because of who's playing with him. If he can get over the hump of coming in a year or two before he was ready. Iverson can do it because . . . he's Allen. Stef and Allen should be battling themselves and against the Game and the pitfalls well into the next millennium. None of which does anything at all for the New York Knickerbockers. Then again, you never know. In a day of free agency, movable talent, it's all in how you put it together.

> > >

Someone once said to me, "Penny Hardaway is too much of a human being to be like Jordan." I think he meant to say "killer instinct." But I think that you have to make a distinction between being a good person and being a winner. A lot of people, when they think of Michael Jordan, the one word they use always is "assassin." He's a cold-blooded killer. Now would you use those words to describe a nice person, a good person? No. But we're talking about athletes engaged in competition. The desire to win. If somebody wins, that means somebody has to lose. To win means you may not have to be nice. There's the conflict of being democratic, Mr. Nice Guy, that's okay, you messed up. Winning is not a democracy. It's not for everybody. Somebody has to take charge. You have to make a distinction between what you do in an athletic arena, a competitive setting, and at home, a social setting. It's different from one's natural persona. But some people say there is a carryover; you can't turn it off and on. Ask some NFL wives or girlfriends, they say. Does competition change one's persona? I can't answer that.

I've shot two commercials for Nike with Penny and Li'l Penny, his highly successful alter ego, with the voice-over provided by Chris Rock, and the would-be love interest played by Tyra Banks. In one spot that I didn't direct, airing during the 1996–97 season, Penny and Li'l Penny are walking along and Li'l Penny tells his human alter ego, "Michael Jordan says you have unlimited potential," and that it was time for him to take over in Orlando, now that Shaq had moved on to L.A. Penny says, "M.J. said that?" Penny has always been a bit in awe of Jordan. Not so Magic. I think Magic's game was what Penny was trying to get on top of. Jordan was another matter. At the All-Star Game during Penny's second year in the league, Jordan snatched off his warm-ups as he was being introduced. Penny looked shocked, bewildered. Later, as they were standing in the line of stars at midcourt, Jordan laughed and smiled and teased and told him, "I do everybody like that. I used to do Dumars like that." Penny said, "Really?" Totally awestruck. You could see it. What Jordan did not say was that he never did the scrubs like that, he never did that to people who could not compete with him. Them he never acknowledged. That's why I say I understand Allen blowing off Jordan when Jordan tried to get inside his head. Jordan is inside Penny's head. But Scottie Pippen says it is Penny who is best in ball now.

Michael Jordan is a great human being off the court, but you're not trying to make best friends on the court, and I think sometimes Penny's a little bit too unselfish and that there are times when you really need to take over a game, if you are one of the few who can do that, which Penny is. Penny demonstrated what he could do when Shaq was out with an injury at the start of the 1995–96 season. And he had demonstrated it to me long before that. I wasn't alone.

"With Penny, as good as he is, I'd have done anything I could to keep that group together," said Larry Brown. "Coaching those kind of kids is, number one, a great responsibility. Sometimes I think when a coach sees they're gifted, they don't keep teaching. With them, as young and as good as they were, with so much ahead of them—yeah, it *would* have been fun to coach them."

Like Jordan, Penny has complete on-court comfort of flexibility. Deep shot, the handle to run point, hops, genius for the angles, can defend in airspace. He has everything Jordan has. Except maybe the mentality. Penny can carry the Magic—but he needs to find someone, like Jordan found Pippen. Now that Shaq's gone, Penny's gotta take over. Penny has to be a leader. Shaq's not there anymore. Penny was under wraps. It's time for him to blossom. Li'l Penny has a crazy kind of confidence. It's been a successful campaign for Nike, but on the court, I don't think the real Penny Hardaway has scratched the surface yet. Under the right circumstances, he could change ball.

Early in 1997 I went down to Orlando to appear in a commercial that would air during the 1997 Super Bowl. The theme was Li'l Penny's Super Bowl Party. A Nike spot, of course, and in it were Tiger Woods, Olympic sprinter Michael Johnson, Ken Griffey Jr., football's Barry Sanders, Lisa Leslie and Dawn Staley off the gold-medal U.S. women's Olympic basketball team of 1996, Jackie Joyner-Kersee, Sergei Fedorov of the NHL, original Iceman himself George Gervin, Juwan Howard, and big 7-7 Gheorghe Muresan of the Bullets, Penny's teammates on the Magic roster—Gerald Wilkins, Horace Grant, Nick Anderson—and Tyra Banks. Li'l Penny knows how to throw a set.

I talked with the Magic players, and with Penny, coming off knee surgery, set to return to the lineup. The Magic players talked about winning the Atlantic Division now that Penny was back. I looked at Penny. The next night would be his first game back, coming off the injured list. He said he was ready. Apparently he was. The Magic promptly won six of their next seven games.

> > >

In 1993 I went to Memphis, to the Pyramid, on the banks of the muddy Mississippi, to see a game between Cincinnati and what was then Memphis State, to see Nick Van Exel, star guard of the Bearcats, and most particularly to see Penny Hardaway, star of Memphis State. Ralph hooked me up. He had done an article on Penny for *Sports Illustrated* and later said I had to meet Penny, watch him play, and meet his grandmother and his mother. But especially meet his grandmother. Mrs. Louise Hardaway was a sharecropper in rural Arkansas for nearly thirty years before she and her husband and children made a lateral move to Memphis in 1951, where they purchased a three-room shotgun house off an alley, with tar-paper walls and no floor, with their entire family fortune of $350. Vast improvements had been made in the place by the time I visited Mrs. Hardaway, but she was still in the same tiny spot. The less fortunate houses on the alley block spoke volumes about the grinding and pitiless nature of poverty's grip on those who would've escaped the hardships of the delta. Mrs. Hardaway's place was a little well-kept rose in a desert. Everybody was telling her she sure wouldn't be poor much longer, but she just laughed and said she never had been, pretty much had what all she needed. A beer every now and then didn't hurt, she said. Otherwise, as long as her Penny was fine, she was fine. She raised him on school lunch cafeteria wages. Mrs. Hardaway may not have been a woman of formal education, but she was a strong, wise black woman whose hands had rocked the cradle of what may one day be greatness. I had a good time. She reminded me of my own grandmothers.

We went to the game at the Pyramid. Coach Larry Finch was accommodating. Coach Bob Huggins, his junior-college behemoths, and the impish Van Exel entered the edifice to torrents of boos. Huggins shot his cuffs, ordered his team to warm up. During the game—Cincinnati won—Penny came on a follow and slammed it through, one of many great plays he made that day. I could see right away he had Total Game. Penny and I met later and promised to keep up.

Later, what was surprising was that Nick slipped a little bit in the draft. The Knicks, along with the rest of the league, knew he was going to be deemed a head case, and he slipped all the way to the second round. Jerry West, the tenacious one, stole him then. I guess Nick missed a couple of planes and had refused to go to some other teams for workouts, and he's had some problems since he's been with the Lakers, most notoriously when he pushed a referee, Ronnie Garretson, over a call he didn't like. That's not really the type of behavior you want from your point guard. But Nicky can light it up. Still, at point, he has to be the one with the calm head.

I've heard it said the Lakers might eventually move Nick over to the two-guard on offense, like they did with Norm Nixon when they got Magic; Kobe Bryant at point. Nick might be like Iverson—they have the scoring mentality of a two-guard, even though they are the size of a point. Nick kind of shoots too much for a one. Kind of? He's launching as soon as he steps on the floor.

I like Penny's game better than Grant Hill's. And I like Grant's game. I don't like how the league and some of the companies he endorses tried to position him at first, as a Goody Two-shoes who doesn't listen to rap music and isn't like "those others." As Les McCann once sang, trying to make it real "Compared to What?" This happened when Michael retired and Grant came into the league—a concerted effort to market a particular image, even though this was another rookie in his first year. There was a time when Jordan was just another rookie. It's part of the process—any process, not just in the NBA. But the campaign worked. Hill was the leading vote-getter for the All-Star Game as a rookie. It pays to advertise. It helps to have a great veteran like the guard Joe Dumars to lean on in times of stress. Penny didn't have that. But he should be able to flourish now that Shaq is no longer there. As I've said, Scottie Pippen has said in private company, on more than one occasion, that at this point, he thinks the best player in the league is Penny. And if you tied Michael Jordan down and gave him sodium pentothal he might admit it too. But that would be the only way Michael would say it. He's not ready to abdicate just yet. With Shaq gone, Penny is going to have to pick it up. He has the game to pick it up. He has the background, the character, to be able to pick it up. But the desire? The will? Penny was one of the few who came into the league ready to learn how to do that. Mrs. Hardaway did that for him. He's fertile ground, but what kind of competitive seed is planted there? Whether being the Man now will change his approach, I don't know. We'll see who's great, who were the people on Orlando who played great when Shaq was there and who have been vaporized since his abrupt departure. Two people at the head of that list in question would be Dennis Scott, who made himself a personal attaché to Shaq, and Anderson, who's got more game than Scott, but can be shaky. It's one thing to put your feet together and shoot threes because the defense has to double Shaq. It's another thing to get your shot off against a defense without help, without screens. A lot of times, people will misread that.

I'll give you an example from football. The Dallas Cowboys won the 1996 Super Bowl over the Pittsburgh Steelers. Dallas had a cornerback named Larry Brown. Not the coach. A decent player. But he was playing on the other side of Deion. So he could play double-teams on his side, because Deion was good enough to cover his man by his lonesome all over the field. So Larry Brown got two interceptions in the Super Bowl, because he had no deep responsibilities. Pittsburgh quarterback Neil O'Donnell gift-wrapped two interceptions right to Brown. And so almost by default, he was the MVP of the Super Bowl, and he got this big free agent offer from the Raiders. Once he got to the Raiders, there was no Deion on the other side. Turned out Brown couldn't beat out either of the Raiders' starting cornerbacks, Albert Lewis or Terry McDaniel. So he became a $2 million a year bench warmer. Likewise, the quarterback who made Brown briefly famous, Neil O'Donnell, was given $5 million a year to play for and perhaps rescue the New York Jets. The Jets finished the season 1–15 with O'Donnell at the helm—although you couldn't really say that, because he missed more than half the season hurt, once injuring his calf while throwing pre-game warm-up passes at Giant Stadium in the Jersey Meadowlands.

You know, if you're a general manager, you've got to take that into consideration before you make some crazy offer to a guy. Why did he succeed? Who were the people around him? One of the definitions of a truly great player is, does he make his teammates better? Deion Sanders did it in football with the other cornerback, Larry Brown. Jerry Rice made all the receivers, backs, and quarterbacks he played with better. But if you answer that question, "No, he doesn't," then you have to question if they are great. Do they make their teammates better?

Penny Hardaway does make his teammates better.

> > >

Work ethic is a large component of being a great player.

That's one of the knocks against Shaq, and it really bothers him, but we're at a point in history where athletes want to sing, they want to rap, they want to act in movies, have their own talks shows, they want to shoot commercials with Pytka and Singleton and Spike and whoever. But back in the day, while they may have wanted to do the equivalent of all that—and they might *not* have—what they *really* wanted to do, what they really *needed* to do, was play basketball well, and do well in their sport, and win, and get paid for that. No one should begrudge any athlete for trying to expand his or her horizons, but at the same time—well, there's no reason why Shaq should be shooting 50 percent from the free-throw line. When a professional athlete neglects his craft in order to take advantage of broader horizons, that's self-defeating. Even doing other things, you have to be more selective. You can't just do a movie because somebody wants you to do a movie. Be selective. What image does this show, not only of me but of everything else around me? You want to talk about keeping it real? Does this vehicle allow me to become better as an actor? Can I act in the first place? Does the role or the video take advantage of my strengths? Many players have the financial wherewithal to pass on a project. We're not talking about struggling actors busing tables and having to take whatever comes down the pike. But looking at some of these films, it seems so. Likewise with recordings.

"That's the real difference between today's ballplayers. Back in my day, the late '70s and early '80s, I really feel we were more skill-oriented," Ice Gervin told me. "Today the players are more athletic, can jump better, strong, big, but their skills are diminished. Guys don't work as hard on their skills. And it *is* a game of skill. Hard work means production. . . . Now it's dunking, and that's it. So then I start wondering about these college coaches. What are you teaching them? You send these kids out here one-dimensional. 'All I want you to do is get the ball off the board.' 'You shoot.' 'You dribble, but I don't want you to shoot.' When you deal with ballplayers like that, it doesn't give them the opportunity to fully play. So a lot of them become frustrated with that old mechanical ball, and they don't want to work on their game, and then that becomes their habit."

All this has to do with being true to your craft. Everything has to come out of that. The Havliceks, the Magic Johnsons—these guys got better as pros. If there was a flaw in their game, they worked hard all during the off-season. Neither Havlicek nor Magic could shoot from the outside when he came into the league. Each coming in a different era, they worked on that. And worked on that. It was between them and the Game. Until, by the mid-point of their careers, they had not only become acceptable outside shooters, they had become outstanding outside shooters. Jordan doesn't even dunk anymore; he's leading the league in scoring with a perimeter game. I have to believe there's more satisfaction for the craftsman in doing something like that than in looking amateurish in some rap video or half-baked film.

If a player has trouble going to his left and they defend him that way, make him go that way, then he's got to work on that. The great players still want to develop their skills into a more multidimensional game where they have no weaknesses, because the NBA is a tough, tough league in which to excel night in, night out. If they see a person has a weakness, they are going to lock in on that weakness, attack it. They are going to keep attacking it until you shore up the weakness or until they force you out of the league. And if you know people are attacking your weakness, and you do nothing to rid yourself of that weakness, what type of athlete—and person—are you?

As the Iceman said, one difference between 1970 and 1997 is that now there may be better athletes who jump higher, run faster, and are bigger and stronger. But mentally, maybe they're not as strong as the older guys were. Today some of these guys just want to get a dunk and they're satisfied. If they can shatter a backboard, they think they've done something. And the media lets them think it. Why? Because that play will be seen all across the country for weeks. And on *SportsCenter*?

Fahgetaboutit! I think the slam-dunk championship eventually came to be a mockery of the league. And now the really big stars don't even participate in that stuff, and I don't know how much longer they can go on with that. Anything stagnant is not going to last.

"We ought to have programs with mentors like Doc, myself, a lot of us, where these young guys have to come in and talk to us," Gervin said. "You still need some guidance and professional direction. Only way you're gonna get it is from guys who've been there. Who can tell you what to do better than a guy who did it fifteen or twenty years, highest level possible, and was successful doing it? Can't find a better guy. Can't go ask a doctor, because I'm not talking about medicine. I'm talking about *bas-ket-ball.* I proved to be one of the best. And now I'm opening my heart and my experience to you, if you need anything pertaining to this game, come ask, and I'll tell you . . . seems like all I'm telling you about is playing, or trying to tell you how to stay out of trouble so you can keep playing. They don't want to hear it, Spike. It makes me sad, yet I've got my own children, and I don't mind raising them. If you don't want to hear it, I'll go on to the next one—won't let one bad apple spoil it. One might say, 'Ice, I'll listen.' That's the one I want to catch.

"That's what I loved about this game, man. This game is all about relationships," Ice Gervin told me. "I made some good ones while I was playing. Yeah, it's a different era now—but it's still *bas-ket-ball.* You've gotta have a certain kind of relationship with teammates and coaches to be successful. 'Let's show the world you're one of the best to ever pick up this ball.' That's what you should be trying to accomplish. Our youngsters need us—more than they think. The NBA needs a mentor program. Sooner or later someone will get ahold of these young guys, and we're going to straighten them out, so they will want to do something with and for themselves on a deeper level."

> > >

Shaq is a great physical specimen. The first time I saw him was down in Louisiana. I was down there to see the Super Bowl between the 49ers and the Denver Broncos, in 1990. We drove down to Baton Rouge to see LSU play. Shaq wasn't even starting that day. Stanley Roberts, now with the L.A. Clippers, was starting, and Chris Jackson, now Mahmoud Abdul-Rauf, was on the team. I went to the locker room afterward and met Shaq. Now that he's left Mickey Mouse Town and gone to L.A., he is going to be distracted even more. You know he is. Still, I'm sure Jack Nicholson and Jerry West will take him. Are you going to win a ring with Shaq? I remember sitting at home and watching the Houston Rockets play the Orlando Magic when the Magic, with Shaquille O'Neal, Horace Grant, and Penny Hardaway, got swept in four games by the Houston Rockets. Shaq seemed too much in awe of Hakeem. Shaq always makes disparaging remarks about Ewing's game. I don't know if it's a fact if he doesn't like Patrick Ewing or his game, but the way he plays against Patrick was the way he needed to play against Hakeem. There is no way that Houston should have swept that Orlando team in four games in 1995. The Magic beat the Bulls that year—the year Jordan came back for the playoffs. Then in 1995–96, in the Eastern Conference finals, the Bulls blew away Orlando, Penny, and Shaq in four games. Horace Grant was hurt, but still. A sweep? When you looked at that team, you saw Shaq, you saw Penny. You said "dynasty." They're going to win, or somebody is going to have to show them why not. Nobody thought, after they got swept by the Bulls, that would be the last time Penny and Shaq would play together. Now Shaq's in L.A. The Magic was broken up.

Things *get* broken up. Things change. Things fall apart, are subverted, and new things are constructed. That's the nature of living. Hoop is no different. My own film crew was broken up. Ernest Dickerson's last film as my DP was five years ago, when he shot *Malcolm X*. Ernest directs his own films. Malik Sayeed, just a young greenhorn when we started, has been doing a great job as my cinematographer. My old buddy Monty Ross lives out in La-La Land, getting a fix on the film business and being a filmmaker from out there. And nowadays I spend as much time in Manhattan as I do in Brooklyn. Things do change. *Subvert the paradigm.* That is progress.

My sister and brothers and I are still my original team, if we are a bit more far-flung now.

My brother Chris lives in Miami. Riding that bike all over Manhattan in the wintertime, all day every day as a bike messenger, it got to be too much for him, and spending so much time out in the cold weather turned him against it on a permanent basis. So Chris is down there somewhere in the geographic fan base of Pat Riley's Miami Heat now. Chris couldn't care less about the Heat, I'm sure. If he ever checks out a box score, any box score at all, then I'm sure it is the one that says "N.Y. Knicks." He's currently unemployed, between jobs, looking for work. I understand now that he has to resolve it himself. My grandmother puts it best: "We're all hoping that Chris will one day find himself."

I have empathy for and with an athlete who doesn't have necessarily the greatest talent, but tries. The great sin is someone who has great talent and wastes it. No matter whether you're an athlete, a singer, an actor, or whatever, to waste a God-given talent is a sin. To be frivolous with it or not try to hone it or, most of all, to not treasure it. Or not take it seriously or develop it.

I'll give you somebody who was and is an overachiever: John Starks. He was someone in the CBA, bagging groceries, and just worked and worked and worked and developed himself into an NBA player. Now, in retrospect, maybe Starks should have never been starter, if you're talking about winning the NBA world title, but at the same time, 1996–97 may be his best season ever. There's nothing wrong with being first man off the bench. John Havlicek was, once.

"Starks, now, I think, has found his best role, because he's explosive and he needs a dramatic entrance," Woody Allen had told me. "Put Starks in, introduce him with the starters, that's one thing, but bring him into the game and let him make his entrance in the second act . . . he's great."

It was also as Larry Brown said: give him the guy who's been through hard times.

> > >

"I grew up in Tulsa. I had hard times," John Starks told me. "Fighting and scrapping with my brothers. My mom had seven children. I was number three—third boy. My two older brothers would get on me, ride me, fight me, beat up on me all the time. I was kind of caught in the middle. Food didn't stay on the table that much either. If you were late to the dinner table, with that many brothers, that was your ass. We had very little money. I know what hunger pangs are. Too many times I knew. My brothers never gave me time to think about it, though. They were athletes. Everything in our family, you had to be tough. You had to be tough. So that's just how I am.

"My oldest brother was an All-America football player at Northeastern University. He got caught up in the drug scene. Kinda just wasted his life away. He's serving time in the penitentiary in Oklahoma. And he was the one who steered me away from trouble, the father figure. He saw my potential, didn't want me to waste it. He should get out of there sometime this year.

"My grandmother and my mother raised all of us. My grandmother taught me about chores, the value of work. We had chores. She would come home late at night from working two jobs, and inspect. If it wasn't done right, you'd get the message, I don't care if it was two o'clock in the morning. Oh, yes, she would get on you. I have washed dishes at two in the morning with a stung backside. Many a time I had the switch taken to me. Nothing like getting hit when you're asleep.

"My mother was a survivor. Trying to raise seven kids on her own. She hustled. She did what she had to do to put food on the table, clothes on our backs.

"I went to Central High. I went out for the high school team my junior year. A partner asked me to come out: 'Man, you're too good to be playing on the streets.' And my brothers said I had the talent. So I went out. Then in a scrimmage I went over this same friend of mine, who was real cool, about 6-4. I went over him for a layup. I was only about 5-11 at the time. The high school coach went off on my friend: 'You should put him on his ass on the ground before you let him do that!' My friend said, 'I'm not trying to hurt John.' I got mad. That's my friend, my partner, I said. Then I went off. My brother was going to kick the coach's ass. So I just didn't play after that.

"In 1983, after I graduated high school, I went to Rogers State Junior College. My first two years weren't good for me. I really wasn't interested in education, just basketball. Then Northern Junior College. But I wasn't ready for it. I got in trouble at both schools, went on back to

Tulsa. I was sitting around, wasn't doing anything. My mother was getting ready to move to California. I didn't want to go out there, and I couldn't be a burden to my grandmother. My mother said, 'You need to get a job.' I started putting in work at the Safeway. Bagging groceries. For $3.35 an hour. Working so hard the older guys told me, 'You need to slow your ass down,' like we had all day. But that's the only way I know. No tips. This is Oklahoma. Got to save every dollar you get your hands on. But I still didn't slow down. I was nineteen, eager. Eager to do something. My grandmother, my brothers, they all said to me, 'If you are going to do something, work hard at it, give it your best.' That's how I was taught. I used to jump and touch the light standards at the Safeway. One of the older guys said, 'Man, you've got too much talent to stay here. You need to go on and go to college, do something with your life.' It was about this time I started going out with my wife, Jackie. She'd been a cheerleader at another JC. She'd left school too because of money problems and was working at a bank. I ran into her at a party. So we started kicking it. She encouraged me.

"Oklahoma JC was my third JC where I played. Ken Trickey, who had been coach at Oral Roberts, was up there then. He was from Tennessee. He was a hustler. His son saw me playing somewhere before. So he came to me and told me I had so much talent, I needed to come and try out, and he would waive the sixty-dollar tryout fee he was charging. I went over there and he had a hundred guys trying out. No way all those guys could play. But the fee wasn't waived for them. So I dominated them. He didn't give me a scholarship, told me I had to get financial aid. I did. Just wanted to be doing something positive. Went up to Idaho. Had a great game. Trickey said, 'Johnny, we've got to get you in there.' I said, 'Just get me on the floor.' We had a great year.

"Then Leonard Hamilton took a chance on me. He's coach at Miami now. He used to be at Oklahoma State. And it was a chance, because I only had one year of eligibility left, had wasted so many. So for one year, I played Division One, in the Big Eight. Went and put in work. That was where Larry Brown saw me. He was coaching Kansas at the time. Every time I played Kansas I gave them numbers. Served the whole Big Eight. That was the year they won it. Larry Brown encouraged me, said if he was going to be an NBA coach again, he'd hide me for a year. Oh, was I serving them at Oklahoma State! I was putting in work. Larry Brown liked what he saw.

"So then I was going to go to Grand Canyon, an NAIA school, just to play for a year, thinking about what Larry Brown said. Paul Westphal was supposed to be the coach at Grand Canyon. He was gone by the time I got there. But Larry Brown had taken the job in San Antonio, and he got me into an NBA camp. He mentioned to one of the coaches at Oklahoma State that he wanted to keep up with me. I called and said he didn't have to hide me out, bring me in now.

"So that's what started me. Went into camp. Put in work. Won the Midwest Review, four teams competing, I was point guard with Vernon Maxwell, Walter Berry, Rocket Rod Foster, Cadillac Anderson. Went in there and put in serious work. Larry wanted to keep me. Scout from Golden State kept coming up to me, 'Who's your agent?' I went and played in the L.A. summer league. Saw the same guy. 'Who's your agent?' 'Don't have one.' 'You need to get one.' Then, San Antonio offered me a contract for $10,000 to come in and make the team. I went to Golden State. Learned a lot in Oakland. The Warriors had Don Nelson coaching. He liked me at first.

"We had a veteran guard named Terry Teagle, 'bout 6-5, long arms, could really rise. Could shoot. Could score. And Don Nelson would not play this man for nothing. We could be up forty, and he wouldn't play him. I didn't know what was going on. Teagle was playing behind Chris Mullin at the time. I saw this man work, work, work every day in practice. Same look on his face. Not getting frustrated with anything, putting in work, like 'Sooner or later I'm going to play.' I said to myself, 'How can he do it?' Eventually Chris went down with an injury. Teagle stepped right in. I mean he was putting up numbers. He had stayed ready. Helped get us into the playoffs. A pro.

"Figured I was next. But Nelson brought in Steve Alford. Gave him minutes. I know I'm better than Alford. He can't play over me. I'm putting in work. Nelson said, 'You should wait your turn.' I would, for a veteran like Teagle. Alford? Killing these boys in practice, couldn't get time on the court. Got hurt in practice. Back. Out for a while. One day in practice at a shootaround I was shooting from off the court because I was pissed off. Nelson said, 'Johnny, if you're not going to shoot on the court, then get your ass out of here!' So I said, 'Fuck you!' I was frustrated. Then Teagle came over, bouncing a ball, not worked up at all. He never got worked up. He said, 'Listen here. I understand you're pissed off. I know what you're feeling. You can see I had to go through the same thing with this man. But you see that man down there? He can blackball your ass from this league. If you're going to shoot, step on the court and shoot the shots. Blow that off.'

"So I listened to him. I knew Nelson wasn't going to keep me. He was bringing in Sarunas Marciulionis for next season. But we made the playoffs. Second round, we got put out. We were going over playoff shares in the locker room. I think it was around $4,000. A lot of money for me. There was an argument about whether I should get a full share. They were qualmin' over $4,000. Ralph Sampson was the main one. We had a heated argument, I'm like 'Ralph, you big ass, you make a million a year, and you're qualming over $4,000? Hey, I got to put food on the table for my family too. Your ass has been on IR the whole damned season!' It hurt my heart.

"I went to try out at Indiana. I put in work, put up numbers, but I'd torn up my ankle in a summer league game and it never got healed. Ended up in the CBA. I put up numbers, put in work, but then I got suspended for bumping a referee. I was playing well, but every time I got ready to get called up, something happened. I had a feeling Nelson put the bad word out on me.

"Then the WBL was formed. World Basketball League. That was the league for players 6-5 and under. Good league. I got called for that, and I put in work in that league. I was putting up numbers. Serving 'em, killing 'em all. I always knew it was a matter of time. Once I first got into San Antonio, I had no doubts. I knew I could make it. I never had doubts. Just a matter of when. Dick McGuire liked what he saw in me. He always liked me. Even when I was in the CBA, he always liked me. They brought me into New York to try out. I had bruised ribs, but I didn't let them know. Had to put in the work. Oh, I was putting in work on them then! John McLeod was here for a minute as the coach. He must've talked to Nelson. I had the feeling Nelson was running me down. McLeod said, 'Talked to Golden State. Don Nelson says you have a problem with trainers. He says you're hard on them.' I said, 'What are you talking about? Go ask your trainers if I'm hard on them. You ever seen me do that?' 'No,' he said. 'You've got a heart like a tiger.'

"So then I made the team, and then Riley came in, and it all worked out for the best.

"I respected Riley so greatly, man, because he was about winning. He's hard on you, and he pushes you to the limit, but his whole purpose is about winning, and as a player I can respect that. Some players might not like it, but growing up, that was the type of environment I had."

I interrupted John here and mentioned some teams and players that seemed to me as if they didn't want to play, or didn't know how to play, and by that I mean trying to win in all aspects, getting better in all aspects.

"Pride," John said to me. "And hard work."

"Did you always have a temper, John?"

"Yeah, I always had a temper. That's just part of me in growing up and being in a family of that many people. Fighting and scrapping for everything we can get, you know. Food. Late to dinner, that's your ass. Now, my wife, she can't understand me either. She says, 'You're crazy in the morning, honey,' and I tell her, 'I'm crazy until I get some food in my belly, 'cause I done had hunger pains too many times.' You had to be tough. Plus my brothers riding me all the time. Beating me all the time. That kind of put the fire in me, you know, doing that, and being competitive all the time. No matter what you do, do your best. Play to win."

Starks was like that too. A couple of years ago he got caught up head-butting Reggie Miller in the playoffs. Reggie Miller bugs the hell out of John Starks. It would've been interesting to see how they would have worked together. I do not think there is any love lost between them. I know there isn't on John's part. So I asked, "Do you think other players know this and try and get under your skin sometimes? Like Reggie Miller maybe, knowing you have a quick trigger?"

"Yeah, Spike. He sees it. He sees it."

"Your nemesis."

"That's my nemesis, all right. He sees it, but I know how to control it against him now, you know. That thing [with the head butt], he seen I wasn't going for what he normally did, so he said, 'Man, you full of shit.' Because he's saying this, doing that, and I'm playing cool. I was really having a good series, in the playoffs, in '95.

"All of a sudden he starts hitting me with cheap shots. I say to myself, 'Okay, John, be cool, mention it to the refs.' You know, take care of the problem like you're supposed to. Tell the ref. Only they don't take care of it. They're like, 'Play on.'

"So Reggie sneaked me one last time. That was it. I lost it all. Went down and scored on him, came back down, he was talkin' shit—you know how you can get so mad you want to hit a man, but I knew, 'If I hit this motherfucker I'm gonna get suspended, kicked out of the series.' Couldn't think of nothing else, so I just head-butted him, you know, just to tap him. Let him know.

"That night, after the game, I grabbed a couple of my teammates—it was Greg Anthony, and Oakley—and we went down to their favorite spot, you know, where they hang out. And it was gonna be on if I had seen Reggie Miller that night. Yeah, it was gonna be real."

"Say the Knicks had gotten Reggie Miller, John—you coming off the bench to replace Reggie Miller. I would have come to practice to see you go up against Reggie every day."

"Yeah, I think about that, Spike. I don't know if I could've handled that one. Yeah, I probably could have played with him—but, I don't know if I could handle that one, though, Spike. That probably would have been a tough one."

It wasn't John Starks's fault that he had to start and try to match up with Michael Jordan. It wasn't his fault that he was the best we had. I'm glad we kept him and let Hubert Davis go to the Toronto Raptors for their number one pick. It was a smart move on both teams' part. Isiah knew there had been a jailbreak; most of the mature NBA-level talent had come out of college when Allen Iverson went number one. The pickings would be pretty slim in 1997. Likewise, paying a rookie bigger money made it less likely that you could go after free agents. And I'd bet that's Isiah's next move (if he gets to make it). On the other hand, the

Knicks are trying to win the NBA title now. Hubert would disappear under playoff-style defensive intensity as applied by the Chicago Bulls or the Houston Rockets. Not that Hubert is a bad player. He can stroke it from deep. But there are levels of the game. Only at the highest level did Hubert disappear. Like Dennis Scott of Orlando. No sin in it. You're as good a basketball player as there is in the world—except the ten that are on the floor right now. You are elite, but they are the fruit of the elite. Good shooter, but in crunch time, Hubert wasn't there on a consistent basis. Hope he does well with Toronto.

But give me a John Starks every time. A lot of people have great talent, but if they have no chemistry, no willingness to be unselfish, to sacrifice some of their personal stats and fame and riches for the collective good, then the team has squat, and the individual also has squat. They have no athletic life worth living. They have press clippings, some trappings of success, and little else. They don't even have love. Not real love, true love, because it is very hard to love somebody selfish like that. You'd have to be a masochist. If people have their own agendas and are not really coming together and aren't going to sacrifice for the greater good of the team, then it's hopeless. And I'd rather have the scrubs. Well, scratch the way I put that. Everybody wants the best players. I'd rather have the best players too. But if they won't have the right mind-set, then you can keep 'em. I'd rather take the scrubs who are going to sacrifice than the superstar who has all this game but only cares about himself.

That's what made that first Knicks World Championship team in 1969–70 so great. That was the epitome of teamwork. All they wanted to do was win, and they didn't care how, and they didn't care who. It's very rare in any sport today to see that type of mentality. You always hear about it, in these different camps, that one star is nothing talking to another star, or another guy who he perceives as a threat to his position, rather than somebody who can help the star win. These things you are able to hide to some degree, but sooner or later that kind of flaw is exposed, especially in the heat of the moment. In a game seven, when stuff like that is there, then that cohesion, that unity is not out there on the floor. It will surface at the worst possible moment, and you come up short. The league is so watered down that you can get by with most of that stuff during the eighty-two-game regular season, but in the playoffs, when the intensity picks up, when there are no more expansion teams or cupcakes on the schedule, that stuff gets exposed.

Scottie Pippen, as great as he is, can pull a Houdini on you. You don't take yourself out of a game. Chris Webber was the coach at Michigan, and they paid for it. He paid for it. Jalen Rose paid for it. Juwan Howard is paying for it. Now C. Web wears black hightops, and is refusing to re-sign with Nike, his stated reason being that few inner-city black kids could afford the $140 retail price. Webber was supposed to be one of the all-time legends. He still might be one day. But I could not help but wonder—is that why he really left Nike? Or was it because he didn't have a campaign like Jordan, like Penny Hardaway, like Reggie Miller? I had shot commercials for all three of them. I didn't shoot Webber's Sittin' 'Round the Barbershop commercials, a campaign that included several players. I liked it. It didn't last that long. The question is, did C. Web leave Nike because of his concern that inner-city kids couldn't afford sneakers or that the sneaker wasn't provided to black vendors by Nike, or because he wasn't the Man? It's a personal question, an individual question. It's supposed to be a team game. Yet I know the human ego is inflatable, deflatable.

It's just more about "me," and I think in many ways, that ends up being sad. Even tragic.

"It *is* sad, and it happens," said Starks. "Not being motivated to play. Not giving the effort. I told some of my own teammates, you've got to look at it like when you were back in high school, when you had the pride, you were glad and proud to put on the jersey, you were a Brave, or whatever you were. That's why I point out New York on my jersey on the court sometimes. I have pride in that. In my team. Go out and exhibit that kind of enthusiasm."

I asked John if some players were getting paid so much money that they didn't care anymore.

"Yeah," he said. "The true player is going to put forth the effort night in and night out. But some think, I've worked all my life to get here, have a nice car, nice house, and they think they've made it now, and they don't put forth the effort. They may play one year, take three years off, play hard for the contract, take another three years off. And that's so sad. Half-assed effort from your teammates. It hurts, man. It hurts. You talk to that player and try to be sympathetic, but I'm not sympathetic to anybody not giving 100 percent on the court."

> > >

The African-American athletes don't know how much power they have, and a lot of times even in their own personal dealings, they give too much power to their agents. They sometimes seem to feel and think that they're working for the agent, when in fact it's the other way around. They are the most visible and most wealthy group of African-Americans going. I went to a football game between the Green Bay Packers and the San Francisco 49ers and spoke to Reggie White early in the 1996 season. I admire Reggie. He is a deeply religious man, has a ministry, and his church in Knoxville, Tennessee, was burned to the ground, one of many black churches in the South that had been burned. Reggie told me, "It's hard, Spike, hard to get the brothers together to do anything, because there is just too much petty jealousy."

Reggie was trying to start a fund, asking all of the players in the NFL to give a portion of their National Football League Players Association dues money to help rebuild these black churches, and he said many of the brothers pooh-poohed it. Reggie said, in some cases, the white players like John Elway were giving more of their dollar than the black players. The black players were saying, "Why should I help you, Reggie? Why should I help you, of all people?" Reggie said he told them this was helping all of us. This was helping everybody. Even the white players could see that. So you see, that's the old Willie Lynch theory that people talk about. The young against the old, the light against the dark, the man against the woman, southern against northern, eastern against western—residual slave mentality. Until we get rid of that mentality, that self-defeating and even murderous methodology, then you know black folks are not going to go too far at all. This comes out of jealousy, and this nonsense has destroyed nations, let alone professional sports franchises. How much am I getting? Why are they getting that much?

Why is he getting more shots than me? Why is he getting shots at all? Why'm I getting only this? How come he has a commercial and I don't? I have more rapping skills than he does. That mentality is a team-killer. It's a people-killer too. And it happens more and more.

After Shaq signed with the Lakers, they raised their ticket prices across the board, which they had to do to help pay his salary. One of the best instances of what happens was when Coca-Cola withdrew their sponsorship of the Lakers. Coke is based in Atlanta. You couldn't even say Pepsi in Atlanta during the Olympics. You had to say, the P-word. Coca-Cola, the primary sponsors of the Olympics in Atlanta, where Shaq was one of the members of the Dream Team, withdrew sponsorship of the Lakers, the L.A. Kings hockey club, and the Great Western Forum itself, because of Shaq. Shaq is a spokesman for Pepsi-Cola. So Coca-Cola took their money out of the Forum, and we'll see if Pepsi is able to make it up, will fill the void Coke left when it pulled out. But that shows the power. The Lakers and Kings and the Forum lose their sponsor, Coke, because the Lakers hired a player who was commercially identified with a competing product. What happens if Nike wants to buy an arena? Does that mean nobody on the team can wear Reeboks? Does that mean the incoming players won't be allowed to wear Adidas? It's getting complicated. You already have major corporate sponsorship for all the parks in big league ball. It used to be the Fabulous Forum. Now it's Great Western Forum. Candlestick Park is 3-Com Park. Capital Centre became USAir Arena, the United Center is in Chicago, and the new arena for the Bullets in D.C. will have MCI, the long-distance phone service company, in its name. And on and on.

I don't even know if there was a preponderance of agents in 1969–70. The players negotiated their own contracts sometimes. Of course that was to their detriment, because the owners would lead them astray, hoodwink and bamboozle them out of their fair compensation. But now maybe it's gone too far the other way. The phrase that was used in the film *Malcolm X* is appropriate. Peter Boyle plays a New York precinct captain, and Malcolm X, as played by Denzel Washington, has the Fruit of Islam standing outside a hospital, where a fellow Muslim brother who has been viciously beaten by police is on the critical list. Behind the stoic

Fruit of Islam, a crowd in Harlem is yelling about justice denied. Boyle's character asks Malcolm to break it up.

"The Fruit of Islam are disciplined men," says Malcolm. "They are not causing trouble."

"But what about those others?" the captain asks.

"The others are your problem," says Malcolm, "but if Brother Johnson dies . . . then I pity you."

The doctor comes out and says the injured man will live. The police captain asks Malcolm to break it up. Denzel-as-Malcolm regards him, levelly.

Denzel-as-Malcolm smiles and, with a simple hand gesture, orders the men to disperse. And then Boyle's character looks at them, at Malcolm X's retreating back. As they leave, he says: "That's too much power for one man to have."

A lot of people feel that way about David Falk now. He has Michael Jordan, which is fine, but so many other people, which may not be so fine.

In an article in the November 17, 1996, *New York Times Magazine*, David Falk, the most powerful agent in basketball, and Michael Jordan's representative, says two things that disturb me about the state of the game. He's not talking about the Game, though: "[In past eras] The teams were famous," Falk explained. "There were great players, but basketball was perceived by companies to be about the team, not the individual."

Falk's newest, latest player is the former Georgetown guard, the number one pick in the 1996 NBA draft, Allen Iverson, the point guard for the Philadelphia 76ers. At the end of the *Times* article, David says, "Allen Iverson doesn't have to play great," to Reebok executives. "He has to be a great personality on the court. He's going to be a fantastic performer."

Now, if your agent is telling you that, then what is a rookie to think? "I have to be a fantastic performer." An individualist, whose goal is antithetical to the kind of team play that is essential to winning—and watchable—basketball. Seems like everybody wants to be that fantastic individual performer now. I think about what Frazier said, about there not being any real basketball players anymore. That's not solely a function of the young players—it is the environment. And it all started, really, when the O'Malleys made the Brooklyn Dodgers the first big-time free agent and took the deal for the L.A. Basin and a ballpark called Chavez Ravine. Ever since then, it's been every man for himself.

But at the same time, I don't want to be guilty of labeling all young players knuckleheads, because that is just not so. A young player like Atlanta's Steve Smith, who donated $2.5 million to his alma mater, Michigan State, is not worthy of the label, while the lunatic of the league, Dennis Rodman, is over thirty-five years old. So, in many cases, it is just a matter of young people still being wet behind the ears and untrained. That's why I agree with Ice about the NBA needing a mentoring program. So maybe they could learn about a man like Curt Flood, who died on Martin Luther King Jr. Day, January 20, 1997. So maybe they can be taught that it wasn't always like this—free agency, fair and huge compensation. Young people just don't get this information by osmosis as much anymore, not the same way Chris and I did when we were young. So if the young people are knuckleheads, we have to face this fact: who were the ones that were supposed to teach them better?

Culturally, the connection between the players and the community at large is there, rock-hard, for the most part, but I don't think the brothers have much to do with the community. It's not just the brothers in basketball; I would say for the most part in all sports. I mean, these guys came from there. That was the fire that forged them. Pete Carrill who used to coach at Princeton, used to rate his players that way. He said he could get by with a player who came from a one-car-garage home; he could make do with that, even though he wouldn't have the same fire and drive, and therefore accumulated ability, as the player who came from a third-floor walk-up or a housing project. Carrill said a player from a family with a two-car garage would be iffy, and a player from a family with a three-car garage—forget it. He wouldn't be able to play competitively in the fire of Division One or the NBA. I mean, these guys came from there, and that's the last place they want to go back, the last place they want to go, and to me that's so very sad.

It's very important for African-Americans to begin to have equity in these leagues, because in America, if you don't own a piece of the rock, then forget about it. In 1996, African-Americans spent an estimated

$380 billion. African-Americans are among the world's biggest consumers. Per capita we buy more movie tickets, more cosmetics, more hair products, more alcohol, more cigarettes, more cars, more shoes, more sneakers, more Hilfiger, more Timberland, mo', mo', and mo'. I mean we just buy, buy, buy, buy, buy, buy, and buy. But the stuff we buy has very little lasting value, and it won't until we begin to own pieces of some of these companies, a piece of this rock. As we get to the next millennium, the twenty-first century, it's got to be about ownership.

The first step is to start people thinking that way—that it's okay to own something. People think that's strange to say. They think the term "slave mentality" is distant, so far apart from them. But there are people alive today whose parents lived in slavery. That's how short a time it's been. The mentality manifests itself in different ways. When Mahmoud Abdul-Rauf had that issue about standing with hand over heart for the playing of the national anthem, maybe that could have been addressed in a different way. Maybe Craig Hodges would not be suing the NBA, saying it blackballed him after the Bulls released him (which, I'm sure, in superstar-personnel terms, Jordan did not object to) and he could not then get another job in the NBA, even though he was a proven three-point shooter, and three times the NBA three-point champion at the All-Star Game. Maybe those kinds of suits and frictions can be more adroitly avoided, but then again, maybe that's wishful thinking.

But then, it wasn't wishful thinking when two African-American businessmen, Peter Bynoe and Bertram Lee, bought a piece of the Denver Nuggets, had operational control, even though Comsat, still the owner of the franchise, had the majority of shares. I'd like to get the real story of what happened. Bynoe was in with Bulls and White Sox owner Jerry Reinsdorf on construction of the new Comiskey Park. Bynoe sold his share of the Nuggets and did pretty well with the sale.

To say an active player can't own is ruinous. Red Grange, after attendance shot up in his rookie year, came in the next year with an agent and said to the NFL, "I want a franchise." He didn't get it, but something amenable was worked out. In today's NBA, a coach can own, the way Riley does in Miami, but a player can't. The NBA Players Association, next time they negotiate a collective bargaining agreement, needs to do something about that. If a coach can be part-owner, why can't a player? They'll say it's opening up another can of worms, guys will be trying to get stats to prove they should own, and it'll be lunch out there. But the thing that counts most to most owners should be winning; it translates into turning extra profits—unless you're oil baron Leon Hess, owner of the dreadful, hapless, pathetic, inexplicable, comatose, disoriented, stupefied, stagnant, lethargic (and all those other things Walt Frazier said) New York Jets.

Seriously, you have to own to care about something in terms of upkeep. Maybe that is just the kind of carrot that would change things for the better, make winning important again. Because how many players are going to be that good, last that long, win that many championships to have the leverage of being able to go in and say, "I want a piece of the rock"? I can think of only two or three who are playing today, and of course, number one on that list is Michael Jeffrey Jordan.

That's one reason why I started the 40 Acres Project Camp. We wanted to show young people that it's okay to take responsibility. That's really keeping it real. Everybody doesn't have the skill to go to ABC camp or Nike Camp, or become a McDonald's All-American. But at the same time, some are just late bloomers. Earl Smith, who runs the camp day to day, has played and coached basketball all his life, since back in the days at Dewey High, and he still thinks he should have been in the NBA. First year, for counselors we had Jerry Stackhouse, Rasheed Wallace, Gary Trent, Joey Brown of Georgetown, and Derrick Anderson of Kentucky. The first two years, we had it at Pratt Institute in Brooklyn. Last year it was held at Stonybrook on Long Island. This is a place to come for five days, have some ball structured, and also try to get them to start thinking of themselves as student athletes. Our campers spend half a day in the classroom, the other half hooping. Nike has been instrumental in helping us pull it off. The point is to get a sense of hard work, unselfishness, team ball.

In September 1996, I did a segment on the baseball villain Albert Belle for HBO's *Real Sports* program, hosted by Bryant Gumbel. The piece caused an uproar among the white media. They took exception to my approach—I didn't crucify the guy. Mark Kriegel, columnist of the *Daily News,* blasted it in a full-page review. I was given an opportunity to respond with a guest column. Here are the last paragraphs from it:

I suspect that the real reason why some people have a problem with the piece is that we pointed out the alarming disparity between the overwhelming number of athletes being black vs. the people who decide who writes, analyzes, and criticizes being mostly white. And that's a problem, but they don't see it that way. I suggest that this imbalance could possibly affect the way some black athletes, such as Belle, are portrayed in the media. If racism, which is as American as apple pie, permeates every aspect of our society, would it be outlandish to speculate that sports journalists would not be immune to this sickness? I don't think so.

Joel Sherman, of the *New York Post,* in an interview with me asked, "Why does Belle think the media is a white monolithic group?" I asked Joel, "How many sportscasters does the *Post* have on staff?" He said, "Twenty-five." I shot back, "How many are white males?" He meekly replied, "Twenty-five."

Looking at the combined writers and editors in sports departments of the four New York dailies, here are the numbers. Read 'em and weep. *New York Post* has zero blacks out of about 40. *Newsday,* 5 out of 60. *New York Times,* 9 out of 60, and the *Daily News,* 5 out of 65. But, let's not just focus on New York. What about the nation? Of the 1,600 daily papers,

only 10 have a black sports columnist. There
are only two black sports editors at major
papers, Garry Howard of the *Milwaukee Journal
Sentinel* and Neal Scarbrough of the *Nashville
Tennessean*. At *Sports Illustrated,* of the 113
editors, writers, and copy editors, only 7 are
black. In baseball, of more than 250 beat writers, a puny 5 are black. Don't shoot the messenger, Kriegel. Facts are facts. Apartheid is
alive and well in the press boxes of the United
States of America.

This article caused a big brouhaha. Leon Carter of the *Daily News,*
along with Bill Rhoden of the *Times* and me, decided we should capital-
ize on this heat and hold a forum on Racism in Sports Journalism. On
December 11, 1996, at the HBO Building, it happened—sponsored by
the Rainbow/Push Coalition, the Sports Task Force of the National
Association of Black Journalists, and the New York Black Sportswriters
Association.

The place was packed and it didn't disappoint. Jesse Jackson put the
entire evening in plain and simple terms, something that everybody
could see. "We have the fascination with athletes. It's not peculiar to our
culture and time. In Biblical times, athletes were seen as being God's
gifted people. You can't decide to be Buck Williams one day, just by
jumping on a wall. You can't decide to have the speed and skill of Deion,
just because you want to have it. You cannot decide to be Mike Tyson.
You can do things to cultivate that, but people who have those skills,
those special abilities, are divinely blessed. And that is why Samson, an
athlete, was seen as the divinely gifted one to represent the strength of a
people. That is why David, the young athlete, was called upon to take on
Goliath. They are not lucky; it's a gift from God. And those who have
appreciation that they are God's gifted and blessed people must behave
that way.

"And Samson, like David, like Jackie Robinson, are the thermometers
of the language of a culture. Jackie Robinson—1947, that was eight

years before Dr. Martin Luther King. Jackie Robinson—the diamond of nine people, the Supreme Court, nine decisions. Nine people make a decision in '54, seven years later. It was on the shoulders of an athlete. And athletes like Jackie were not merely champions, they were heroes. When champions win ball games, the people put them on their shoulders. But when heroes win, they put the people on their shoulders."

With those stirring, eloquent words the good Reverend had me fired up. I was ready. I proposed a hypothetical question to one of the panelists, New York Knicks veteran Buck Williams. I said, "Buck, what would happen if all the Knicks got together and decided to boycott the *New York Post,* not speak to them until they hire an African-American sportswriter, can this happen?" Buck replied, "If Patrick and Herb Williams said, let's do this, it would get done; the team would follow. I'm ready." The auditorium was abuzz with his answer. This is what I wanted to hear. I knew the *Post* would have to do something.

He added, however, that the chances would be slim for this to happen. The NBA Players Association is a sleeping giant. Most brothers in the league don't trust each other, don't trust black people in general. That's why in a league that is 80 percent black, over 90 percent of the athletes have white agents, white lawyers, white financial planners, et cetera, et cetera, et cetera.

Nonetheless, I'm optimistic that there will be a movement as we step into the twenty-first century. Conscious brothers like Buck Williams, Charlie Smith, and Reggie White are starting to make moves. That's what's exciting to me. These athletes have a great legacy to live up to from Joe Louis, Jackie Robinson, Muhammad Ali, Tommie Smith, John Carlos, up to the giant Curt Flood. Nobody would be making the money they're making now if Curt hadn't taken on baseball and the reserve clause himself. He didn't do that by being a handkerchief-head, shuffling Negro, worrying about his contract or endorsements. That activism, I believe, isn't dead. It can be rekindled.

> > >

Shortly after the forum, I received a phone call from the editor of the *New York Post,* Ken Chandler. He asked me to turn him on to qualified black sportswriters. I had to laugh out loud. What happened was that he had gotten a letter from Jesse, threatening a major boycott, and heard about the Knicks scenario, and he was scared. But aside from that, his hiring policy was indefensible. Think of all the black or Latin athletes on the Jets, Giants, Yankees, Mets, Knicks, Nets, not even to mention the visiting teams, and think of the racial makeup of the most diverse city in the world, and you don't have one woman, Asian, Latino, or African-American in their entire sports department. Is this Birmingham, Alabama, in the '60s under Bull Connor, or is this New York City?

Guess what? The *New York Post* hired George Willis, an African-American from the *New York Times* and gave him his own column. We did that. We had a hammer and were ready to use it. The *Post* would never have done that by themselves, they had to be shamed into it. It's just one position, one job—but it's a start. And as Jesse said, maybe that will be one fewer sports journalist "who will portray blacks who are less intelligent, less hardworking, less universal, less patriotic, and more violent than white athletes."

What would happen if the Griffeys, Jordans, Tysons, Sanderses, Ewings, Whites, Woods, Belles, O'Neals, and Bondses got together, realized their collective power, and used it effectively? Fahgetaboutit. You may think I'm dreaming, but I believe there was a time when some of our ancestors thought we would never escape bondage either. In the next millennium, it will be about ownership. We make up the cattle— that's what the players are—to be bought, sold, traded at will. When will we ever own a professional sports franchise?

> > >

Shortly after I rode with Michael Jordan from the Berto Center in suburban Chicago, I went to Indiana to shoot a Nike commercial with Reggie Miller. The 1996–97 season had begun. Don't ask me why Nike waited three years to do this. I read the scripts for the commercial and I thought they were pretty funny, and Reggie was very agreeable. We had squashed whatever difficulties there had been between us in the wake of that "Chokers!" game.

We arrived and sat in the stands at Market Square Arena and watched the morning practice. Big Rik Smits was just back from having surgery on both feet, riding a stationary bike. Dampier, the big 6-11 rookie, was moving people from underneath the boards like a backhoe. Dale Davis was cleaning everything off the boards, and his extended elbows were teaching the usual lessons. Coach Brown was running the practice almost quietly. Later, Miller said that was only because I was there. Heywoode Workman sat on the side. Brown knew what he had there. He was trying to work in Travis Best at lead guard. Travis has offensive potential. I watched as Donnie Walsh sat with me in the stands and discussed the team's prospects. Indiana's assistant coaches include Billy King and Gar Heard. Gar Heard will always be remembered for that long jumper he made to force triple overtime in that playoff game between the Phoenix Suns and the Celtics at the old Boston Garden in 1976. King, a very personable young man, went to Duke and was known as a defensive specialist, was being groomed, perhaps to be an NBA coach one day, but I'd also heard the league itself was seeking him for its office in the liaison position of vice president of operations.

But I was most interested to see how the 6-7 newcomers would look. This is what Brown had meant as the Answer for Pippen, Kukoc, Jordan . . . the Pacers had Jerome Allen in camp, a great guy, smart, fun, willing, all of that. Went to Penn. Everything going for him, except for the fact he was neither tall nor strong nor quick nor experienced enough to guard any of the Bulls outside.

The practice was frantic, hotly contested on the boards. Eddie Johnson, a tall veteran shooter on his last legs, sat out. He needed every bit of tread that was left on his tires. He smiled as Jalen Rose kept up a running commentary with himself as the Pacers scrimmaged. Jalen had little or no defensive technique. He turned his head away from the ball too much. Coach Brown was constantly telling him something. Later, Coach Brown called Reggie Miller's name. "Reggie." No answer from Reggie. "Reggie." No answer. "Reggie Miller." Miller looked up then. None too quick though. I got the feeling there was no love lost between Reggie and Coach Larry Brown.

I was glad to see Reggie, and he seemed content enough to be shooting the commercial. The Pacers had lost their first two games of the season. No one in Indiana seemed particularly worried. They had gone 1–6 to begin the previous season. They were a team of veterans. They knew when they had to have their game on. In May and June. That's when they played for keeps.

"When are you guys going to start playing, Reggie? January?"

"March," said Reggie Miller, and we laughed.

"People talk about the regular season, how many games you win. Home-court advantage. It doesn't matter," Miller says. "What matters is winning in the playoffs." Later he began the drudgery of shooting the commercial. The creative directors at Weiden & Kennedy had come up with some more good lines, some funny lines. I was no longer playing Mars Blackmon, but myself—Spike Lee, Knicks fan.

One scene: I had a telephone and walked up to Reggie as he was shooting free throws: "It's the police. They found your shot."

Reggie kept up a running commentary between takes, and we shot him playing Around the World, making deep three after deep three after deep three, amazing the small group of observers who watched the shoot. All-day deal. After practice I asked Coach Brown about the Bulls.

"I don't think anybody is going to beat Chicago as long as Michael and Scottie are there, Spike," Larry Brown told me. "I really believe that. Michael's will to win . . ."

His voice had trailed off. I couldn't believe what he was saying.

"Why even coach, then?" I asked.

"Well, that doesn't mean you don't try, Spike. I saw Michael at Chapel Hill during his retirement. He gave me a two-year window to win a title. But we couldn't close the deal."

"Can L.J. play defense?" I asked, referring to Larry Johnson, recently signed with the Knicks.

"I think he'll learn. When you put a priority on something, it's different. If you don't ask players to do something, sometimes they don't. If you make that a priority and they see a chance of winning, there's a lot of things these guys can do. Oakley, Ward, and Buck won't command the ball. They won't care. Neither should Childs. When you look at Allan Houston, L.J., and Patrick, you've got two post-up players there who demand double-teams, so you're gonna get your shots if you're on the floor with them. Charlie Ward and Childs won't have to look for their shots. They'll be there. The Knicks have quality people. They helped themselves because one of those guys from the Bulls is going to have to guard Larry in the post. Seattle won two games off the Bulls in the finals, but I didn't think they matched up best. I was surprised Orlando didn't do better.

"Again, I think maybe they had internal problems," Brown said, not realizing he was echoing what Jordan had said about the Pacers. "I was disappointed watching Orlando against Chicago in the '96 playoffs, especially after the way Orlando handled us. . . . With Penny, as good as he is . . ."

As the shoot went on, it came out that the Pacers had just made a trade. Had they brought in another 6-7 perimeter player to give them a better matchup with Chicago? No. They had traded Reggie Williams to the New Jersey Nets for Vincent Askew. At the airport, I saw Williams and his wife, Kathy. He seemed mystified at why he'd been traded. "My shot was going. They said they didn't have scoring. Here I was," said Williams. Reggie's numbers had been slipping for several years.

"He came into the league insecure," said a friend of mine. "And he never got over it. His attitude, even after a loss, became 'Hey, I got mine.' Meaning not stats but money."

I listened to Reggie: "Against the Bulls, what you need is perimeter defenders who can also score."

The Pacers had said they needed more strength.

"Against Scottie Pippen?" Reggie Williams asked. I had no answer for that.

Larry Brown is not one for reflections either. There is no time during the NBA season. He was putting an edge on the Pacers. On December 4, 1996, Indiana dismantled Vancouver—the "hapless" Grizzlies, in the lingo—at Vancouver, 127–80. Reggie Miller had 36 points. Twelve Pacers scored. That's supposed to be the name of the game, winning, and that means beating the Bulls. Is the object of the game to beat the Bulls? In a way that I had never considered when I was young, I was part of the Answer now—part of the market forces helping shape the league. If a player gets a commercial, it's better than beating

Jordan. Not like the old days. Nor, perhaps, should it be. I don't want to be too nostalgic about the olden days. But they had their moments. Like in the spring of 1970, when a group of twelve men, a "very bright team," got together and said, let's do it. Now things would work out anew. I thought of what Coach Larry Brown said: he thought Chicago wouldn't be beaten as long as Jordan was there. I couldn't believe he said that.

"Well, that doesn't mean you don't try, Spike."

On January 21, 1997, the day after Curt Flood died, the Bulls and the Knicks met for the first time during the regular season, at Air's Crib, the United Center. Before the game, Coach Van Gundy's comments to me about Michael Jordan being a con man, how he psychologically softened the opposition up, had been repeated by him—they *were* good comments, after all—and were given serious airplay in Chicago. And it was fuel for Michael Jordan's fire. He torched the Knicks for 51 points in an 88–87 Bulls win. At one point Michael yelled at me, "Spike, put on your sneakers and come out here and get some of this shit." I said nada, not a peep. He kept up a running commentary at Coach Van Gundy the entire evening, and after his last game-clinching basket, he turned, stood, and just let Van Gundy have it. Coach Van Gundy turned his back and walked away. As Jordan went past me before going into the Bulls' locker room (of course I was there, what do you think?), he said, "Spike, tell your coach to shut the fuck up."

I think Jeff Van Gundy is a good coach, and what he said about Jordan is true, but don't tell the press that. Don't say anything to Jordan about Jordan. I know I never have during a game from the best seats in the house. Pippen, Miller, oh yeah. Money, Black Jesus? Hell, no. Mum's the word. Money was upset by Van Gundy's comments. Phil Jackson, never one to miss an opportunity to stick a knife in about the Knicks, said, "It was probably a tactical mistake by the coach of the Knicks to attack Michael personally . . . for having his character attacked before the ball game in the papers." But the Knicks did not move the ball well on offense that night. We kept forcing it to Ewing as the first option. In the last minute of the game, with the Knicks down by three, Allan Houston had a wide-open look at a 3-pointer, but Chris Childs chose to pass the ball down low to Ewing. The last time we'd gone to the NBA finals, in 1994, it was another Knick, Starks, who took the critical shot, and Patrick Ewing was then free to crash the boards and pound the offensive rebound home for the game-winner. With the team we have now constructed—with Allan Houston, Larry Johnson, Chris Childs, John Starks—that is how we should play. The open man takes the shot. We don't have the most athletic team in the NBA, but a team of good shooters. It was January. It was early. We'd see if these Knicks would learn to play Knick ball, team ball, by the playoffs. Against Jordan and the Chicago Bulls, it was our only way.

Despite the fact Money scored 51 points, the game was still there for the Knicks to win. We came back from 17 down in the fourth quarter. The rest of the entire Bulls team only scored 37 points. The Knicks have to score more than 87 against Michael to win. It's getting frustrating as hell, flying to Chicago, sitting front row in the United Center, and losing. Shit. After the game Money told the Bulls' beat writers, "I don't know how [Spike Lee] keeps on getting those [front row] seats. People in Chicago should be sitting there." Well, Michael, if you read this book you'll find out.

> > >

Growing up in Brooklyn, New York, dreaming that I'd be in major league baseball or the NBA seems like it happened eons ago. I've just turned forty and I'm not a kid anymore. But somehow over the years I've still been able to maintain my love for sports—in particular basketball. It's funny how things turned out. All my heroes, all the great players who I patterned myself after, all my heroes who I lived and died with, I've been able to meet. And I'm happy to say they all turned out to be great human beings, when I finally met them. I've been lucky. I've been blessed.

After any game, as Tonya and I walk across the baseline of the court, I think about my mother, my brothers, my sister, my youth, and the youth of my children. The Game will dance in their blood, too. I look up at the blue seats, the nosebleed section, and see me and Chris cheering, my father and Uncle Cliff and Uncle Len acting as if they didn't care, when we knew they did. I look back down as the teams run off the court, changing before my eyes. They call it morphing now. It can be done with computer-generated imaging. It used to be day-dreaming, and you did it only with imagination. I see Alcindor and O, West and the Dipper, Pearl, Hondo, and the Doctor. I see Reggie Miller, Reggie Lewis, and Pete Maravich. I see Bird, Magic, 'Nard. I see Isiah and Dumars, interchangeably. I see Shaq, Penny, Allen, Stef; I see Starks jump from outside the lane and rise over three Bulls and throw down the dunk. I see Michael Jordan. He doesn't change at all. Right behind him, I see Caz hugging Dave the Rave; Phil Jackson in street clothes, taking pictures; Clyde, Dick, Bradley, and DeBusschere leaping off the court and out through the dark, square passageway. Willis is already back there. He gave it his all. I think of the challenges and the changes; I think it is not all good. It has been corrupted. It isn't being maintained. But still, even thinking this, I see what I see, and a voice in my head that I cannot always control keeps saying, over and over, *"Great game, Spike . . . great game. . . ."*

GLOSSARY

Airball (n.) A shot that hits no part of the net, rim, or backboard.

All ball (n., exclamation) 1. A clean blocked shot, or clean steal, without a foul committed by defensive player making the block or getting the steal. 2. Purity of game, without frills.

Ball game (n.) 1. An organized game, at any level. 2. Exclamation used when a play is made to seal the outcome of a game as either victory or loss—e.g., the Knicks are up by two, Allan Houston pulls up . . . "Yess! Ball game!" 3. A relationship.

Bang (v.) To use arms or hips to roughly displace an opponent's position or balance.

Blank See "Airball."

Blow up (v.) 1. To become well known. 2. To receive favorable notices. 3. To become profitable. 4. (*Archaic*) To lose one's cool, to make mistakes under pressure.

Board (n., v.) 1. The backboard. 2. The act of rebounding. 3. A rebound.

Bounce (n., v.) 1. A dribble. 2. Ball-handling ability—e.g., Isiah had great bounce.

Bow up, bow your neck (v.) 1. To strengthen one's resolve in the face of misfortune or adversity. 2. To become stronger and tougher in the face of adverse circumstances.

Box (n.) 1. The three-second area. 2. The square painted or taped above the rim.

Box out (v.) To keep a defender or rebounder away from the goal with the use of one's body; to prevent rebounding by the other team—e.g., "It's hard to box out Rodman because he's such a quick jumper, quick to the ball, and he's so active."

Brick (n.) A ball shot off the mark, off the rim, not in the cylinder (see "Clank").

Busted up (v.) Injured.

Candy (n.) 1. An easy shot. 2. A poor defender. 3. One who allows himself to be used.

Change ball (v.) When a player, or a player's talent, is so great, either combined or in an individual area, that the manner in which the game is played is altered—e.g., "Dr. J changed ball; after him, everybody started dunking," or "Michael Jordan changed ball because he was multidimensional in space," or "If Penny played with Michael Jordan and Scottie Pippen, that would change ball," or "Do you think Shaq's got the game to change ball by himself?"

Clank (n., v.) 1. A shot that hits the rim without entering the cylinder or having any chance to go in. 2. A player who launches such a shot. 3. A player with no ball-handling capabilities. 3. A player who commits turnovers. 4. A slow-footed player—e.g., "Gheorghe Muresan is good to have around, he'll fool you, he can score, but in the end, he's still a clank."

Clear out (n., v.) 1. When a team moves all its players to one side and allows one man with the ball to try to score one-on-one against a defender. 2. What people do if they are fired.

Cut (n.) 1. To make a sharp change of direction in order to escape a defender, usually toward the basket—e.g., "A good back cut by Derrick McKey got him open for a layup." 2. Well-defined muscularity—e.g., "Mailman is cut, but Mason is *swole*." 3. Female pulchritude.

D (n.) Defense. Configuration, alignments used to prevent opposition from scoring—e.g., "The Clippers never heard of D," or "They hardly play D out west."

Dap (n.) An act of etiquette, similar to handshake, this via open hand slap to extended palm, or one fist hit atop fist of the person being greeted. Also called "giving five" or "pound"—e.g., "When did they start giving dap after they made free throws?"

Decent (adj.) Average—e.g., "Marcus Camby is decent, but not nice yet."

Deep (n.) See "Downtown."

Deny (v.) 1. To prevent an uncontested shot. 2. To keep a favorable position.

Down low (n.) 1. The area around the basket end of the painted three-second lane area. 2. The place where the dirty work is done.

Downtown (n.) Behind the three-point line—e.g., "Reggie Miller can see from downtown."

Drop (v.) 1. To score points—e.g., "Michael Finley dropped 30 on Orlando."

Dunk (v., n.) 1. The act of throwing the ball down through the rim and basket. 2. Such a shot. (Also *cram, throwdown, slam, jam, stuff, slam dunk.*) 3. Easy pickings.

D up (v.) 1. Admonition to stop other team from scoring. 2. To play good defense—e.g., "Mookie Blaylock can D up on a rookie and shut him down."

Face (adv.) Formerly "in your face." Exclamation after a goal scored over a defender despite defender's best attempts to close in and deny or block the shot.

Fraud (n.) A player who has made the professional league for reasons that must be political, because a good reason cannot be ascertained from his lack of playing ability—e.g., "Yo, man, Yinka Dare is a fraud," or "So? There's one fraud on every roster."

Garbage (n.) 1. See "Brick." 2. A weak shot attempt. 3. A player of very limited capabilities.

Get mine (n., v.) 1. When in the course of a game a player asks for help from a teammate in covering his opponent. 2. When one asks a friend to keep an eye out for transgressions.

Got game Having an array of talents—e.g., "Terrell Brandon's got game."

Got nothing 1. A weak attempt. 2. A player who mounts weak attempts.

Got yours (n., v., exclamation) 1. When during the course of a game a player tells a teammate he is picking up responsibility for the teammate's defensive assignment. 2. When one tells a friend he or she will keep an eye on somebody for the friend's benefit.

Grab (n., v.) 1. A blocked shot. 2. The act of blocking a shot.

Grille (n.) The human face—e.g., "Olajuwon slammed on C. Web's grille."

Handle (n.) Ball-handling ability—e.g., "Jason Kidd has all kinds of handle."

Hole (n.) The rim of the basket—e.g., "Terrell Brandon will take it to the hole."

Hop, hops (n.) Jumping ability—e.g., "Dr. J could hop. He had serious hops."

Hot (adj.) Making at least three consecutive shots.

j (n.) A jump shot.

Lift (n., v.) 1. Jumping ability—e.g., "Shawn Kemp and Antonio McDyess have lift." 2. To jump—e.g., "Sir Charles lifted and grabbed the Admiral's dunk attempt."

Lob (v., n.) 1. To toss the ball over the defense so a teammate may catch the ball either to advance it or to score—e.g., "Nick lobbed to Shaq over Kevin Garnett." 2. The toss itself. 3. Taking a defender for granted—e.g., "Nick thinks he can just get the lob on Marbury any time," or "Hey, are you just going to let that person just lob on you like that?"

Look, look at it (v., n.) 1. To gaze at the rim in preparation for shooting —e.g., "Oakley has to look at the basket to keep the defense honest, because they're playing back off him." 2. An open shot—e.g., "Reggie Williams hasn't been getting good looks because of Jordan's D."

Low block (n.) The area near the basket, just to either side of the three-second lane, so called because of the blocks that separate free-throw positions painted on both sides of the lane.

Money (n.) 1. Mars Blackmon and Ron Harper's name for Jordan. 2. A sure shot.

Nasty (adj.) Very creative and overpowering—e.g., "That was a nasty dunk that Spree threw down on Mailman," or "Michael's getting nasty."

Nice (adj.) 1. Good but not great yet. 2. Dependable, steady, predictable—e.g., "Damon Stoudamire is nice," or "Mark Jackson is nice on the offensive end." 3. Proven—e.g., "Tim Hardaway's crossover dribble is nice," or "Patrick Ewing's pogo jump shot is nice."

No D (n.) 1. Lack of defense. 2. Ernie DiGregorio. 3. A player who plays poor defense.

Out high (n.) The area between the top of the key and the half-court line.

Pick (n., v.) 1. When a player's stationary body position is used to impede the progress of a defender. 2. A steal. 3. To make a steal— e.g., "Gary Payton will pick your dribble."

Pill (n.) The basketball.

Pin (v.) To block a shot and hold it against the backboard without goaltending.

Pin down, pin-down (v., n.) 1. To gain advantage over a defender by keeping his body under the basket. 2. The act of gaining such advantage.

Post up (n., v.) Positioning to attempt to score from close to the basket.

Pure candy (n.) 1. A hopelessly poor defender or a hopelessly ineffectual offensive player—e.g., "Dennis Scott is like radar from deep, but he's pure candy on D. He can't stop anybody from scoring." 2. Someone who lets you get away with anything.

Rack (n.) The rim and the bracket attaching it to the backboard.

Rise (n., v.) 1. Jumping ability. 2. To jump—e.g., "Yeah, but David Thompson had the rise of life. He could rise and is probably rising up on somebody somewhere right now."

Rock (n.) The basketball.

Run (n., v.) 1. An organized or unorganized game of basketball. 2. A trip or journey.

Screen (n., v.) See "Pick," definition 1.

See (v.) Ability to shoot—e.g., "Mahmoud Abdul-Rauf, Dell Curry, Dale Ellis, and Glen Rice can all see from downtown," or "Mark Price could see before he got busted up."

Spacing (n.) The distance and balance that should be kept between teammates in offensive and defensive patterns and configurations.

Special (adj., n.) 1. Having total game. 2. Endowed with the ability to win and have others accept this ability—e.g., "Penny Hardaway is special; even Pippen can't stop him," or "Larry Bird and Magic Johnson were special," or "Walt Frazier was special to me," or,

"Iverson might be special, but Cedric Ceballos and Danny Manning are not special. They are nice." 3. One with so much ability he can dog you and remain on good terms with you.

Spot up (v.) To go to a spot on the floor where one is comfortable shooting and preparing to shoot before one receives the ball.

Square (n.) See "Box," definition 2.

Square up (v.) To set one's body facing the goal, in preparation to shoot—e.g., "If you let a good three-point shooter like Steve Smith get squared up, he can hurt you."

Stay down (v.) Usually given as an instruction imploring defensive players to play in front of the offensive team, semi-allowing jump shots but preventing drives to the basket—e.g., "You've got to stay down against Jimmy Jackson, because he likes to go to the hole, cram, and dangle."

Stay up (v.) Usually given as an instruction imploring defensive players to play tight on the offensive team, preventing long jump shots—e.g., "You've got to stay up against Allan Houston."

Stop, stopper (n., v.) 1. The act of preventing the other team from scoring so as to regain possession of the ball without allowing points—e.g., "Stops win championships." 2. To prevent a player from scoring. 3. A defensive player. 4. One who prevents relationships.

Stroke (n.) 1. Shooting motion—e.g., "Juwan Howard has a nice stroke." 2. What a coach has when a player with a poor stroke starts firing from out high.

Sweet (adj.) 1. Gracefully efficient, artful—e.g., "Jerry Stackhouse is sweet," or "Glen Rice has a sweet stroke," or "Mash put a sweet move on Plastic Man and left him there."

The truth (n.) 1. Michael Jordan. 2. A common nickname, often misplaced.

Touch (n.) A combination of skills and experience that give a shooter the ability to make baskets consistently, from long distance or short. Touch has nothing to do with dunking—e.g., "Shaq has no touch from the free-throw line," or "Kukoc has a streaky touch from deep."

Touch him (n., v.) 1. Playing up close on a good outside shooter, or a hot shooter, to prevent a good look at the basket. 2. To play close to someone.

Trash (n.) 1. See "Garbage." 2. Slightly worse than garbage—e.g., "The Bulls are about to kill Michael Jordan. He doesn't have much help. They've got some trash on their bench."

Two-game, two-man game (n.) 1. When two offensive players share a side and pass the ball in and out to each other, seeking a shot for one—e.g., "With Shaq and Penny running the two-man game, how did Orlando ever get swept, lose four games in a row?" 2. Monogamy.

Unconscious (n.) A shooter who hasn't missed in recent memory.

Up top (n.) See "Out high."

Warm (adj.) Making two consecutive shots.

Went off, got off (v.) Having dominated a phase of the game for a period of time—e.g., "Scottie Pippen went off on Seattle," or "Oakley got off on the boards."

Zoned, in the zone (adj.) Having made four consecutive shots. At least.

INDEX

ABOUT THE AUTHORS

Spike Lee is one of America's most acclaimed and prolific directors. The founder of 40 Acres and a Mule Filmworks, he has directed ten feature films, including *She's Gotta Have It, Do The Right Thing, Malcolm X,* and *Clockers,* and more than sixty music videos and commercials. He is also the author of six film-related books. He lives in Brooklyn, New York, with his wife, Tonya, and their daughter, Satchel.

Ralph Wiley is a seasoned journalist and author. He spent seven years with the *Oakland Tribune,* nine years with *Sports Illustrated,* and is the author of five highly acclaimed books, including *Serenity: A Boxing Memoir, Why Black People Tend to Shout,* and *Dark Witness.* He collaborated with Spike Lee on *By Any Means Necessary: The Trials and Tribulations of Making Malcolm X.* He lives in Washington, D.C.

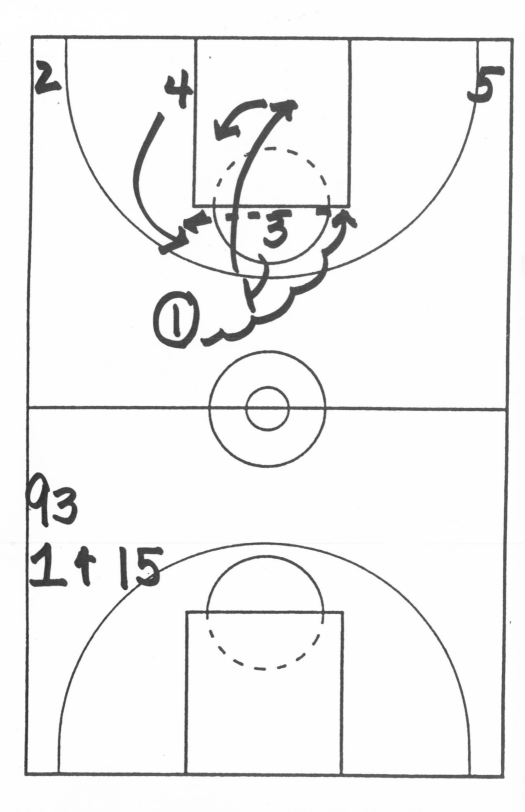